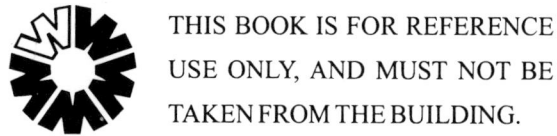
Smarter Choices
Changing the Way We Travel

Volume 1 final report

METROPOLITAN BOROUGH OF WIRRAL

EDUCATION & CULTURAL
SERVICES DEPARTMENT

Sally Cairns, ESRC Transport Studies Unit, University College London
Lynn Sloman, Transport for Quality of Life
Carey Newson, Transport for Quality of Life
Jillian Anable, The Centre for Transport Policy, The Robert Gordon University,
Aberdeen
Alistair Kirkbride, Eco-Logica
Phil Goodwin, ESRC Transport Studies Unit, University College London

October 2004

Department for Transport
Great Minster House
76 Marsham Street
London SW1P 4DR
Telephone 020 7944 8300
Web site www.dft.gov.uk

This report is accompanied by the following volume:

Jillian Anable, Alistair Kirkbride, Lynn Sloman, Carey Newson, Sally Cairns and Phil Goodwin (2004) *Smarter Choices - Changing the Way We Travel, Volume 2: Case study report.* Report published by the Department for Transport, London on 20 July 2004, available via the Sustainable Travel section of www.dft.gov.uk

Smarter Choices - Changing the Way We Travel is the title chosen for publication of the final report of the research project *The influence of soft factor interventions on travel demand.*

To order further copies of this publication or to arrange a standing order for all the department's publications contact:

DfT Publications
PO Box 236
Wetherby LS23 7NB
Tel: 0870 1226 236
Fax: 0870 1226 237
Textphone: 0870 1207 405
Email: dft@twoten.press.net
or online via www.publications.dft.gov.uk.

ISBN 1 904763 46 4 (2 volume set)

If you would like to be informed in advance of forthcoming Department for Transport titles, or would like to arrange a standing order for all of our publications, call 020 7944 4668.

Printed in Great Britain on material containing 75% post-consumer waste and 25% ECF pulp.

October 2004

Product Code 45 TA 02286

Contents

Acknowledgements

We gratefully acknowledge the many contributions made by organisations and individuals consulted as part of the research, and by the authors of previous studies and literature reviews which we have cited. Specific acknowledgements are given at the end of each chapter.

We have made extensive use of our own previous work including research by Lynn Sloman funded by the Royal Commission for the Exhibition of 1851 on the traffic impact of soft factors and local transport schemes (in part previously published as 'Less Traffic Where People Live'); and by Sally Cairns and Phil Goodwin as part of the research programme of TSU supported by the Economic and Social Research Council, and particularly research on school and workplace travel plans funded by the DfT (and managed by Transport 2000 Trust), on car dependence funded by the RAC Foundation, on travel demand analysis funded by DfT and its predecessors, and on home shopping funded by EUCAR.

Summary

In recent years, there has been growing interest in a range of initiatives which are now widely described as 'soft' transport policy measures. These seek to give better information and opportunities, aimed at helping people to choose to reduce their car use while enhancing the attractiveness of alternatives. They are fairly new as part of mainstream transport policy, mostly relatively uncontroversial, and often popular. They include:

- Workplace and school travel plans;
- Personalised travel planning, travel awareness campaigns, and public transport information and marketing;
- Car clubs and car sharing schemes;
- Teleworking, teleconferencing and home shopping.

This report draws on earlier studies of the impact of soft measures, new evidence from the UK and abroad, case study interviews relating to 24 specific initiatives, and the experience of commercial, public and voluntary stakeholders involved in organising such schemes. Each of the soft factors is analysed separately, followed by an assessment of their combined potential impact.

The assessment focuses on two different policy scenarios for the next ten years. The **'high intensity'** scenario identifies the potential provided by a significant expansion of activity to a much more widespread implementation of present good practice, albeit to a realistic level which still recognises the constraints of money and other resources, and variation in the suitability and effectiveness of soft factors according to local circumstances. The **'low intensity'** scenario is broadly defined as a projection of the present (2003-4) levels of local and national activity on soft measures.

The main features of the high intensity scenario would be

- A reduction in peak period urban traffic of about 21% (off-peak 13%);
- A reduction of peak period non-urban traffic of about 14% (off-peak 7%);
- A nationwide reduction in all traffic of about 11%.

These projected changes in traffic levels are quite large (though consistent with other evidence on behavioural change at the individual level), and would produce substantial reductions in congestion. However, this would tend to attract more car use, by other people, which could offset the impact of those who reduce their car use unless there are measures in place to prevent this. Therefore, those experienced in the implementation of soft factors locally usually emphasise that success depends on some or all of such supportive policies as re-allocation of road capacity and other measures to improve public transport service levels, parking control, traffic calming, pedestrianisation, cycle networks, congestion charging or other traffic restraint, other use of transport prices and fares, speed regulation, or stronger legal enforcement levels. The report also records a number of suggestions about local and national policy measures that could facilitate the expansion of soft measures.

The effects of the low intensity scenario, in which soft factors are not given increased policy priority compared with present practice, are estimated to be considerably less than those of the high intensity scenario, including a reduction in peak period urban traffic of about 5%, and a nationwide reduction in all traffic of 2%-3%. These smaller figures also assume that sufficient other supporting policies are used to prevent induced traffic from eroding the effects, notably at peak periods and in congested conditions. Without these supportive measures, the effects could be lower, temporary, and perhaps invisible.

Previous advice given by the Department for Transport in relation to multi-modal studies was that soft factors might achieve a nationwide traffic reduction of about 5%. The policy assumptions underpinning this advice were similar to those used in our low intensity scenario: our estimate is slightly less, but the difference is probably within the range of error of such projections.

The public expenditure cost of achieving reduced car use by soft measures, on average, is estimated at about 1.5 pence per car kilometre, i.e. £15 for removing each 1000 vehicle kilometres of traffic. Current official practice calculates the benefit of reduced traffic congestion, on average, to be about 15p per car kilometre removed, and more than three times this level in congested urban conditions. Thus every £1 spent on well-designed soft measures could bring about £10 of benefit in reduced congestion alone, more in the most congested conditions, and with further potential gains from environmental improvements and other effects, provided that the tendency of induced traffic to erode such benefits is controlled. There are also opportunities for private business expenditure on some soft measures, which can result in offsetting cost savings.

Much of the experience of implementing soft factors is recent, and the evidence is of variable quality. Therefore, there are inevitably uncertainties in the results. With this caveat, the main conclusion is that, provided they are implemented within a supportive policy context, soft measures can be sufficiently effective in facilitating choices to reduce car use, and offer sufficiently good value for money, that they merit serious consideration for an expanded role in local and national transport strategy.

1. Introduction

1.1 Background to discussion of 'soft factors'

In recent years there has been growing interest in a range of transport policy initiatives which are aimed at producing more reliable information, better informed traveller attitudes, and more benign or efficient ways of travelling. In transport policy discussions, these are now widely described as 'soft' factor interventions.

A clear or consistent definition has not yet been developed to identify what constitutes a 'soft' measure. The word 'soft' is sometimes used to distinguish these initiatives from 'hard' measures such as physical improvements to transport infrastructure or operations, traffic engineering, control of road space and changes in price, although some soft factors do include elements of this nature. (For example, workplace travel plans often including parking management). 'Soft' also refers to the nature of the traveller response, with initiatives often addressing psychological motivations for travel choice as well as economic ones. There is an emphasis on management and marketing activities rather than operations and investment. And there is also often the observation that these measures are largely or entirely omitted from established modelling and appraisal techniques, which deal with measures that are assumed to be more reliably understood. However, not all soft measures show all of these attributes, and various earlier studies have defined and dealt with different combinations of soft measures.

Out of many potential lists, definitions and groupings of soft measures, the measures included in this study were defined in the original project brief, as follows:

- workplace travel plans;
- school travel plans;
- personalised travel planning;
- public transport information and marketing;
- travel awareness campaigns;
- car clubs;
- car sharing schemes;
- teleworking;
- teleconferencing, and
- home shopping.

This is the list which we use as the basis of this report. We do not assume that it is a final and complete listing of all such factors, which no doubt will evolve as further understanding and practice develops.

Such policies, separately or together, have been undertaken for a wide range of different objectives including reducing congestion; increasing revenue for transport companies; improving health by encouraging physical activity; improving social inclusion; reducing environmental damage and saving commercial costs for employers. The most common specific feature linking these different policies has been that they have the potential to impact on levels of car use.

Although some of these activities have a very long history, mainstream analyses of specific initiatives, and their implications for policy, mainly date from the late 1990s. The current study collates and builds on this evidence, reviews current practice and experience at the local level in the UK and from some other countries, and comes to a broad view about the prospects for these policy instruments in the UK. Although there is much accumulating evidence, it is still early days for soft factors, and the picture is changing rapidly as information and understanding grows, and agencies develop better skills in implementing them. Consequently, all the conclusions in this report are subject to change as experience deepens.

1.2 Aims and objectives

The Department for Transport and its predecessors have commissioned a number of reviews of evidence in this field, reviewed in Chapter 2, of which the most recent had been a study by Halcrow (2001, 2002). This was used to inform Departmental advice to the Multi-Modal Studies teams, who were guided towards a conclusion that the total potential effect of soft factor interventions could be, on average, a traffic reduction of around 5%. This figure was widely discussed, with a number of criticisms that it under-estimated the potential effect in the light of accumulating new evidence. Therefore the Department decided to take understanding of soft measures further by a new review of all available evidence as published in the UK and overseas literature, together with a series of case studies involving visits and interviews with local authority and other staff actively involved in developing current work. A brief was put out to tender in Spring 2003, and the present team of six individual specialists, co-ordinated by the ESRC Transport Studies Unit at University College London and the independent consultancy Transport for Quality of Life, were selected to carry out the study.

The project brief established that the main objective was to collate and collect evidence from a diverse set of sources, including new case studies, about the effects and effectiveness of these measures at present, and their potential in the future. The study was intended to help to inform decisions on the importance that should be attached to such interventions, future levels of resourcing, and the development of the National Transport Model. Four main dimensions of evidence were defined:

- What interventions are being used, and where?
- What have they achieved in terms of modal shift for different types of journey?
- What other effects have followed?
- What is their cost effectiveness?

In addition, the project aimed to refine understanding of the effectiveness of these measures in different types of areas and for different trip types (purpose, length etc), where such information could be obtained.

It was recognised that this was just about the earliest stage when such an approach could be expected to be feasible. Local authorities were three years into the implementation of their first Local Transport Plans, though some authorities have been actively encouraging travel plan development for schools and workplaces for longer. The appointment of local authority school and workplace travel plan co-ordinators through the Government's bursary scheme began in 2001. Through their Annual Progress Reports, local authorities identified that there would be over 2000 employer travel plans and over 3000 school travel plans in place or planned by the end of 2003.

But there were, and are, still real-world limits on the amount of existing experience of different soft factor interventions (and in particular, on introducing combinations of such factors in a concerted fashion), which limit the scope of the study's conclusions and recommendations.

1.3 Methodology

There were two main activities undertaken in the study, a literature review and a series of local case studies, with a considerable effort devoted to seek to integrate and compare the results of these two strands of work.

The **literature review** took the broadest view possible about sources of information, with particular attention, where feasible, to results of actual practical experience on the ground, including evidence on the importance of surrounding conditions, complementary policies, conditions affecting success and failure, the separate impacts of individual initiatives, and the combined effects of packages of measures. We paid attention to seven important 'overview' studies which themselves had sought to come to a view about the overall impact of soft measures. We also went back to their original source material, and new published evidence, which dealt with specific individual soft factor measures. The overview studies are compared in Chapter 2, and the information about individual soft factors are summarised in separate chapters on each measure.

The **case studies** aimed, as far as possible, to add detailed information, not yet widely available, about:

- what soft factor interventions are being used in different types of area;
- the size of the intervention (how many people have been affected);
- effects of the initiative on car use;
- likely changes in impact over time;
- what other effects have been achieved, such as improved accessibility;
- what resources have been needed to achieve these effects;
- any synergy between the intervention and other soft or hard measures;
- data on trends in car traffic levels available from other sources;
- the likely costs, and impacts, of scaling up interventions over the long term.

An initial list of potential case study interview locations for each soft factor was drawn up based on the project team's knowledge, strengthened by consultation with experts and the Department for Transport. This produced a long-list of about 60 potential case studies. Telephone conversations, web searches and analyses of local authority progress reports were then used to obtain further information about each suggested location and organisation.

Following this trawl, and discussion with the steering group, the 24 case study interview locations were finalised as shown in the following table.

Table 1.1: Case studies examined in the project

Case study area / organisation	Soft factor									
	Workplace travel plans	School travel plans	Personalised travel planning	Public transport information & marketing	Travel awareness	Car-sharing	Car clubs	Telework	Teleconferencing	Home shopping
Bristol	X		X				X			
Birmingham	X									
Cambridgeshire	X									
Nottingham	X		X	X						(X)[1]
Buckinghamshire	X	X				X				
Merseyside	X	X								
Gloucester			X							
Brighton				X						
S Yorkshire PTE				X						
York	X	X			X					
Milton Keynes						X				
Edinburgh							X			
British Telecom								X	X	

In making these choices, key priorities identified with the steering group were that the selection should aim for a balance between metropolitan, urban and shire areas; that more than one measure should be investigated in at least some of the case study areas to seek insight into synergy between measures; and that the selection should include some examples of local authorities which have been less successful in a particular field. (This was taken to mean that they had tried to implement a particular measure but not made great progress, rather than that they had not shown any interest in the measure at all).

A further constraint was that the authority should have carried out formal monitoring and/or have other relevant data available. It should be noted many local authorities lack adequate data about the effects of initiatives that they are undertaking. This is partly because the cost of thorough monitoring is often large compared with the cost of the initiative itself, meaning that there is understandably less enthusiasm for undertaking such monitoring in local authorities, than is considered desirable by research institutes. In addition, some soft factors are at a very early stage of development in the UK and have only been trialled by a few local authorities in total.

---

[1] This material was available from a TransportEnergy Best Practice case study: we did not undertake our own additional interviews.

Having chosen the case studies, a discussion guide was developed for each soft factor, and interviews took place between July and September 2003. Initial interviews were usually with 1-3 people (including both local authority, and initiative-related staff, from the local public transport or car club operator, or PTE, or associated consultancy etc.). Follow-up work usually involved contact with further staff from relevant organisations, and a number of rounds of consultation and redrafting with all those involved – up to a further 30 email and telephone contacts per soft factor interview.

A separate volume (Anable et al, 2004) contains the full case study interview reports. In the present volume, the case study material is organised on a thematic basis, related to each of the soft measures, and integrated with the relevant specific literature from other areas, in the UK and internationally, which is mostly also of a case-study character.

1.4 General approach and caveats

Following this introduction, Chapter 2 summarises the previous UK 'overview' studies on this topic. Chapters 3-12 take each of the soft measures in turn, reporting (as far as possible in a standard format) the results of both the available literature and our own case studies. Chapter 13 looks at the combined potential impact of the different soft measures in the future, and their associated costs. Finally, Chapter 14 provides an overview of the main conclusions from the study, including the main policy implications that emerge.

At this stage we highlight some differences in the form of analysis in the different chapters, and the caveats which should be applied to them.

As far as possible, the main body of evidence in Chapters 2-12 relates to published information and case study evidence, where we have sought to summarise the data as accurately as possible – including the judgements and analyses made by the authors of the source documents, and by those involved in local initiatives, but with the minimum reliance on our own judgement. These chapters have been checked with the many case study interviewees and other experts who have contributed to the study, to ensure their robustness, and their helpful comments are gratefully acknowledged. Each chapter includes a list of those who have helped throughout the study, though with no implication that they have a responsibility for the analysis and conclusions that the chapter contains.

We then add our own judgements and analyses, identified separately from the source information, at two points.

In each chapter, we make calculations about the impact of the appropriate soft measure on car use, and the costs of achieving that, in order to calculate a figure for the cost per vehicle kilometre reduced. This is based on the case study experiences and also on the wider literature, with our own judgements on how to reconcile or synthesise this evidence. To the extent that the rather different nature of each of the soft measures allows, we have adopted a common approach in all the chapters, usually including treatment of build-up and decay rates of spending and effects over time, and inclusion of discount rates for annualisation of capital costs in line with Treasury guidance on public sector investment appraisal. Additional external benefits (such as time savings, accident reductions, health and environmental impacts, social inclusion gains etc.) have been briefly noted where evidence exists, but not monetised nor included in a social cost-benefit appraisal. In some cases, we have drawn on the National Travel Survey to provide a basis for current travel habits. We have aimed to draw on the 1999/2001 results for consistency, although it has occasionally been necessary to use results from 1998/2000, or 2002.

These calculations come together in chapter 13, where we give our own judgement of the future potential of soft measures to affect traffic levels. Two different scenarios are defined. The first scenario, which we call 'low intensity', is a projection of the present rate of expenditure and level of commitment, taking account of the important initiatives which already exist, and will no doubt continue, by the most committed local authorities, and of commercial initiatives being undertaken by companies. The second, which we call 'high intensity', is based on an expansion of activity, commitment and resources to a substantially higher level, which would still be consistent with practical and realistic experience, and feasible levels of expenditure, given the known constraints of staffing and funding generally.

As discussed in each of the chapters as relevant, and in considerably more detail in chapter 14, there are a number of important caveats and methodological difficulties which all studies in this area have needed to consider. In summary, these are as follows:
- Travellers may adjust their behaviour in many different ways apart from the switch in mode of transport which is often the main focus of policy attention. Some of these responses change the average distance of journeys, and in this case, it is not correct to calculate directly from mode switch to traffic impact.
- Travellers do not adjust their behaviour instantaneously. Therefore any before-and-after results, and model forecasts, need to assess as to whether the estimated effect has fully settled down, or is still in an uncompleted process of change.
- Much attention has been given to the logical likelihood, and strong judgements of those with local experience, of 'synergy' or interactions in effect among the various soft factors, and between soft and hard factors.
- Interpretations of empirical results need to make allowance for the extent and type of change that would have happened anyway, even without the intervention.
- Many studies have only measured some dimensions of behaviour (for example, changes in trips, but not mileage).
- Not all studies have used control groups or locations as part of the process of estimating impacts, and even where this has been done, it has often been difficult to ensure that the control groups are completely valid.

Wherever possible, we have sought additional evidence to enable us to take these issues into account. But where evidence has been lacking, it is still necessary to consider these issues, since to ignore them would almost certainly introduce bias into the calculations, one way or the other.

When in doubt, our general stance has been to err on the side of caution – i.e. to assume that effects on behaviour are at the lower end of a potential range, as opposed to the higher end. The cumulative effect of this approach has meant that we are fairly confident that we have not overestimated the potential impact of soft measures. This applies to both the low and high intensity scenarios. As a result, the estimated effects of the high intensity scenario have already been discounted to allow a degree of caution: the two scenarios should not be interpreted as a low and high bound of possible effect, the truth being somewhere in the middle. Rather they are both cautious estimates of the effect of two different policy choices.

A final caveat that we should make, of a quite different kind, relates to treatment of the surrounding policy context in which an expansion of soft policies might take place. A critical issue is whether the effect of even the most successful soft measures might be offset by induced traffic. In order not to confuse the analysis, we have adopted the assumption that *sufficient* supportive measures will be put in place not to obscure the impacts of soft factors, either by eroding or enhancing them.

This is a convenient neutral assumption for the analysis, and we have not attempted to define exactly what package of supportive measures would be capable of producing such a result in practice: its purpose is only to allow the potential impact of soft measures to be defined in themselves. However, to avoid misunderstanding, we note that this is not an implied policy recommendation. In practice one would, of course, expect a different condition to be applied, since the scale of the supportive measures sensibly chosen would not be that which just maintains the impact of the soft measures and no more, but would be at a level which takes into account the costs and benefits of those measures themselves.

Thus we make, at this point, an initial statement of our approach, which will be discussed in detail recurrently during the report.

In accordance with the spirit of our brief, we have sought to use the results from the literature and the case studies to identify the maximum reasonable potential scope for soft factor interventions, given a serious commitment of intent and a coherent general policy approach, but within the bounds of political feasibility, sensible amounts of resources, and a cautious interpretation of the evidence. Thus the potential we have identified does presuppose that this whole approach is treated as a serious and important arm of transport policy, both at the local level, where many of the soft policies are implemented, and also at national level, in setting a strategic context, giving clear signals, and addressing practical constraints. However, it is not intended to be outside the range of what willing and committed local and national agencies could realistically achieve, in the world as it really exists.

We emphasise that our conclusions are therefore about a *potential*, not a forecast. Whether this potential is considered desirable or not depends on policy judgements. If it is considered desirable, whether it is realised or not depends on the degree of commitment and consistent application of soft factor interventions which is secured in practice. These are issues of political will rather than research or modelling.

2. Overview of other soft factor studies

In addition to an extensive literature reporting evidence on specific measures, which is discussed in Chapters 3-12, there have been seven previous studies which themselves reviewed national and international evidence in order to make estimates of the overall effect of a combination of soft measures on traffic levels in British conditions. These have been undertaken by NERA (1997, 2000), WS Atkins (1999), Halcrow Group (2001, 2002), SWTAR (2002), Transport for Quality of Life (2003), Steer Davies Gleave (2003) and Transport for London (2003).

2.1 NERA (1997, 2000)

Dodgson et al from NERA (National Economic Research Associates) produced a report for the RAC in 1997 entitled 'Motors or Modems'. This reviewed earlier studies, and carried out market research surveys, of teleworking, teleconferencing and 'teleservices' which included teleshopping, telebanking and information services such as the Internet. Although the title of the report referred to 'business travel', it included commuting, shopping trips and freight movement. Results of the surveys gave estimated effects on trip rates, which were then inserted in NERA's traffic model, somewhat similar to the Department for Transport's National Transport Model (NTM). They suggested that telecommunications would result in traffic flows 'below otherwise forecast' of 6.1% to 9.7% by 2007[1], and 9.2% to 16.2% by 2017. The assessments were revised in 2000, for the RAC Foundation and the Motorists' Forum. Revisions were apparently more optimistic for commuting, and less so for car business travel, though revision of the scenario dates makes direct comparison difficult.

We have seen no critique of these results. The suggestion of a large effect from telecommunications has also been made by others, as discussed in Chapters 10 to 12.

2.2 WS Atkins (1999)

The first overview commissioned by the DETR (Department of Environment, Transport and the Regions) was carried out by WS Atkins (1999), to assess the effect of the new transport agenda set out in the White Paper 'A New Deal for Transport' (DETR 1998). The phrase 'soft factors' had not yet come into use: the report used the phrase 'individual action' with much the same meaning, including workplace travel plans, school travel plans, publicity, teleworking, travel awareness and similar measures. The evidence base was slim, the local authority case studies mentioned mostly being local transport plan (LTP) targets rather than completed initiatives, and few references were cited[2].

---

[1] They describe this as giving a 41% to 69% 'reduction in congestion', which, in the context, probably means by comparison with free-flow conditions, and without any offsetting induced traffic.

[2] The local authority case studies were Bexhill & Hastings, Eastbourne, Swindon, Chester, Northumberland, Derbyshire, Norwich, Bristol, North Lincolnshire, Portsmouth, Hampshire and Cambridgeshire, and 'a particularly good example of current practice' being Nottingham. Most of the LTP targets were expressed in terms of uptake or awareness, but Swindon mentioned a 25% reduction

WS Atkins suggested that of the measures they reviewed, workplace and school travel plans, 'can be seen as the most tangible of the various forms of travel awareness and substitution measures' and the quantitative parts of their review used these as a proxy for all the other measures. The objective was to calculate a series of factors to be used for adjusting traffic forecasts, separately for each type of initiative not included in the DETR's (then) traffic forecasting model, and separately for different types of area. The calculations proceeded from assumptions for a credible target level, the proportion of trips in the peak, the proportion in scope, and three levels of intensity of the initiative.

The resulting factors were then applied to the proportion of trips in each time period that would be targeted by the schemes, for each of 11 National Road Traffic Forecast area types (London, conurbations, large towns, etc), or combinations. Under many of the assumptions being made at that time about the extent of implementation, the effects on traffic were expected to be invisibly small for most places and times: the maximum potential, with widespread application, at high intensity, was estimated as a reduction of traffic of 8.8% by 2010 for larger towns and cities, in the absence of any other measure such as intensified charging or improvements to alternatives. Aware that they had not taken account of a number of potential initiatives, WS Atkins suggested that the figure could conceivably be increased by wider initiatives especially aimed at short trips, but commented 'the empirical evidence for doing this successfully is extremely weak at the present time'.

An important part of the WS Atkins methodology was to combine these estimates with others which they called local action measures, meaning improvements to public transport and walking facilities, parking restraint, reallocation of road capacity, road user charging, highway and traffic control improvements, and land use policies. These were converted into generalised cost equivalents and modelled using a 'ready reckoner', intended to provide an aggregate approximation to reassignment, mode switching, redistribution and trip suppression/generation[3].

WS Atkins gave precedence to these local policies over individual action, arguing that they would have the potential to influence a larger number of people, and therefore only allowed for a net impact of individual measures in cases where the adjustment factor calculated or assumed was greater than that already achieved by the local policies. In other words, once a given proportion of the trips had been diverted from car by, say, road user charging, they were no longer available to be diverted by other measures. Table 2.1 summarises their 2010 estimates on maximum implementation.

---

in car commuting by its own employees, Northumberland sought a 20% shift from car among participating employers, and Nottingham sought a 30% reduction in car trips to work and had 'already achieved 17% since 1996'.

[3] No details of the operation of the ready reckoner are included in the Final Report and Appendices of this project, beyond some statements that it is based on processing information from a number of other models which were assumed to be fit for purpose, with linear interpolation of their results. The implication is that it is a spreadsheet with a series of generalised cost elasticities and cross-elasticities. The authors comment 'the body of evidence on which the ready reckoner is founded does not reliably support the forecasting of traffic reductions beyond 25%', and they therefore imposed an upper threshold of 25% for the combined effect of all the local action policies.

Table 2.1: W S Atkins summary results

	Peak	Interpeak	Off-peak	Weekend
Local policy alone Larger urban (1-8) Small urban/rural	-21% to -25% -1% to -3%	-7% to -15% -1% to -13%	-3% to -5% -1%	-4% to -10% -1% to -2%
Individual action alone Larger urban (1-8) Small urban/rural	-9% -2%	-4% -1%	-4% -1%	0 0

Because, in general, the calculated local policy impact is greater than the individual action impact, the former dominates and the combined figure given by WS Atkins is generally just the same as the local policy figure alone. However, the report notes that an alternative approach would be to assume that some motorists are sensitive to one sort of instrument and others to another, and in the extreme the effects would be combined to give a greater total. These figures are not estimated in their report, but a procedure is suggested to enable readers to calculate it themselves.

WS Atkins note that their approach is subject to a number of caveats and very tentative assumptions, due to the limited data then available. It is also likely that the calculations in the ready reckoner would have been informed by the generally rather low sensitivities to policy instruments that were used within DETR forecasts at the time, compared with the revised figures now used within NTM. It is therefore possible that a re-application of this technique, with updated elasticities, would show greater reductions in traffic.

The general approach encompasses many features that are desirable, including allowance for a number of different types of behavioural response, a relationship between intensity of implementation and impact (apparently including a relationship with expenditure levels, though details are not available), and scope for varying the treatment of synergy. Most important, it allows direct calculation of differential effects in different types of area, which all subsequent reviews have referred to but not as systematically or coherently calculated.

In summary, WS Atkins proposed that, by 2010, workplace travel plans and school travel plans would be capable of reducing peak traffic levels by roundly 2% for rural areas and small towns, and by up to 9% for larger towns and cities, though they suggest that this reduction, and more, could alternatively be achieved by intensive application of local authority policies on transport facilities and pricing. No national totals, or 24-hour totals, were produced. All figures cited were applied to specific types of area and specific times.

The study does not seem to be widely known, and we have not seen any published comments or criticisms of it.

2.3 Halcrow Group Ltd (2001, 2002)

Using a different form of presentation, most of the figures suggested by Halcrow (2001, 2002) relate to national totals, with few specific figures relating to types of road or times of day, and none comparable with the WS Atkins format. The focus of their discussion and conclusions relates to trunk roads. This is because the study was commissioned by Department of Transport, Local Government and the Regions (DLTR) to make an assessment of the impact of soft factors with special reference to the Multi-Modal Studies. This led to Halcrow primarily examining the potential impacts of vehicle traffic on trunk roads, with only passing comments on urban and local travel.

Halcrow's initial 2001 report was criticised by a number of commentators, notably James (2002) for the South West Round Table on Sustainable Development, following which a 2002 version, with small revisions, was produced by Halcrow at the request of DfT, and is used in this section.

Halcrow used a longer list of soft factors than WS Atkins, and by then had access to many more empirical results, although Bayliss (2004) reports that there were still major concerns, at the time, about the lack of empirical evidence on which to base conclusions. Results were most commonly expressed as an estimate of traffic reduction from policies implemented over the next 10-15 years, measured in national vehicle kilometres per year on all roads, but expressed as though calculated with traffic levels for the year 2000.

Our summary of the main conclusions of the Halcrow review is as follows, using their list of factors which includes some outside the scope of our work.

- **Negligible net effects on travel demand:** e-commerce, internet shopping, visitor travel plans, car clubs (except for a few inner city areas), improved public transport interchange; general public transport marketing; land-use policies, local sourcing of goods, oil supplies and new automotive technology.

- **Some net effect but not significant for multi-modal studies:** school travel plans (0.45 bn veh km); measures to increase walking and cycling (up to 3bn veh km, but Halcrow identified this estimate as unreliable).

- **Material effects on travel demand, and relevant to multi-modal studies:** teleworking (5bn veh km); video-conferencing (2.5bn veh km); workplace travel plans (3.25-5.25 bn veh km); public transport fares and ticketing (figure obscure); individualised marketing (2 bn veh km); bus quality partnerships (2bn veh km).

Halcrow translate their figures into percentage traffic reductions at the national level, which are consequently all rather small numbers. For example, the 0.45 billion vehicle kilometre reduction attributed to school travel plans is described as 0.1% of total road traffic, and the 3.25 to 5.25 billion vehicle kilometre reduction from workplace travel plans as 0.8% to 1.2% of total traffic volumes. Thus the potential effect of these two instruments is assessed as roundly 1% traffic reduction overall.

These are the two instruments which dominate the WS Atkins assessment discussed above. They do not give a total figure, but, inspection of their figures suggests that it must be in the order of 4%. Prima facie, the Halcrow assessment is of an effect approximately one quarter as big as the Atkins one, for the factors contained in both.

Halcrow concluded that the combined overall effect of soft measures will be too small to have much general importance, although allowing, in principle, for bigger effects in specific locations of interest. Their order of magnitude informed Departmental advice to the Multi-Modal Studies teams, who were guided towards a total potential effect of around 5%[4].

The report was widely noticed, and rather controversial. All of those who commented in any detail on it, including James (2002) below and three peer reviewers, concluded that it underestimated the potential:

- Goodwin (2002) suggested that Halcrow's results were likely to be subject to a methodological bias for three reasons: (a) their interpretation of the evidence had not allowed for the time period of build-up of behavioural response, and had therefore underestimated longer-term effects; (b) their calculations of traffic impact had only allowed for the effect of mode switch within a fixed trip matrix, and had therefore underestimated the results of changes in journey length; (c) there was inadequate treatment of synergy.

- Bonsall (2002) concludes that the Halcrow approach gives a 'low-side impression of the potential contribution that an appropriate combination of measures could have – particularly in the context of a determined effort to use all the currently available levers'.

- Headicar (2002) argues that the Halcrow approach is essentially based on a presumption that declared Government policy positions will not be implemented. He notes that this presumption might be true, but precludes effective assessment of the evidence on whether to do so.

Further discussion during our study with David Bayliss of Halcrow clarifies some of the difference between the Halcrow estimates and its critics, which had not been fully understood at the time (including by the present authors), and which closely relates to the distinction between high and low intensity implementation of soft factors defined in chapter 1. Bayliss (2004) reports that they were essentially answering the question 'what could reasonably be relied on to reduce demand for trunk transport capacity?', not 'what could soft measures achieve if their full potential was effectively achieved?', which was the focus of some other studies. Not surprisingly, this gives a lower answer. He also emphasises (as, indeed, did many of the interviewees from our case study areas as reported in chapters 3-12) that it is important not to expect too

---

[4] This figure was implied, but not stated, in their report. Sloman (2003) calculated the figure from their conclusions, and in evidence to the House of Commons Select Committee on Transport (2003), Mr MacMillan for the DfT said that the Department thought it reasonable "to assume that soft measures could get you into a position where you had reduced travel overall by some five per cent" (p37 and evidence Q171). The Select Committee reported that specific studies had assumed between 1% and 10%, which is consistent with an assumption of 5% average overall.

much from soft measures on their own, without supporting hard measures, as this might have the counter-productive effect of reducing the incentive to carry out the supporting measures which are, in fact, crucial to success.

The Halcrow estimates were therefore based on the policy presumption that – broadly speaking – no great increase in priority or government attention would be given to this area, which reflected their interpretation of stated policy at the time. This is approximately equivalent to the definition we have adopted for our low intensity scenario.

2.4 SWTAR (2002)

James (2002) produced a critique of the Halcrow figures, at the request of the South West Transport Activists' Round Table (SWTAR), who were concerned about its implications for the local multi modal study. In his critique, he made alternative suggestions about the potential impact of each soft factor in the Halcrow report, essentially using the same framework and presentation as Halcrow, but interpreting the evidence and potential differently. His assessments for impacts in 2015, as summarised by Sloman (2003) were as follows:

- Teleworking –3%
- Workplace travel plans –2.4%
- Public transport marketing and ticketing –2%
- Land use effects –2%
- School travel plans –1.3%
- Internet shopping –1.2%
- Videoconferencing –1.2%
- Cycling –1.2%
- Car clubs, public transport interchanges and information, bus quality partnerships and promotion of walking, less than -1% each.

This gives a total potential traffic reduction broadly in the range 15% to 20%, without adjusting the figures upwards for synergy or downwards for double counting. This, like WS Atkins, implies a figure of three to four times as large as Halcrow's total potential effect of up to 5%.

His figure was about the same as W S Atkins for the two measures common to both.

In the light of the clarification of the basis for Halcrow's calculations discussed above, it is interesting that James actually suggested that Halcrow's own forecast would have come to an 11% reduction if they had combined their figures in a different, but in James' view more defensible, way, relating to the treatment of some mathematical corrections, inclusion of some 'negligable' but not zero aspects, and land-use planning impacts. The use of these alternative calculations would reduce the underlying difference between the Halcrow and James figures, for reasons quite apart from the policy scenarios under consideration.

2.5 Transport for Quality of Life (2003)

A further review of evidence was carried out by Sloman (2003) of Transport for Quality of Life, funded by the Royal Commission for the Exhibition of 1851, and using a wider range of more recent empirical evidence than was used by the earlier studies. In her approach, no specific importance was attributed to the difference between 'soft' and other measures, and the main focus was on the potential impacts in 2010 of implementing a coherent package of many different types of local policy instruments, including measures to promote walking and cycling.

Sloman suggested the following range of impacts:

- **Bus quality partnerships**: average patronage increase 18% short term, 36% medium term, with assumed 33% switched from car.

- **Workplace travel plans**: average reduction in commuter cars of 14 per 100 staff

- **School travel plans**: decreases in car use of between 8% to 52% for individual schools (including two where no change took place, and one increase)

- **Individualised marketing and travel blending**: for urban areas, individualised marketing typically cuts car use by 7% to 14%.

- **Car clubs**: on average 1/3 of car club members give up a car on joining, and reduce their car use by 2/3.

Putting these results together with experience on walking and cycling increases, and some other measures, Tables 2.2 to 2.4 show a summary of her estimates of the effect of modest and more ambitious implementation of policies, at national level and for the West Midlands conurbation.

Note that the figures here are expressed as a percentage of car 'travel', which, in this context, refers to trips in most of the cases. WS Atkins and Halcrow both quote their results in terms of vehicle kilometres, though not calculated in the same way – Atkins intending to take account of changes in trip length, and Halcrow taking account in differences in average trip length for different purposes, but not changes in these brought about by the measures. Comparing the results therefore needs some care. Sloman's figures for travel *ought* to be comparable with Halcrow's for kilometres, since neither adjust for changes in journey length: her overall national figure of 5% for 'enlightened business as usual' is close to Halcrow's full effect figure. On the basis of the discussion above, her figures for travel plans and school travel plans seem rather less than those of WS Atkins, probably because the latter include some allowance for journey length changes.

Table 2.2 Reductions in national car travel demand under each scenario (%)

	'Enlightened business as usual'	'Ambitious change'
Better bus services	-0.5	**-0.9**
Light rail systems	-0.03	**-0.03**
Community rail partnerships	-0.1	**-0.3**
Workplace travel plans	-1.0	**-2.1**
Teleworking	-1.6	**-2.8**
School travel plans	-0.4	**-1.3**
Individual marketing	-0.8	**-1.6**
Car clubs	-0.02	**-0.04**
More cycling	-0.3	**-1.2**
More walking[5]	-0.1	**-0.2**
Total	-4.9	-10.5

Table 2.3 Reductions in car travel demand in the West Midlands metropolitan area (%)

	'Enlightened business as usual'	'Ambitious change'
Bus and tram improvements	- 2.3	**- 6.5**
Workplace travel plans	- 3.4	**- 6.9**
Teleworking	- 5.2	**- 9.4**
School travel plans	- 0.9	**- 2.8**
Individual marketing	- 2.7	**- 5.5**
More cycling	- 0.3	**- 1.2**
Car clubs	- 0.14	**- 0.3**
More walking	- 0.1	**- 0.2**
Total	- 15.1	- 32.8

[5] The estimate for "more walking" is a net figure, excluding impacts from school travel plans and individual marketing. If these are included, the total reduction in car travel demand arising from shift to walking is 0.7 per cent (enlightened business as usual) or 1.65 per cent (ambitious change).

Table 2.4 Ambitious change scenario: Effect on distance travelled as a car driver (per person per year), according to journey purpose

	Before		Reduction in mileage in ambitious change scenario (as percentage of total car travel demand)											After
	Car driver km per person per year	% of total car mileage	Bus quality partnerships	Light rail	Rail partnerships	Workplace travel plans	Teleworking	School travel plans	Individual marketing	Car clubs	More cycling	More walking	Total	Car driver km per person per year
Commuting	1450	25.6	0.3	0.01		2.1	2.8		0.2	0.01	0.4		5.82	1120
Visiting friends at home	864	15.2	0.1						0.3		0.1		0.50	836
Business	840	14.8							0.1	0.01	0.1		0.21	828
Shopping	686	12.1	0.3	0.01	0.1				0.3	0.01	0.2	0.1	1.02	628
Other escort	426	7.5							0.1				0.10	421
Personal business	406	7.1	0.1	0.01					0.2	0.01		0.1	0.42	382
Holiday / day trip	385	6.8			0.2				0.2				0.40	362
Sport / entertainment	307	5.4							0.1		0.1		0.20	296
Visiting friends elsewhere	145	2.6							0.1		0.2		0.30	128
Escort education	111	2.0						1.3					1.30	37
Education	42	0.7	0.1								0.1		0.20	30
Other	13	0.2											0.00	13
Total	**5674**	**100.0**	**0.9**	**0.03**	**0.3**	**2.1**	**2.8**	**1.3**	**1.6**	**0.04**	**1.2**	**0.2**	**10.47**	**5080**
													Car driver kilometres saved per person per year	594

In summary, Sloman's estimates, based on two scenarios about less or more intensive application, suggest that national car travel would reduce by 5% or 11% respectively. Applying such policies to the West Midlands conurbation, as an example of conditions in which considerably more than average effects should be obtainable, produced estimated reductions in car travel demand (before allowing for induced traffic effects) of 15% or 33% respectively. To enable comparison with the results of other studies, we have recalculated these figures expressing them as a percentage of all motorised traffic. The national estimate is a reduction of 4% or 8.5%, and the estimated effect in the West Midlands is to reduce motorised traffic by 12% or 26% under the two scenarios.

We are not aware of any written critique of these figures.

2.6 Steer Davies Gleave (2003)

An SDG study used much the same general background literature as the others and indeed cited Halcrow and Sloman among its sources. The application was much more focussed. The study was commissioned by a group of environmental agencies as a study of alternatives to a major proposed road expansion in Dorset, and the objective was to consider the combined effects of available soft (and other related) factors in very specific local conditions relevant to the proposed Weymouth Relief Road. Therefore the traffic levels and demand structure of particular roads and time periods were the base, and national totals irrelevant.

A long list of measures, both hard and soft, were included in the policy discussion, but estimates were only made for the effects of four factors, namely personalised travel planning, workplace and school travel plans, and bus quality partnerships, the first of these then being substantially discounted in order to avoid double-counting. Estimated total impacts ranged between 6% and 19% during peak hours, and it was assumed that measures could be realistically implemented within 2-3 years.

We are aware of continuing discussions in the region about the policy argument, but have not seen any detailed critique of the numbers.

2.7 Transport for London (2003)

Transport for London is currently developing its road strategy and initiated an internal review of the potential impact of soft factors. The sources used are much the same as the other studies (although including some additional references based on their own work in London), and expressing all the estimated results as a proportion of peak period traffic levels in Greater London. Results were quoted as ranges, in this case representing both an element of uncertainty in the figures, and also the effects of more or less energetic implementation, with no specified timescale. The combined effect was estimated as a potential of 8%-17% traffic reduction, with strong caveats about the problem that induced traffic would be particularly prone to erode these numbers given the level of congestion in London. The London-wide figure does not exactly correspond with 'best local', since it is itself an average within which there would be local variation.

2.8 Summary of the overview studies

Thus we have examples of more and less well documented, more and less controversial, and more and less comprehensive estimates of the impact of soft measures, using a range of definitions, assumptions and evidence. Table 2.5 compares the figures they suggested. Before taking account of the differences in definitions, approaches and policy assumptions, the picture is that Dodgson et al, WS Atkins, James, Sloman, SDG and TfL all come up with a range for the overall figures in which only the lower bounds are comparable with the Halcrow-based guideline figures. The two measures which were common to all except one of the studies are workplace and school travel plans, so estimates for these two are identified separately to ease comparison. The same pattern is shown of a wide range, bounded by the Halcrow study at the low end. We note also that the various estimates of the effects of individual components vary significantly between studies even when the estimated total is similar.

A substantial part of the apparent difference between Halcrow and the other studies derives from the assumptions about intensity of implementation, not from a different assessment of the inherent potential for change. This may be seen from the closeness of the lower bound of Sloman's figures, to Halcrow's, and from the upward revision of Halcrow suggested by James which would put their figure within the same range as the others.

At face value, taking the 17 upper and lower bounds given in these seven separate published estimates of the overall effect of differently defined packages of such measures, we observe a lowest figure of 4% of traffic and a highest of 20% overall, and up to about 30% for some specific urban locations (although the latter figure also includes also the effect of additional supporting hard measures). We can then separate out the results according to their (approximate) correspondence with the low and high intensity scenarios we are interested in, as defined in Chapter 1. The low intensity figures comprise Halcrow, the 'business as usual' scenario of Sloman, and the lower bound of some other studies, all suggesting a national figure of 4%-5%. The rest are more closely comparable with potential of a higher intensity scenario. These have a central range broadly suggesting 10% to 15% for national impact, and 15% to 20% for best local impact.

It is interesting to compare these figures with earlier research in a review published by Goodwin et al (1995), based on a quite different methodology considering the inherent characteristics of car trips rather than the policy effects of any specific initiatives. This concluded that some 20% of car trips were not locked in to car use, and could be reduced by reasonably accessible measures: seeking reductions greater than this would be possible, but increasingly difficult and so require greater effort or initiative. This conclusion is broadly consistent with the orders of magnitude of the studies reviewed.

Two measures, workplace and school travel plans, were common to six of the seven studies, the estimated effect ranging from the lowest figure of about 1% of traffic, to the highest in the best specific local circumstances of 9%. The central estimates for workplace and school travel plans, taking these studies together, were 3% of traffic nationally and 8% in the best local conditions.

Table 2.5 Summary of 'combined effect' literature results

Study	NERA et al (1997)	WS Atkins (1999)	Halcrow (2001, 2002)	SWTAR (2002)	Transport for Quality of Life (2003)	Steer Davies Gleave (2003)	Transport for London (2003)
Factors included	All telecommunications (telecommuting, teleshopping, teleconferencing, freight operations)	Workplace and school travel plans, improvements to public transport and walking facilities, public transport fares, parking restraint, reallocation of road capacity, road user charging, highway and traffic control improvements, land use policies.	Workplace and school travel plans, visitor travel plans, bus quality partnerships, improved public transport interchange, general public transport marketing, public transport fares and ticketing, individualised marketing, car clubs, teleworking, video-conferencing, home shopping, measures to increase walking and cycling, land-use policies, local sourcing of goods, oil supplies and new automotive technology.	Workplace and school travel plans, bus quality partnerships, public transport interchange, public transport marketing and ticketing, public transport information, car clubs, teleworking, videoconferencing, internet shopping, cycling, promotion of walking, land use effects.	Workplace and school travel plans, bus quality partnerships, local rail improvements, individual marketing, car clubs, teleworking, promotion of walking and cycling.	Workplace and school travel plans, bus quality partnerships. (Visitor travel plans, rail improvements, parking restraint considered but impacts not estimated. Individual travel planning estimated but largely discounted to avoid double counting.)	Workplace and school travel plans, individualised marketing, car clubs, car sharing, teleworking, videoconferencing, e-shopping, promoting cycling, promoting walking, travel awareness campaigns.
Maximum combined potential of all included measures							
National	**-6% to −16%**	-15% to -20%	-5%	**-15% to −20%**	**-4% to -9%**	not estimated	**-8% to -17% London-wide**
Best Local	not estimated	**-25% to -32%**	not estimated	not estimated	**-12% to -26%**	**-15% to -19%**	
Maximum potential of work and school travel plans only							
National	not estimated	-4%	-1%	**-3.7%**	**-1% to -3%**	not estimated	**-2% to -4% London-wide**
Best Local	not estimated	**-9%**	not estimated	not estimated	**-3% to -8%**	**-12% to -15%**	

Bold figures as stated explicitly in sources, others inferred. Sloman's figures as in source but recalculated as % of total traffic.

Apart from the policy context, the biggest apparent differences between the studies arise from presentation. Figures expressed as a percentage of total national traffic inevitably appear small, and those expressed as a percentage of traffic in specific contexts, e.g. urban peak periods, are substantially higher. The national total calculations will have merit for certain purposes, notably calculation of carbon dioxide emissions, but for nearly all policies aimed at transport objectives such as congestion, mobility, social inclusion, local air quality or other environmental impacts, revenue generation, cost minimisation and economic impacts, it is the effects in a specific context that are more useful.

From this point of view, the form of analysis reported by WS Atkins, SDG, TfL and Sloman's local application, seem likely to be more useful than the form used by Halcrow, James, and Sloman's national application. In chapters 13 and 14, as far as possible, we therefore report results in both national and context-specific formats.

2.9 Conclusion

As a conclusion to this chapter, we note that there are a range of different estimates that have been given in earlier studies, the differences being related to issues of measurement and definition; differences in assessment of the realistic pace of future policy initiatives and market developments; differences between 'expected' and 'potential' outcomes; and differences in the range of measures included in the studies.

The lowest estimates of effect that have been given are, to all material purposes, close to zero. Such figures tend to emerge when it is assumed that there will be little momentum in such policies, when the impacts of specific factors are averaged over 24 hour, national traffic flows, and/or when caveats are made about induced traffic. At the other extreme, the highest figures suggested have approached car use reductions of up to a third, these being discussed as a result of the simultaneous application of many different consistent initiatives (including, it should be emphasised, supporting 'hard' measures), and expressed as a proportion of the traffic levels in a specific locality, by journey purpose and by time of day.

Given these differences, and the sharpness of the debate which has surrounded them, there is in fact a surprisingly consistent underlying picture that emerges from the various studies, and which we judge to express the measure of professional consensus that exists from those who have carried out the earlier studies. This suggests that at the lower intensity application, and/or without support from complementary hard measures, there is scope for soft measures to reduce traffic levels, but not very much: perhaps 4% or 5% at the national level, with a range around this according to local circumstances. With higher intensity application (and emphasising the importance of supportive hard measures either by assumption or explicitly) there is an estimated potential for soft factor interventions to reduce traffic levels by 10% to 15% as a national average, and 15% to 20% in favourable local conditions. And there are some estimates that, in very specific circumstances, figures higher than this are not impossible.

These figures act as useful hypotheses, or tests, against which our own estimates can be compared.

2.10 Acknowledgements

We gratefully acknowledge the contribution to this chapter made by the work of the following:

Individual	*Organisation*
John Dodgson	NERA
Andy Southern Tony Meehan	WS Atkins
David Bayliss	Halcrow Group Ltd
Alan James	South West Activists' Round Table
Lynn Sloman	Transport for Quality of Life
Tom Cohen	Steer Davies Gleave
Patrick Allcorn	Transport for London
Peter Bonsall	University of Leeds
Peter Headicar	Oxford Brookes University

2.11 References

Bayliss D (2004) personal correspondence.

Bonsall P (2003) *Peer review of Halcrow (2002)*, Department for Transport, London, unpublished.

DETR (1998) *A new deal for transport. Better for everyone.* DETR, London.

Dodgson J, Sandbach J, McKinnon A, Shurmer M, van Dijk T, & Lane B (1997) *Motors or Modems*, National Economic Research Associates, London

Dodgson J, Pacey J, Begg M (2000) *Motors and Modems Revisited*, National Economic Research Associates, London

Goodwin P (ed) et al (1995) *Car Dependence.* RAC Foundation for Motoring and the Environment, London.

Goodwin P (2003) *Peer review of Halcrow (2002)*, Department for Transport, London, unpublished

Halcrow Group (2000, 2002) *Multi-modal studies: soft factors likely to affect travel demand, update final report*, Department for transport, London

Headicar P (2003) *Peer review of Halcrow (2002)*, Department for Transport, London, unpublished

House of Commons Transport Committee (2003) *Jam tomorrow? the multi-modal study investment plans*, TSO London

James, A. (2002) *Review of Halcrow soft factors report*, South West Transport Activists Roundtable, and personal correspondence 2004.

Cairns S, Sloman L, Newson C, Anable J, Kirkbride A & Goodwin P (2004*)*
'Smarter Choices – Changing the Way We Travel'

Overview of other
soft factor studies

Sloman L (2003) *Less traffic where people live: how local transport schemes can help cut traffic*, Transport for Quality of Life, Machynlleth

Steer Davies Gleave (2003) *Weymouth relief road: alternatives to the proposed scheme.* SDG, London.

Transport for London (2003) *Soft options – review of studies.* Cited with permission, unpublished committee report

W S Atkins (1999) *Assessing the effect of transport white paper policies on national traffic*, Final Report and Appendices, DETR, London

3.   Workplace travel plans

3.1   Introduction

Commuting to work by car makes up a large proportion of all car traffic, particularly during the morning and evening peak periods. In the early 1990s, the idea of workplace travel planning began to gain ground in Britain, based on successful experience in the Netherlands and the US. A workplace travel plan can be described as a package of measures put in place by an employer to try and encourage more sustainable travel, usually meaning less car use, particularly less single occupancy car use. Travel plans usually primarily aim to address the commuting habits of employees, although many also incorporate measures aimed at travel during the course of work, including business and delivery travel, and also travel by patients, students, shoppers, tourists, or other visitors to the employer's site. Local authorities are often involved in both developing their own travel plan, and also encouraging other employers to develop their own, site-specific travel plans. Local authorities have developed a range of measures to encourage the development of travel plans, (as discussed in section 3.7).

The biggest study so far of British workplace travel plans was carried out by Cairns, Davies, Newson and Swiderska (2002). This reviewed existing literature and added its own new results based on analysis of best practice in 20 organisations, employing over 69,000 staff.

There is also valuable research on travel plan effectiveness from the Netherlands and US. Other British studies have examined the differing levels of take-up of travel planning in the private and public sectors, and between large and smaller organisations.

As background to the current study, we were interested in evidence from the literature on the following questions:
- How effective are workplace travel plans?
- What take-up of workplace travel plans is there already?
- What are typical costs of workplace travel plan initiatives?

In later parts of the chapter, this information is analysed in conjunction with the interview information from seven local authorities about their travel plan work, and their plans for the future.

3.2   Literature evidence about the effectiveness of workplace travel plans

The British study of 20 organisations implementing workplace travel plans (Cairns et al. 2002) looked at a range of private and public sector organisations, all selected as examples of good practice in workplace travel planning. It found substantial variation in their effects on car use. At one extreme, the mobile phone company Orange had cut the number of staff driving to work from 79% to 27%. This extremely good result was in part due to re-location from a business park to a city centre site close to a rail station. At the other extreme, Boots headquarters in Nottingham had cut car drivers from 65% to only 62%, whilst coping with a large influx of staff from a town centre site to its main offices on an out-of-town business park.

Table 3.1 shows the changes in car use achieved at the different organisations involved in the study.

Table 3.1: Changes in commuter car use at British organisations with travel plans

Organisation	Cars per 100 staff*~		%-point shift	%change
	Before	**After**		
Orange (Temple Point)	79	27	52	-66
Bluewater	69	31	38	-55
Plymouth Hospitals NHS Trust	>78	<54	>24	>-31
Computer Associates	89	74	15	-17
Buckinghamshire County Council	71	56	15	-21
Addenbrooke's NHS Trust	<74	<60	>14	>-19
Wycombe District Council	77	65	12	-16
Orange (Almondsbury Park)	92	80	12	-13
Nottingham City Hospital NHS Trust	73	61	12	-16
Marks and Spencer Financial Services	<95	<83	>12	>-13
BP	84	72	12	-14
Vodafone	<84	<75	>9	>-11
University of Bristol	44	35	9	-20
Egg	62	53	9	-15
AstraZeneca	<90	<82	>8	>-9
Government Office for the East Midlands	<45	<38	>7	>-16
Pfizer	75	68	7	-9
Agilent Technologies	71	65	6	-8
Stockley Park	<88	<84	>4	>-5
Oxford Radcliffe Hospitals NHS Trust (JR site)	58	54	4	-7
Boots	65	62	3	-5
Average	74	61	> -14	> -18
National Travel Survey comparison	59			

Reproduced from Cairns et al. (2002)
* 'Cars per 100 staff' relates to the number of commuter cars arriving per 100 staff at the time of the earliest and latest monitoring at each organisation. Staff who were parking off-site were counted as bringing a car. Staff using Park-and-Ride services for commuting were not counted as bringing a car.
~ Where inequality signs have been used, changes in car numbers have usually been inferred from figures about the total proportion of staff commuting by car. This usually gives a conservative estimate of change, as it does not allow for reductions in the number of commuter cars arriving per 100 staff achieved by increased car sharing, or, in the case of Vodafone, increasing proportions of people who only commute by car for some days each week.

Taken overall, the 20 organisations had reduced the number of cars driven to work by 14 for every 100 staff. This represented an average reduction of 18% in the proportion of commuter journeys being made as a car driver. This is the average – the medians were similar, with a median reduction of at least 12 cars per 100 staff, and a median percentage reduction of at least 15%, showing that even after giving less emphasis to the few extreme cases, organisations were typically achieving sizeable cuts in car use.

On average, the organisations had nearly doubled the proportion of staff commuting by bus, train, cycling and walking. Car sharing had also been successful. Several organisations mentioned that some staff had given up a second car as a result of the travel plan.

A number of factors were examined, to try and identify why some travel plans were more successful than others. In general, the study found very few generalisations that could be made – for example, some organisations had achieved success by focusing on a range of modes, whilst others had been relatively successful by only focusing on one, such as train use or car sharing. There were examples of considerable success from all types of geographical location. It was shown that being located in an urban area meant that an organisation was likely to start with a lower level of car use, but it did not determine the degree of change or the 'end' level of car use that it could achieve – instead, the quality of the plan was likely to 'over-ride' the location effect. All of the travel plans had involved some 'real' changes in employees travel options, such that it was not possible to assess the effects of plans that were about awareness raising only. However, the one factor that did emerge as being important was parking. Specifically, for the 13 travel plans which had addressed parking, either by restricting the number of staff entitled to park in the organisation's car park, introducing charges or providing specific incentives payments to those giving up a parking space, the average reduction in the proportion of commuter journeys being made as a car driver was >24%, and the median was 17%. For the 8 travel plans which had not addressed parking, the average reduction in the proportion of commuter journeys being made as a car driver was >10%, and the median was 9%.

There is more evidence about the effectiveness of British travel plans from a separate study by Napier University, Open University and WS Atkins (2001). This assessed government department travel plans, based on issues of process rather than on actual 'before' and 'after' monitoring of car use. Aspects of each travel plan were awarded points on a weighted system (for example, a maximum of 250 points for 'plans and measures', 100 points for monitoring, and so on). Using the framework, the study assessed a sample of government department travel plans and found that they achieved an average score of 29%. This study highlights the problem that organisations can be required to draw up a travel plan, but it is more difficult to oblige them to make it a *good* travel plan.

Detailed evaluation of the effects of travel planning in the US and the Netherlands is reported by Organisational Coaching/Schreffler (1996). Their research involved a comparison of 20 paired case studies from the two countries. The organisations examined included a large hospital, a large manufacturer, a government (local/national) organisation or utility, a bank, insurance or telecommunications organisation, a major university, an airport, a consultancy firm and a smaller employer with less than 250 employees. Examples chosen were all considered to be 'success stories'. Results from both countries showed considerable reductions in car travel with remarkably similar averages across the two sets of case studies. Programmes in the US revealed a range of vehicle trip reduction rates from 6% to 49% with an average of 19%. For programmes in the Netherlands, where reductions were recorded in vehicle kilometres, the range was from 6% to 32% with an average reduction of 20%.

A study by Shoup (1997) focussed on the role of financial incentives in changing travel behaviour. It looked at eight Californian employers, who were required by law to offer a cash allowance as an alternative to free parking at work. This cash-out programme reduced the proportion of people driving alone to work by between 3% and 22%, with an average reduction of 13%. The average reduction in vehicle miles travelled was 12%.

A study of 49 US employers by TCRP (1994) (reported in Organisational Coaching / Schreffler 1996) found an average vehicle trip reduction of 15.3%. It was able to demonstrate that workplace travel programmes combining 'sticks' and 'carrots' were the most effective. Employers providing only information did not realise any trip reduction results. Those providing commute alternatives (such as van pools) realised an average 8.5% reduction, while those providing financial incentives (such as transit subsidies) realised an average 16.4% reduction. Employers providing *both* financial incentives *and* services realised the largest reduction in vehicle use, at an average of 24.5%.

The conclusion that travel plans combining both sticks and carrots are the most effective is echoed in a Dutch study by Ligtermoet (1998). This included a review of other Dutch data plus new results from 40 Dutch organisations. Plans with 'basic' measures (such as car-sharing schemes) achieved vehicle kilometre reductions of 6-8% (or 10% if only the sample 40 organisations are considered). Plans with 'luxury' measures (such as public transport subsidies) and / or 'push' measures (such as parking management) achieved reductions in the range 15 – 20% (or 23% if only the sample 40 organisations are considered).

In another review of Dutch travel plan experience, Touwen (1999) concluded that travel plans consisting of communication/marketing measures, basic measures such as car pooling and cycle leasing, and organisational measures such as flexitime achieved an average reduction of 8% in kilometres travelled by employees driving alone to work. If luxury measures (such as company buses) and disincentive measures (principally parking management) were added, the average reduction was about 20%.

The findings of the studies described above are summarised in the table below. In brief, they suggest that travel plans typically reduce car use by 15-20%, with perhaps higher reductions of 20-25% from plans incorporating measures such as parking management and bus subsidy, and perhaps lower reductions of 5-15% for plans that do not incorporate such measures, However, all plans are individual, and results vary significantly from organisation to organisation.

Table 3.2 Summary of literature evidence about the effects of travel plans

Study	Conclusion
Cairns et al (2002)	A selection of good practice travel plans reduced commuter car driving by an average of at least* 18%. Plans which included parking management measures achieved an average reduction of car driving of >24%, compared with >10% for those that did not.
Organisational Coaching and Shreffler (1996)	Successful travel plans in the US typically reduce vehicle trips by 19%. Successful travel plans in the Netherlands typically reduce vehicle mileage by 20%.
Shoup (1997)	Eight Californian employers offering cash for parking had reduced single occupancy driving by an average of 13% and vehicle miles by 12%.
TCRP (1994)	49 US employers with travel plans had achieved an average vehicle trip reduction of 15%. Averages for different types of plans were: 9% if offering commuting alternatives only (such as van pools)

	16% if offering financial incentives only (such as bus fare subsidy) 25% if offering financial incentives and services
Ligtermoet (1998)	40 Dutch employers (plus an unspecified numbers of others from review work) provided information about different types of plans. This suggested average reductions in vehicle kilometres of: 6-10% for plans with 'basic' measures 15-23% for plans with 'luxury' measures
Touwen (1999)	Information from different types of Dutch travel plan suggested average reductions in single occupancy vehicle kilometres of: 8% for plans with 'basic' measures 20% for plans with 'luxury' measures

* Data and analysis in several of the cases were judged to lead to an underestimate (of unknown size) of the effects of the travel plan work on car commuting, as discussed further in the footnote to table 3.1.

3.3 Literature evidence about take-up of workplace travel plans

Adoption of travel plans in Britain is growing fast, particularly amongst public sector employers.

A study published in 1998 (University of Westminster 1998) found that only 3% of local authorities had implemented a travel plan on a permanent basis and 4% on a trial basis.

Three years later, a survey by Steer Davies Gleave (2001) found a substantial increase in take-up. SDG surveyed 388 local authorities, and (randomly selected) 1000 businesses, 60 hospitals and 40 higher education establishments to gauge take-up of travel plans by these organisations. They found:

- Of the 289 local authorities responding, 24% had a travel plan in place and 45% were developing one.
- Out of 554 businesses responding, only 7% had a travel plan or were developing one. However, larger businesses were much more likely to have a travel plan. Amongst businesses with over 300 staff, 21% already had a travel plan and 10% were considering one.
- Out of 45 hospitals responding, 62% had a travel plan in place or were in the process of developing one, and another 22% were thinking about doing so.
- Of the 29 higher education establishments responding, 52% had a travel plan or were in the process of developing one, and another 10% were thinking about doing so.

Research by Addison and Fraser in 2002 further highlighted that the planning process is increasingly being used as a mechanism for requiring travel plans. This should provide a further spur to travel plan development (although their research also showed that local authority use of the planning system is very varied across the country, and there are concerns about the meaningfulness of planning requirements, given difficulties with monitoring and enforcement). This issue is discussed further in section 3.9.3.

Data supplied for this project by the Department for Transport shows that local authorities expect take-up of travel plans to continue to grow, in both public and private sectors. Table 3.3 shows local authority's predictions of the number of travel plans likely to be implemented between 2001/02 and 2006/07, based on their annual progress reports. The figures suggest about two-thirds of shire district local authorities will have a travel plan by 2006. It is not possible to estimate the proportion of highway authorities that will have a travel plan because the data is reported per work site rather than per authority, but the figure is likely to be as high or higher. Figures for further and higher education establishments suggest slightly over half will have a travel plan by 2006. Figures for hospitals suggest lower take-up, which is surprising given the requirement from the NHS Executive for them to consider their traffic impact. However, other data supplied by NHS Estates indicates that 27% of hospital sites had already implemented a travel plan by 2002/03 (and the difference between the two sets of figures may be an artefact of how local authorities are reporting hospital travel plans to the Department for Transport). Figures for employers suggest about 3600 will have implemented a travel plan by 2006. If we assume almost all these travel plans will be at work sites with over 100 staff, the proportion of larger (>100 staff) workplaces with a travel plan in 2006 will be 11%.

Table 3.3: Number of travel plans local authorities expect to implement between now and 2006

	01-02	02-03	03-04	04-05	05-06	06-07	total with travel plans	number of organisations in England	% with travel plan by 2006-07
Local highway authority site	28	53	65	48	45	16	255*	150	
Shire district	18	36	34	27	20	12	147	238	62%
Further/higher education establishments	28	43	75	51	47	23	267	519	51%
Hospitals	52	68	55	35	33	16	259	1200	22%~
Employers	401	688	656	695	708	421	3569	31,376#	11%#
Total	527	888	885	856	853	488	4497		

Figures are based on Department for Transport analysis of local authority annual progress reports.

* Figures for local highway authority travel plans are reported per site rather than per authority, so it is not possible to estimate the proportion of highway authorities with travel plans.

~ Figures for hospitals may underestimate the proportion covered by a travel plan (possibly because local authorities report one travel plan for a hospital with several sites). Data supplied by NHS Estates suggests 126 Trusts had implemented travel plans by 2002/03, at 322 hospital sites out of 1200, or 27% of hospitals.

Figure is for the number of workplace sites with 100 or more staff, based on the assumption that almost all travel plans are likely to be implemented at these larger sites. Hence figure of 11% is the number of work sites of over 100 staff with travel plans by 2006-07.

These figures are approximate, being based on informed guesses by local authorities. However, they are consistent with the general picture emerging from the University of Westminster and Steer Davies Gleave studies, namely that, proportionally, take-up of travel plans is higher in the public sector than in the private sector; that take-up is growing fast; but that there are a still a large number of organisations without travel plans that could be encouraged to develop them. Meanwhile, the largest *number* of plans being developed is in the private sector. It is notable that local authorities are predicting fewer travel plans being implemented in 2006/07 than in previous years. This is probably because local authorities simply did not know at the time they completed their APR returns how many travel plans might be implemented several years in the future. However, there is a concern that the fall-off might be because local authorities judge that by 2006 they will have reached most of the easy targets. If this is the case, and if further expansion of travel plan activity is considered to be desirable, further incentives and encouragement might be needed to persuade employers (especially in the private sector) to adopt travel plans.

Finally, Rye (2002) used the SDG data on take-up in different sectors to estimate the current effect of travel plans on total distance travelled to work by car. He assumed that travel plans were reducing car use for the trip to work by an average of 6%. (This is probably a reasonable assumption in the early days of most travel plan programmes, although, as highlighted in section 3.2, it would be inappropriate for more mature and well-developed plans). Applying this figure across 62% of hospitals, 40% of higher education institutions, 60% of government organisations and 11% of larger private sector companies, he concluded that workplace travel plans may already be affecting roughly 12% of the workforce and reducing car trips (and car mileage) for the journey to work by roughly 0.7%. His calculation was about the national impact of travel planning, and did not attempt to distinguish between areas where travel planning has been intensively promoted and those where it has not yet been developed.

3.4 Typical costs of workplace travel plans

Cairns et al. (2002) included some information on the average cost to an organisation of implementing a travel plan. The lowest gross annual cost was £2 per full-time equivalent employee (at Agilent Technologies, where the most successful measures were a 33% discount on train fares and service improvements, paid for by ScotRail as part of a partnership arrangement). The highest annual cost was £431 per full-time equivalent employee (at Vodafone, which had 10 dedicated bus services and payments for staff who gave up their parking permits). The median annual running cost was £47 per full-time equivalent employee, which is notably cheaper than the £300-500 often quoted as the annual cost of running a parking space.

Six organisations had considerably reduced their costs by recycling car park revenues, with four reducing their costs to zero. The cost of the travel plan did not relate directly to the degree of change that was achieved, or the overall level of car use at the end. Rather, it was the appropriateness of the measures and overall strategy that was the key to travel plan effectiveness.

In the US, the review of previous research by Organisational Coaching / Schreffler (1996) found that the annual cost of transportation demand management (TDM) programmes ranged from $8 to $105 per employee, but in most cases was closer to $30. Some TDM programmes realised net savings through parking income. However, the 20 paired Dutch and US companies examined in the same study had spent rather more than this. Their costs were in the range $100 - $200, with an average of $187.

3.5   Selection of workplace travel case studies

To complement the evidence from the literature review, we carried out interviews with seven local authorities involved in promoting travel plans in their area. In selecting travel plan case studies, there were many potential local authorities to choose from. However, rather fewer were able to provide data to show what their travel plan work was achieving. This is partly because good travel plan work involves engaging with an organisation which then also puts its own resources and staff time into sustainable travel. It can therefore be difficult for the local authority to identify how much any change in travel can be attributed to their input (as opposed to changes introduced by the organisation). Also, it may be difficult to disentangle travel plan work from other initiatives that are taking place in the area. On one level, travel plan work is distinctive in that it involves taking an organisational/employee perspective - and it is presumed to be relatively effective precisely because it aims to address problems at that level of detail. However, many of the solutions, such as altering bus services or road conditions around a site, may be done as part of other work taking place through the local transport plan anyway. Local authorities also stress that all organisations are different, which makes them reluctant to produce averaged or generalised results from a number of organisations. Finally, it should be noted that although workplace travel plan work is relatively widespread, the resources and staff dedicated to it still tend to be relatively small scale which, apart from anything else, limits the ability of those involved to undertake staff travel monitoring.

Our final selection of workplace travel plan case studies was based on a combination of those places which were known to have a reasonable amount of data about the effects of their work, and those places which were undertaking work on other soft factor initiatives as well as workplace travel plans (on the basis that this might provide interesting insights about the synergies between initiatives).

The final places chosen to study workplace travel plans were:
- Birmingham
- Bristol
- Buckinghamshire
- Cambridgeshire
- Merseyside
- Nottingham
- York

During the case study selection process, we also collected some information about Surrey.

Some case studies about other soft factors also provided insights on factors influencing travel to work:
- the car sharing schemes in Milton Keynes and Buckinghamshire
- the use of personalised journey plans as part of South Yorkshire PTE's Travel Options Planning Service (TOPS)
- tele-working and tele-conferencing at British Telecom
- elements of the travel awareness campaign in York.

3.6 Details of chosen workplace travel case studies

Some key features of the seven workplace travel plan case studies are summarised here. In the next section we look in more detail at the different approaches they adopted.

Birmingham: Birmingham City Council co-ordinates an initiative called Company TravelWise. The council's approach is to offer companies a menu of options that the council can provide, rather than expecting each company to develop its own travel plan. Some 165 companies are affiliated to Company TravelWise.

Bristol: Bristol City Council's workplace travel plan programme currently involves contact with 85 employers. The programme involves development and support for travel plan networks as well as advice to individual employers to develop their own plans. There is an award scheme for companies which have successfully cut car commuting, and grants to enable employers to develop particular measures.

Buckinghamshire: Buckinghamshire County Council's workplace travel plan initiative is branded 'Travel Choice'. One of its notable successes is the county's travel plan for its own staff, which has cut single-occupancy car commuting from 71.3% to 49.4% over five years. Having proved the concept can be successful via their own plan, the council is now working with another 32 companies and organisations based in the county.

Cambridgeshire: A 'Travel for Work Partnership' is jointly funded by the county council, two district councils, the University, Addenbrooke's Hospital and the Primary Care Trust. At the time of the interview, 44 members of the partnership were considered to be developing travel plans, and most of the commentary in this chapter is about their work. Meanwhile, another 50 – 60 employers have separately been engaged in travel planning via the planning system.

Merseyside: Workplace travel planning is co-ordinated through a partnership between the five Merseyside local authorities and Merseytravel, known as Merseyside Travelwise. Following a major expansion of staff in 2001, Merseyside Travelwise is now developing travel plans with 57 organisations.

Nottingham: Nottingham was a pioneer of the workplace travel planning concept, with the introduction of its first plans in the early 1990s. There are now 25 organisations with active travel plans (35 in the Greater Nottingham LTP area) and the council has specifically prioritised working in depth with these organisations, in preference to engaging with an increasing number. The city's plan to introduce a workplace parking levy is encouraging employers to invest in travel plans.

York: Although the council had only had a dedicated workplace travel co-ordinator for six months at the time of our interview, 30 York employers were engaged in travel planning at some level.

3.7 Tactics used to promote workplace travel plans

The tactics used to promote workplace travel plans showed some variation between the different case studies. Some authorities engage in intensive work with a small number of organisations, while others adopt a broad-brush approach, providing information and general support to many companies.

York is a good example of a local authority with an intensive approach. The council carries out staff travel surveys for companies, gives detailed feedback on the results and advises on the best initiatives to start with. It can assist companies in drawing up a plan, and can also help secure grants, for example from the DfT cycle projects fund.

In contrast, Birmingham has more of a broad brush approach. Rather than working with individual companies to draw up a tailored workplace travel plan, the council has developed a standard travel plan, Company TravelWise, and companies are invited to implement the elements of it that they are attracted to. Some companies simply want to receive public transport information mailings from the council, CENTRO and Travel West Midlands, while others request specific help from the TravelWise team, for example in resolving a problem with bus routes, or poor access from a business park to a station. Where such help is requested, the TravelWise team are eager to provide it: the broad-brush approach sits alongside tailored support where it is requested.

Whichever approach is adopted, it is clear that in order to 'get a foot in the door' with companies, the local authorities need to be able to offer something in return. Sometimes interest is generated by parking problems or local authority restrictions on parking. The local authorities are also usually able to offer incentives to engage companies in travel planning. The main incentives used are described in more detail below, and include:
- Discounts on public transport, and spending on public transport infrastructure
- Information about public transport
- Cycle initiatives
- Walking initiatives
- Centrally co-ordinated car-sharing schemes
- Grants to develop travel plans, or to provide specific infrastructure.
- Attachment of conditions to planning permission

Alongside these incentives, all the case studies used various publicity techniques to attract the interest of companies, and offered networking opportunities to support companies in developing their travel plans.

- **Discounts on public transport and spending on infrastructure**
In three of the case studies, the local authority had negotiated special deals with public transport operators, which were available to some or all organisations with travel plans.

In Birmingham, the partnership between the council, CENTRO and Travel West Midlands has made it possible to offer a 50% discount on an annual season ticket to staff at companies affiliated to Company TravelWise, if they give up driving to work.

In York, the main bus company, First York, offers a six-month free bus pass to commuters who give up driving to work.

In Buckinghamshire, the county council has negotiated a 34% discount with Chiltern Railways, and a 50% discount with Arriva. Discounts were available to family members as well as employees, and covered all journeys, not just the journey to work. This was a particularly good deal, but required negotiation on an organisation by organisation basis. At the time of the interview, the Council had also helped to negotiate discounts for the police, and for the private company Ercol.

In Cambridgeshire, the council had worked in partnership with Addenbrooke's Hospital to build a new bus station on the hospital site, which has resulted in a large increase in bus use.

- **Information about public transport**

Birmingham organises regular mailings of public transport timetables and other information to Company TravelWise affiliates. All affiliates are also offered branded Company TravelWise notice-boards, for displaying information. In York, individual journey planners for employees are free, and the council is piloting customised public transport information with a 'lifestyle' leaflet promoting buses to Norwich Union. In Buckinghamshire, providing organisations with public transport information (and persuading them to display it), was seen as a good way of starting a dialogue with an organisation without scaring them off. South Yorkshire PTE has developed tailored public transport information for workplaces as a key part of its general public transport promotion work.

- **Cycling initiatives**

In Bristol, the local authority has a service level agreement of £30,000 a year with local organisation Lifecycle to provide 125 adult cycle training sessions, up to two Sheffield racks per SME, to work with up to 12 employers on Bicycle User Groups and to provide tailored cycle route advice to individuals. Organisations can then opt to receive these services. In Cambridgeshire, the Travel for Work partnership has helped in the development and distribution of a cycle route map, runs adult cycle training sessions and has a specific grants scheme for installing cycle parking.

Various local authorities have also negotiated discounts on cycle equipment for travel plan organisations. In Cambridgeshire, the Travel for Work Partnership has negotiated discounts for members at local cycle shops. In Birmingham, about 20 of the companies affiliated to Company TravelWise are termed 'support companies'. These companies offer discounts to Company TravelWise affiliates for equipment such as cycle parking stands.

- **Walking initiatives**

Local authorities were promoting walking in different ways. Buckinghamshire was piloting a 'walk-share' scheme, to match people who might want to walk together (for example, for security reasons, particularly on winter evenings). In Merseyside and York, there has been a lot of awareness-raising work relating to the health benefits of walking. For example, Merseyside produces walking maps with 'calorie counts' used for different routes. In Nottingham, Nottingham City Hospital has worked in partnership with the council on pedestrian improvements.

- **Car-sharing**

County-wide car-sharing schemes operate in Cambridgeshire and Buckinghamshire, and a city-wide scheme operates in York. In Bristol, a car-share scheme has been developed for the Temple Quay central business site. The Milton Keynes car share scheme is aimed at journeys to work in the central business area.

- **Grants to assist in developing travel plans**

In Nottingham, the county and city councils have set up a grant scheme, TransACT, to encourage small and medium businesses to develop travel plans. Companies receive up to £20,000 to fund works arising from travel plans. In Bristol, companies can receive grants of up to £5000 to fund 40-50% of the costs of their travel plan initiatives. In Buckinghamshire, the council has held prize draws for companies, with the prize being a covered cycle shelter, and in Cambridgeshire, there is a grant scheme for cycle parking. Merseyside had not introduced a grants system at the time of the case study interview, but was planning to do so.

- **Planning permission**

Attitudes varied to the use of the planning system to promote travel planning. For example, in Birmingham, it was used very proactively – as all planning approvals for developments with 50 or more employees include a condition that the company must join Company TravelWise. In contrast, Nottingham tries to avoid securing travel plans through the development process, preferring that travel plans are entered into voluntarily on the basis of 'business benefits'. This issue is discussed in more detail in section 3.9.3.

- **Publicity and information**

Buckinghamshire has placed strong emphasis on 'feel-good' publicity to attract interest in travel plans and increase brand recognition of Travel Choice. This has included events such as Green Roadshows, business breakfast and dinners, advertising (on bus backs, and at cinemas) and a wide range of promotional materials such as branded Frisbees and post-it pads.

The Cambridgeshire Travel for Work Partnership has a dedicated website, regular newsletters and various email circulation groups. Buckinghamshire, Nottingham and Merseyside have all produced their own guides for employers, explaining how to draw up a travel plan.

All the case study authorities considered that an important part of their work is to meet with employers, and many mentioned that they often attended meetings with employees to provide information, for example about public transport options.

However, some, such as Cambridgeshire, mentioned that they are still relatively reactive in terms of who they work with, due to resource constraints, and are careful not to 'over-advertise', for fear that they would not be able to meet demand. Nottingham has decided that local authority time is best spent working with the 25 largest employers in the city, and is concentrating time and effort on those companies.

- **Commuter planner clubs and forums**

Most of the case study authorities organise regular meetings of employers to share ideas about travel plans. In Nottingham, a Commuter Planners Club meets quarterly, and there are also sub-groups bringing together employers from a particular geographical area to tackle issues of common interest. For example, employers based near the train station have worked with Central Trains on promotions.

Bristol has similar networking opportunities, with an Avon Green Commuter Club and sub-groups such as the Temple Quay Employers Group. Birmingham has set up groups or clusters of companies, some of which focus on a particular geographical area while others are sector specific – for example, there is a hospital group and there are plans for a college group.

- **Monitoring**

The local authorities' approach to monitoring progress was quite variable. Some offered to undertake travel surveys as part of the 'package' that they could offer to organisations. Others did not. This issue is discussed further in section 3.10.

3.8 Staffing and budgets for workplace travel planning

The seven workplace travel plan case studies had quite similar staffing levels and budgets. These are illustrated in table 3.4.

3.8.1 Current budgets

Total annual expenditure (including staff costs within the local authority *and* in outside agencies such as the PTE in Birmingham) lay within the range £52,000 - £200,000. The lowest spending authority was York, which is also the smallest area in terms of population and workforce. The highest spending authority was Nottingham, which has a substantial programme of travel planning grants to businesses.

In some local authorities, almost all the budget was consumed by staff salary costs, with little left over for publicity materials or other incentives to encourage take-up of travel plans. The most marked example of this was in Birmingham, where Company TravelWise had no dedicated budget (although this was due to change). About £12,000 a year was secured from other budgets within the local authority and from external sponsorship, for information materials and Company TravelWise noticeboards. At the other end of the spectrum, Nottingham allocated £100,000 a year to its grant scheme to encourage small and medium sized enterprises to develop travel plans. Clearly local authorities where there is less funding available to promote workplace travel plans are likely to have to find other tactics to interest companies in adoption of travel planning measures: examples include the discounts on public transport travel negotiated in York and Birmingham, and the proactive approach to incorporating travel planning into planning conditions in York and Cambridgeshire.

Table 3.4: Comparison of staffing and budgets for workplace travel plans (summer 2003)

	Birmingham[3]	Bristol[4]	Buckinghamshire[5]	Cambridgeshire (TfW)[6]	Merseyside[7]	Nottingham[8]	York[9]
Length of time scheme has been running	5 years	5 years	5 years (3 mainly)	6 years	5 years (2 mainly)	8 years	5 years (1 mainly)
Number of companies local authority is working with	145	60	33	44	57	35	30
Number of employees in companies with WTP	136,000	29,960	21,700	34,000	55,870	52,000	26,187
Proportion of workforce covered by travel plans	29%	13%	11%	12 or 29%	8%	28%	29%
Staff time in local authority / PTE and outside agencies initially[1]	1 fte	0.25 fte	1 fte	1 fte	1 fte	1 fte	0.3 fte
Staff time in local authority / PTE and outside agencies once scheme established	3 fte	1.25 fte	1.5 fte	1.6 fte	3 fte	3 fte	1.5 fte
Estimated expenditure in first *intensive* year[2] — Capital	0	0	£14,000	0	0	0	0
Estimated expenditure in first *intensive* year[2] — Revenue	£27,000	£10,000	£77,500	£25,000	£98,000	£25,000	£52,000
Estimated expenditure in most recent year — Capital	0	0	£25,000	0	0	0	0
Estimated expenditure in most recent year — Revenue	£97,000	£130,000	£82,500	£57,500	£98,000	£200,000	£52,000

1 'Staff time initially' gives staff time when the local authority first began travel planning.

2 'First intensive year' is usually the year when the local authority first began travel planning, but for Buckinghamshire, Merseyside and York it is the year when the authority significantly scaled up its activity.

3 Birmingham first year expenditure assumes one full-time post, estimated at £25,000, plus small additional costs. Expenditure in most recent year includes estimated £25,000 for one post at CENTRO as well as city council costs.

4 Bristol first year expenditure assumes a quarter of a full-time post plus £4000 for promotional work. Most recent year figure includes £65,000 for salaries and £65,000 for grants and promotional materials.

5 Buckinghamshire began workplace travel planning roughly five years ago, and initial staff time refers to this date. Expenditure figures cover only the period of more intensive activity, from about 2000 when the county started promoting travel plans to other organisations (not just its own staff). Estimates of first intensive year expenditure are based on 2001/02 figures to which are added cost of 1.5 staff posts at an estimated £25,000 per post. Current year expenditure estimates are based on figures for 2003/04 plus 1.5 staff posts at £25,000 per post.

6 All figures relate to Cambridgeshire Travel for Work initiative only: council planning department work and Travel Choices personalised travel planning initiative excluded. Lower figure for proportion of workforce covered by travel plans relates to workforce for entire county; higher figure for workforce in Cambridge City and South Cambridgeshire, where most travel planning work has been focussed. First year expenditure assumes one full-time post estimated at £25,000. Expenditure in most recent year includes £35,500 for the Travel for Work Partnership (which includes staff costs) and £22,000 for individual projects.

7 Merseyside began travel planning five years ago, and initial staff time refers to this date. Expenditure figures cover only the recent period of more intensive activity, when there have been three fte staff delivering workplace travel plans as part of a team of seven. Expenditure has been calculated by assuming that 3/7ths of the total revenue budget for travel planning in Merseyside is for workplace travel work.

8 Nottingham first year expenditure assumes one staff post at £25,000. Current year expenditure includes actual cost of workplace travel staff, including the TransACT co-ordinator at the Chamber of Commerce.

9 York began travel planning five years ago, and initial staff time refers to this date. Expenditure figures cover only the period of more intensive activity of nearly one year during which a full-time staff member has been in post.

We compared funding levels for workplace travel planning with those for school travel planning in Buckinghamshire, Merseyside and York. All three areas have given a lower priority, in terms of budget and staffing, to workplace travel. Even leaving aside capital funding (which tends to be higher for school travel work because it includes safe routes infrastructure), revenue funding for promotional work was lower for workplaces than for schools. In Buckinghamshire, annual revenue spending on workplace travel plans is £82,500, compared to an estimated £184,500 on school travel. In Merseyside, revenue spending on workplace travel plans is £98,000, compared to an estimated £156,000 on school travel. In York, revenue spending on workplace travel plans is £52,000, compared to £63,000 on school travel. These disparities seem surprising when one reflects that travel to work accounts for a far greater proportion of mileage than travel to school, and the potential to affect overall traffic levels is therefore greater.

3.8.2 Current levels of staffing

Most of the case studies had between one and two full-time equivalent posts dedicated to workplace travel plans within the local authority. In Birmingham and Nottingham there were additional posts in outside agencies (the PTE and the Chamber of Commerce respectively) with which the local authority was working closely, bringing the team of people promoting workplace travel planning to three. Merseyside Travelwise had the largest complement of in-house staff dedicated to travel planning: out of seven travel planning staff, there were two full-time posts dedicated to workplace travel plans, and two other staff working some of the time on workplace travel.

Partnerships with other agencies were common. For example, as highlighted, in Birmingham the local authority works closely with staff from CENTRO and the local bus operator Travel West Midlands, and in Nottingham the local authority funds a post in the Chamber of Commerce to administer their travel planning grants scheme. In Cambridgeshire, much of the proactive promotion of travel plans is carried out by the Cambridgeshire Travel for Work Partnership, which is jointly funded by three local authorities, two health bodies and the university.

In several cases, additional staff had been recruited relatively recently. For example, in York, a full time member of staff had only become dedicated to working on workplace travel plans within the previous six months (at the time of our interview). Generally, staffing levels were increasing, but the withdrawal of the DfT bursaries at the time interviews were carried out was giving rise to anxiety that some staff posts would be lost.

Cambridgeshire was able to provide some comparative data on staffing levels, based on a review that they had carried out of travel plan activity by other local authorities. This suggests that across the country, local authority staffing levels for travel planning are generally somewhat lower than those reported from our case studies. Of ten local authorities for which data had been gathered (none of them the same as our case studies), seven had the equivalent of 1 full-time post, two had 0.5 or 0.6 fte posts, and one had 2 fte posts.

3.8.3 Changes over time in staffing and budgets

When the case study local authorities began their travel planning work, they all spent quite low sums of money, with typically one full-time or part-time staff post and a revenue budget of a few thousand pounds. There was little up-front expenditure which might be considered as a capital cost. Although all the case studies have been involved in some form of travel planning work for between five and eight years at the time of our interviews, several had only recently increased staffing to the level at which it became possible to engage in a thorough way with a significant number of companies. This is one reason why some local authorities were able to report rather few 'after' monitoring results, as discussed later.

3.8.4 Costs per employee

It is interesting to see how the cost per employee targeted varies between the case study areas. Data for this is shown in table 3.5. Birmingham, which has reached many people relatively quickly, is working with employees at a cost of 70 pence a head. In contrast, Buckinghamshire is still at the stage of persuading employers to engage with them, such that overall costs are relatively expensive – approximately £5 per employee. Cambridgeshire, York and Merseyside are all operating at a cost of about £2 per head, whilst Bristol and Nottingham (who both now offer a grants scheme for employers) are spending about £4 a head. It could be argued that once travel planning work is underway, initial costs will work out at £2 per head, but that as additional incentives are needed to engage more 'reluctant' employers or to encourage the implementation of more substantial measures, the cost will rise to about £4 per head.

Table 3.5: Cost of workplace travel plans per employee targeted

	Cost per employee targeted (£)
Birmingham	0.7
Bristol	4.3
Buckinghamshire	5.0
Cambridgeshire	1.7
Merseyside	1.8
Nottingham	3.8
York	2.0

Calculation based on expenditure (capital + revenue) in current year and staff affected by travel plans in current year

It should be noted that this is the cost to the local authority of encouraging the take-up of travel plans amongst other organisations. This is different to the costs quoted in section 3.4, which related to the typical costs *to the employer* of implementing a travel plan. In many cases, the costs to the employer are likely to be greater, since the travel plan is likely to involve the introduction and facilitation of alternative travel options. However, as discussed in 3.4 and in the chapters on telework and teleconferencing, there is also the opportunity for the employer to recoup their costs through parking revenues, better use of site space etc., and some employers have managed to introduce very cheap but effective travel plans, via, for example, negotiation of public transport discounts with operators in return for agreeing to market their services to staff.

3.9 Comparison of case study findings on the scale of workplace travel planning

3.9.1 Number of employees and companies engaged in travel planning

The scale of local authorities' travel planning work can be assessed either in terms of the number of organisations they are working with, or the number of staff covered. The scale of work in the case study areas at the time of our interviews is shown in table 3.6.

Table 3.6: Summary of local authority engagement on travel plans (summer 2003)

Location	Number of staff in companies with WTP	Number of companies local authority is working with	% staff	% companies
Birmingham	136,000	145 (+20*)	29	0.5-0.6
Bristol	29,960	60 (+25#)	13	--
Buckinghamshire	21,700	33	11	--
Cambridgeshire	34,000	44 (+16*)	29 or 12~	0.5 or 0.3
Merseyside	55,870	57	8	--
Nottingham	52,000	35 (+265#)	28	0.5
City of York	26,187	30	29	0.6

*These are support companies – e.g. cycle shops – and non employer steering group members such as Cambridge cycling campaign.
These are members of travel plan networks who are largely inactive, or with whom the council has little involvement
~ First figure is the % of employees in the two main target districts (Cambridge City and South Cambridgeshire). The second figure is for the percentage of all employees in the county.

Most city authorities (Nottingham, Birmingham and York) had managed to engage organisations representing about 30% of staff. Bristol's engagement had been relatively lower, with 13% of staff affected.

In contrast, the larger authorities (Cambridgeshire, Merseyside and Buckinghamshire) had engaged organisations representing 8-12% of employees (although in Cambridgeshire the proportion of employees engaged in travel planning rises to 29% if one looks only at the City and South Cambridgeshire, where most travel planning work is concentrated). It should be noted that Birmingham, although a larger authority, had engaged with a large proportion of its organisations and workforce, presumably due to its distinctive broad-brush approach.

In total, there are about 2.2 million employees in the seven areas, of which about 356,000 (16%) had become engaged in travel plans by summer 2003.

All locations had engaged with only small fraction of total companies in their local area, and preferred to concentrate their efforts on the larger employers.

It is difficult to compare these with the national figures given in section 3.3, where the data provides information about engagement levels of different types of organisation, rather than proportions of employees. However, a tentative suggestion would be that some of our case study areas have already managed to achieve above average take up of travel plans (compared to local authority estimates for 2006), particularly in urban areas. This issue is discussed further in section 3.9.5.

3.9.2 Evolution of approach

Table 3.7 explains how the different local authorities have developed their work on travel plans over time.

Table 3.7: Details of the evolution of local authority approaches to travel planning

Location	
Birmingham	The city council began writing its own travel plan in 1997. In 1998, the standard 'Company TravelWise' service was launched. By 2001, 101 organisations were affiliated. By summer 2003, there were 165 affiliated organisations. The council has deliberately prioritised breadth over depth. There is no specific targeting – involvement is voluntary or via the planning process. Larger organisations show more interest - most of the top 100 employers in the city are members. The council is now developing groups of workplaces, including sector-specific (e.g. hospital and college groups) and area-based groups (e.g. Castle Bromwich, with Jaguar, Goodyear and Baxi Fires).
Bristol	Bristol began work on travel planning in 1997/98, and began to develop networks including the 'Green Commuter Club'. In 2000, 26 organisations were involved. By 2002, this had grown to 69, and by summer 2003, there were 85 members of the club. The LTP indicated 9 major target sites – Temple Quay (town centre business site); United Bristol Hospital Trust; Bristol University; City of Bristol College; Bristol City Council; Central city area; Cabot Business Park; Southmead and Blackberry Hill hospitals; and Avonmouth & Brislington trading estates. In general the approach is to target major employers, key sites such as hospitals, and major leisure complexes. There has also been an emphasis on the public admin/banking/insurance industries (50% employees) and hotels/manufacturing sector (33% employees). A recent priority is the tourist businesses along the harbour side. Increasing interest in travel planning has meant that the authority is now developing a more reactive approach, and is working with organisations involved through the planning process.
Buckinghamshire	The county started with work on its own travel plan in 1998. It was expected that many organisations outside the local authority would want to work with them to develop travel plans but this did not turn out to be the case. The lack of interest has led, instead, to intensive work with fewer organisations. In 2000/01, they were working with 11 organisations, whilst by 2001/02, 19 travel plans had been introduced. In 2002/03, 24 plans had been implemented – and by summer 2003, the total was 33. In 2003, they were proactive in targeting all businesses with >100 staff (around 80 in total), with a 20% response rate. They are also targeting local

	business parks, including Cressex Globe Park and Slough Trading Estate. They feel that there are particular opportunities when a company relocates. They also try to engage organisations at a relatively low level (e.g. persuading them to display public transport information) and then build on the relationship. Their work tends to focus on organisations in the urban centres of Aylesbury, High Wycombe and Amersham. They have had problems engaging with the health sector.
Cambridgeshire	The Travel for Work Partnership was set up in 1997, as a development of the Cambridgeshire Cycle Friendly Employers Partnership. By 1998, there were 25-30 members, and numbers have grown gradually since then. In general, they have found that there is more interest from larger organisations and public sector organisations. Their work is mainly focused on Cambridge City and South Cambridgeshire – the economically booming parts of the county. There has also been close involvement of the health sector.
Merseyside	In 1998, a member of staff was appointed to work on sustainable travel issues, including some travel plan work. In 1999, a second staff member was appointed (with a similarly broad remit). Work on travel plans really took off with the appointment of 2 bursary post holders specifically for travel plans in 2001. Merseyside now targets all partner local authorities, health and education sites; large employers; tourism and leisure sites; and strategic investment/Objective 1 areas. When a dialogue begins with an employer, the team works intensively with that employer, although it is hoped that there will be spill-over into other organisations in the local area.
Nottingham	Nottingham has specifically focused their work on the 25 largest organisations and would probably dedicate additional resources to working more intensively with them rather than working with new organisations. Work in the area began with the County Council's travel plan in 1992. In 1995, the City (and county) set up a 'Commuter Planners Club'. Initially, this had 10 members (representing 10-15,000 staff) – cherry picked to be the largest employers in the city. By summer 2003, there were 300 members, although only 35 were attending regularly. Two city based sub-groups of the club were set up in 1999 (South Side and North Side Employers Groups). Area wide travel plans are now also being completed for business parks and clusters of companies. For example, organisations near the train station worked with Central Trains on promotions, and one – Capital One – now has more than 15% staff arriving by train.
City of York	Some work on travel plans has taken place since 1998, but a dedicated officer was only appointed in 2003. In 2000, there were 5 organisations with travel plans and 16 developing them. By 2002, there were 12 with plans and 11 developing them (representing 24000 or 27% of employees). By summer 2003, there were about 30 organisations involved in travel planning. Initially, large public sector employers were targeted. This was

	followed by targetting all employers with over 300 staff. The rationale was that it was easier to find the right person to work with; these organisations were more likely to have problems with recruiting and parking; and the council's intervention was more likely to be effective. The City prioritised intensive working with these organisations. They are now starting to work with smaller employers and business parks and may go for a more broad brush approach. Over time, their approach has become more focused, putting more emphasis on 'health and lifestyle', and carefully tailored individual advice such as journey planners for employees.

The information from table 3.7 provides the following insights:

- At least two local authorities (Birmingham and Buckinghamshire) started work by developing travel plans for their own local authority
- At least four local authorities have engaged organisations by developing networks of interested employers - specifically, the Company TravelWise scheme in Birmingham, the Green Commuters Club in Bristol, the Travel for Work Partnership in Cambridgeshire, and the Commuters Planners Club in Nottingham.
- Nottingham was the earliest to start work on travel planning (1995). It was followed by Bristol (1997), Birmingham (1997) and Cambridgeshire (1997). Although the other three authorities (Buckinghamshire, Merseyside and York) theoretically began work around the same time, in practice major work on travel planning has only taken place in these areas in the last few years.
- All local authorities are seeing a growth in the number of employers that they engage with. However, Nottingham has developed a unique approach, in that it is choosing to concentrate the majority of its efforts on the top 25 largest employers.
- As travel planning work has developed, those responsible are increasingly engaging with the planning system (as discussed in more detail in section 3.9.3). Several are also choosing to set up sector-specific or area-based groups (including business parks), for example in Birmingham, Bristol, Buckinghamshire and Nottingham.
- All local authorities are targeting larger organisations and public sector organisations. The majority have been successful at engaging with the health sector, although Buckinghamshire has had problems with this.
- Work is often focused on areas of economic growth. In some cases, particularly Bristol and Merseyside, initiatives are taking place in partnership with regeneration work, although in Merseyside there has been some concern about conflicting objectives, which is in the process of being resolved.

Figures 3.1 and 3.2 show how the numbers of engaged organisations and employees have changed over time. Almost all local authorities are engaging an increasing number of organisations over time. The rate of growth is similar in six of the case study areas, but much higher in Birmingham, where the council's distinctive approach has led to engagement with a far higher number of employers and employees.

Figure 3.1: Growth in number of employers covered by travel planning work

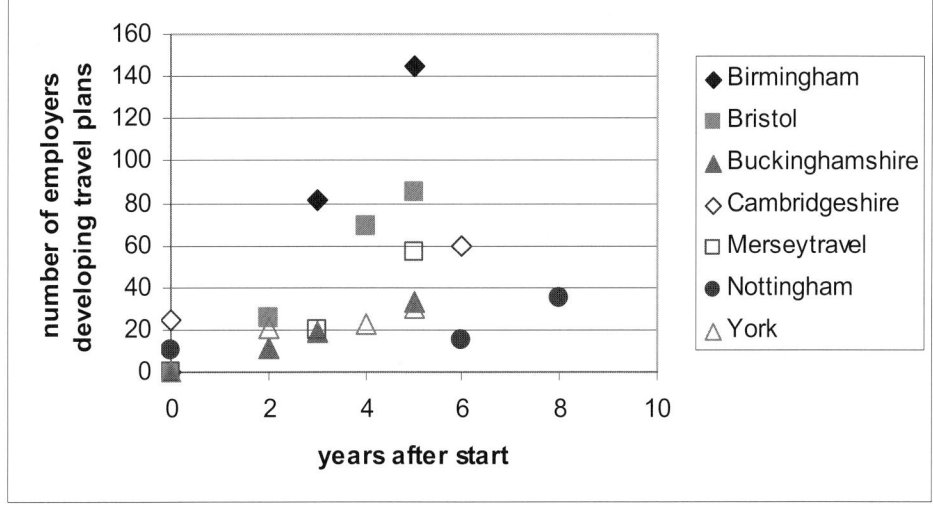

Figure 3.2: Growth in number of employees covered by travel planning work

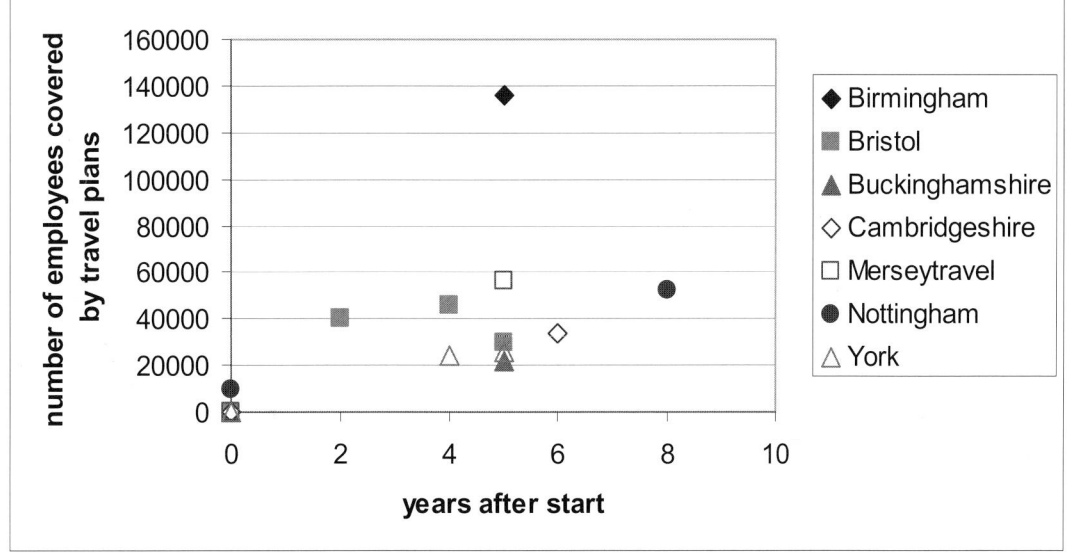

3.9.3 Use of the planning system

It is now useful to look at how the planning system is used in relation to travel planning, since this is becoming an increasingly important mechanism for engaging organisations, as examined in depth in recent Department for Transport research by Addison and Fraser (2002). The experience of our case study areas is summarised in table 3.8.

Table 3.8: Use of the planning process (summer 2003)

Location	
Birmingham	53% of organisations have been involved due to planning requirement. Planning conditions are used to require all new developments that will have 50+ employees to join Company TravelWise. If a company is already a member, the planning condition will require them to remain active in Company TravelWise. Companies are also asked to produce reports of activity.

Bristol	Travel planning conditions are increasingly being included in section 106 agreements.
Buckinghamshire	Planning applications that are expected to generate significant traffic are generally required to include a commitment to a travel plan. However, this is sometimes difficult to achieve because the county is not the planning authority, and not all district councils are as proactive as they might be in ensuring a travel plan is made a planning condition.
Cambridgeshire	The planning process is used to require travel plans and developer contributions to travel measures. Different levels of commitment to travel planning are required, depending on the nature of the development. However, there is little link between development control and the Travel for Work Partnership at present – organisations required to implement travel plans as a planning condition are left to undertake the implementation themselves.
Merseyside	There have been a few occasions when S106 agreements have been used to require travel plans, although the system is not well developed. There have also been concerns about mismatching between the aims of travel planning and attracting inward investment. Supplementary Planning Guidance is being drawn up to address this.
Nottingham	The city council prefers travel plans to be entered into voluntarily. Seven of the 25 large employers have been subject to planning requirements (largely relating to parking allocations), although they were already engaged in travel plan work. Planning applications for new developments with more than 50 parking spaces are referred to the Transport Partnership Officer for comment.
City of York	The travel plan officer scrutinises all planning applications and advises on inclusion of travel plan issues in planning conditions. She spends 10-15% of her time on this work, and perhaps another 10% on issues (including enforcement) relating to old planning permissions with travel plan conditions.

In summary, all local authorities use the planning system to require travel plans. However the approach taken was very different in different locations at the time of our interviews. In Bristol, Buckinghamshire and Merseyside, the approach was still relatively informal, although in Merseyside, supplementary planning guidance was being drawn up due to concerns about streamlining travel planning with regeneration work. The approach was more formal in the other four authorities although different approaches were still taken.

Both Birmingham and Nottingham had guidelines regarding use of planning conditions. In Nottingham, all proposals for new developments with more than 50 parking spaces were being referred to the travel plans officer for consideration. However Nottingham prefers that the planning system is used as little as possible, believing that travel plans are more effective if they are entered into voluntarily. In Birmingham, all developments that will have more than 50 employees are required to join Company TravelWise. This has been a major means of recruiting organisations to Company TravelWise.

In Cambridgeshire, the planning system was also being used to involve developers in travel work. There are guidelines for developer contributions (a fixed fee per trip generated, with the amount depending on location). However no formal link was being made between a planning condition to draw up a workplace travel plan and referral to the Travel for Work Partnership.

The most intensive use of the planning system was in York, where the travel plan officer scrutinises all planning applications and advises on the inclusion of travel plan initiatives in planning conditions.

3.9.4 Quality of travel plans

We were interested in the proportion of travel plans in each case study area that were felt by the interviewees to be 'fully-fledged', including some degree of parking management, since these are the travel plans that are likely to deliver the greatest reduction in car use. Table 3.9 shows the breakdown of employers and staff covered by fully-fledged travel plans, those with more limited travel work not including parking management, and those just starting a travel plan. The figures are approximate, and discussion of this point led several local authorities to express concern that no clear definition exists of what constitutes an effective travel plan.

Table 3.9: Breakdown of organisations involved based on their degree of involvement in travel planning work (summer 2003)

Location		Considering or starting plan	Some travel work (but not parking management)			Fully fledged travel plan including parking management
Birmingham~	Employers	10%	60%			30%
Bristol*	Employers	30%	30%			39%
	Staff	7%	48%			46%
Buckinghamshire	Employers	18%	42%			39%
	Staff	38%	6%			55%
Cambridgeshire	Employers	59%	12%			29%
	Staff	36%	1%			63%
Merseyside	Staff	7%	38% - some work but mainly awareness raising or only a few initiatives		12%	42%
Nottingham	Employers	29%#	--			71%
	Staff	4%				96%
City of York	Employers	30%	13% some work; 43% full travel plan without parking management			13%
	Staff	46%	1% some travel work; 19% full travel plan without parking management			34%

~ Figures for Birmingham based on the council's frequency of contact with organisations
* Figures for Bristol are based on the length of time companies have been developing travel plans
# Figures for Nottingham assume 35 engaged organisations. There are another 265 CPC members.

At the time of our interviews, both Cambridgeshire and Nottingham were planning to develop the Department for Transport travel planning evaluation tool, in order to provide themselves with some way of assessing travel plan quality. In the case of Nottingham, this was linked to their need to assess whether to award companies rebates on the workplace parking levy. In Cambridgeshire, the aim was to develop an accreditation scheme for travel plans which could assist the planning division with their work.

Table 3.9 demonstrates that local authorities have focused on working with larger organisations first. They also appear to have been relatively successful. By summer 2003, between 34% and 96% of staff that have been affected by travel plan work were considered to be in organisations with fully fledged travel plans including parking management. After this, they appeared to fall into two groups. In Buckinghamshire, Cambridgeshire, York and, to some extent, Merseyside, about a third to half of all staff covered by travel plans were working for organisations which were just starting out. In Bristol, Nottingham (and possibly Birmingham), rather few staff were working for organisations which were at this early stage.

3.9.5 Types of organisation engaged in travel planning

Local authorities were also asked to give the breakdown of the different kinds organisations that they are working with. The results are shown in table 3.10.

Table 3.10 demonstrates that, proportionally, engagement is generally higher with public sector organisations, although numerically, local authorities are typically dealing with larger numbers of private companies. The majority of local authorities themselves have travel plans, and a significant fraction of both the health and education sectors have plans (typically between 29 and 80%). Engagement with larger organisations is relatively successful (possibly in the order of 20 to 40% of organisations with more than 300 staff), typically representing engagement with 10-30 companies per se. Most local authorities are also working with small and medium enterprises, although usually only a tiny fraction of the total number. It is notable that Birmingham is working with considerably more than any of the other local authorities, presumably because of its distinctive approach. As mentioned previously, several local authorities have chosen to focus on business parks as key target areas. It should be noted that several interviewees highlighted the problem of whether a travel plan should be defined by organisation or by work site – which explains, for example, why the figures in the local authority column are significantly different.

As discussed earlier, comparisons with national data (as given in section 3.3) are problematic, as the data are in different formats. However, we tentatively suggest that our case study areas are doing at least as well, if not better, in terms of their level of engagement with organisations in their area.

Table 3.10 Breakdown of organisations involved in travel planning by sector (summer 2003)

Location	LA	Ed.	NHS	GP	Public	<300	>300	Other
Birmingham	1 (100%)	12 (80%)	12 (60%)	4	16	65	33	2
Bristol	33 sites	2	3	n/a	12	13	22	
Buckinghamshire	2 (40%~)	3	3	1	2	10	9	2
Cambridgeshire*	5 (100% or 83%)	5 (2%*)	6 (29% or 14%)	2 (3%)	8 (2%)	4 (<0.1%)	11 (31% or 20%)	3
Merseyside	6 (100%)	11	12	n/a	n/a	36		n/a
Nottingham	1 (100%)	4	2	n/a	n/a	n/a	25~	n/a
City of York	1 (100%)	3-6 (38-60%)	6 (66%)	0	7	5	8 (36%)	n/a

Notes:

LA = Local authority

Ed = Further / higher education

NHS = Health (excluding GP surgeries)

GP = GP surgeries

Public = Other public sector or voluntary organisation

<300 = Private sector organisation with <300 staff

>300 = Private sector organisation with >300 staff

Where a percentage is given in brackets after the total, this refers to total proportion of organisations of that type which the local authority has engaged with. For Cambridgeshire, figures are given for both the proportion of organisations in the two districts where most of the work has taken place, and for the county as a whole.

* for Cambridgeshire, percentage figures were derived from comparisons with the number of workplace business units. This may have led to some data oddities – in particular, the figure for engagement with higher education establishments may be misleadingly low, as the university travel plan probably covers a number of 'workplace business units'.

~ These figures are inferred from the case studies, rather than being reported directly by interviewees.

3.9.6 Summary of case study data about the scale of travel plan work

Typically, local authorities representing urban areas had managed to engage with organisations employing about 30% of staff, whilst the larger, county authorities had engaged with organisations employing 8-12% of staff. Despite its size, Birmingham had managed to engage with organisations representing a relatively high proportion of staff, given its distinctive approach. Averaged overall, about 16% of the workforce in our case study areas was working for organisations with travel plans by summer 2003. Many authorities had begun by developing their own travel plan and/or developing a network for employers, and are now developing more sophisticated strategies, including use of the planning system, and encouraging sector specific or area based groups of employers to work together, partly as a way of reaching small and medium sized enterprises. In terms of travel plan quality, all case study areas felt that at least a third of staff covered by travel plans were in organisations with relatively fully-fledged plans. However, there was then a divide, where some authorities were working with a considerable number of organisations that were just starting out, whilst other authorities were building on earlier work with organisations that already have travel plans. Nottingham was distinctive in its explicit prioritisation of intensification at organisations with existing travel plans (and relative disinterest in engaging new organisations). In terms of the types of organisations involved, the case study data reflect national figures suggesting that, proportionally, engagement with the public sector is greater, whilst numerically, authorities are working with larger numbers of private companies. Information from two areas suggested that the authorities had managed to engage with approximately 20-40% of companies involving more than 300 people. This compares with national data suggesting that local authorities aim to engage with 11% of companies employing more than 100 staff by 2006.

3.10 Comparison of findings about the effects of workplace travel plans on car use

3.10.1 Effects of travel planning amongst engaged organisations

Many local authorities have limited monitoring data about the effect of their travel plan work. This may be due to resource limitations, reliance on individual companies to administer surveys (who may be reluctant to do so) and concerns about the reliability of data received from companies. Local authorities may also be reluctant to take the credit for what individual organisations achieve (since the organisation has often put in its own resources), or to compare organisations, given their differing nature. In particular, Nottingham was concerned with reliability of results (given that organisations might have an incentive to report a particular result in relation to the workplace parking levy); York and Cambridgeshire were reluctant to attribute the achievements of individual organisations solely to the travel plan work of the local authority; and most of the case study areas highlighted that different organisations faced different opportunities and constraints.

In York, Cambridgeshire and Birmingham, survey work is done for the organisations who participate in travel planning work, with the analysis taking place at the local authority. In Bristol, organisations undertake their own survey work, but the results are assessed as part of the council's awards scheme. In Nottingham and Merseyside, the local authority relies on results submitted by individual organisations, based on survey work that they have undertaken themselves. Buckinghamshire was still developing its monitoring programme, but had detailed results for its own staff.

In looking at the effect of travel plan work, we were interested both in results or estimates of the overall effect across all organisations, and data from individual organisations. All case study locations were able to provide data for individual organisations, and these are given in table 3.11. The data for Birmingham is for organisations with at least a 10% response rate to a survey carried out by the local authority. Merseyside, Buckinghamshire and York only had data about one travel plan organisation. Nottingham and Bristol provided results for those organisations where information was readily available, which were probably those that were performing well. Cambridgeshire provided data for a selection of organisations which had reasonable response rates for their general survey and for Addenbrooke's, the flagship organisation in their area.

Table 3.11: Results from individual organisations about commuter journeys

Organisation	Staff	Car driver or SOV		Car share or 'multi-mode'		Cars per 100 staff		% point Change	% change
		Before	After	Before	After	Before	After		
Birmingham									
Priory Hospital 1998-2001	300	79	59	10	5	84	61.5	**-22.5**	**-26.8**
Northfield Medical Centre 1999-2001	50	86	59	2	21	87	69.5	**-17.5**	**-20.1**
WS Atkins 2001-2003	767*	53	30	--	--	53	30	**-23.0**	**-43.3**
City council economic development department 1999-2003	387*	50	29	22	32	61	45	**-16.0**	**-26.2**
City council transportation department 1997-2001	578*	48	35	20	34	58	52	**-6.0**	**-10.3**
Dental hospital 1998-2001	400	34	28	15	23	41.5	39.5	**-2.0**	**-4.8**
Royal Orthopaedic hospital 2000-2002	500	62	74	17	8	70.5	78	**+7.5**	**+10.6**
Compass Group 1999-2003	520*	61	69	9	16	65.5	77	**+11.5**	**+17.6**
HM Prison 1999-2001	650	64	90	19	0	73.5	90	**+16.5**	**+22.4**
Bristol									
Orange	700	60	27	--	--	60	27	**-33.0**	**-55.0**
Norwich Union	1300	37	21	--	--	37	21	**-16.0**	**-43.2**
University of Bristol	5000	36	32	--	--	36	32	**-4.0**	**-11.1**
Arup	109	41	38	--	--	41	38	**-3.0**	**-7.3**
Buckinghamshire									
Buckinghamshire County Council 1998-2003	2200	71.3	49.4	--	7	71.3	52.9	**-18.4**	**-25.8**
Cambridgeshire									
Addenbrookes NHS Trust 1993-2002~	4977	<74.0	42.0	--	7	<74.0	<49	**>-25.0**	**>-33.8**
Government Office for East of England 2001-2002	290	69.5	42.5	3.4	11.9	71.2	47.7	**-23.5**	**-33.0**
Cambridge City Council 2000-2002	800	34.7	30.8	22.2	6.1	45.8	33.9	**-11.9**	**-26.0**
Chamber of Commerce 2001-2002	18	56.6	49.5	18.9	10.8	66.1	54.7	**-11.4**	**-17.2**
Cambridge University 2000-2002	6250*	35.7	27	10	8.6	40.7	31.3	**-9.4**	**-23.1**
Cambridgeshire County Council (county hall) 1999-2002	1100	51.0	44.0	15.0	15.3	58.5	51.7	**-6.9**	**-11.7**
Generics 2000-2002	220	65.7	67.5	14.3	7.4	72.9	71.2	**-1.7**	**-2.3**
Merseyside									
St Helen's College 1999-2002	800	77	63	13	17	83.5	71.5	**-12.0**	**-14.4**
Nottingham									
Nottingham City Hospital NHS Trust 1997-2000	3500	72	55	2	11	73	60.5	**-12.5**	**-17.1**
Government Office for the East Midlands 1997-1999#	245	<45	<38	--	--	<45	<38	**-7.0**	**-15.6**
Boots	7500	--	--	--	--	65	62	**-3.0**	**-4.6**
City of York									
Local Government Ombudsman 1998 -2002	85	73	68	5	6	75.5	71	**-4.5**	**-6.0**

* = staff numbers have changed between the first and second surveys – where this has occurred, an average of the staff totals has been included here.

All Birmingham surveys have a 'multi-mode' category. This is given in the 'Car share or other column'. A conservative estimate would be that the majority of these people travel by car. An optimistic estimate would be that the majority of these people do not travel by car. Therefore, we have taken a mid-way estimate – assuming that at any one time, perhaps half of these people are likely to be driving to work.

~ GOEM (Nottingham) only has figures for all car users.

In the first survey at Addenbrooke's, car users were not separated. To ensure that the results are not overstated, we have used the figures for overall car users for the latest survey results too. In reality, if car sharing has increased as a result of the travel plan work, greater change will have been achieved than is recorded here.

Only one authority – Cambridgeshire – has aimed to collect results about the overall effect of its travel plan work, although there have been some problems with interpreting the results of its annual survey. Meanwhile, the Nottingham interviewee gave his opinion about the overall effect of work, Merseyside had an opinion about 'common' modal shifts achieved, and Birmingham has a target that they expect all affiliated organisations to aim for. These estimates of overall effect are reported in table 3.12. The results in table 3.11 were also used to derive average results for each case study area, which are given in table 3.12. None of these averages should be taken at face value, as every local authority involved would want to put caveats on them. However, given the lack of more robust information, they provide a starting point for understanding what travel planning can achieve.

Table 3.12: Averaged results from individual organisations
(note caveats given in text)

	Total staff	Change in number of cars per 100 staff*	% change*	% change, weighted by staff numbers
Overall average	33,169	-9.8	-15.8	-17.8
Birmingham average	4152	-5.7	-8.7	-7.5
Bristol average	7109	-14.0	-32.2	-21.3
Cambridgeshire average	12,555	-12.9	-21.0	-27.3
Nottingham average	11,245	-7.5	-12.3	-8.7
Buckinghamshire	2200	-18.4	-25.8	--
Merseyside	800	-12.0	-14.4	--
York	85	-4.5	-6.0	--
Nottingham opinion	*10-15% reduction in SOV trips from 'good' travel plan*			
Merseyside opinion	*10% reduction in SOV trips over 2-3 years common.*			
Birmingham target	*All affiliated organisations to reduce car use by 10%*			

* The figures in these columns have been calculated by averaging the before and after 'cars per 100 staff' for the companies involved, and then calculating the changes in the averages. (Simply averaging the percentage changes produces similar results – for example, for the overall average, the average change in the number of cars per 100 staff would be -9.9, and the percentage change would be -16.6%.)

Averaged across all 26 organisations (representing over 33,000 staff), the weighted average reduction in traffic was 17.8%. This is remarkably close to the 18% reduction recorded in Cairns et al. (2002). Although seven of the organisations were the same in both studies, this should not have affected the overall results. This is because only the three from Nottingham are reporting the same results as in Cairns et al. (2002). The two from Bristol are reported here as achieving less than in that study (presumably due to use of different survey periods), and Buckinghamshire County Council and Addenbrooke's are reported as achieving more than in that study, as they have undertaken surveys after 2002. Moreover, it is notable that these results are drawn from a range of different types of local authority area, including the conurbations of Merseyside and Birmingham, the historic towns of Nottingham and York, and the mix of urban and rural situations comprising Buckinghamshire and Cambridgeshire. (These areas also vary considerably in relative wealth and levels of car ownership).

For the four case study areas with data from several organisations, the area-wide average varied from -7.5% to -27.3%. These figures should not be taken as implying greater success in some case study areas than others, since they are based on few data points. However, it is interesting that Birmingham, with its distinctive broad-brush approach, had the lowest area-wide average. This is compensated for by the fact that Birmingham city council is working with a greater number of employees than any other case study area. Looking at the data for the individual organisations we were given, Bristol and Cambridgeshire had high area-wide averages of 20–30%. In Bristol, the high average may be because the organisations that have been quoted are considered to be success stories. However, it is notable that Bristol provided information about four organisations in the process of developing travel plans with equally ambitious targets (North Bristol NHS Trust: >10,900 staff, 10% cut in SOV trips; UBHT: 5000 staff, 11.4% cut in SOV trips; IKEA: 600 staff, 25% cut in SOV trips; BBC: 900 staff, 35% cut in SOV trips). In Cambridgeshire, the high level of achievement may be because organisations become part of the Travel for Work Partnership on a voluntary basis, and would therefore be expected to start with a positive motivation to make a difference to travel habits. (Results were not available for Cambridgeshire organisations that became involved via the planning system).

Three local authorities - Buckinghamshire, Merseyside and York - could only provide information about one organisation. This is because they have started major work on travel planning relatively recently. Although Buckinghamshire started travel plan work in 1998, it took two years and 13 committee reports before it was possible to implement a plan for the council itself, and work with other organisations only started subsequently. Substantial work in Merseyside only began with the appointment of two bursary post holders for workplace travel plans in 2001, whilst a dedicated officer for travel plan work was only appointed in York in 2003. Given the recent nature of their work, it is encouraging that they are already able to report results from organisations which have achieved a measurable reduction in traffic.

As well as the average results, it is also interesting to look at the distribution of individual travel plan results. It is immediately apparent that the achievements of employers differ widely. In some cases, a travel plan appears to have had no effect as car driving has increased (three examples from Birmingham). Others have achieved a modest reduction in car driving (three organisations report reductions of less than 5%) or more substantial reductions. Specifically, there were 18 organisations which had reduced car driving by more than 10%, including 9 organisations which reduced car driving by more than a quarter. The distribution of results for the 26 organisations is illustrated in Figure 3.3.

Figure 3.3: Distribution of individual travel plan results

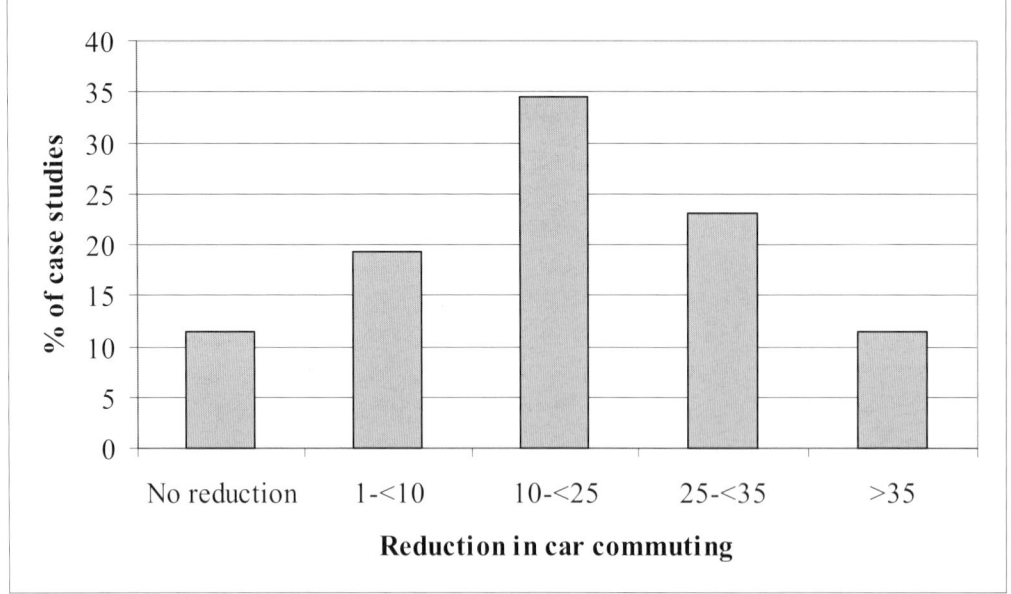

This distribution demonstrates clearly that the overall average result (17.8%) is not giving a biased reflection of what travel plans can achieve, as individual plans are relatively uniformly distributed around that point. Clearly, there are some high performers (achieving traffic reductions of over 35%), and some disappointments (where travel planning appears to have made no difference), however the majority reduce traffic by between 1% and 35% with a typical plan achieving reductions in the range 10-25%. One caveat, however, is that these are all, almost certainly, relatively well developed plans and would not include the typical experience from organisations which are only just beginning their work.

Finally, as highlighted in the introduction, it should be noted that travel plan work is not always aimed only at the commuter journey. Many organisations also aim to affect business mileage. For example, in Bristol, the Environment Agency (Westbury site) aims to reduce business mileage by 10%, whilst Faber Maunsell aims to reduce business mileage by 5%. Bristol Zoo is reporting reductions in car travel from its travel plan, which aims to affect over 700,000 visitors per annum.

In summary, then, the results support the conclusion of the literature review outlined in section 3.2 and summarised in table 3.2 - that fully fledged travel plans typically reduce car driving by an average of 15-20% at individual sites. The results lend weight to the argument that these are not 'freak' outcomes achieved at a few successful companies, but that this scale of car use reduction is occurring at many locations where travel plans have been introduced.

3.10.2 Effects of travel planning on overall levels of commuter traffic

The previous section demonstrates the considerable success the case study areas have had in influencing car use amongst the organisations with which they are working. But how much impact has this had on overall levels of commuter traffic?

To estimate this, we used two approaches, set out in table 3.13. These are based on information from the case study interviewees about (a) the overall proportion of their workforces that were engaged in travel planning, and (b) what proportion of travel plans are fully-fledged as opposed to being at a more basic stage.

The first approach (model A) assumed that the average effectiveness of travel plans across all organisations engaged so far was to reduce car use by 5% overall. This provides a lower bound for estimates of overall impact. This is extremely conservative, since we know that much higher reductions in car use are reported from surveys of individual firms in the case study areas, and it is lower, even, than the average result achieved by surveyed employers in Birmingham (-7.5%), with its relatively broad brush approach.

The second approach (model B) assumed employees in organisations with fully fledged travel plans (including parking management) reduced their car use by 18%, whilst those in organisations actively undertaking travel work achieved reductions of 10%. Organisations at the early stages of travel planning work are assumed to have made no difference to the travel of their employees. Again, this is still a relatively conservative scenario, since the literature suggests that even basic travel plans can be expected to reduce car use by 6-10%, whilst fully fledged travel plans with parking management will typically achieve reductions in the order of 20-25%. We use this model to avoid overstating the effects of current work. We note that it clearly underestimates the future potential of travel planning work since, with the exception of Nottingham, very few areas consider that the majority of travel plans in their area are fully developed.

Overall, so far, travel planning may have reduced overall levels of car commuting by 0.4 – 1.5% using our conservative assumptions (model A), or by 0.7 – 3.3% under model B.

Interestingly, the models imply both broad-brush and targeted approaches can work well. In their target areas, according to our calculations, both Birmingham with its extensive broad-brush approach and Cambridgeshire, with its more narrowly focused, but in-depth approach, have achieved about the same (3.3% reduction in model B).

Table 3.13 Effect of travel planning on overall levels of commuter traffic

	Birmingham	Bristol	Buckinghamshire	Cambridgeshire A~	Merseyside	Nottingham	York
Proportion of workforce affected by travel plans	29%	13%	11%	29%	8%	28%	29%
Model A (all travel plans reduce car use by 5%)							
Reduction in commuter traffic +	1.5%	0.7%	0.6%	1.5%	0.4%	1.4%	1.5%
Model B							
Proportion of fully-fledged travel plans (-18%)	30%*	46%	55%	63%	42%	96%	34%
Proportion actively undertaking travel work (-10%)	60%*	48%	6%	1%	12%	0%	20%
Proportion with travel work just starting (0%)	10%*	6%	39%	36%	46%	4%	46%
Reduction in commuter traffic +	3.3%	1.7%	1.2%	3.3%	0.7%	4.8%	2.4%

~ Cambridgeshire A: calculations are based on the districts of Cambridge City and South Cambridgeshire, where most work has taken place.

+ In model A, reduction in commuter traffic = 0.05 x proportion of workforce affected by travel plans. In model B, reduction in commuter traffic = [proportion of 'good' travel plans x 0.18 + proportion of 'average' travel plans x 0.10] x proportion of workforce affected by travel plans.

* Reflects frequency of contact between employers and Birmingham city council, rather than quality of travel plan.

3.11 Other effects of workplace travel planning

As well as effects on car use, various other benefits were reported from the travel plan work. These included:

- **Increases in bus use and associated ticket revenue.**

- **Increases in walking and cycling, with associated health gains.**

- **Improved social inclusion.**
Travel planning was closely associated with the WorkWise scheme in Birmingham, the Joblink scheme in Merseyside, a WorkWise project in Meadows in Nottingham, and the regeneration of the Avonmouth area in Bristol. All these initiatives aim to increase access to work (and travel plans have provided one way of entering into communications with employers).

- **Better conditions for employees.**
Flexible work patterns and occasional work from home have made childcare arrangements easier. Employees are reported to have experienced less commuting stress. Bicycle user groups and car sharing schemes were felt to have improved social interaction.

- **Improved staff recruitment and retention.**
Improvements in travel options, combined with the benefits reported in the previous bullet are reported to make an employer more attractive to new staff and to improve employee retention. For example, Computer Associates, a business software company based in Berkshire (whose travel plan was reviewed by Cairns et al 2002), estimate that staff turnover has reduced from 15% p.a. to 7.5% p.a. as a result of their travel plan (according to PR material produced by the car share software company JamBusters, who have worked with Computer Associates).

- **Good PR for businesses.**
For example, Norwich Union in York received positive PR from funding a bus service.

- **The opportunity to contribute to environmental management standards such as ISO 14001.**
Corus Rail and Portakabin in York had used their travel plan work for this, as had St Helens College in Merseyside.

- **Financial savings.**
For example, Buckinghamshire County Council estimated that it had saved £60,000 - £75,000 on annual parking costs.

- **Better estate management**.
For example, Addenbrooke's Hospital in Cambridgeshire was able to develop its site more intensively as less space was needed for car parking.

- **Less noise, congestion and pollution, and better conditions for freight distribution, associated with reductions in car use.**

- **Better security and less fear of crime from better car parking management.**

There are also a number of reported benefits that arise from synergy between travel plans and other transport initiatives. These are discussed in the next section.

3.12 Synergies between workplace travel planning and other policies

The case study local authorities identifed various examples of synergy between workplace travel planning and other policies.

First, car restraint measures were seen as an important lever to persuade employers to draw up travel plans. In Buckinghamshire, restrictions on town centre parking coupled with car parking charges for county council employees had increased the effectiveness of the council's own travel plan. In Birmingham, high long-stay parking charges have encouraged employers to join Company TravelWise. In York, the lack of town centre parking has encouraged people to leave the car at home.
Interviewees felt that further traffic restraint would increase the effectiveness of travel plans. The workplace parking levy was mentioned in Nottingham as a future key policy; road user charging in Bristol was highlighted as a useful potential measure that would stimulate travel planning; and in Cambridgeshire, interviewees felt that both road user charging and the workplace parking levy would be helpful.

Second, measures to improve alternative modes had made travel plans more effective. Such measures included area-wide car sharing schemes; showcase bus routes; cycle routes; improvements in public transport, cycling and walking information; and improvements in pedestrian infrastructure. For example, employees at Nestlé in York will benefit from a planned new cycle route, whilst pedestrian improvements around York station have made people feel that it is safer to take the train and walk to the city centre. Bus showcase routes were mentioned as helpful in Birmingham, Bristol and Merseyside. In Merseyside, walking promotion measures such as calorie count walk maps and 'Walkabout' guides were seen as usefully contributing to travel plan work.

Travel plans have also benefited from wider travel awareness campaigns. Notably, the Big Wheel campaign in Nottingham and the travel awareness work in York were both mentioned as making it easier to work with employers (and travel plans are seen as one strand of work that takes place under their 'umbrella').

Conversely, travel plans have acted as an umbrella for other soft initiatives. For example, a citywide commuter car sharing scheme has been established in Cambridgeshire, whilst a business park car sharing scheme has been established for Temple Quay in Bristol. In Birmingham, the national 'Share-a-journey' site is marketed to employers as part of the 'Company Travelwise' package. Personalised travel planning is also being undertaken for commuter journeys in Cambridgeshire, with two of the lead organisations that have been involved in travel plan work. In Buckinghamshire, the authority is investigating and developing tele-centres (for teleworking and video-conferencing) which they can then make available to other employers.

Travel plans have also acted as a conduit to promote other schemes. Examples include the health promotion campaigns in Merseyside, and the Joblink and Workwise bus services in Merseyside and Birmingham respectively. For example, the Joblink services now serve Jaguar cars and Liverpool John Lennon airport. In many cases, the travel plan work has provided opportunities for information dissemination to employees about new or improved bus services or cycle routes.

It was felt that travel plans had funded or initiated schemes with wider benefit. For example, Somerfield/Wincanton at Lea Green, St Helens, are intending to put a bus turnaround on their site for buses which serve the Parr Strategic Investment Area. In Cambridgeshire, buses funded for Alconbury airfield operate as public services; an increase in frequency of the 113 public service from Haver Hill to Addenbrooke's hospital has benefitted all users of the route; and private shuttle bus services from Cambridge train station to the Genome Campus at Hinxton Hall operate as public services in the opposite direction.

Synergy between promoting workplace travel plans and school travel plans has been variable, however there are clearly opportunities for promoting both at once. For example, in Merseyside, these initiatives are undertaken in parallel, and there is a degree of a 'informal neighbourhood targeting' to try and achieve synergistic benefits by working with both schools and workplaces in the same area.

Finally, interviewees felt that as the concept of travel planning has become more familiar, it has also become more acceptable. For example, in Buckinghamshire, the interviewee felt that far fewer people were opposed the concept of travel planning than when the work started. In Bristol, attendance at Green Commuter Club meetings is steadily increasing.

3.13 Relationship between spending and impact for workplace travel planning

In setting out to evaluate the relationship between costs, scale of travel plan work and effectiveness, we used a similar model to that used to assess the impact of travel planning on overall levels of commuter traffic. The calculation is set out in table 3.14.

As discussed in section 3.10.2, the first approach (model A) assumes that the average effectiveness of travel plans is to reduce car use by 5% overall. The second approach (model B) assumes employees in organisations with fully fledged travel plans have reduced their car use by 18%, whilst those in organisations actively undertaking travel work achieve reductions of 10%. Organisations at the early stages of travel planning work are assumed to have made no difference to the travel of their employees. As highlighted previously, model A is extremely conservative, whilst model B is less so, although it may still be an underestimate of what travel planning has achieved[1].

---

[1] Neither model should be taken as an indication of what travel planning can achieve, since much work is still at a relatively early stage, as discussed earlier in section 3.10.

Table 3.14 Calculation of cost-impact ratios for workplace travel plans

	Birming-ham	Bristol	Bucking-hamshire	Cambridge A~	Merseyside	Nottingham	York
length of time scheme has been running intensively (years)	5	5	3	6	2	8	1
estimated total expenditure, with capital costs annualised # (£)	310,000	350,000	243,700	247,500	196,000	900,000	52,000
staff affected by travel plan in current year	136,000	29,960	21,700	34,000	55,870	52,000	26,187
% driving (2001 census)	56	51	72	52	55	45	48
number of drivers affected by travel plans +	76160	15160	15624	17748	30617	23244	12622
Model A							
driver reduction (all travel plans -5%) ++	3808	758	781	887	1531	1162	631
kilometres saved in current year ##	27052032	5384747	5549645	6304090	10875073	8256269	4483382
total kilometres saved **	108208128	21538987	16648934	28368403	27187683	45409478	8966764
cost per kilometre saved (pence)	0.3	0.6	1.5	0.9	0.7	2.0	0.6
Model B							
good travel plans (-18%)	30%*	46%	55%	63%	42%	96%	34%
average travel plans (-10%)	60%*	48%	6%	1%	12%	0%	20%
travel work just starting (0%)	10%*	7%	38%	36%	45%	4%	46%
driver reduction ++	8682	1983	1641	2030	2682	4017	1025
kilometres saved in current year ##	61678633	14086498	11654254	14423757	19053128	28533665	7281012
total kilometres saved **	246714532	56345990	34962762	64906907	47632820	156935157	14562025
cost per kilometre saved (pence)	0.1	0.6	0.7	0.4	0.4	0.6	0.4

~ Cambridgeshire A: calculations are based on the districts of Cambridge City and South Cambridgeshire, where most work has taken place.

Total expenditure is estimated, assuming linear growth from expenditure in first intensive year to expenditure in current year, with capital costs annualised at 3.5%. The expenditure data used as the basis for this calculation are given in table 3.2.

+ 'Number of drivers affected by travel plans' is calculated by applying the percentage of people driving according to the 2001 census figures to the total number of staff affected by travel plans.

++ In Model A, driver reduction = 0.05 x number of drivers affected by travel plans. In model B, driver reduction = [proportion of 'good' travel plans x 0.18 + proportion of 'average' travel plans x 0.10] x number of drivers affected by travel plans.

'kilometres saved in current year' is derived by assuming that each driver was previously driving for 240 working days and making a daily round trip of 29.6kms, (the average distance of a commuter journey by car according to the 2001 'Travel to work in GB' personal travel factsheet produced by the DfT and ONS).

** 'total kilometres saved' assumes linear behaviour change in car kilometres saved, from zero in year 1 to current year figure, plus some behaviour change in future years, declining by 40% per year after current year if no further money is spent.

* Reflects frequency of contact between employers and Birmingham city council, rather than quality of travel plan.

For both models, cost was taken as the total expenditure over the period the programme had been running. This was estimated from case study data on expenditure in the first intensive year and the current year of each workplace travel programme, with the assumption that expenditure grew linearly between the two. All expenditure was treated as revenue, except for Buckinghamshire where there were some capital costs. These were annualised at 3.5%.

We also assumed that impact increased linearly, from zero in the first intensive year to current levels. Even if no more money were to be spent, we assumed there would be some impact in subsequent years, but this would decline at the rate of 40% a year.

Cost-impact ratios range from 0.3 pence to 2 pence per kilometre saved in model A, or 0.1 pence to 0.7 pence in model B. Differences in cost per kilometre probably relate to a range of factors, including whether the area is easy or difficult territory for travel planning; congestion levels (and hence willingness of employers to become involved); the proportion of the workforce based in larger, more-easily targeted organisations; and how far advanced travel planning work is, with costs appearing higher in both early and later stages.

We were also interested in how much the case study authorities might need to spend in order to influence the entire workforce. Here, we made the assumption that costs per head would be about £2, as suggested in section 3.8.4. No allowance was made either for the greater difficulties in engaging more reluctant employers over time, nor for reduced difficulties due to snowball effects among residents' and employers' networks. The results are shown in table 3.15. They show that in every case, greater funding is likely to be necessary to roll out travel planning programmes to sections of the workforce who are not presently targeted. The budget in Nottingham would have to at least double; budgets in York, Bristol, Buckinghamshire and Cambridge City / South Cambridgeshire would have to increase four times; and budgets in Birmingham, Merseyside and the county of Cambridgeshire would have to increase by a factor of ten or more.

Table 3.15: Budget needed to work with entire workforce in case study area, compared to current budget

	Total workforce in area	Annual budget required to work with whole workforce * (£)	Ratio of required budget to current budget
Birmingham	475000	950000	9.8
Bristol	231800	463600	3.6
Buckinghamshire	205902	411804	3.8
Cambridgeshire A ~	118396	236792	4.1
Cambridgeshire	275685	551370	9.6
Merseyside	700000	1400000	14.3
Nottingham	188000	376000	1.9
York	90000	180000	3.5

* 'Annual budget required to work with whole workforce' based on spending £2 per head.
~ Figures for Cambridgeshire A are based on the districts of Cambridge City and South Cambridgeshire, where most work has taken place.

3.14 Future impact of workplace travel plans

The future impact of workplace travel planning depends on:
- The number of workplaces where it is appropriate and effective, and the proportion of the workforce that these cover
- The effectiveness of travel plans at these organisations.

3.14.1 What proportion of the workforce might be covered by travel plans?

In trying to understand what proportion of the workforce might be covered by travel plans in future, we asked case study interviewees two sets of questions: first, how much impact did they think their work might have by 2006 and 2011 under currently planned resources; and second, what might be possible by these dates if resources were not a constraint.

Unsurprisingly, interviewees found it quite difficult to predict future levels of implementation, particularly for the more distant date. However, three local authorities, York, Buckinghamshire and Birmingham, were able to provide some information on this.

York: In York, the interviewee estimated that by 2006 there would be full travel plans for 30 organisations, with some 20 organisations at an earlier stage of development, and that travel plans would cover some 35% of the workforce, in line with the council's target. By 2011, the coverage would not be much higher – perhaps 40% of the workforce might be covered by a travel plan. This assessment was based on the assumption that resources would stay the same as at present, at least until 2006. If resources were not a constraint, the council could develop travel plan work more rapidly, and extend it to more small organisations, perhaps covering 40% of employees by 2006.

Buckinghamshire: In Buckinghamshire, the interviewee suggested that the council might be working with 75 organisations by 2006. New organisations might be smaller than those with which the county is already working, with an average of, say, 75 staff. Travel plans would cover about 25,000 people, or 12% of the workforce by 2006. By 2011, workplace travel plans might be in place for 150 organisations, covering 30,000 employees or 15% of the workforce. Again, this assessment was based on the assumption that resources would remain roughly the same as at present, with 1.5 fte staff in the council promoting workplace travel planning.

Birmingham: In Birmingham, the interviewee estimated that about 300 companies, covering 180,000 – 200,000 employees, or 40% of the workforce, might be engaged in Company TravelWise by 2006. By 2011, the scheme might cover 500 companies and 220,000 employees, or 46% of the workforce. This is in line with the targets in the West Midlands Local Transport Plan, for 40% of the workforce to be affiliated to Company TravelWise by 2006 and 50% by 2011. It was based on the assumption that the number of staff promoting travel planning might increase to about 4 – 6 by 2006, and 6 – 8 by 2011.

The growth rates predicted by interviewees in all three case studies are slower than growth rates achieved in those areas to date. This seems to be because interviewees felt that they were already working with most of the larger companies, and that extending travel planning to smaller organisations would pose greater challenges and require more intensive work. (However, it may also be that natural conservatism crept in, with interviewees finding it difficult to envisage working with many more organisations than at present.) If this is right, it suggests that there may be an upper limit to the proportion of the workforce that can be readily targeted, and that this upper limit lies somewhere between 15% (the Buckinghamshire estimate) and 40 – 50% (the estimates in York and Birmingham), perhaps depending on the type of area and the nature of the workforce.

3.14.2 Future effectiveness of travel plans

In five of the case study interviews, interviewees highlighted the potential to increase the effectiveness of travel plans over time.

From the York, Buckinghamshire and Birmingham estimates discussed in section 3.14.2, it seems that some local authorities will reach an upper limit of companies that they consider are worth targeting. After this, several mentioned that they will specifically turn their attention to improving the effectiveness of existing travel plans as the best way of achieving further results. The Nottingham interviewee corroborated this view, since Nottingham's whole approach is to focus on the 25 largest companies in the city with active travel plans (who are responsible for about 80% of all the car parking spaces). Nottingham's aim is to increase the effectiveness of the initiatives at these organisations, rather than spread travel planning to more companies, and there is clearly felt to be the potential to increase the effectiveness of the travel plans at these locations.

The York interviewee suggested that the proportion of companies with parking management as an element in their travel plan was likely to increase over time. This would result in an increase in average travel plan effectiveness.

The Birmingham interviewee cautioned that repeat monitoring at individual companies could show car driver mode share going up as well as down. However, where the trend is in the wrong direction he aims to understand the reasons for this and works with the company to tackle them as far as possible.

3.14.3 Future resources for travel planning

Local authorities were asked about their 'fantasy' budgets for travel plan work: that is, what level of staff and resources they would ideally like by 2006 and 2011, and how much they thought could be achieved with this level of support. The opinions of those authorities which felt able to comment are summarised in table 3.16. All local authorities felt that resource constraints were the key issue in how their work could or would be scaled up. Nonetheless, it is interesting that even the most 'extravagant' wish list would only result in costs of under £500,000 by 2011 – a relatively modest sum compared to other schemes being undertaken by the local authority. It may be that many travel planners have become rather used to operating on a shoe string, and find it difficult to think big about scaling up their work. Staffing levels were put at between 2.5 and 14 staff (though the figures may not be strictly comparable for the different case studies since some include staff time in non-dedicated travel planning posts, for example in development control.)

Table 3.16: Ideal level of resources by 2006 and 2011, and what it might achieve

	Birmingham	Bristol	Buckinghamshire	Cambridgeshire~	York
2006					
Number of staff promoting travel planning	4 – 6	7		11	
Budget			£90,000	£350,000	
Number of companies with travel plans	300	120*	75		45
Number of staff covered by travel plans	180–200,000		25,000		
Proportion of workforce covered by travel plans	40%		12%		40%
2011					
Number of staff promoting travel planning	6-8	7		14	2.5
Budget				£455,000	£104,000#
Number of companies with travel plans	500	220*	150		
Number of staff covered by travel plans	220,000		30,000		
Proportion of workforce covered by travel plans	46%+		15%		40%

~ Figures are for both the Travel for Work partnership and the planning division of the local authority
* Based on interviewee's view that about 20 organisations per year may become involved in travel planning through planning obligations. Others are likely to become involved independently of planning obligations.
# Based on interviewee's view that approximately double the current budget would be needed to cover 40% of the workforce.
+ Based on interviewee's estimate. The West Midlands local authorities have recently set a target that 50% of employees should be covered by a travel plan by 2011.

3.15   Key issues for scaling up workplace travel planning

The case study interviewees identified similar issues as likely to influence the success of travel plans in future.

- **More demand management measures, including more support from central government for promoting more sustainable transport**
It was felt that more 'stick' measures would get more businesses involved in travel planning, as discussed in section 3.12. Specifically, in Nottingham, it was felt that the introduction of the workplace parking levy would lead to increased priority for commuting issues; Bristol felt that the proposals for road user charging, if implemented, would have a big effect; and Cambridgeshire felt that road user charging or some form of workplace parking levy would both encourage more companies to get involved.

Interviewees also felt their job would be easier if they were 'backed up' more by the government, with more visionary and supportive messages and policies about sustainable transport in general and travel plans in particular. It was felt that when councils were preparing to take politically tough decisions, such as the introduction of the parking levy in Nottingham, they needed more overt support. The government could also help by engaging with business organisations, developers and trade unions to encourage them to support travel plans.

- **Poor quality alternatives to driving**

Lack of the right 'hard' infrastructure, such as cycle parking and poor quality bus services, was identified as a constraint by three case study interviewees. The Bristol interviewee highlighted the difficulties caused by inadequate co-ordination of bus services, particularly when bus companies altered routes or fares, while the Merseyside interviewee felt that the existence of the PTE made travel planning work easier.

- **Need for more fiscal incentives**

Four interviewees suggested central government could encourage greater take-up and effectiveness of travel plans by reforming the tax system so that travel plan incentives were not taxed, and so a greater distinction was drawn between more and less polluting forms of transport. The Buckinghamshire interviewee said he would like to be able to say to companies: 'if you are doing x, y or z as part of your travel plan, you can get a 10% reduction on business rates.' Merseytravel pointed to their plans to introduce a grants scheme for businesses as likely to increase the number of companies engaged in travel planning.

- **Planning conditions and requirements for companies to have a travel plan**

While the role of the planning system was welcomed, one interviewee commented that revisions to PPG13 to make it 'sharper, with less room for interpretation' would be helpful. It was also suggested that legislation requiring all organisations to have a travel plan (similar to regulations on disability access and affordable housing) would be very helpful. Meanwhile, the York interviewee suggested a requirement for companies to increase the cost of workplace parking, or to buy pool cars, might be enforced through better use of planning obligations. It was also suggested that travel plan measures could come about through environmental management systems, if certification required them and companies refused to use other companies without certification.

- **Funding**

Increased staff resources would enable travel plan officers in local authorities to spend more time supporting individual organisations. For example, the Cambridgeshire interviewees suggested that increased staff resources would enable them to be far more proactive, to work with all the big organisations and business parks, and probably a number of other organisations, and to 'test the boundaries' in terms of what they expected of developers. In many of our case studies, constraints on funding, and the overemphasis on capital funding were highlighted as inhibiting the development of travel planning. The loss of travel plan bursary posts was felt to be unhelpful, both because it 'sent the wrong message' about the importance of travel plans, and because it had been one way of addressing shortages of revenue funding. The Cycle Projects Fund was welcomed as an effective way of motivating employers, and it was suggested that a repeat cycle projects fund and a walking fund would be helpful.

- **Area wide approach**

Travel planning might become more commonplace in smaller organisations if it was part of a neighbourhood or area-wide approach. As discussed in section 3.9.2, such clustering is developing in Birmingham, Bristol, Buckinghamshire and Nottingham. In Merseyside, areas are being targeted for workplace and school travel plans at the same time.

3.16 Policy implications relating to workplace travel

- The potential to offer further tax incentives for workplace travel plans could be examined. Rebates on business rates may be one possible mechanism to explore.
- There is potential to strengthen the wording in PPG13 to help local councils enforce effective travel plans as part of new developments.
- National government could give greater explicit support for policies aimed at car restraint and traffic management, to help bolster local authorities who undertake such policies – which may, in turn, help to motivate organisations to become involved in travel planning.
- Nationally led education of developers, trade unions and public transport operators about travel planning could be useful.
- Dedicated cycling and walking funds could provide an incentive for companies to become involved in workplace travel planning.
- The government could consider whether to require all organisations to develop travel plans. One interviewee commented that although this might be initially resisted, it would become accepted, as with legislation on disability and affordable housing.
- Following loss of the travel plan bursaries, there is a risk that fewer local authorities will employ dedicated travel plan officers. Mechanisms for increasing the revenue funding allocated by local authorities to travel planning could be considered.
- There is a disparity between the resources allocated to workplace travel planning and those for school travel planning in some local authorities. There could be substantial traffic reduction benefits if resources for workplace travel planning were increased to match those for school travel.
- Local authorities could be encouraged to introduce standard monitoring systems for travel plans, to make it easier to assess the value of this work.
- There may be opportunities to strengthen the links between travel planning and environmental management standards such as ISO14001.
- As experience of using the planning process grows, local authorities would appreciate greater sharing of information.
- As travel planning develops, it may be appropriate for local authorities to develop area–based strategies, which can engage small and medium enterprises, and which dovetail with improvements to infrastructure and public transport which may be taking place for other reasons.

3.17 Acknowledgements

We would like to thank the following people for their help with the workplace travel plan case studies:

Individual	Organisation
Graham Amis	Cambridgeshire County Council
Rosemary Bryant	Buckinghamshire County Council
Sarah Collins	Cambridgeshire County Council
Paul Cook	Cambridgeshire County Council
Mike Cooper	Birmingham City Council
Helen Davies	Birmingham City Council
Sarah Dewar	Merseyside TravelWise
Stefan Dimic	Buckinghamshire County Council
Mike Ginger	Bristol City Council
Will Haywood	Cambridgeshire County Council
Wyn Hughes	Addenbrooke's NHS Trust, Cambridge
Daniel Johnson	City of York Council
Jeremy Prince	Nottingham City Council
Helene Vergereau	City of York Council
Mark Webb	Cambridgeshire Travel for Work Partnership
Joseph Whelan	Cambridgeshire County Council
Barbara Wilcox	Cambridgeshire County Council
Eileen Woods	Cambridgeshire County Council
Tim Carter	Cambridgeshire County Council

In addition to the main case study interviewees, we would like to thank:

Individual	Organisation
Lyndon Mendes	Surrey County Council
Margaret Longes	Department for Transport

3.18 References

Addison L & Fraser J (2002) *Using the planning process to secure travel plans.* Report by Addison & Associates for the Department for Transport, London.

Cairns S, Davis A, Newson C and Swiderska C (2002) *Making travel plans work: research report.* Report by Transport 2000, ESRC Transport Studies Unit UCL and Adrian Davis Associates for Department for Transport

Ligtermoet D (1998) *Zeven jaar vervoermanagement: synthese van ervaringen Report to Adviesdienst Verkeer en Vervoer* Netherlands Ministry of Transport, The Hague

Napier University Transport Research Institute, Open University and WS Atkins (2001) *Evaluation of Government Departments' Travel Plans* Report for DETR, unpublished

Organizational Coaching and Schreffler E (1996) *Effective TDM at worksites in the Netherlands and the US*

Rye (2002) Travel plans: do they work? *Transport Policy* 9(4) 287-298

Shoup D (1997) Evaluating the effects of cashing out employer-paid parking: eight case studies *Transport Policy* 4(4) 201-216

Steer Davies Gleave (2001) *Take up and effectiveness of travel plans and travel awareness campaigns* Report for DETR

Transit Co-operative Research Program (1994) *Cost effectiveness of TDM programs* working paper #2, COMSIS Corporation

Touwen, M. (1999) *Travel planning in the Randstad: an evaluation based on ReMOVE.* Report to Netherlands Ministry of Transport, The Hague

University of Westminster (1998) *Levels of activity relating to safer routes to school type projects and green transport plans.* Report for DETR

4.   School travel plans

4.1 Introduction

The 'school run' accounts for a small proportion of all car traffic on the road, but, in urban areas, it is a significant contributor to peak hour congestion. In Britain, the proportion of children, especially younger children, being driven to school has risen significantly over the last 25 years. Research by Bradshaw and Atkins (1996) found that car escort trips were increasing even when car ownership was held constant: for example, amongst two-car households the proportion of primary-age children escorted to school by car rose from 38% to 53% in the two decades after 1975. According to the National Travel Survey, the proportion of children travelling to school by car increased from 16% in 1985/86 to 28% in 1999/2001 (although it should be noted that this is a slight decline, from 29% in 1995/97, offering some hope that the situation may be stabilising or even reversing).

There has been considerable interest in the 'school run' for a number of reasons. Originally, interest in school travel was generated by concerns about children's safety, and loss of independent mobility (as highlighted by Hillman et al, 1990). Since that time, there has also been increasing concern about the congestion impacts, particularly in the immediate vicinity of schools. Measures to encourage non-car travel to school are also perceived to be important because sustainable patterns of travel behaviour may be carried into adult lives (and conversely, children who never travel by bike or bus are less likely to switch to these modes in adult life). There may also be health benefits from encouraging walking and cycling, an issue which is gaining particular interest given concerns about the growth in childhood obesity.

Initially work on school travel primarily focused on physical street improvements, such as traffic calming, 20mph zones, cycle lanes and safe crossings. Over time, the approach has developed to include a greater concentration on consultation with the school and local community, education and information measures, road safety training, changes within the school and initiatives such as 'walking buses' and, more recently, 'cycle trains'. These involve volunteer parents escorting groups of children by foot or by bike on a fixed route. Measures to encourage bus use are also often promoted: for example personalised timetable information, discount tickets, new bus services and dedicated school buses. The current focus includes each school drawing up a 'school travel plan' in partnership with their local authority, as part of developing their own, individual long-term strategy to address school travel issues.

The issue of school travel has also increased in political importance. Following on from the 1998 Integrated Transport White Paper, a school travel advisory group was set up (STAG). In 2001, funding was made available for the three year appointment of 57 travel co-ordinators to work in local authorities on school travel, and a further 17 co-ordinators to focus on both school and workplace travel. An advice scheme, whereby schools could request five days of free advice on their situation, was also established and by February 2003, more than 200 schools had received advice under the scheme. In September 2003, the government announced a major new initiative to address travel to school, which was particularly significant because the initiative is a joint one between the departments of Transport and Education. In support of the initiative, £7.5 million per year has been allocated for at least two years to fund more local authority based school travel advisers, and regional travel advisers have been appointed, based in each government office region. Local authority schools with an authorised travel plan have also become eligible for capital funding (approximately £5000 per primary school and £10,000 per secondary school) to fund their travel work. New legislation is also being discussed, which will enable local education authorities to pilot new arrangements for statutory transport and school hours.

At the same time as the increase in political interest in the topic, there has also been additional research commissioned. Specifically, a major study entitled 'Making School Travel Plans Work' is in progress. This has involved interviews with 30 schools (chosen to represent good practice), and their 23 associated local authorities. The study aims to examine what has been achieved, and the factors which have been responsible for success or failure. It will lead to good practice guidance. As discussed in section 4.5, there has been some overlap with this project, and both projects have been able to draw from each other. In particular, section 4.9 has been able to benefit from some of the findings of 'Making School Travel Plans Work'.

4.2 Literature evidence about the traffic impacts of school travel work

In terms of research evidence about the effects of school travel work, there have been a number of studies, which have included an assessment of where the greatest impact can be made, what individual schools are achieving, and what particular types of school travel initiatives are achieving. Details are given below and summarised in table 1.

Research commissioned by the AA Foundation For Road Safety Research undertaken by Bradshaw and Jones (2000) concluded that improvements to public transport offer the greatest potential to reduce car escort mileage (as opposed to car *trips*), because most car mileage for this journey purpose is on trips too long to be walked or cycled.

Sloman (2003) reported before and after monitoring data on 17 school travel plans, gathered from a variety of sources. There was considerable variation in outcomes: at 13 of the schools, the number of cars arriving per 100 pupils declined by between 4 and 23, equivalent to reductions in car use of between 8% and 52%. However, the three schools with the lowest 'before' car mode share (all under 10%) failed to achieve any further reduction (and in one case, car mode share slightly increased). There was also one further school where there was no reduction in car use.

In research commissioned by DTLR (2001), four local authorities felt they had sufficient experience to estimate the reduction in car travel at targeted schools as a result of school travel plans. Hertfordshire gave an estimate of 30%, Derby City Council estimated 20%, Manchester City Council estimated 11% and North Tyneside Council estimated 10%.

European projects have also reported car use reductions. In the Swedish city of Lund, for example, where a walk and cycle to school project combined hard engineering measures with information for parents, road safety training and health promotion, the percentage of parents driving their children to school fell from 17% to 13%, a reduction of 23.5% (Hyllenius, 2003).

A report from the MOST project (Mobility Management Strategies for the Next Decades) on demonstration projects in Limburg, Belgium and Surrey in the UK, found promotion of cycling and walking for school children worked well, providing the safety concerns of parents were taken into account. Car free action days or weeks motivated high proportions of pupils and parents to change their travel behaviour and were popular among parents. Longer term experience showed a typical percentage reduction in car use of between 6 and 16%, but with reductions as high as 42% in some cases, (Wilhelm 2003).

In contrast to these studies, a recent evaluation of the effects of site specific advice provided by two part-time school travel co-ordinators to schools in Camden and Islington, found no evidence of changes in children's travel patterns, or reductions in parental fears about children's safety, (Rowland et al 2003). This randomised controlled trial compared the results of 16 hours of expert advice in 11 schools that had received the intervention, with results in 10 schools that had not. One year on, nine of the 'intervention schools had developed travel plans, but without obvious beneficial impacts. However, many of the actions listed in these school travel plans had yet to be implemented, and the researchers themselves commented that the changes needed to make a difference "were unlikely to be implemented within the project time frame". Consequently, the value of these results is unclear.

Table 4.1: Literature evidence about the effects of school travel work on car use

Source	Finding
Bradshaw & Jones (2000)	Greatest reductions in mileage likely to come from public transport improvements
Sloman (2003)	Monitoring data from 17 school travel plans showed a car use increase at one, no change at three and reductions of between 8% and 52% at the others.
DTLR (2001)	Four local authority estimates of the typical change in car use from travel plans were between 10% and 30%.
Hyllenius (2003)	School travel work in Lund has reduced car use by 24%
Wilhelm (2003)	Projects in Limburg, Belgium and Surrey,UK have typically reduced car use by 6-16%, but with reductions as high as 42%
Rowland et al (2003)	No change in travel behaviour or parental perceptions of safety following one years work at 11 schools in Camden.

In addition to evaluations of general school travel work, there have also been evaluations of particular types of initiatives:

- **Yellow buses**: a recent evaluation of the introduction of yellow buses into the UK shows that they generally become well used, and can be effective at reducing car use, particularly at primary schools (SDG, 2004). The original pilot projects evaluated by SDG were in Wrexham (North Wales), Runneymede (Surrey) and Hebden Bridge (North Yorkshire). Surveys after the introduction of the yellow buses took place in September 2002 and May 2003. Car use at both the evaluated primary schools reduced (from 45% to 34% at Wrexham Primary and 40% to 36% at Hebden Bridge Primary – comparative reductions of 24% and 10%

respectively). Results at the two evaluated secondary schools were more mixed (at Wrexham Secondary car use increased, whilst at Runnymede Secondary, there was an initial dip in car use, from 38% to 33% by September 02, although car use had returned to previous levels by May 03). The SDG report also reported on other surveys of the impacts of introducing yellow buses. At Standish Community High school in Wigan, 135 students now have yellow bus passes, 31% of which previously travelled to school by car. In Ilkley, where yellow buses have been introduced at primary schools, 64% of users previously travelled to school by car. Some other areas reported that yellow bus use had not achieved modal shift, although this was for a range of reasons (yellow buses were introduced for children already entitled to statutory transport; no promotion of services took place due to limited capacity; services introduced to control costs only).

- **Walking buses in New Zealand**: An evaluation carried out in four schools in Christchurch, New Zealand covered 13 walking buses. Of the 112 children involved, 40% were not previously walking to school, (O'Fallon, 2001).

- **Walking buses in Hertfordshire**: A postal survey of schools with walking buses has been carried out in Hertfordshire (Mackett et al, 2003). According to walking bus coordinators, 62% of the children now travelling this way used to travel to school by car (though not necessarily every day). The survey found the 'buses' frequently folded because of a lack of volunteers or coordinators, but that the majority achieved their objectives, which mostly involved shifting children from car to walking. The work also suggested that there may be a natural age limit for children participating (with the peak in interest being amongst children aged 6-7).

- **Walk to School week in Hertfordshire**: Hertfordshire have also been involved in the TAPESTRY EU project (Tapestry 2003), which included an assessment of their Walk to School week campaign, as carried out in May 2002. This work is discussed further in the travel awareness chapter. In brief, it involved an evaluation at 11 schools which received the campaign, comparing them with 2 control schools which did not. As well as achieving changes in attitudes, there was a small (1.3%) increase in the proportion of children walking to school at least once a week in the campaign schools compared with a small (1.3%) decline in the proportion at control schools. At both types of schools, 10%-15% of respondents said that their child walked to school more compared to the same time last year (and the researchers argued that national press and countywide publicity about walking to school had probably affected parents even when their school has not been directly engaged in Walk to School week).

4.3 Literature evidence about other effects from school travel work

In addition to evidence about the impact of school travel work on modal shift, there has also been considerable interest in other potential impacts from such work, although there has been less research to evaluate these.

In particular, there has been interest in the safety benefits that can be achieved from the engineering work that often takes place as part of school travel plans. The UK has relatively high pedestrian casualties rates compared to other European countries such as the Netherlands, Denmark and Sweden. The Transport Select Committee report on Road Traffic Speed concluded that one contributory factor was a relative lack of speed reduction measures in the UK (DTLR 2002). It also highlighted that addressing this issue could be effective at achieving similar results in England, as shown by the experience of cities such as Gloucester, Hull and York. In Hull, for example, well engineered 20mph zones have achieved a 74% reduction in child pedestrian accidents. In Gloucester, a Department for Transport funded five year Safer City project involving extensive speed management and physical speed reduction measures, resulted in a 24% decline in child pedestrian casualties between 1996 and 2000. Both these cities were considered as potential case studies for this project, as discussed in section 4.5.

The safety benefits of encouraging more children to cycle have also been highlighted by a number of commentators, as, in general, higher levels of cycling seem to result in lower accident rates. In the Netherlands the level of cycle traffic increased by 30% between 1980 and 1990, yet annual cyclists' deaths fell (Dutch Ministry for Transport, 1999). In York, too, where there has been consistent investment in traffic calming and cycling infrastructure, a ten year period has seen casualties reduced by 30%, while peak-hour cycling has increased by 10%, (DfT 2000). Wardlaw (2002) compared cycling statistics from the UK with France, Denmark, Germany and the Netherlands, and concluded that "cycling gets safer as it becomes more popular", and that "there is no known example in recent decades when an increase in cycling has led to an increase in cycle deaths". An international survey of travel by 10-14-year-olds, using comparable data from 8 countries has also shown that higher levels of cycling amongst this age group are linked with fewer accidents per kilometre cycled (Christie et al 2004).

There is also a growing body of evidence about the health benefits of encouraging children not to travel by car. Evidence from Sustrans (2003) suggests that there may be a correlation between levels of cycling in different European countries and weight problems in children. The International Obesity TaskForce also highlights that changes in children travel habits may be contributing to the growth in obesity, and that measures to encourage more walking and cycling to school should be part of the solution (IOTF, 2002).

Research undertaken by UCL in Hertfordshire has also examined the role of the school journey in children's physical activity (Mackett et al, 2003b). The work involved 149 children from Hertfordshire schools from years 6 (age 10/11) and 8 (age 12/13). These children were fitted with activity monitors, and monitored over a 4-day period. Key results of this work are as follows:
- Children are typically over 20% less active on weekend days compared to weekdays which may partly reflect the lack of travelling to school
- A typical one-way trip to school by car (18 activity calories) gives less than half the amount of physical activity of travelling by bus (40 activity calories) or on foot (48 activity calories)
- On average, children gain 9% of their physical activity travelling to and from school

- On average, children use more calories travelling to or from school than they do from two hours of PE. This is particularly true for older children who do not travel to school by car.

Finally, there have been various studies showing that reducing car use for the school run could be popular amongst parents and children. Specifically, a study carried out in Spring 2000 demonstrated that school travel work can help to satisfy children's travel preferences. The survey was undertaken by Carrick James Market Research for the 'Are you doing your bit' campaign (DETR 2000). It involved interviews with 769 children aged 7 to 11 at 40 locations across England. The results showed that, of children travelling to school by car, 17% would prefer to walk all the way and 21% would prefer to cycle. In addition, a higher proportion of children travelling on foot, 57%, liked their current method of transport compared to 43% of those going by car. Meanwhile, a survey for the Department for Transport (2002) found that 65% of parents taking their children to school by car would prefer not to drive, but feel that they have no alternative.

Further benefits from school travel work, in addition to health and safety gains, have emerged through the case study examination, and these are discussed in more detail in section 4.10.

4.4 National evidence about the scale of school travel work

It is notable that, although there has been interest in school travel in the UK since the mid-1980s, widespread practical work with schools is relatively recent. According to a 2001 DTLR report, at that time only 4-5% of schools had implemented a travel plan, with a comparable proportion having one 'firmly planned'. Meanwhile, comparisons are often made with European practice. For example, the city of Odense in Denmark has implemented more than 200 projects to improve safety for school pupils over the last 20 years (for example, traffic calming, traffic islands and cycle lanes), and consequently has high levels of cycling, and significantly reduced accident rates (Andersen, undated).

Whilst the UK has been relatively slow to introduce widespread practical work with schools, there has been relatively rapid progress in the last few years. Based on analysis of Local Transport Plan annual progress reports, the Department for Transport has provided data for this project about the current and future number of school travel plans to be implemented. This has been combined with DfES data about total numbers of schools to give the following two tables showing the scale of school travel plan implementation in 2003 and 2006.

Table 4.2: Number of school travel plans in England in 2003

Government Office region	Total number of schools*	Total number of school travel plans implemented by 2003~	Implied % schools with a school travel plan by 2003
North East	1209	379	31
North West	3370	385	11
Yorkshire & Humber	2389	299	13
East Midlands	2198	312	14
West Midlands	2496	347	14
East of England	2745	235	9
South East	3763	759	20
South West	2562	393	15
Total	*20732*	*3109*	*15*

* Data from National Statistics (2003) *Statistics of Eduction: Schools in England.* London: TSO. Data includes primary, middle, secondary and independent schools. It excludes nursery schools, special schools, pupil referral units, city technology colleges and academies.

~ Data supplied by DfT based on local transport plan annual progress reports.

Table 4.3: Number of school travel plans in England proposed by 2006

Government Office region	Total number of schools*	Total number of school travel plans to be implemented by 2006~	Implied % schools with a school travel plan by 2006
North East	1209	676	56
North West	3370	618	18
Yorkshire & Humber	2389	522	22
East Midlands	2198	611	28
West Midlands	2496	759	30
East of England	2745	475	17
South East	3763	1367	36
South West	2562	819	32
Total	*20732*	*5847*	*28*

* Data from National Statistics (2003) *Statistics of Eduction: Schools in England.* London: TSO. Data includes primary, middle, secondary and independent schools. It excludes nursery schools, special schools, pupil referral units, city technology colleges and academies.

~ Data supplied by DfT based on local transport plan annual progress reports.

Department for Transport figures also give some indication of numbers of school travel plans being implemented over time. These are as follows:

Figure 4.1: Number of school travel plans being implemented over time in England.

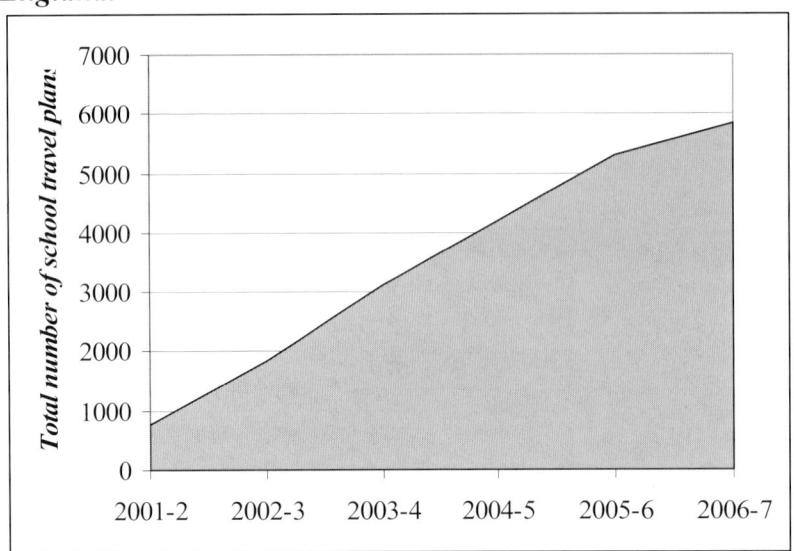

Taken together, these figures imply that, nationally, by 2003, about 15% of schools had travel plans, although the proportion ranged from 9% in the East of England, to 31% in the North East. By 2006, about 28% are expected to have travel plans, with the proportion ranging from 17% in the East of England, to 56% in the North East. It also appears that, nearing 2005, local authorities anticipate that there may be a slowing down of the number of schools involved. It is hard to assess why – possibly it may reflect that they expect all the 'easy targets' will have been reached, or possibly it may reflect that there is an anticipated shift from working with primaries to working with secondaries (who are likely to be more labour intensive per school given their greater size). However, it would be unwise to read too much into what are currently speculative forecasts – especially as many local authorities have only just started to make work in this area a mainstream activity in the last few years.

4.5   Selection of school travel case studies

The preceding sections provide evidence from the literature and national statistics about school travel work. In addition, three local authority case studies of school travel work were examined in detail.

In selecting case studies for this project, there were a number of authorities which were known to have undertaken impressive work on school travel or related work on improving safety in residential areas. Consequently, the following authorities were contacted:
- Buckinghamshire County Council
- Cambridge County Council
- Cornwall County Council
- Gloucestershire County Council
- Hertfordshire County Council
- Hull City Council
- Merseyside
- Oxfordshire County Council

- Sandwell Metropolitan Borough Council
- Surrey County Council, and
- York City Council

In the end, three of these, Buckinghamshire, Merseyside and York were chosen. The main reason was that, at the time, these authorities appeared to have the best available data about the results of their work. The majority of the others did not, at the time, have specific results available.

It should be noted that Gloucester and Hull councils were contacted because of their extensive work on traffic calming, speed management and traffic safety, rather than because of their work on school travel. It was interesting that neither authority has particularly linked these initiatives with school travel work. Indeed, in Hull, there has been little development of school travel plans. In Gloucester, work on school travel is still at an early stage and there were no available data about the effects of their school travel work. However, in a survey of 972 residents in Hull living in areas where 20mph zones had been introduced, 52% of respondents said they thought that more children played in the street since traffic calming was introduced, and 23% said that they walked or cycled more often, (Kirby, 2002). The Gloucester Safer City report (2001) highlighted that the number of parents who said that they let their child go to school on their own had risen from 32% in 1996 to 49% in 2001.

Since the soft factors project interviews took place, the interviews for the parallel 'Making School Travel Plans Work' have taken place with 23 local authorities (including Buckinghamshire, Merseyside and York). In some cases, these have been able to draw on more recently available data from authorities that were initially contacted for the soft factors project. In other cases, authorities were not initially approached for the soft factors project but have emerged as useful sources of information and insight. The data from all 23 authorities is analysed in relation to the effects of their work on car use in section 4.9. Meanwhile, the rest of the chapter concentrates on the evidence provided by Buckinghamshire, Merseyside and York.

4.6 Details of chosen school travel case studies

The 3 case studies which provide the main evidence for this chapter have interesting and contrasting histories and approaches to the school travel issue. These can be summarised as follows:

York: York began its school travel work with a strong focus on safety, including road safety training, infrastructure and and engineering work designed to reduce traffic danger. This approach has continued. In addition, the city has a strong history of cycling, and this is also reflected in its work which is partially guided by its stretched public service agreement target to increase the number of children who normally cycled to school in years groups 6-9, from 5.8% in 1999 to 10.3% by December 2005.

Buckinghamshire: Buckinghamshire initially began its school travel work by focusing on infrastructure, but now believes the most effective way of achieving modal shift is to focus on non infrastructure measures and small scale work. Consequently, it has prioritised this type of work with schools. It has developed a grading system (levels 1, 2 and 3) for travel plans, where schools achieving a level 3 travel plan are eligible to apply to an awards scheme to get measures at their school funded.

Merseyside: Merseyside has been working on school travel for some time, however there was a major increase in staffing in 2001, when the number of staff involved increased from less than two to a team of seven people, helped by funding from the Department of Transport, the PTE and the Health Action Zone. This team now works across the five local authorities based in the area; the work is gaining significant impetus; and has many dimensions of interest including strong health links and work in extremely deprived areas.

4.7   Staffing and budgets for school travel work

Data about local authority staffing and budgets are given in table 4.4.

Table 4.4: Staffing and budgets for school travel work (summer 2003)

		Bucks	Merseyside	York
Length of time scheme has been running		4 years	5 years (2 years intensively)	5 years (with early work dating back 8 years)
Number of primary and secondary schools worked with		142	124	43
Number of primary and secondary school pupils covered by travel plans		47,000	43,000	17,609
Staff time in local authority / PTE initially		1 fte	0.5 fte	4.6 fte
Staff time in local authority / PTE once scheme established		6.5 fte[1]	5 fte[2]	7.0 fte[3]
Expenditure in first 'intensive' year	Capital	£0[4]	£644,500	£520,000
	Revenue	£25,000[5]	£156,000[6]	£7,000
Expenditure in most recent year	Capital	£89,000	£644,500	£628,000
	Revenue	£184,500[5]	£156,000[6]	£62,629

[1] School travel plan co-ordinators and school travel initiative officers

[2] This includes 4 full-time equivalent posts in Merseytravel and one post in Knowsley Council.

[3] This includes staff time promoting school travel plans, providing engineering measures (safe routes to school and school safety zones), installing cycle parking, and cycle and pedestrian training

[4] Although there was capital spending in Buckinghamshire originally, this work is no longer considered to be part of the school travel approach, and has therefore not been included above.

[5] Staff costs have been calculated by assuming an average staff salary of £25,000

[6] This has been calculated by assuming that 4/7ths of the total revenue budget for travel planning in Merseyside are for school work, and adding an assumed salary of £25,000 for the school travel advisor in Knowsley.

At the time of our interviews, work on school travel plans had been going on for between four and five years in all the case study areas, although York has a longer track record of work on safe routes to school engineering measures (which dates back to 1995), and Merseyside has only begun to work intensively with schools in the last few years.

Staffing levels in the three case study areas were similar, at between 4 and 7 full-time equivalent posts. However, the way in which these staff were deployed differed between the case studies. In Buckinghamshire and Merseyside, all staff posts were focussed on developing travel plans – that is, primarily on non-infrastructure measures. In contrast, York had only one staff post developing travel plans, with the rest involved in engineering measures, road safety, installation of cycle parking, or pedestrian and cycle training. (It should be noted that engineering time spent in local authorities across Merseyside has not been included in these figures).

The number of schools engaged and budgets were also very different between the case study areas. In particular, Buckinghamshire had engaged with a high number of schools, it had a relatively low budget, most of which was revenue, and these characteristics undoubtedly related to its focus on non engineering measures. In contrast, York had engaged with far fewer schools, its budget was far higher and the majority of this funding was capital money. Again, this clearly related to its focus on engineering measures. Merseyside appeared to represent a midway scenario, engaging with a high number of schools, with reasonably substantial revenue and capital budgets. (It should be noted that statements in this paragraph relate to absolute levels of engagement, as opposed proportional levels of engagement, which are explored in the next section). In general, it is accepted that engineering measures are relatively expensive (per school) compared with non engineering measures, although there are strong arguments that both are essential.

The three school travel plan case study areas were also case studies for their workplace travel plan activity. This is reported in chapter 3, but it is noteworthy that all three authorities have given a higher priority, in terms of budget and staffing, to school travel work than they have given to workplace travel. In York, total spending on workplace travel plans, including staff costs, was £52,000 in the most recent year, while total spending on school travel programmes was £691,000. In Buckinghamshire, total spending on workplace travel plans was £108,000, compared to an estimated £273,500 on school travel. In Merseyside, total spending on workplace travel plans was £98,000, compared to an estimated £156,000 on school travel plans plus a further £644,500 for safe routes work at local authority level. Whatever the reasons, for the disparity, school travel plan co-ordinators in those authorities were working actively with a much higher proportion of school pupils than workplace travel plan co-ordinators were with employees. In other words, the increased resources allocated to school travel plans had translated into greater activity and more impact.

We were also interested in estimating the costs of school travel work in terms of each affected pupil. Table 4.5 shows the revenue costs per pupil targeted.

Table 4.5: Revenue cost of school travel plans per affected pupil

	Revenue cost per pupil (£)
Buckinghamshire	£3.93
Merseyside	£3.63
York	£3.56

Calculation based on revenue expenditure and pupils affected by travel work, in current year.

Revenue costs were similar in all three case study areas, at about £3.50 - £4 per pupil. This is comparable to the upper end of the range of costs per employee targeted for workplace travel plans. The fact that the figures are at the higher end of the range may reflect that local authorities are almost solely responsible for the inputs to schools, whereas workplaces will also usually put in some of their own resources too.

Moreover, in addition to revenue costs, it is important to add in the capital costs of 'safe routes' infrastructure such as pedestrian crossings, traffic calming and cycle lanes. These costs are likely to vary from school to school. Using data from the parallel project for the Department for Transport (Making School Travel Plans Work), we were able to estimate infrastructure costs per school and per pupil. These are shown in table 4.6. Provisional figures show capital costs per school ranging from £30,000 to £75,000, and capital costs per 'pupil place' ranging from £32 to £243, with an average of £95. It should be noted that none of the eight schools on which this calculation was based had received comprehensive 'safe routes' treatments, and that the costs of providing these would be higher. For example, the £30,000 spent at Broke Hall primary school in Suffolk was enough to pay for one zebra crossing and footway improvements. However, the interviewee in Buckinghamshire highlighted that in some instances, a small scale measure – such as widening a pavement – may be sufficient to address particular parental concerns, although others would undoubtedly argue that this is not always the case. Clearly, the extent and scale of engineering work needed is likely to vary from school to school.

Table 4.6: Capital cost of school travel infrastructure

School	Number of pupil places	Total capital spent on safe routes infrastructure (£)	Capital cost per pupil place (£)
Park Brow, Knowsley	386	30,000	78
St Sebastians, Merseyside	309	75,000	243
Holmemead, Bedfordshire	530	60,000	113
Knowles Hill, Devon	1156	65,000	56
Watchfield, Oxfordshire	312	35,000	112
Kesgrave, Suffolk	1450	46,000	32
Broke Hall, Suffolk	541	30,000	55
St Michaels, South Gloucestershire	585	40,000	68

Data drawn from 'Making School Travel Plans Work' case studies

4.8 Case study data about the scale of school travel work

In addition to information about staffing and budgets, there was evidence from our case studies about the level of their involvement in school travel work. This forms a useful comparison with the national figures discussed in section 4.4. A summary of the results are given in the following three tables.

Table 4.7: Proportions of schools involved in travel work in case study areas (summer 2003)

Location	Number of schools in the area*	Proportion currently working with	Predicted proportion working with in 2006.
Buckinghamshire	221	64% (142)	80% (55% at level 3, 15% at level 2 and 10% at level 1)
Merseyside	582	21%(124)	25%
York	73	59% (43)	75%

* Defined as primary plus secondary

Table 4.8: Primary and secondary school involvement in case study areas (summer 2003)

Location	% primary schools	% primary school pupils	% secondary schools	% secondary school students
Buckinghamshire	64%	62%	65%	64%
Merseyside*	23%	n/a	14%	n/a
York	55%	61%	73%	76%

* Figures for Merseyside calculated on the basis that 15% of total schools are secondaries, in line with the regional average for the North West.

Table 4.9: Levels of school involvement in travel planning work (summer 2003)

Location	% pupils in schools….		
	Developing plan	Plan agreed and/or some measures in place	Fully fledged plan inc. engineering measures
Buckinghamshire	74%	15%	11%
Merseyside*	46%	18%	35%
York	31%	54%	15%

* Done on basis of school numbers rather than pupil numbers, as pupil numbers were not available.

These figures suggest that both York and Buckinghamshire have already engaged a far higher proportion of schools than the national average (59% and 64% respectively), and have higher expectations about future levels of engagement by 2006 (75% and 80% respectively). In contrast, levels of engagement in Merseyside were closer to the national average, (21% in 2003 and 25% in 2006). This probably reflects the fact that both York and Buckinghamshire have been engaged in serious school travel work for a longer time period and that they can be considered to be relatively 'early developers 'as far as school travel work is concerned. Meanwhile, work in Merseyside is more in line with national trends.

In all three areas, levels of engagement with primaries and secondaries were roughly similar, although York has put more emphasis on secondary schools and Merseyside has put more emphasis on primaries.

In all three areas, much of the school travel work is at an early stage – and, in Buckinghamshire, the interviewee highlighted that a lot of their work will involve upgrading work at existing schools that they engage with, as well as engaging new schools. The proportion of schools considered to have fully fledged travel plans in Merseyside seemed surprisingly high compared with Buckinghamshire and York, given the large number that they are working with and the relatively short period that they have been working with schools intensively. Possibly, this implies that the interviewees in the different areas interpreted the question differently.

If it is true that York and Buckinghamshire are early developers – whilst Merseyside's development is more recent – this implies that the plateauing of school travel plan work suggested by the local transport plan annual progress reports (at 30-40% of all schools) is unlikely to happen. Instead, as authorities gain more experience, the number of schools that they feel able to engage with seems likely to increase over time.

4.9   Effects of school travel work on car use

4.9.1 Available data about the traffic impacts of school travel work

As highlighted in section 4.5, this project was able to draw on preliminary data from the parallel Department for Transport 'Making School Travel Plans Work' project, which involved interviews with 23 local authorities (including Buckinghamshire, Merseyside and York). However, although all of these authorities collect information about travel to school, the number with usable results was more limited.

At the time of our assessment, data were available from 12 authorities that could provide information about 'all' schools in their area (or at least, a representative sample of schools). Nine of these had data about how modal choice for travel to school had changed, whilst 10 had information about the current proportion of journeys to school made by car. In section 4.9.2, this information is analysed to assess how individual authorities are performing.

At the time of our assessment, data were also received from 8 authorities about particular categories of school that have been involved in school travel initiatives. The nature of this information, and what it shows, is discussed further in section 4.9.3. It is relatively disparate, however, there seem to be some general findings, whose credibility are perhaps enhanced by the fact they derive from such different sources.

4.9.2 Effects of school travel work on car use to 'all' schools

Information from authorities that had data about travel to all schools (or a representative sample of schools), and relevant data for regional comparisons is given in Table 4.10.

Table 4.10: Local authority results and trends in their region.

Local authority		% car use in most recent survey	% change in car use	Region	% car travel in 1999/01 NTS
Bath & NE Somerset (2001-2002)		--	"Slight" decline	GOSW	34
Bradford City (2000-2002)		36.7	+7.3	GOYH	25
Buckinghamshire (2002-2003)		37	-5-18	GOSE	37
Cambridgeshire (2002)		26.8	--	GOE	36
Devon County (2001-2003)		34	-3	GOSW	34
Norfolk County (1999)		34	--	GOE	36
Nottingham City (01/02-02/03)	Primary	32	+7	GOEM	44
	Secondary	15	-17	GOEM	17
Greater Nottingham (01/02-02/03)	Primary	37	+6	GOEM	44
	Secondary	15	-17	GOEM	17
Oxfordshire (2000)		27	--	GOSE	37
Shropshire (2000-2002)	Primary	48	+12	GOWM	38
	Secondary	17	-11	GOWM	17
South Gloucestershire (1999-2003)		--	0	GOSW	34
Suffolk (1999-2001)		30.5	0	GOE	36
York (1999-2002)	Primary	38.6	+11.9	GOYH	28
	Secondary	22.7	+0.4	GOYH	21
	All	28.6	+9.6	GOYH	25

Of authorities that conduct regular surveys of all schools, and which had data that they considered to be at least partially comparable over a period of time:

- 2 were reporting increases in car use (Bradford 7.3% over two years, York 9.6% over three years, with most of the increase occurring at primary schools)
- 2 were reporting stable levels of car use (Suffolk over two years, South Gloucestershire over four years)
- 3 were reporting declines in car use (Bath and North East Somerset "slight" decline over one year; Devon -3% over two years and Buckinghamshire, between -5 and -18% over one year) [1]
- 2 were reporting increases in car use at primary schools whilst reductions at secondary schools (Nottingham over one year: primaries + 6-7%, secondaries -17%; Shropshire over two years: primaries +12%, secondaries -11%) [2].

---

[1] 18% is the reduction in the proportion of students reporting that they go to school by car. In the 2003 survey, inclusion of a new park and walk category allows for some ambiguity when making comparisons between surveys. Employing the most pessimistic assumptions suggests that it is possible that total car use has only reduced by 5% overall.

[2] It should be noted that, apart from York, these were the only authorities breaking down their data into trends for primary and secondary schools. Hence, it is entirely plausible that in other authorities, travel trends are also more favourable at secondary schools compared with primary schools. However, examination of the individual case studies for the 'Making School Travel Plans Work' project has suggested that there has been considerable success at particular primary schools – indicating that there is no particular reason to assume that focusing on secondaries will be a more successful strategy. Instead, it may be that travel to secondary schools is being influenced nationally by factors such as

As a comparison with these results, National Travel Survey data for 1996/98 and 1999/01 (a period of three years) shows that car use has been stable across all schools, with an underlying pattern of an 8% increase in car use to primary schools and 10% decline in car use for travel to secondary schools.

Overall levels of car use in survey areas can also be compared with regional averages since in some cases, the main effect of the local authority's work has been to keep car use at a low level for school travel in general (as opposed to achieving particular reductions). Making these comparisons is not straightforward. For example, travel patterns are often different in urban and rural areas, and, whilst most regions will include a mixture of area types, many local authorities may be predominantly urban or rural. It is also possible for the local economic circumstances of a particular city to vary markedly from those of the surrounding area. Nonetheless, given those caveats, the following comparisons emerge.

Nottingham City and its surrounding area, Oxfordshire, Cambridgeshire, Suffolk, and, to a lesser extent, Norfolk, have all succeeded in keeping car use below the regional average.

In contrast, the average level of car use for school journeys in Bradford City and primary school journeys in Shropshire and York appear to be significantly higher than the regional average. (It should be noted that car use in Bradford is apparently rising very rapidly generally, which may mean that this is a case in point where the city is performing differently to the region).

In summary then, information from 12 areas which are all engaged in school travel work seems to suggest a mixed picture. Some (Buckinghamshire, Devon and Bath & NE Somerset) have managed to reduce car use overall. Others (Oxfordshire, Cambridgeshire Nottinghamshire and Suffolk) are holding car use at below the regional average. However, others have had less success in making an area wide impact – notably (and surprisingly) York (all schools, particularly primaries), Bradford (all schools) and Shropshire (primary schools).

This may relate to other factors 'confusing' trends, or the extent and depth of the work. Clearly local authorities vary significantly in terms of the number of schools that they have managed to engage with so far, the intensity and nature of their work, the amount of area wide initiatives they run that will affect all schools in their area etc..

It is interesting that Buckinghamshire has prioritised non engineering measures, whilst York has prioritised safer routes work, and that both authorities agree that, if the aim is short-term modal shift, Buckinghamshire's approach may be better. However, York justify their approach on safety grounds and the fact that it is expected to deliver longer term effects. Until these measures have been in place for a longer time period, it is impossible to properly assess the relative long term impacts of these two approaches.

---

media condemnation of the school run, whereas local authorities' achievements at particular schools are more likely to be contingent on the policies adopted.

4.9.3 Effects of school travel work on car use to 'engaged' schools

At the time of our assessment, 8 authorities had 'before and after' data about schools which had been engaged in school travel initiatives in some way. It should be noted that authorities varied in the schools they chose to report on. In some cases, it was schools that had reached a certain level or were involved in a certain programme; in some, it was simply the schools that they had available data about; and in some, it was schools that they were proud of. Specfically, information was received about the following:

Buckinghamshire:
- All schools involved in the county wide 'Go for Gold' walking incentive scheme (number unknown)
- All schools which had reached 'Level 3' (i.e. fully fledged travel plan) and which had available data at the time of the interview (6 schools).

Cambridgeshire:
- Private schools and sixth form colleges prepared to be part of a partnership (CTEEP) that wanted to address travel, with repeat surveys undertaken in 2001 and 2003 at 7 private schools and 1 sixth form college.
- LEA schools which had been the focus of safer routes to schools work, compared with those that had not (numbers of each unknown)
- Schools taking part in Walk to School week in May and October 2002 (67 schools in May and 33 in October).

Hertfordshire:
- All schools which the local authority had received several years of data from. This constituted a total of 17 schools, including 15 that have been involved in their 'safer routes to school' programme.

York
- 60 schools that responded to their 'all schools' surveys undertaken in December 1999 and 2002
- Comparisons of changes in travel behaviour at schools where particular measures (school travel plans, new cycle parking and safety work) had been introduced between 1999 and 2002 (compared to schools where such measures were not introduced in that period). It should be noted that, in York, safety work for primaries involves the introduction of 'safety zones' outside the school entrance, whilst safety work for secondaries involves the introduction of safer routes measures.

Merseyside
- All schools for which the authority had available 'before and after' data. At all of these schools, MerseyTravel had started some school travel work, although the extent of work undertaken by the time of the surveys varied significantly (39 schools).

Knowsley

- All schools where the authority had more than one year of data (3 schools). The authority had undertaken work at all three schools, although one was still to implement its main measures at the time of the survey work.

Cornwall

- Results from a cluster of four schools that the authority had worked with in Falmouth.

Devon

- Results from 9 schools which the council considers to be exemplars of 'good practice' school travel work, although one of these schools was still at a fairly early stage of its work when the surveys were undertaken.

In addition, there were available data from all the individual schools contacted as part of the 'Making School Travel Plans Work' project. Information about individual schools from both phases of the project is relevant:

- In the early work, all schools nominated by school travel experts as 'good practice' examples were asked to complete a survey about their work. Eventually, 80 schools supplied usable before and after data (according to returns received by 3/9/03).
- Of the 30 schools then selected as representatives of good practice, 28 have usable 'before and after' data.

For all the data sources reported above, it is probable that the schools reported were keen to be involved in school travel work (i.e. there was a degree of self selection), either because of traffic problems, or other concerns such as safety, sustainability, health and environmental considerations. Hence, it cannot be argued that their experience would inevitably translate to 'all' schools. However, there is some evidence that, as an increasing number of schools become involved in school travel work in a given area, others, that were initially reluctant, become keener to be involved too. In addition, the different data sources do provide insight into some schools with intensive travel work, and some schools that will have had a much lesser degree of involvement, making some generalisation possible.

For schools involved in initiatives, the following results emerged:

- High proportions of these schools typically achieved reductions in car use: 89% of 'good practice' schools in Devon; 88% of schools in the CTEEP partnership in Cambridgeshire; 83% of Level 3 schools in Buckinghamshire; > 80% of safer routes schools in Hertfordshire; 75% of schools in the Falmouth cluster in Cornwall; 66% of all schools with results in Knowsley; and somewhere between 62 and 77% of schools in Merseyside (depending on how account is taken of car-sharing and park-and-walk trips)[3].

---

[3] In the case of Knowsley, the '33%' school without a traffic reduction was still awaiting the implementation of its main school travel measures, whilst, in Buckinghamshire, the '17%' school seems to have achieved a significant car use reduction in the first few years of its work, but car use has since risen again. These examples highlight that the situation will, of course, vary over time – schools at the early stages of work, and schools which have undertaken travel work which has since lapsed, may both be less likely to be showing traffic reductions.

- Reductions in car use of 20% or more are not uncommon for schools involved in initiatives, including reports of 8 schools (89%) in Devon; 6 or 7 schools (75/88%) in Cambridgeshire; 2 or 5 schools (33%/83%) in Buckinghamshire; 2 schools (50%) in Cornwall; 4 schools (27%) in Hertfordshire; and 6 or 9 schools (15/23%) in Merseyside[4].

- Several authorities quoted schools where car use had more than halved, including 2 schools in Buckinghamshire; 1 school in Devon and (possibly) 2 in Merseyside (depending on the magnitude of the car use component of the park and walk trips made to these schools).

Notably, of the 80 individual schools with data which responded to the 'Making School Travel Plans Work' project survey, 61 (76%) of these had achieved reductions in total car use. Thirty-three (41%) appeared to have achieved reductions in total car use in excess of 20%, and 8 (10%) appeared to have more than halved overall car use[5].

Of the 28 individual schools with data selected to be representative of good practice, 26 (93%) have achieved reductions in total car use, with 14 (50%) achieving reductions in excess of 20%, and 2 (7%) achieving cuts of more than 50%.

In terms of the total numbers of schools for which there are reports of measured changes in car use, the following emerges[6]:

- In terms of schools with data showing a reduction in car use, there were 26 of the case study schools from the 'Making School Travel Plans Work' project, a further 71-77 from the local authority reports, and a further 20 from the 'Making School Travel Plans Work' shortlisting process. This makes a total of 117-123 schools where car use is reported as having reduced. There are probably considerably more examples than this, both because the 'Making School Travel Plans Work'

---

[4] Buckinghamshire, Merseyside and Cambridgeshire included survey categories of car sharing, park and walk or both. In these cases, in the absence of actual information, conservative assumptions were made about how much of these trips should be counted as car use, in order to avoid the risk of over-estimating the traffic reduction achieved. These assumptions were that each car sharer accounts for half a car, and that 75% of every park and walk trip is made by car. When these assumptions are applied, the degree of reduction in car use achieved at some schools reduces. Consequently, two figures are given for each of these authorities. The larger number refers to the number of schools where the proportion of children reporting that they simply come to school by car has reduced by 20% or more. The smaller number refers to the number of schools where, after making conservative assumptions about the amount of more sustainable travel that will still involve car use, total car use has still probably reduced by 20% or more.

[5] These figures relate to 'total' car use – which was calculated using the same assumptions as those described in footnote 4, for those cases where the school provided data which enabled consideration of car sharing or park and walk.

[6] To calculate the figures from this section, data were amalgamated from the 30 individual 'Making School Travel Plans Work' schools selected to represent good practice, the local authority reports, and the data for the 80 individual schools received in the first phase of the 'Making School Travel Plans Work' project. Data were carefully checked to avoid double counting. Where there were differences in the results for the same school (due, for example, to differences in the time period of change being reported for that school), the data about the 30 individual schools was treated as the most reliable, then the local authority reports, and only then the results received in the initial phase of the 'Making School Travel Plans Work' project. For the local authority reports, two figures are given – because, in some cases, it was possible to calculate what individual schools had achieved in two different ways (either changes in conventional car use or, using assumptions, changes in total car use). The figures from the other two sources should relate to changes in total car use at the individual schools.

survey process is unlikely to have picked up every possible national example, and also (probably more importantly) because many schools are undertaking high quality school travel work but have simply not monitored the effects of their work.

- In terms of schools with data showing a reduction in car use of more than 20%, there were 14 of the case study schools from the 'Making School Travel Plans Work' project, a further 20-30 from the local authority reports, and a further 8 from the 'Making School Travel Plans Work' shortlisting process, making a total of 42-52 schools where car use has reduced by over 20%.
- In terms of schools with data showing that car use had reduced by 50% or more, there were 2 of the case study schools from the 'Making School Travel Plans Work' project, further 1-3 from the local authority reports, and a further 3 from the 'Making School Travel Plans Work' shortlisting process. This makes a total of 6-8 schools where car use has more than halved. Clearly, this implies that managing to reduce car use this substantially is quite rare – although there are enough reports to provide confidence that it can happen.

There were also results particular to the initiatives that schools had been involved in. Throughout the rest of this section, the terms 'conventional car use' and 'total car use' are used. Changes in 'conventional car use' are defined as changes in the number of children who record themselves as coming 'by car' in travel surveys. Changes in 'total car use' have usually been calculated by combining different categories of travel, to allow for the fact that some children have transferred to means of travel which still involve some car use – in particular, children who now arrive at school by car sharing or undertaking park and walk. As previously, calculations conservatively assume that each car sharer accounts for half a car, and that 75% of every park and walk trip is made by car.

The results about schools involved in particular initiatives show the following:
- At Buckinghamshire, all schools involved in Go for Gold have reduced car use by an average of 22%. Schools achieving what the authority regards as a Level 3 travel plan have reduced conventional car use by an average of 39% and total car use (calculated using pessimistic assumptions) by 21%.
- In Cambridgeshire, the 8 CTEEP schools have reduced conventional car use by an average of 32% and total car use by 22%; schools involved in the 2002 safe routes to school programme had car use which is 28% lower than those which were not; and, after Walk to School week (which reduces car use by about a quarter) car use remained 11% lower three weeks after the May week (67 schools involved) and 2% lower a fortnight after the October week (32 schools involved).
- For the 9 schools quoted from Devon, an average car use reduction of 28% was achieved.
- For the 4 schools involved in the Falmouth cluster in Cornwall, an average car use reduction of 19% was achieved.
- For the 39 Merseyside schools that had been engaged in school travel work in some capacity, conventional car use reduced by an average of 10.2%, whilst, using pessimistic assumptions, total car use reduced by 3.3%
- For schools in York, calculations suggest that, on average, primaries with school travel plans had car use which was 15% lower than it would otherwise have been; primaries with new cycle parking had car use which was 21% lower than it would otherwise have been; and secondary schools with safer routes work had car use which was 8% lower than it would otherwise have been.

These results suggest that when local authorities engage with schools (that are happy to be involved), there will inevitably be some schools that do not achieve positive modal shift. However, a high proportion (somewhere between 60 and 90%) can be expected to achieve positive modal shift, and there are more than an hundred schools around the country where this has occurred. Moreover, a significant percentage of them can be expected to reduce car use by over a fifth – for all schools that are engaged with, the proportion is likely to be somewhere between 15 and 40%[7].

Taking this data, the implied overall reduction in traffic that might occur across all engaged schools is likely to be in the order of 8-15%[8]. Notably, this is reasonably consistent with the previous results about all schools quoted for Buckinghamshire in section 4.9.2, where conventional car use had reduced by 18%, and using pessimistic assumptions (necessitated by the lack of any park and walk category in surveys prior to 2003), total car use had declined by at least 5%. For Merseyside, the results for all 39 schools were slightly lower (conventional car use reducing by 10% and total car use reducing by at least 3%), which is consistent with the evidence that their average degree of engagement with the surveyed schools has probably been less.

Meanwhile, for schools that are engaged in intensive programmes or that reach a certain 'level', achieving an average reduction in car use across all schools of over a fifth is common, as shown by the results from schools in Devon, the Falmouth cluster in Cornwall, the CTEEP partnership schools and safer routes schools in Cambridgeshire, Level 3 schools in Buckinghamshire and the 28 individual schools surveyed for the 'Making School Travel Plans Work' project. There are also a number of rarer cases where car use has actually halved – indicating that very dramatic levels of change can be achieved.

Meanwhile, the experience of Buckinghamshire and Cambridgeshire highlights that promotional programmes aiming to involve a large number of schools (such as the Go for Gold walking incentive scheme and Walk to School week) can also have substantial effects.

4.9.4. Overall effects of school travel work on car use

In terms of reductions in car use for school travel across the whole of a local authority area, there is a mixed picture. Some have managed to reduce car use overall, whilst others are holding car use at below the regional average. However, other areas have

---

[7] The 60-90% range is the full range from all the examples – Merseyside provides the lower end of the range whilst figures of more than 80% were derived from five different sources – making the higher end of the range credible. For the 15-40% range – 15% is the lowest figure derived from any local authority. There were a number of figures greater than 40% quoted that could have been used for the higher end of the range, however, given the sources (and number of schools involved), it was less clear that this figure was representative. Consequently, 40% has been chosen as a more credible figure – deriving from the data about 80 individual schools originally submitted for the 'Making School Travel Plans Work' project.

[8] This has been calculated by assuming a) that 40% of schools experience no modal shift, 45% experience a car use reduction of between 0 and 20% (i.e. on average, 10%), and that 15% experience a car use reduction of over 20% (assumed, conservatively, to be an average of 25%); and b) that 10% of schools experience no modal shift, 50% experience a car use reduction of between 0 and 20% (i.e. on average, 10%), and that 40% experience a car use reduction of over 20% (assumed, conservatively, to be an average of 25%).

had less success in making an area wide impact. There is some (tentative) evidence, which suggests that prioritising awareness raising and incentive schemes may be more effective at delivering short term modal shift, than engineering work designed to improve safety. However, many authorities are prioritising safety work, in order to reduce accident risk, because they believe it to be a necessary condition for sustained and long term modal shift, and, in some cases, because the consultation process for introducing engineering work is seen as an awareness raising mechanism anyway.

In terms of the degree of modal shift - when local authorities engage with schools (that are happy to be involved), not all schools will reduce car use. However, a high proportion (between 60% and 90%) can be expected to achieve positive modal shift, and a significant percentage can be expected to reduce car use by over a fifth – for all schools that are engaged with, the proportion is likely to be somewhere between 15 and 40%. This leads to a range of 'typical' profiles for local authority work on school travel, as shown in Figure 4.2.

These profiles imply that the overall effect of car use at all engaged schools is likely to be a reduction in the order of 8-15%. It should be noted that these profiles relate to schools that are involved in school travel work, not all schools in the area. Moreover, they relate to the profile for schools where travel work has developed sufficiently that it could be expected to have made an impact. (Clearly, in an authority where the majority of schools are only just starting work, the effects on travel are unlikely to immediately materialise.) It also presupposes that contextual factors remain relatively constant – for example, that there has not been a major cut in school bus provision across the authority which could have a major counterproductive effect on school travel work.

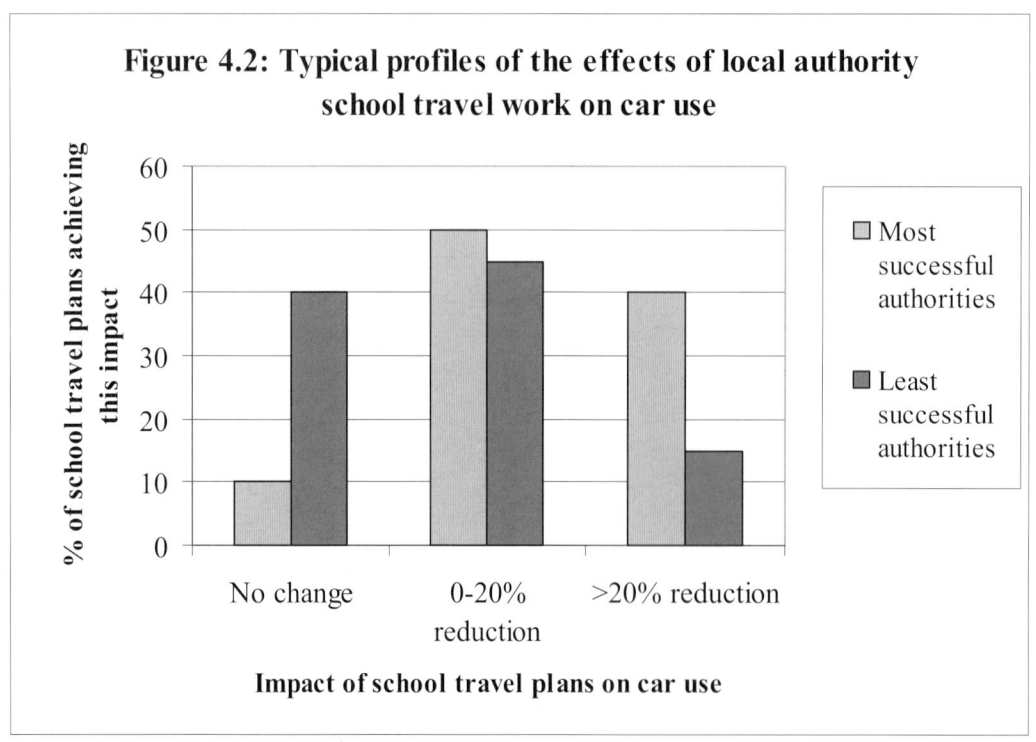

Figure 4.2: Typical profiles of the effects of local authority school travel work on car use

These profiles relate to the effects from 'typical' school travel work. Meanwhile, for schools that are engaged in intensive programmes or that reach a certain 'level', average reductions in car use of over a fifth are common. There are also a number of rarer cases where car use has actually halved – indicating that very dramatic levels of change can be achieved.

In addition, promotional programmes aiming to involve a large number of schools (such as walking incentive schemes and Walk to School week) can also have substantial effects.

These findings are broadly consistent with the literature reviewed in section 4.2.

There is one final issue in relation to the car use reductions achieved by school travel – namely the proportion of car journeys which will still be made because the parent continues to make the trip. This may apply particularly to journeys where the parent is driving to work, and was previously dropping the child at school on the way to work. There has been little direct investigation of this issue, although there have been some assessments of how many school journeys are simply home-school-home. According to NTS data quoted by Bradshaw and Jones (2000), only about a third of school escort journeys made by car are not made solely for the school run, although they also quote a number of other surveys which suggest different results. It must undoubtedly be the case that some car journeys are still made – however, the number of these is important in terms of how seriously this issue needs to be considered. In addition, the extent to which the school run is causing deviation in route is significant – since most school journeys are relatively short, it is plausible that the home-school-work deviation is nearly equivalent in distance to a home-school-home trip anyway. Finally, a number of commentators have highlighted that the need to undertake the school run is often seen as a constraint on why travel to work by an alternative means is not possible. Consequently, initiatives aimed at addressing school travel could, in some cases, make travelling to work by an alternative means more viable. It is notable that two of the case study areas are starting to link their work on school and workplace travel, as discussed in section 4.11.

4.10 Other effects from school travel work

In addition to achieving modal shift, school travel work is commonly associated with achieving a wide range of benefits. These were identified in the literature and the three project case studies as follows:

- **Improved safety**: school travel work can result in reductions in both the perceived danger of travel near schools and actual accidents. Specifically, in York, the introduction of school safety zones around primary schools appear to have approximately halved the number of 8-9-year-olds reporting that they have been involved in a traffic accident (from 6.0% to 3.6%). In Merseyside, there have also been improvements in accident rates, with the number of children killed or seriously injured in road traffic accidents reducing from 216 (1994-98 average) to 137 in 2001, although it is difficult to know how much of this reduction can be attributed to school travel work.

- **Improvements in road safety skills**: school travel work can help to improve pupils' road safety skills. For example, in Buckinghamshire, walking incentive schemes are associated with pedestrian training, cycle trains are associated with cycle training and the county is also piloting a sixth form drivers scheme.

- **Increased independence for children**: improvements in both safety and pupils road safety skills can, in turn, increase parental confidence about letting their children travel by themselves and result in increased independence.

- **Health and fitness benefits:** increases in walking and cycling are generally associated with health and fitness benefits. As discussed in section 4.3, work in Hertfordshire is quantifying the extent of these benefits.

- **Improved attendance and ability to learn**: school travel schemes are often associated with benefits for children's general education. Specifically, schemes in Merseyside have been associated with improved attendance and punctuality at school. There are also numerous anecdotal reports that children are brighter and more alert when they arrive if they have walked or cycled, and more able to settle down and learn if they have 'burnt off excess energy'. (It has been hypothesised that this may be particularly true for children with attention deficit disorder).

- **Greater knowledge of environmental and citizenship issues**: school travel work can be associated with particular educational benefits, in terms of improved awareness about environmental issues and citizenship. This was identified as particular benefit in Buckinghamshire. Where pupils are engaged in consultation and their ideas are taken on board, this can also resulting improvements in self-esteem. There has been school travel work specifically aiming to involve children with low self-esteem in Devon, with positive results reported.

- **Community benefits**: school travel work is often associated with improved community integration and empowerment, with spin-off benefits in the wider area. These benefits were specifically mentioned by all three case studies. In particular, in Merseyside, it was mentioned that school travel work often helps parents and neighbours to get to know each other, that children from local areas now play out with each other more, and that parents become active in school and community activities often the first time. At one school (St Sebastians) school travel work has resulted in new lighting in the surrounding area which has benefited far more people than just the school pupils, and the IT room has been opened to the whole community outside school hours.

- **Increased social inclusion**: school travel work is seen as socially inclusive, providing options which are available to all, and, in some cases, local authorities are specifically targeting more deprived areas to improve their options. Again, the social inclusion benefits of school travel work were mentioned by all three case studies. Specifically, in Buckinghamshire, travel plans were described as "a great leveller", on the basis that everybody can enjoy the health benefits of walking and cycling, and that they have enabled the team to look at safety issues for groups who might otherwise not come forward. In York, there are specific examples where school travel work has helped socially deprived areas, including reducing congestion for one school that is an area with pockets of deprivation; and improving access routes to 2 colleges whose catchment areas include more socially excluded students. The cycle maintenance training project in York is also being run in the 4 most deprived secondary schools of York.

- **Increased awareness of the potential for change**: specific school travel work can also raise general awareness of school travel issues. For example, in Buckinghamshire, the interviewee commented that people were initially unaware about potential initiatives, such as walking buses. Now, however, there is greater familiarity, which is resulting in more schools requesting measures that will benefit their pupils. In a Mori survey in October 2002, safe routes to school came out as a top priority for local transport (identified by 36% of respondents).

4.11 Synergies between school travel work and other policies and issues

There are various synergies involved in school travel work.

First, school travel work clearly benefits from related measures, including measures to improve alternative options to the car and measures to manage the car. Specifically:

- in Buckinghamshire, the introduction of special parking measures in High Wycombe in Aylesbury were seen as something that has encouraged parents to think twice about driving. For example, Hamilton School in High Wycombe now requires parents who drive to have a parking permit and to park in a specific area.
- In York, schools were seen as having benefited from the development of pedestrian and cycle networks, park and ride sites, village safety plans, speed management initiatives and public transport initiatives.

In all areas, road safety measures are commonly seen as complementary with school travel work.

It was also noted that school travel work can increase the acceptability of such hard measures. For example, in York, the interviewee commented that in the context of school safety zones or safe routes to school, people are more inclined to support traffic calming or the extension of cycle paths where they might otherwise oppose them.

School travel work can also benefit from other soft initiatives. Specifically, improvements in public transport information and marketing were mentioned as a useful synergetic policy initiative occurring in Merseyside. There is also a growing tendency for some areas to link their work on schools and workplaces, in order to enhance their effects. Specifically:

- in Merseyside, the same team is working on school and workplace travel plans and they are deliberately starting to informally target schools and workplaces in particular neighbourhoods at the same time, to try and maximise the benefits of their work
- in York, the interviewee reported on work at a primary school, where a new cycle path has provided to link to two main arterial routes and good off-road cycle routes. As a result, the school reports that many parents are cycling to school with their children and then carrying on to work in town, rather than travelling by car.

As well as synergy with other initiatives, there are also examples of specific soft measures being specially adapted for school travel work. Specifically:

- in Buckinghamshire, the Bucks CarShare scheme is now being publicised for schools, including providing sixth formers with information.
- in York, at the time of the interview, the council was planning to produce individualised journey planners for children starting secondary school.
- in Buckinghamshire, at the time of the interview, the council was about to start work on personalised travel planning for students over the age of 16, to raise awareness of public transport options for students travelling long distances to school, as they have identified lack of awareness of public transport amongst such students as a particular issue.

School travel work was also seen as a good way of raising awareness and increasing the acceptability of more sustainable transport policies. The Merseyside interviewee expressed frustration that the work was not given high priority, given that it has this effect.

Finally, school travel work clearly has synergistic benefits with other areas of policy, including health and education. It is notable that in York, a member of the primary care trust was originally involved, and in Merseyside, some of the funding comes from the Health Action Zone.

4.12 Relationship between school travel work spending and impact

In setting out to evaluate the relationship between spending, scale of school travel plan work and effectiveness, we used the local authority figures about the proportions of schools that they had engaged with. However, we did not use their assessments of how advanced their travel plan work was, as we were not convinced that interpretation of 'travel plan level' was consistent across authorities. Instead, to calculate impacts, we used the data range suggested by work in a number of authorities. This suggests that, at current levels of engagement, typically, 10-40% of schools with travel work will not achieve positive modal shift, 45-50% will reduce traffic by between 0 and 20%, and 15-40% will cut traffic by over 20%, with some schools achieving reductions in traffic of 50% or more. Crudely averaging these results suggests that travel work might be expected to cut traffic levels by between 8% and 15% - figures which are approximately in line with the averages produced by Buckinghamshire and Merseyside. Consequently, we developed two models – one of which assumed that the average cut in car use achieved by the local authorities was 8%; the other assuming that the average cut in car use was 15%.

We assumed that at the schools where school travel work has taken place, behaviour change has grown linearly from zero when the programme was established, to the position in the current year. We further assumed that the total investment so far would result in behaviour change in subsequent years, but that this would decline at a rate of 40% per year.

The cost of achieving this behaviour change was taken as the *total* spending on revenue and capital. Revenue expenditure was calculated over the years the programme had been running (estimated on the assumption that expenditure grew linearly between the first and current years).The capital costs of infrastructure measures were annualised at 3.5% for the period that the school travel work had been taking place.

Table 4.11 sets out the calculation of costs and impacts.

Table 4.11: Calculation of cost-impact ratios for school travel plans

	Bucking-hamshire	Merseyside	York
length of time scheme has been running (years)	4	2	5
estimated total expenditure, with capital costs annualised # (£)	£429,465	£379,673	£465,973
pupils affected by travel plan in current year	47000	43000	17609
% travelling by car*	39	45	26
number of pupils travelling by car affected by travel plans	18330	19350	4578
Model A: low estimate – 8%			
kilometres saved in current year ~	4692480	4953600	1172055
total kilometres saved +	16423680	9907200	4688220
cost per kilometre saved (pence)	2.6	3.8	9.9
Model B: high estimate – 15%			
kilometres saved in current year ~	8798400	9288000	2197603
total kilometres saved +	30794400	18576000	8790413
cost per kilometre saved	1.4	2.0	5.3

Total expenditure is estimated, assuming linear growth from expenditure in first year to expenditure in current year, with capital costs annualised at 3.5%. The expenditure data used as the basis for this calculation are given in table 4.4.

* For Buckinghamshire and York, this is the earliest car mode share for all schools recorded in a county wide survey (1999 in both cases). For Merseyside, it is the average figure for all the schools that Merseyside has engaged with (2001/02) – it does not include any car use associated with park and walk, given that this cannot be calculated specifically. (This makes our estimate of cost relatively conservative – i.e. it potentially errs on the side of 'expensive').

~ In calculating car mileage saved per year, we assumed 200 school days per year. 1999/2001 NTS data gives the average journey to school distance by car as 4km. Hence annual car distance saved for each pupil who stops travelling by car = 200 x 8 x 2 = 3200 km per year. This assumes two return trips from home to school each day. As discussed in section 4.9.4, it should be noted that some car escort trips would be made anyway, as they are part of a journey elsewhere. However, given an absence of data, the issue of deviation and the fact that there could be some traffic gains in the opposite direction – from work journeys previously made by car converting to other means, no account of the issue is taken.

+ 'total kilometres saved' assumes linear behaviour change in car kilometres saved, from zero in year 1 to current year figure, plus some behaviour change in future years, declining by 40% per year after current year if no further money is spent.

This table shows that cost-impact ratios range from 3-10 pence per kilometre saved under the more conservative assumption of travel plan effectiveness (model A), or 1 - 5 pence with the less conservative assumption (model B). The figures for York are higher than Merseyside and Buckinghamshire, largely because lower car mode share in York means that the number of car escort trips available to be influenced at each school is smaller.

However, it should be noted that this method of calculation (employed throughout the report) to some extent 'disguises' the up-front investment in capital expenditure needed. Evidence from 'Making school travel plans work' suggests that most authorities see engineering measures as an important part of their work with schools. They are needed as a way of engaging schools, allaying (justified) parental concerns about road safety, maximising the effects of softer measures and locking in long-term benefits.

Consequently, as an alternative way of assessing costs, we also looked at how much revenue and capital funding the case study authorities might need to spend in order to influence the entire school population (table 4.12).

Table 4.12: Revenue and capital budgets needed to work with all schools in case study areas, compared to current budgets (summer 2003)

	Total pupils in area	Annual revenue budget required to work with all pupils *(£)	Ratio of required revenue to current revenue budget	Total capital spend required to deliver some safe routes measures to all schools+	Number of years required to deliver some safe routes measures to all schools, with current capital budgets
Buckinghamshire	74847	£299,388	1.6	£7,110,465	36
Merseyside	240000~	£960,000	6.2	£22,800,000	35
York	26179	£104,716	1.7	£2,487,005	4

~ Figure for total pupils in Merseyside is an estimate, based on number of schools
* Annual revenue budget required to work with all pupils based on spending £4 per head
+ Capital spend required to deliver some safe routes measures (but not comprehensive safe routes treatment) to all schools in the local authority area, based on a capital spend of £95 per pupil place.

For revenue costs, we assumed local authorities would need to spend roughly £4 per head each year. Under this assumption, budgets need to rise slightly in Buckinghamshire and York (to 1.6 and 1.7 times the 2003 revenue budget, respectively). Merseyside, with its much larger school population, requires a budget about six times the current figure. Although current budgets are not sufficient to reach the whole school population in any of the case study areas, they are much closer to the necessary sum than for workplace travel plans.

For capital spend, we made the assumption that infrastructure spending of £95 per pupil place is required to provide a basic level of safer infrastructure. Under this assumption, the current rate of capital investment in York would be sufficient to provide some basic 'safe routes' measures at every school within about four years. (This makes no allowance for the measures already in place in York.) However, capital investment at current levels in Merseyside and Buckinghamshire would take about 35 years to provide basic 'safe routes' measures at every school. Put another way, the capital budgets in these areas would have to nearly quadruple to be able to provide basic infrastructure improvements for every school within the next decade, if that was what the authorities concerned wished to do.[9]

---

[9] Recent additional funding provided by the Department for Transport directly to schools will help provide some 'micro' infrastructure such as cycle shelters, but will not be sufficient to fund safe routes infrastructure such as traffic calming and cycle lanes.

4.13 Future impact of school travel work

The future impact of school travel work depends on the number of schools where school travel work would be appropriate and effective, and the average effectiveness of travel plans at these schools. These issues are discussed below.

4.13.1 What proportion of schools might be covered by travel plans?

The three case studies gave varying estimates of the proportion of schools that might be covered by travel plans in future, but all were reasonably confident that coverage would grow substantially.

Buckinghamshire: In Buckinghamshire, the interviewee estimated that 55% of schools would have fully-fledged 'level 3' travel plans by 2006, with 15% of schools at level 2 and 10% at level 1. About 20% of schools would not have a travel plan. By 2011, she felt that 95% of schools would have a fully-fledged level 3 travel plan. Consequently, only 5% were not expected to be involved in travel planning. It was anticipated that these schools would be much more difficult to engage with, for various reasons. These estimates were based on the assumption that resources for school travel planning would remain at least the same as at present.

Merseyside: Merseyside has a target that about 25% of schools will have a travel plan by 2006. This is based on the assumption that resources will remain about the same as at present, and on a pragmatic assessment of the rate at which schools become engaged with the programme. No assessment was made of the likely take-up of travel plans in 2011.

York: In York, the interviewee estimated that about 75% of schools would have a travel plan by 2006, with 100% coverage by 2011. She also felt that the proportion of schools with physical 'safe route to school' engineering measures would increase. About 20% of schools might have safe routes by 2006, rising to about 75% by 2011. Again, this was based on the assumption that resources would remain about the same as at present.

Taken overall, assuming current levels of resources, Merseyside aims to reach 25% of schools by 2006, whilst the goals are much higher for Buckinghamshire (80%) and York (75%). Moreover, both Buckinghamshire and York expect to have achieved 95-100% coverage by 2011. Buckinghamshire andYork also expect the proportion of 'fully-fledged' travel plans to increase – with 95% of Buckinghamshire schools to have level 3 travel plans and 75% of schools in York to have safer routes work, by 2011. The future effectiveness of travel plans is discussed below.

4.13.2. Future effectiveness of school travel plans

York: The York interviewee felt that if funding for school travel plan work was increased, the council would be able to offer a higher quality of intervention for each school. They would work with the same number of schools, but the behaviour change achieved would be greater. She estimated that if resources were not a constraint, it would be possible to halve levels of car use at half of all schools (presumably with smaller reductions in car use at other schools). This estimate was based on the proportion of schools and communities that have the interest and capacity to become actively involved in school travel planning, and her perception of the possible behavioural change that can be achieved. We infer that it would imply a reduction in overall car mode share for children travelling to school in York from 29% (the figure for 2002) to 22% or less. To achieve this maximum impact, the York interviewee suggested the council would need to increase its staffing from seven full-time staff to nine full-time staff working on school travel planning and safe routes, and also increase the associated capital funding.

Buckinghamshire: in Buckinghamshire, it was reported that, for schools with fully-fledged 'level 3' travel plans, the average reduction in car use was between 21% and 39% (depending on the magnitude of the car component of park-and-walk trips). At present less than 20% of schools in the county have a level 3 travel plan, but if 95% had a travel plan at this level (which the interviewee suggested would be possible by 2011), we estimate overall car mode share for the trip to school in Buckinghamshire could fall from the current figure of 37% to somewhere between 29% and 23%. This assumes the effectiveness of level 3 travel plans at individual schools would average about the same as they do now.

In summary, then, evidence from both Buckinghamshire and York suggests that, in the future, it would be feasible for a very significant proportion of schools in these areas to have travel plans, resulting in very substantial reductions in car use.

4.14 Key issues for scaling up work on school travel

In general, interviewees seemed positive and optimistic about the potential to scale up delivery of travel plans. The main issues likely to influence the success of school travel planning were as follows.

- **Willingness of schools to engage with the process**

All the interviewees pointed out that their work could only be effective if schools were willing to engage with the travel planning process. The Buckinghamshire interviewee also highlighted that schools need a certain amount of time to introduce travel plans, and that, to some extent, this will also condition the speed of progress. One interviewee suggested that schools should be required by OFSTED to draw up travel plans, as part of their health and safety responsibilities to their pupils. Others have suggested that there should at least be clear criteria within OFSTED whereby schools with travel plans will always receive positive feedback for good work, (as opposed to the current situation where OFSTED inspectors can choose whether or not to comment on school travel work. There are reports of schools losing motivation because their travel work, which has been commended in other contexts, has not been acknowledged in their OFSTED report at all).

- **Funding**

Lack of funding was raised as an issue less often than by workplace travel plan co-ordinators, reflecting the fact that in general, the school travel plan case studies had allocated quite significant resources to their work with schools. Nevertheless, one interviewee pointed out that long-term security of funding was vital to permit strategic planning of school travel planning work. Capital funding for associated infrastructure has also been highlighted as important, particularly as this is seen as one of the concrete benefits that local authorities can offer schools in return for their engagement.

- **Use of the planning system**

The Buckinghamshire interviewee pointed out that in two-tier authorities (where the highway authority is not the same body as the planning authority), the planning system is not always used as effectively as it could be to require schools to adopt travel plans. Government could help by reviewing and strengthening PPG13, to encourage more consistent interpretation by planning authorities.

- **Restraint measures**

Two interviewees felt that the absence of traffic restraint measures, such as parking management, and lack of political will to re-allocate roadspace to pedestrians and cyclists, meant school travel plans were less effective than they could be. The fact that every school has to make a special case for 20mph limits and/or parking enforcement outside the school gates was also raised. It was argued that the position should be reversed, with guidance highlighting that such measures should be regarded as the norm – with schools only needing to make a special case if they want higher speed limits or a lack of parking measures.

- **Parental preference**

One interviewee pointed out that national policy to increase parental choice of schools has made it more difficult to get pupils to school by bus, foot or cycle, and that this is likely to limit the effectiveness of school travel plans. Several interviewees argued that their education authorities needed to be made more aware of school travel plan work in general.

- **Advertising and marketing**

One interviewee argued that the Advertising Standards Agency could help by stopping advertising based on the school run, together with advertisements that denigrate cyclists and give unrealistic glamour to car use.

4.15 Policy implications relating to school travel

Our interviewees felt that the following policy measures would be helpful in encouraging more widespread and effective school travel work:
- The possibility of requiring schools to adopt travel plans, as part of their health and safety responsibilities to pupils, could be explored. As a minimum, OSFTED could be required to acknowledge good school travel work.
- There may be potential to strengthen the wording in PPG13 to encourage more consistent application by planning authorities in relation to schools.
- Encouraging local authorities to consider school travel work as a reasonably long-term programme would help to provide the security of funding and other resources that permit strategic planning.
- To ensure that school travel work is successful, it is important that local authorities plan appropriate revenue and capital budgets that allow measures to be implemented which emerge from school travel planning.

- National government could provide a stronger policy steer about the desirability of traffic restraint measures outside schools, such as parking restrictions or speed limits or traffic calming.
- The transport implications (including the costs) of parental choice and increasingly specialised schools need to be factored into policy decisions on these topics.

4.16 Acknowledgements

We would like to thank the following people for their help with the school travel plan case studies:

Individual	Organisation
Catherine Rawas	Buckinghamshire County Council
Jane Woods	Buckinghamshire County Council
Catherine Heinemeyer	City of York Council
Daniel Johnson	City of York Council
Sarah Dewar	Merseyside TravelWise

In addition to the main case study interviewees, we would like to express our grateful thanks to the project team for 'Making School Travel Plans Work' and their interviewees. We would also like to thank:

Individual	Organisation
Barbara Wilcox	Cambridgeshire County Council
Kirsty Gilliland	Cambridgeshire County Council
Hannah Moore	Cambridgeshire County Council
Margaret Longes	Department for Transport

4.17 References:

Andersen T (undated) *Safe routes give healthy cycling children*
http://www.cyclecity.dk/eng_safe%20routes.asp

Bradshaw B and Atkins S (1996) *The use of public transport for school journeys in London* in PTRC 24th Annual Meeting Seminar F

Bradshaw R & Jones P *(2000) The Family and the School Run: What Would Make a Real Difference?*, University of Westminster, Scoping Report to the AA Foundation for Road Safety Research, June 2000.

Christie N, Towner E, Cairns S & Ward H (2004) *Children's Road Traffic Safety: an international survey of policy and practice.* Report coordinated by the University of Surrey for the Department of Transport and OECD Child Traffic Safety Expert Group.

Department for Transport (2000) *Tomorrow's roads: safer for everyone, The Government's road safety strategy and casualty reduction targets for 2010*, Department for Transport, London.

Department for Transport (2002) *Assessment of attitudes to, and potential take-up of, additional home to school transport.* Department for Transport, London.

DETR (2000) *'Are you doing your bit' research amongst children.* Research conducted by Carrick James Market Research, management summary RS4531.

DTLR (2001) *Levels of activity relating to school travel plans and initiatives.* Report commissioned from TRL and Adrian Davis Associates

DTLR (2001) *Gloucester safer city.* Authors unknown. Report to the DTLR

DTLR (2002) *Road Traffic Speed, Ninth Report of Session 2001-2002*, DTLR Committee, House of Commons, June.

Dutch Ministry for Transport *(1999) The Dutch Bicycle Master Plan*, Public Works and Water Management, The Hague.

Hillman M, Adams J, and Whitelegg J (1990) *One False Move: a study of children's independent mobility*, Policy Studies Institute, London.

Hyllenius P (2003) *Soft measures affect traffic in Lund – effects from two years work with sustainable transport system in Lund*, , Trivector Traffic AB, Lund, Sweden, Workshop paper at ECOMM 2003

International Obesity Taskforce (2002) *Obesity in Europe: the case for action.* European Association for the Study of Obesity, London.

Kirby T (2002) *Kingston upon Hull: the 20mph city.* Speeds for people conference, November 2002.

Mackett RL, Lucas L, Paskins J and Turbin J (2003) *Walking buses in Hertfordshire - results from a postal survey*, report from the ongoing research project: 'Reducing children's car use: the health and potential car dependency impacts', Centre for Transport Studies, University College London, 2003.

Mackett RL, Lucas L, Paskins J & Turbin J (2003b) *The health benefits of walking to school,* paper for the SUSTRANS national conference, Leicester, September.

O'Fallon, 2001, reported in *A methodology for evaluating walking buses as an instrument of urban transport policy*, Roger L Mackett, Lindsey Lucas, James Paskins and Jill Turbin Centre for Transport Studies, University College London, paper for the WCTR Special Interest Group 10 (Urban Transport Policy Instruments) First Annual Conference, held in Leeds, July 2002

Rowland D, DiGuiseppi C, Gross M, Afolabi E & Roberts I (2003) *Randomised controlled trial of site specific advice on school travel patterns*, Archives of Disease in Childhood, 2003; 88:8-11

SDG (2004) *Evaluation of the First Yellow Bus Pilot Schemes.* Report for the Department for Transport, London.

Sloman L (2003) *Less Traffic where people live: how local transport schemes can help cut traffic.* Report supported by the Royal Commission for the Exhibition of 1851, Transport for Quality of Life and Transport 2000, London.

Sustrans (2003) *Submission to the House of Commons Health Committee Inquiry into Obesity*, Sustrans, Bristol.

TAPESTRY project papers, Hertfordshire case study, CD-ROM, September 2003.

Wardlaw M (2002) *Assessing the actual risks faced by cyclists.* Traffic Engineering + Control 43 (11), pp420-424

Wilhelm A (2003) *Results from the MOST practice: schools, tourism, hospitals, site development, events, mobility consulting*, Austrian Mobility Research, Graz, Austria, Workshop paper at ECOMM 2003.

5. Personalised travel planning

5.1 Introduction

There has been much interest recently in the use of direct techniques in which information is provided to individuals or households aimed at enabling them to choose a different pattern of travel behaviour which brings them benefits as well as reducing car use and/or increasing the use of more sustainable transport modes. These approaches have developed from commercial marketing techniques aimed at increasing public transport use, and public sector campaigns aimed at raising community understanding or awareness of environmental aspects of transport.

At present, the field is led by two commercial organisations, operating independently and in competition with each other: Socialdata, based in Germany, and Steer Davies Gleave, based in the UK. The most widely cited experience has been built up in projects carried out by both organisations in Australia, where there has been a quite vigorous debate about effectiveness and results. There are a growing number of applications in the UK, other European countries and the USA, which have not usually aroused the same debate. Recently a larger number of companies have started supplying services to carry these initiatives out, with a wider range of styles, and we assume that, as the market matures, this trend will develop further.

There are some differences between the styles and emphasis of the two companies, and a number of their survey techniques and strategic approaches are patented or use registered trade names: it is not our intention here to take a view as to the competition between them.

We briefly summarise the two approaches, though acknowledging that, in practice, both are rather flexible in adapting to specific locations and tasks, and there is not a strict dividing line.

Socialdata calls its approach 'IndiMark' (individualised marketing). Its first applications were aimed at increasing public transport use by providing very specific information, motivation, and system experience, relating to public transport services. These were mostly aimed at those infrequent users who indicated that they would be interested to receive it. The assumption was that they generally had low and inaccurate information about services, and would use them more when it became clear that the services were better than they had thought. Under the 'TravelSmart' brand in Australia and the UK, the approach was extended to encouraging a mode shift of specific journeys from car to public transport, walking or cycling. There is no explicit intention to reduce travel, although this may occur as a consequence. Instead, the main focus is on targeting the easiest car trips to shift, by the people most ready to do so. The main data required is to identify the likely switchers, monitoring being carried out in separate surveys, passenger counts and other measures as appropriate.

Steer Davies Gleave initially developed an approach which it called 'Travel Blending'. This subsequently evolved to a package of techniques described as 'Living Neighbourhoods' or, more recently, 'Living Change'. Stopher (2004) describes Living Neighbourhoods / Living Change as a 'community development' approach, which starts with a conversation about travel with a representative of a household, as a result of which various tools are offered to help households solve the frustrations they face about travel. The tools include:

- Ideas Tool (ideas for changing current travel, activities or timing of activities)
- Travel Blending, which involves completion of a travel diary, following which tips and suggestions are given on how to reduce travel
- Personalised journey plans
- Brochures, dealing with how to save time or money, reduce environmental impacts, make travel less stressful, and become more independent (for older people and youg people)
- Local activity guides and Kids activity pages
- Reinforcement e.g. free public transport ticket
- Loan-a-bike.

Individualised marketing is mainly aimed at achieving mode shift from driving to walking, cycling, public transport or car-sharing, and generally reported overall trip rates remain about the same. In contrast, Living Change seeks to reduce the overall need for travel, through combining or 'blending' activities or destinations, as well as stimulating modal shift.

The success of both techniques must manifestly be influenced by the quality of alternative modes or opportunities on offer, but until now, most reported experience of personalised travel planning initiatives is about interventions which have not depended on making real improvements to alternative transport options.

The next section discusses the available literature about personalised travel planning, focusing primarily on international experience. Subsequent sections integrate this material with detailed analysis of UK information.

5.2 Literature evidence on the effectiveness of personalised travel planning

5.2.1 The evidence base

The largest proportion of source information comes from technical reports or public presentations written by the two consultants, sometimes with collaborators and/or their clients, who are mostly local government agencies. These reports have been brought together in two overview reviews (with considerably overlapping material) by Steer Davies Gleave (2001) for the DfT, and by Perkins (2003) for the Australian National Greenhouse Strategy, and in turn summarised by Sloman (2003). Unpublished information on some of the most recent projects was made available to us by Sustrans and Steer Davies Gleave. In addition, a seminar at University College London in June 2003 brought together many of those actively involved for a discussion mainly about the Australian results, from which an exchange of papers was arranged.

Because these papers report results from different stages of the work on each project, there have been some discrepancies in figures on (for example) sample sizes, success rates, calculated trip rates, etc. Resolution of these discrepancies requires a level of detailed analysis of source data that cannot be done within this project, but mostly they are very small and well within the level of rounding which seems appropriate to the subject. Some larger discrepancies have arisen from alternative interpretations of monitoring data, and we comment on these where they appear significant.

Halcrow (2002) suggested that these initiatives could reduce car use nationally by up to two billion vehicle kilometres a year, based on influencing 50% of people living in 25% of residential areas, at a cost of over £100 million. Sloman (2003) suggested an impact over twice as great (5.2 billion vehicle kilometres) based on reaching 50% of people in cities over 250,000 population. The two estimates also used different assumptions about the effectiveness of personalised travel planning.

5.2.2 Evidence about impacts on car use

This section reviews evidence from the literature about the impacts of individualised marketing, and then examines evidence on the impacts of early travel blending projects and more recent Living Neighbourhood / Living Change programmes.

Individualised marketing
The largest applications of individualised marketing so far have been in Perth, Western Australia. The first large-scale application was in the suburb of South Perth in 2000, and involved contact with 15,300 households (35,000 people). Random sample surveys before and after the project showed a fall in car driver trips from 60% to 52% (a 14% fall in car driver trips). Vehicle kilometres fell by 17% (Brög 2002, John 2002a,b). Follow-up monitoring a year later found that the modal shift was sustained.

The second large-scale application in Perth was in the suburb of Cambridge in 2001/02, and involved contact with 9400 households, or 24,000 people (James 2003a,c). Here, car driver mode share fell from 60% to 56%, accompanied by a 7% fall in car driver trips. The TravelSmart programme has subsequently been delivered to the suburb of Marangaroo (10,000 people) and City of Subiaco (15,000 people), and is being delivered to parts of the Cities of Melville and Fremantle (40,000 people). In Marangaroo car driver trips fell by 4%. Results for the other areas were not available at the time of our inquiry.

James (2003b) noted that the result of the large scale application in Perth (a 14% reduction in car driver trips) was larger than that seen in a preceding pilot (-10%), and that a similar effect (greater change when the initiative was scaled up) occurred in Viernheim in Germany. It is also notable that, in Perth, the greatest shift in modal share has been to walking (+2%-points in the pilot and +4%-points in the large scale trial).

James (2003c) reported data on public transport patronage in areas which had been targeted by the TravelSmart programme. Figure 5.1 reproduces his graphs, using data based on automatic counts of public transport boardings.

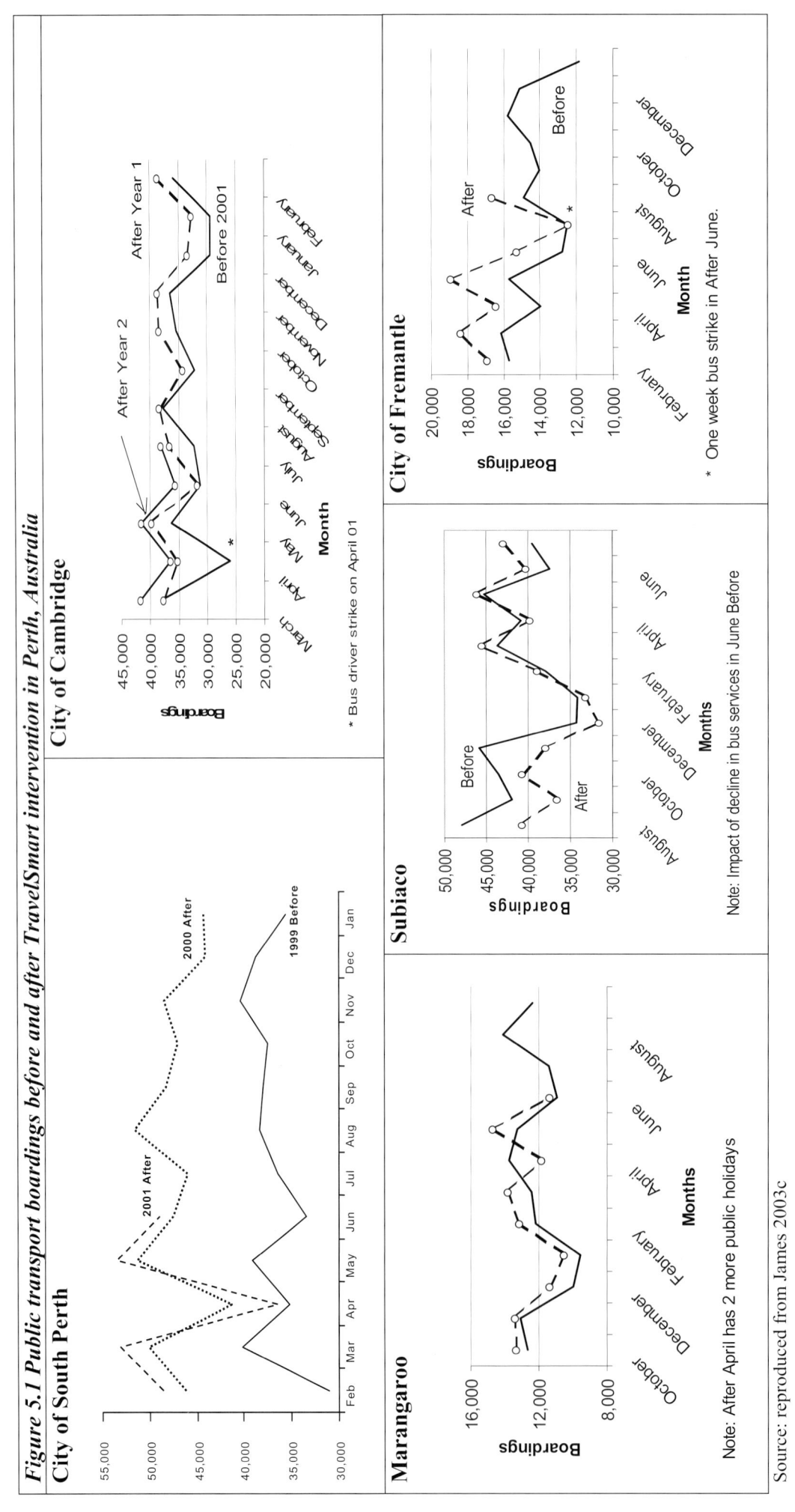

Figure 5.1 Public transport boardings before and after TravelSmart intervention in Perth, Australia

Source: reproduced from James 2003c

The average increases in public transport boardings were 17% in South Perth; 11% in Cambridge; 5% in Marangaroo; and 12% in Fremantle. In Subiaco, a reduction in bus services prior to the TravelSmart project led to a 15% fall in patronage. After TravelSmart, public transport boardings were 4% higher than before the bus service reductions, suggesting TravelSmart had delivered a 19% increase in patronage.

Results were reported by Roth et al (2003) relating to the behaviour of different groups within the Perth large scale trial. These show that people who were not interested in receiving further information about travel had stable car use (59% of all trips being made as a car driver); people who were already regular users of more sustainable modes, some of whom wanted information, reduced their car use by 12% (from 57% to 50%) whilst regular car users who wanted further information reduced their car trips by 25% (from 61% to 46%). Aggregated together, these results lead to the 14% reduction in car driver trips reported as the headline result of the initiative.

In the UK, pilot individualised marketing projects in Frome and Gloucester, each involving about 500 people, have delivered net reductions in car driver trips of 6% (Frome) and 9% (Gloucester) (Sustrans 2002). Results from individualised marketing in Bristol suggest a fall in car driver trips of 5% in one area and 10% in another. An individualised marketing pilot project in London has reduced car driver trips by 11%, with another potentially reducing them by 16%. UK results are discussed in more detail in section 5.7.

Meanwhile, individualised marketing projects from Germany have shown comparable results. Available results from other countries are summarised in Table 5.1.

Table 5.1: Effect of individualised marketing programmes on car use in other countries

Location	Size of programme	Car driver mode share before	Car driver mode share after	Fall in car driver trips*	Source
South Perth (suburb of Perth, Australia)	15,300 households / 35000 people	60	52	-14%	Brög (2002)
Nürnberg (Germany)^		44	38	-14%	UITP (undated)
Goteburg (Sweden)	large scale			-13%	James (2003b)
Viernheim (Germany)	large scale			-12%	James (2003b)
Brisbane (Australia)	Pilot			-10%	James (2003b)
South Perth (suburb of Perth, Australia)	Pilot			-10%	James (2003b)
Portland (USA)	Pilot			-8%	James (2003b)
Kassel (Germany)^	not known	48	44	-8%	UITP (undated)
Viernheim (Germany)	Pilot			-8%	James (2003b)
Cambridge (suburb of Perth, Australia)	9400 households / 24,000 people	60	56	-7%	James (2003a)
Marangaroo (suburb of Perth, Australia)	10,000 people			-4%	James (2003c)
Breisgau-Hochschwarzwald (Germany) ~	not known	44	43	-2%	Socialdata (2003)

Emmendingen (Germany) ~	not known	44	43	-2%	Socialdata (2003)

* Note that this figure is not calculated from the two previous columns, but is drawn separately from the available source data.

^Pilots in Nürnberg and Kassel used an early prototype of the IndiMark methodology, which has been developed considerably since.

~ Projects in Breisgau-Hochschwarzwald and Emmendingen had the objective of increasing public transport use, not reducing car travel

Travel blending

Travel blending provides personalised information to participants based on a completed 'before' travel diary, which then serves also as information to be compared with an 'after' diary. As discussed in section 5.1, travel blending was initially developed as a freestanding intervention, but more recently has been used as one element of Living Change / Living Neighbourhood projects. Results of early travel blending interventions reported in SDG (2001) point to reductions in car driver trips of over 10% for the people who complete both diaries. Typically about 40% of those recruited complete both the 'before' and 'after' diaries.

Early experience of travel blending included projects in Nottingham and Leeds. In Nottingham in 1997, car driver trips fell by 8% amongst those completing both diaries and 3% overall (SDG 2001), whilst in Leeds in 1998, car driver trips fell by 6% amongst those completing both diaries and 2% overall (Jopson 1998). Available summary statistics of experience from other countries are shown in table 5.2.

Table 5.2: Effect of travel blending programmes on car use in other countries

Location	Size of programme	Fall in car driver trips*	Source
Adelaide pilot (Australia)	not known	-15%	SDG (2001)
Adelaide, Christie's Beach (Australia)	1000 households	-15%	SDG (2001)
New Jersey (USA)	212 households	-14%	SDG (2001)
Adelaide, Dulwich (Australia)	1000 households	-10%	SDG (2001)
Brisbane, Holland Park (Australia)	600 households	-9%	SDG (2001)

* The impacts on participants completing both travel diaries.

Living Neighbourhood / Living Change programmes

Living Change programmes have been developed in Adelaide (in 2002), Melbourne (2003) and Canberra (2004), and in three towns in Scotland (Bishopbriggs, Inverurie and Paisley) during 2003.

External evaluations of all four programmes have been or are being carried out. At the time of writing, an evaluation was available for the Adelaide project and a draft final report was made available to us for the Scottish work. Results were not yet available for the projects in Melbourne and Canberra.

The Adelaide project took place in the suburb of Mitcham and targeted approximately 350 households (Transport Planning Agency S Australia 2004, SDG 2004). Evaluation using before and after surveys in Mitcham and in a control area was carried out by Booz Allen Hamilton on behalf of the South Australia government. Within the programme area (Mitcham), surveys were carried out both with households which had participated in the intervention, and with those which had not.

The results were not conclusive: within the programme area, car driver trips fell by 7% between the before and after surveys, but when compared with the control area car driver trips showed no signficant change. However, comparisons between the programme and control areas showed a statistically significant increase in public transport travel, with bus trips increased by 48% and train trips increased by 84%. The Scottish project, branded 'Stepchange', involved approaches to households, workplaces and schools in the three pilot towns (Bishopbriggs, Paisley and Inverurie). A total of 3139 households were approached, of whom 1745 were engaged in conversation or an activity, and 984 took one or more of the offered tools (similar to those described in section 5.1). In addition, the project targeted people at eight workplaces and six schools in the pilot towns. SDG (2004) reports that in total, around 4000 households were involved in some way. The initiative took place alongside an intensive media relations campaign. Unfortunately, evaluation of before and after surveys by the Scottish Institute for Sustainable Technology has so far proved inconclusive. However, the project is to be extended, with the next stage involving a large-scale application in an area of Aberdeen (10,000 households), and two smaller projects involving around 2000 households (SDG 2004).

Overview of reported personalised travel planning results

Before summarising the overall evidence in the literature on the effects of personalised travel planning, a few words of caution are necessary. First, it should be noted that the quoted changes in car use for individualised marketing, travel blending and Living Change are not comparable. Evaluations of individualised marketing and Living Change quote results based on the entire responding population approached, whereas early travel blending results were quoted for participants who had completed both travel diaries. Second, there has been a vigorous debate about the effectiveness of different personalised travel planning techniques: for example Stopher (2003) has raised queries about the statistical validity of the results quoted for individualised marketing projects, and his comments have been rebutted by its proponents, notably Roth et al (2003). Finally, some but not all of those involved in personalised travel programmes (e.g. SDG 2004) have cautioned that survey respondent attrition rates and lack of willingness to complete surveys may pose significant challenges to the collection of reliable findings. These and other issues related to the reporting of results are discussed further in section 5.7.3

Bearing in mind these issues of data validity (which, incidentally, may also apply to a greater or lesser extent to the monitoring of other soft factors), results so far available suggest that personalised travel planning may lead to reductions in car driver trips of 7-15% amongst targeted populations in urban areas (according to trials in Germany, Australia, USA and the UK), with rather lower reductions in car driver trips (2 – 6%) reported from a smaller number of more rural trials. Even where challenges have been made claiming that these results overstate the efficacy of personalised travel planning, alternative figures suggested, while lower, are still within the same range as the figures quoted above, and evidence that personalised travel planning can reduce car use by a significant amount is accepted by those who challenge the technique as well as its supporters.

5.2.3 Change in impact over time

One further concern which has been expressed about personalised travel planning is that its effects may be short-lived, if people may quickly slide back into their old travel habits once the monitoring is over. There is some evidence to suggest that this may not usually be the case. In Perth, follow-up monitoring two years after the pilot individualised marketing project found the change in travel behaviour had been sustained. Follow-up monitoring was also carried out in Nürnberg, Germany, two years after the individualised marketing project, and in Kassel, Germany, four years after the project. In both places, the initial increase in public transport use was still evident two or four years later. Travel blending in Adelaide, Australia, showed continued change after the project was completed. A sample of participants interviewed six months after the initial programme had reduced their car use by a further 5% as a result of a combination of factors: people 'taking a while to get round to it'; developing other measures themselves; changing school or job; or moving house, (Ampt et al. 1998).

5.2.4 Journey purpose

It is interesting to see which journey purposes are most affected by personalised travel planning. In the Nürnberg and Kassel individualised marketing projects, the greatest increase in public transport use was for shopping and leisure trips, which accounted for more than 70% of the behaviour change.

5.2.5 Costs of personalised travel planning

SDG (2001) reported that the cost of travel blending at that time was about £44 per household, or £15 per person. This included the cost of becoming familiar with the neighbourhood, setting up a project team, recruitment, running costs (the intervention itself costing £17 per household), meetings and reporting. The figure included monitoring costs. SDG (2004) report that more recent work may have enabled them to find significant cost reductions for their work. The cost of individualised marketing is discussed in more detail in section 5.5.2 and 5.11.3.

5.3   Selection of personalised travel planning case studies

As highlighted above, there has been some experience of personalised travel planning in the UK. However, initial trials were small and sparse, including, for example, trials of travel blending on 100 households in Nottingham in 1997 (reported by SDG 2001) and 132 households in Leeds in 1998 (reported by Jopson 1998).

Following the success of the individualised marketing work in Australia, the charity Sustrans championed the concept in this country, stimulating the individualised marketing projects which have taken place in Gloucester and Frome. These were completed between 2001 and 2002.

Since then, there has been a substantial increase in work in this area. The Department for Transport has now funded 14 projects (in 14 different areas of the country). Some have used personalised travel planning, while others have focussed on personalised journey plans for specific journeys (either nominated by the recipient, or to a particular destination such as a workplace or school). Others have offered information specifically to people undergoing a lifestyle change (such as those starting work).

In addition, Transport for London funded four pilot projects as part of a 'Travel Options' programme, which have collectively targeted 4000 households. Each of the London projects deliberately uses a different balance of consultants and approaches, in order to test the effectiveness of different methods[1].
Steer Davies Gleave has been working on the Stepchange project, grant aided by the Scottish Executive, which is intended to develop a Scottish approach to voluntary travel behaviour change, encompassing personalised travel planning but also some elements of workplace and school travel planning.

The completion of these projects will provide a huge fund of information and insights, to enable a better assessment of the effectiveness of personalised travel planning techniques. Meanwhile, initiatives which are primarily focused on alternative approaches (e.g. workplace travel planning or public transport information provision) are also starting to include elements of personalised travel planning as one of their tools for intervention, as discussed in Chapters 3 and 6 respectively.

At the time of selecting case studies for this research work (spring 2003), most of the personalised travel planning work in the UK was too recent to have generated any results. In particular, the Department for Transport pilots were only launched in December 2002, and the first results from the London and Scottish studies only became available towards the end of our study. As case studies had to be UK based and to either already have results, or to be likely to produce some within the timescale of our research, this situation posed severe constraints on our choice of case studies. The case studies do not therefore reflect the full range of personalised travel planning techniques as currently being applied in different locations and by different researchers and consultants.

Our selected case studies were as follows:

- *Gloucester*
This was one of the original Sustrans case study areas which subsequently decided to scale up its work.

- *Bristol*
This is part of the DfT pilot programme, but began personalised travel planning work before becoming part of this programme, meaning that initial results were available.

- *Nottingham*
This was the focus of a travel blending experiment in 1997. In addition, their involvement in individualised marketing during the period of our study was led by

---

[1] Socialdata applied their IndiMark approach in Kingston; Steer Davies Gleave offered generic local travel and amenity information (a 'travel guide') and personalised journey plans in Enfield; Colin Buchanan used a version of individualised marketing in Southwark but focused particularly on car owning households; and Peter Brett Associates provided locally specific (but not individually tailored) information to a full sample of households in Lambeth.

Bruce James, who was primarily responsible for the individualised marketing work that was undertaken in Perth.

A further interview was also undertaken with James Ryle, at Sustrans, who has helped to lead much of the individualised marketing work taking place in the UK at the moment.

From the other case studies, there was some relevant information from:

- Cambridgeshire, where there is a joint initiative called 'Travel Choices' taking place between the County Council and Addenbrooke's NHS Trust, which aims to provide personalised journey planning advice to new employees.
- York, where the city council is involved in a project on 'intelligent travel' in partnership with Norwich Union, First Group and Halfords, investigating the most effective ways of providing people with individual information, and
- South Yorkshire, where the Information Development team of the Passenger Transport Executive provides personalised journey plans to individuals and to staff at client organisations. This work is discussed in more detail in Chapter 6.

As part of the shortlisting process, we also collected some limited information about:

- the 14 Department for Transport pilot projects, (DfT, 2002).
- the 4 Transport for London projects (including interim results, as reported in Allcorn et al 2003).
- pilot projects previously undertaken in Frome and Leeds (as reported by Sustrans 2002 and Jopson 1998, respectively).

5.4 Details of chosen personalised travel planning case studies

Gloucester: Gloucester was the focus of one of the original Sustrans pilot projects, which constituted an individualised marketing initiative involving about 500 people in the suburb of Quedgeley, a few miles south of the city centre. This was followed by a large-scale project which aimed to reach all 10,000 people (4631 households) in the same suburb. This was the first large-scale application of individualised marketing in the UK. The marketing phase of the large-scale project was completed in summer 2003. The budget was £168,600.

Bristol: The first individualised marketing project in Bristol was carried out as part of the EU VIVALDI programme in the relatively low-income edge of city Hartcliffe and Bishopsworth wards. It was carried out in two phases, each targeting about 2500 people. Phase 1 marketing was in September 2002 and phase 2 marketing was in September 2003. The project was aimed at increasing social inclusion (by increasing awareness of travel opportunities), and was also designed to coincide with the introduction of 'Showcase' bus improvements along a corridor passing through the wards. The city subsequently received funding from the Department for Transport for a separate project targeting about 5000 people in a contrasting high-income area, Bishopston. Marketing in this area took place in April-June 2003.

Nottingham: Nottingham was originally involved in a travel blending experiment in 1997. It is currently participating in one of the Department for Transport's 14 personalised travel planning projects. Preparatory work started early in 2003, targeting two contrasting socio-demographic areas of the city, linked by a newly improved bus route. In total, 1000 people are being contacted in these two areas. The project is due to be completed in late 2004. The budget is £68,000.

5.5 Staffing and budgets for personalised travel planning

5.5.1 Staff time required from local authorities for personalised travel planning

The personalised travel planning interventions in the three case study areas have all been managed by Sustrans and Socialdata, using their TravelSmart individualised marketing technique.

Staff time requirements within the local authorities have varied from very low levels in Gloucester to quite high time commitments over short time periods in Nottingham and Bristol. In Gloucester, the city and county councils together estimated that they had committed no more than £3000-worth of staff time to the pilot project and 100 hours of staff time to the large-scale project.

In Nottingham, the cost of local authority staff time for the project was put at about £3000 per month. One person spends about half her time on the programme, with another staff member and a consultant (Bruce James) each allocating about a third of their time to the project, equivalent to 1.2 fte staff in total.

In Bristol, four or five council officers were involved in the few weeks of the intense campaigning phases of the first individualised marketing project, equivalent to 2.5 full-time equivalent posts for that period, and this level of staff commitment continued in subsequent phases. There have been three campaign phases (of approximately 2 months each) which have taken place over about 18 months.

In all three areas, day-to-day project management has rested with Sustrans and Socialdata, and their staff costs have been covered in the consultancy fees paid to them by the local authorities.

Broadly, the impression is that where day-to-day management is contracted out, personalised travel planning interventions require relatively limited staff time from within the local authority, although this might change if the one-off pilot programmes were expanded to large-scale rolling programmes.

5.5.2 Project costs for personalised travel planning

Project costs have been met by grants from a variety of sources, but especially the Department for Transport pilot programme, and from the local authorities' own revenue budgets.

The costs of the projects may be divided into three parts:

- Monitoring of the impact of the intervention. All projects involve 'before' and 'after' monitoring of the target group and a control group. In Gloucester, an in-depth attitudinal survey of 100 people was also carried out.
- The marketing campaign, including telephone contact, postal follow-up and face-to-face contact.
- Preparation and provision of gifts and information materials (for example, bus stop timetables; local travel maps; bicycle bells), project management and dissemination of findings. As far as possible, the projects used existing, readily available, information materials, but some additional materials have been prepared.

Table 5.3 compares the budgets for the case study projects, and the cost per person targeted. Where possible, monitoring, marketing and other costs have been disaggregated.

More limited information about budgets was also available from some other schemes:
- In Frome, 500 people were targeted, with a total project budget of £72,000, implying an average cost per person of £144. This cost included evaluation surveys of the target group and a control population, the development of a new walking, cycling and public transport guide for Frome and the surrounding area and TravelSmart website resources.
- In the Cambridgeshire 'Travel Choices' project, 1500 new employees are being targeted. The original project budget (including funding for local authority staff time) was £100,550, implying an average cost per person of £67.
- Nottingham has estimated that a large-scale individualised marketing programme covering 161,800 people in five areas would cost about £2,310,000, or £14 per head.
- Transport for London has estimated that a large-scale Travel Options programme (which is based on individualised marketing) covering 120,000 – 150,000 people would cost £1.3 million, or £9 - £11 per head.

Table 5.3: Comparison of budgets for personalised travel planning projects

	Gloucester pilot project	Gloucester large-scale project	Bristol VIVALDI phase 1	Bristol VIVALDI phase 2	Bristol Bishopston	Nottingham
When marketing intervention took place	Oct 2001	July 2003	Sept 2002	Sept 2003	May 2003	Sept 2003
Number of people targeted~	500	10,000	2500	2500	5364	1000
Number of people in 'before' survey *	871	Not known	862	Not known	Not known	1350
Staff time / cost within local authority	Equivalent to £3000	100 hours	The equivalent of 2.5 fte staff during campaign phases of the programme			£3000 per month, or 1.2 fte
Monitoring costs	£18,000	£37,600				£41,000
Marketing costs	£12,000	£65,000				£27,000
Other costs +		£66,000				
Total cost #	**£30,000**	**£168,600**	**£100,000**		**£100,000**	**£68,000**
Monitoring cost per person surveyed	£21					£30
Marketing cost per person targeted	£24	£13				£27
Total cost per person targeted	**£60**	**£17**	**£20**		**£19**	**£68**

~ Number of people targeted is the total number of individuals approached (including those who wished to receive assistance or information and those who did not).

* Number of people in 'before' survey includes people in target group (who will later be offered the marketing intervention) and a control group. The number of people in the 'after' survey tends to be slightly smaller than the number in the 'before' survey due to people dropping out.

+ Other costs include production of new information materials; management; and dissemination of findings.

Total cost does not include local authority staff time in managing the project, except in Nottingham where some staff time costs were included.

Finally, we have some limited information about the costs of the other personalised travel planning projects supported by the Department for Transport. This is summarised in table 5.4. These projects are using a range of techniques and in some cases targeting specific journey purposes (for example journeys to workplaces, schools and colleges).

Table 5.4: Costs of other pilot projects funded by Department for Transport

Initiative	Size of target group	DfT contribution	Cost per person targeted *
West Sussex County Council	2400 students	£25,000	£21
Oldham Metropolitan Borough	2000 individuals	£50,000	£50
Hampshire County Council	8870 staff and students	£50,000	£11
York city council	2100 households (4800 people implied)	£49,900	£21
Northumberland County Council	2000 households along corridor (4600 people implied)	£42,000	£18
North Yorkshire County Council	>1000 students	£20,000	£40
Worcestershire County Council	2500 hospital staff	£30,000	£24
Bracknell Forest Borough Council	2000 staff	£50,000	£50
South Yorkshire PTE	3000 residents	£50,000	£33
Durham	300 business park employees	£20,000	£133

* A household occupancy of 2.3 residents has been used to convert households into individuals. It is assumed that each organisation has contributed matched funding equal to the DfT grant.

Taken together, the data on costs suggests that:
- The *monitoring* cost of an individualised marketing initiative is in the order of £20 to £30 per person surveyed.
- The cost of the *marketing* element of an individualised marketing intervention ranges from perhaps £10 to £30 per head. This is particularly influenced by the scale of the programme, and by whether new information materials are produced.
- The cost of undertaking a personalised travel planning initiative ranges from £10 per head to £140 per head, but is typically in the range of £10 to £70 per head. Costs tend to be higher where the development of new materials is involved.

In addition, larger scale initiatives tend to be cheaper than pilot programmes. For example, it is notable that the Gloucester pilot programme, which targeted 500 people, cost £60 per person, whilst the Gloucester large-scale project, which targeted 10,000 people, cost £17 per person. Large-scale marketing programmes are likely to be cheaper than pilot programmes for three reasons:
- In contrast to pilot studies, before and after monitoring is only ever carried out on a sample of the targeted population. Given that statistical reliability always

depends on the absolute (not relative) sample size, monitoring costs do not need to rise directly in proportion to the number of people targeted.

- Large-scale programmes offer general economies of scale in production of resources and materials.
- Project staff are likely to become more practiced in applying the technique, and more familiar with an area and its access and transport opportunities, in a large-scale application.

Given these factors, Sustrans estimates that the unit cost of large-scale individualised marketing interventions may fall below that seen in the Gloucester large-scale programme. They suggest that a project covering 30,000 people would cost £30 per household, or £13 per person (assuming an average household size of 2.3). This would cover the cost of marketing, one 'before' and two 'after' surveys, and promotional materials, but does not include the cost of preparing new information materials. This is remarkably similar to the SDG estimate given in section 5.2.5, that travel blending costs £44 per household or £15 per person, where the intervention itself costs £17 per household, (although SDG 2004 report that they may now be able to deliver their personalised travel planning interventions for less). These figures are also similar to those estimated for the large scale projections in Nottingham (£14 per head) and London (£9-11 per head). The Nottingham interviewee has subsequently suggested that it might be necessary to add on a further £10 per household (or £4 per person) to include the costs of local authority time and improvements to the marketing materials available.

Only some of the figures above include staff time within the local authority, as this seems to vary so much within the local authorities examined in our case studies. The largest project, in Gloucester, was estimated to require only 100 hours of local authority staff time (or about three weeks' work), whereas the Bristol project involved the equivalent of 2.5 full-time staff during the brief but intensive campaign phases lasting about two months each.

In general, for a local authority running a personalised travel planning programme *for the first time*, there may be complicating factors. These may include gaining acceptance of the programme within the local authority; securing funds and meeting the requirements of different funding bodies; and designing an experimental programme to compare results between different target groups. However, once experience of such programmes has increased, the staff time requirements are likely to fall, particularly if the programme is implemented by an outside agency.

5.6 Comparison of findings on scale of implementation

The scale of the case study initiatives and other personalised travel planning projects is summarised in tables 5.5 and 5.6.

Table 5.5: Scale of personalised travel planning interventions

	Size of target group	Size of 'before' monitoring survey (target + control)	Number of people receiving information materials
Gloucester pilot	515 people target; 496 people reached	871 people	187 people (38% of those reached)*
Gloucester large-scale	4631 households/ 10,000 people target; 4069 households reached		2018 households (50% of those reached)*
Bristol VIVALDI phase 1	1192 households/ 2500 people target; 867 households reached	862 people	232 households (27% of those reached)*
Bristol VIVALDI phase 2	2500 people target		
Bristol Bishopston	5364 people target		
Nottingham travel blending 1997	100 employees + their households	200 people	100 (all involved in travel diary process)
Nottingham	1000 people target	1350 people	
South Yorkshire personalised journey planners	n/a	n/a	1300 journey planners provided since 2001 (335 for individuals; 998 via 9 organisations)
Cambridgeshire 'Travel Choices'	1500 new employees		
Leeds travel blending 1998	132 households / 296 people		296 (all involved in travel diary process)
Frome pilot	553 people target; 503 reached		282 people (56% of those reached)*
Southwark TfL pilot	1000 households target; 1800 contacts attempted, of which 257 car-owning households reached		
Lambeth TfL pilot	1000 households target; 30,000 contacts attempted		
Kingston TfL pilot	1000 households target; 1100 attempted contacts;1008 reached	1300 households	793 households (79% of those reached)*
Enfield TfL pilot	1000 households target; 2619 attempted contacts; 977 contacts made	565 households	235 received initial travel guide
Stepchange pilot in Scotland	4000 households involved, including 3139 households directly approached		Of households approached, 1754 engaged in an activity (56%), of whom 984 requested an offered 'tool' (31%)

* In these cases, a further number of people, who were already using environmentally friendly modes and did not require further information, were sent a small gift as a 'thank you'. The number receiving gifts only ranged from 52 (in the Bristol VIVALDI phase 1 project) to 195 (in the Kingston TfL pilot).

Table 5.6: Scale and target audience for other personalised travel planning projects funded by the Department for Transport*

Initiative	Size of target group
West Sussex County Council	2400 school students from eight schools
Oldham Metropolitan Borough	2000 individuals from 4 organisations (a hospital, College, a primary care trust, and private company)
Hampshire County Council	8870 staff and students from 4 sites (a hospital, a college, the constabulary headquarters and the County Council)
York City Council	2100 households (4800 people implied) from three contrasting areas of the city
Northumberland County Council	2000 households along a high-quality public transport and cycling corridor (4600 people implied)
North Yorkshire County Council	>1000 students from 4 schools
Worcestershire County Council	2500 hospital staff
Bracknell Forest Borough Council	2000 staff from companies that are part of the local business travel forum
South Yorkshire PTE	3000 residents in an area well served by public transport
Durham	300 business park employees

*Figures are based on the targets set by each project prior to implementation. Several projects note that additional people will be involved other than the direct target group. In particular, this seems to be considered to be the case for the schools projects. In West Sussex, a further 600 family members were expected to be influenced, whilst in North Yorkshire, the initiative expected to potentially reach 2300 people. Some projects have subsequently reported difficulties reaching their targets: for example, the Oldham trial finished in April 2004 and had recruited 1300 people compared to the target of 2000.

The tables suggest that:

- Over 67,000 people had been directly involved in personalised travel planning in the UK, or were in the process of being targeted, by summer 2003.
- Personalised travel planning initiatives are usually relatively successful at establishing contact with enough households to approximately meet their targets, although some initiatives have reported problems.
- For individualised marketing initiatives, typically between a quarter and three-quarters of people contacted request information materials. It is notable that in Gloucester, there were a large proportion of ex-directory households and so the project team made far more door-to-door contacts, instead of the more usual process of establishing contact by telephone. This is felt to have led to a greater number of requests for information materials than usual.
- Most personalised travel planning initiatives are still relatively small, pilot experiments (involving 1-2000 people), although this is starting to change.

5.7 Comparison of findings on effects on car use

5.7.1 Headline effects on mode choice

As discussed in section 5.2.2, understanding and comparing the effects of personalised travel planning projects is complex, not least because the reporting styles depend on the technique used. This means that results of different projects are not directly comparable. A further difficulty is that headline results which are, at first sight, simple, may be the partial product of quite sophisticated statistical adjustments. These issues are explored in more detail in section 5.7.3.

Tables 5.7 to 5.10 summarise the available headline results from UK initiatives involving a range of personalised travel planning techniques including individualised marketing, travel blending and personalised journey planners.

Table 5.7: Effect of individualised marketing projects in the UK

		Mode share without individualised marketing (%)	Mode share with individualised marketing (%)	Change in trips per person per year (%)~
Gloucester pilot	Car driver	44	40	-9
	Car passenger	23	22	-6
	Walk	27	30	+10
	Bicycle	2	3	+133
	Public transport	4	5	+41
	Motorbike	1	1	-33
Gloucester large-scale	Car driver	49	45	-9
	Car passenger	20	19	-5
	Walk	22	25	+12
	Bicycle	3	4	+35
	Public transport	5	6	+18
	Motorbike	1	1	0
Bristol VIVALDI phase 1	Car driver	46	43	-5
	Car passenger	23	22	-3
	Walk	19	21	+8
	Bicycle	0	0	0
	Public transport	11	13	+23
	Motorbike	1	1	0
Bristol Bishopston	Car driver	37	34	-10
	Car passenger	15	14	-7
	Walk	37	39	+6
	Bicycle	4	6	+51
	Public transport	6	7	+18
	Motorbike	1	0	-67
Frome	Car driver	44	41	-6
	Car passenger	21	19	-7
	Walk	30	33	+11
	Bicycle	0	1	+60
	Public transport	5	6	+10
	Motorbike	0	0	-50
Kingston TfL pilot interim results	Car driver	42	37	-11
	Car passenger	17	15	-9
	Walk	21	24	+14
	Bicycle	3	5	+75
	Public transport	16	18	+16
	Motorbike	1	1	-33

Southwark TfL pilot interim results*	Car driver	41	34	-16
	Car passenger	8	8	-3
	Walk	19	32	n/a
	Bicycle	5	4	n/a
	Public transport	22	19	n/a
	Other	4	5	n/a

~ Note that this column is not generated from the preceding two columns but is separately quoted in the source documentation.

* It is unclear whether changes in the behaviour of the control group have been taken into account in the same way as in other individualised marketing projects. Changes in trip rates have been calculated from interim source data in Allcorn et al (2003), which show that the number of trips made as a car driver fell from 149 to 125, and as a car passenger, from 30 to 29.

Table 5.8: Effect of travel blending projects

		Effect on all people approached*	Effect on participants completing both travel diaries
Nottingham 1997	Car driver trips	-3.3%	-7.6%
	Car driver miles	-6.2%	-4.2%
	Car hours	-4.8%	-11.8%
Leeds 1998	Car driver trips	-2.0%	-5.6%
	Car driver miles	-0.6%	-1.7%
	Car hours	-0.7%	-2.7%

* See explanation given in section 5.7.3 as to how this column is calculated

Table 5.9: Effect of personalised journey planners

South Yorkshire	750 personalised journey plans supplied in 2001 and updated in 2002	Type of trip affected:	Change in trips per person
		Bus trips	+18%
		Train trips	+10%
		Tram trips	+12%
South Yorkshire	250 personalised journey plans supplied to Meadowhall shopping centre senior staff	Shift from car to bus	+19%
Enfield TfL pilot	See table 5.10: this project included use of personalised journey plans coupled with generic travel and amenity information		

Table 5.10: Additional data from Transport for London pilot projects

		Mode share 'before' (%)	Mode share 'after' (%)
Enfield pilot interim results*	Car (driver or passenger)	37	26
	Walk	38	43
	Bicycle	1	1
	Public transport	23	28
	Motorbike	1	0
	Taxi / minicab	1	1
	Other	0	2

Lambeth pilot interim results	Car driver	25	24
	Car passenger	7	7
	Walk	30	28
	Bicycle	2	3
	Public transport	28	33

* Interim source data from Allcorn et al (2003) shows a 19% reduction in car trips (driver and passenger combined), from 58 to 47.

The results from tables 5.7 to 5.10 suggest the following:

- All personalised travel planning initiatives have achieved reductions in car use.
- In the UK so far, individualised marketing initiatives have reduced car driver trips by between 5% and 16%.
- The results from travel blending initiatives perhaps look less promising, although this may be because of the small-scale and early nature of the initiatives for which we had data.
- Some forms of initiative appear to be less successful. In particular, the Lambeth pilot, where all households were given local information (which was not individually tailored) has only reduce car driver mode share by 1%-point overall, although it is notable that initial levels of car use were already low, and this still represents a 4% decline in car driving.
- Most of the initiatives have had a positive effect on walking.
- Some of the initiatives have had a positive effect on cycling.
- Most of the initiatives have increased public transport use. Notably, in Bristol, the control and target groups were selected from an area where improvements to local bus routes were taking place. Additional data suggests that, although both groups increased their bus use, individualised marketing has more than doubled the increase in bus use that would have resulted from the bus improvements alone.

On the basis of the data above, our initial conclusion from the literature seems relatively robust – namely that personalised travel planning typically reduces car driver trips amongst targeted populations by 7-15% in urban areas, and (based on rather less evidence and therefore a considerably less certain conclusion) by 2-6% in rural areas. The caveat is that initiatives do not always achieve this degree of success, as highlighted by the evidence from Leeds and Lambeth. Allcorn et al (2003) also highlight that their pilot work has shown that the specific context where personalised travel planning takes place will alter the nature of the initiative that will achieve maximum effect. For example, London residents were relatively uninterested in receiving test public transport tickets and home visits, compared with levels of interest experienced elsewhere.

While most of the data given above relates to car trips, there was some information about effects on car mileage from Gloucester and Frome. In the Gloucester pilot project, the distance travelled by car fell from 21 km to 19 km per person per day as a result of the individualised marketing, a fall of about 9%. In Frome, the distance travelled by car fell by about 6%. These figures are of the same order as the reduction in car *trips,* suggesting that both long and short car trips are equally susceptible to influence.

5.7.2 Effects on mode choice according to trip purpose and length

There was also information about the types of trips that were affected. In Gloucester, car use went down for all journey purposes except education. Commenting on Gloucester and Frome, Sustrans felt that there was proportionally more travel behaviour change at off-peak times, for shopping and leisure journeys. This is consistent with the German experience reported in section 5.2.4. However, other personalised travel planning projects have successfully targeted peak-hour travel. The personalised journey planners supplied in South Yorkshire are mainly for work journeys, and have clearly had a substantial effect on the travel behaviour of staff at Meadowhall shopping centre. At least five of the DfT pilot projects are focusing on commuters (with two - Cambridgeshire and Bracknell Forest - targeting people when they change job, as they are assumed to be most susceptible to behaviour change at this time). Two other DfT projects are focusing on the journey to school.

One further dimension of changing travel behaviour was reporting of greater use of local facilities. In particular, in Gloucester, a greater proportion of trips were made within the case study area after the intervention (an increase from 43% to 45%). This finding is consistent with the recorded increases in walking.

The following limited conclusions emerge in relation to these results only:
- Individualised marketing appears to have greater effects on off-peak journeys such as shopping and leisure trips. However, other personalised travel planning initiatives have effectively targeted the work journey, and existing pilot projects consider that it is valuable to focus on work and school journeys, as well as other types of trip.
- There may be some increase in the use of local facilities, and a reduction in the use of facilities which are further away.

5.7.3 Adjustments to the data

All the UK personalised travel planning projects for which results are available show reductions in car use, many of which are impressive. However, a note of caution is necessary about the difficulties of interpreting and comparing data.

First, as discussed in section 5.2.2, some travel blending results in the published literature relate only to participants who have completed both 'before' and 'after' travel diaries. There may be a substantial drop-out rate between the two diaries, and it is not possible to say whether, or how, behaviour has changed amongst those who do not complete the second diary. The data in table 5.8 shows the effect of the intervention on participants who have completed both diaries, and on 'average' participants, including those who did not complete the second diary. For the average data, it is assumed that participants who only complete one diary have not changed their behaviour. Non-respondents are assigned the travel behaviour of all those who complete the first diary (and their behaviour is also assumed to remain unchanged). This method could result in headline figures which are either an overestimate or an underestimate of the effects of the initiative on the travel behaviour of the whole group.

Second, the calculation of behaviour change for individualised marketing involves a series of quite complex statistical adjustments, which may make a substantial difference to the reported results. For the Gloucester pilot project, these were as follows:

- A transfer factor was applied to the 'before' data for the target group, reflecting changes in travel behaviour between the 'before' and 'after' surveys in the control group. This is based on the assumption that changes in the control group between the two surveys would also have taken place in the target group. In the Gloucester pilot project, this adjustment takes car driver mode share in the target group from 43% (before, unadjusted) to 44% (before, corrected by control group effects).
- The 'after' data for the target group and the control group was weighted in two ways: first by trip purpose, so that the distribution of trip purposes is the same as in the 'before' data; and second (for the target group only), the 'after' data is adjusted so that the proportion of respondents requesting information is the same as actually observed in the marketing campaign. In the Gloucester pilot project, this adjustment takes the target group car driver mode share from 41% (after, un-weighted) to 40% (after, weighted).

If these adjustments were not made, the reduction of car driver trips in the Gloucester pilot project would still be significant, at about 5%, but less than the reported figure of 9%.

To some extent, personalised travel planning monitoring is often a victim of its own attempt to be rigorous. Of all the soft factors, personalised travel planning is perhaps the one where monitoring methodologies are most developed, where more than one dimension of travel behaviour is commonly measured and where the use of control groups helps to address some of the difficulties with assessing impacts that are discussed in chapters 1 and 14. However, the complexity of the processes and adjustments involved; the fact that those advocating the initiatives are sometimes also responsible for monitoring them; and the fact that the data is largely the preserve of commercial companies, released in a variety of formats, with a range of detail, and only sometimes subject to independent auditing has led to a lack of confidence in conclusions amongst some professionals. Hence, one priority for work in this area is a greater degree of independent monitoring and analysis.

5.8 Other effects of personalised travel planning

The following additional benefits are quoted for personalised travel planning:
- Reduced car use, which leads to lower road capacity requirements, reduced emissions of local air pollutants and greenhouse gases, fewer road casualties, and lower private vehicle running costs for the individual.
- Increased walking and cycling, which has associated health and fitness benefits.
- Increased public transport use, which results in additional revenue for public transport operators.
- Increased viability of local shops and businesses, which was mentioned as a potential benefit in Gloucester.
- Improved interaction by different players in the community, which was mentioned in Gloucester and Nottingham.

- Positive attitudes towards the initiative, as people feel that they have been helped by the provision of information. For example it was noted that the Gloucester initiative had not attracted any negative media comment.

The issue of social inclusion was also raised in relation to personalised travel planning. In Bristol, the work has deliberately targeted a deprived area, partly as a way of trying to highlight travel opportunities to people, and hence, for example, expand their range of perceived available job opportunities. The initiative seems to have been successful. However, the Nottingham interviewee felt that individualised marketing was likely to be most successful in middle-class areas.

In addition to these effects, there were also a number of synergies identified between personalised travel planning and other transport policies.

5.9 Synergies between personalised travel planning and other policies

There were some synergistic effects which all interviewees agreed about:

- **Some alternative transport modes need to be good quality for personalised travel planning to work.**
The success of personalised travel planning partly depends on the quality of transport alternatives in the area, which will, in turn, partly be determined by 'hard measures'. In Bristol, the range of other initiatives taking place was seen as a good rationale for also undertaking personalised travel planning.

- **Improvements in transport alternatives are not necessary for personalised travel planning to work.**
Where (some) alternative modes are of reasonable quality, it is not necessary to *change* hard measures in order for personalised travel planning to have an effect. In Gloucester and Frome, there were no major changes during the period of individualised marketing, such that the reduction in car use can be attributed to the individualised marketing initiative alone.

- **Personalised travel planning can increase the impact of public transport improvements.**
Notably, the Bristol experience seems to suggest that combining personalised travel planning with public transport improvements produces a greater increase in public transport trips than if the public transport improvements are undertaken in isolation. First Bus has been involved in the scheme, providing information materials and trial tickets.

- **High quality information about alternative modes is important.**
Personalised travel planning requires the availability of high-quality information about alternative modes. Therefore it can act as a catalyst to generate this information, or alternatively is considerably cheaper where this information already exists.

- **Personalised travel planning can provide information about public attitudes.**
The process of personalised travel planning can generate useful information about public attitudes towards different modes, which can be used to inform and prioritise transport planning. This was mentioned as a particular benefit in Gloucester.

- **There is potential synergy with health promotion.**
In Gloucester, officers felt that there was the potential to work with health promotion bodies, to see how individualised marketing could help achieve the twin objectives of reducing car use and promoting healthier lifestyles. (However, in Nottingham, it was noted that if a participant is already fairly active, changes in travel may make little difference to overall fitness).

Two other issues were also raised:

- **Initiative duplication**
The travel blending experiment in Nottingham was considered to have been less effective than comparable work that took place in Adelaide (Australia) because the subjects had already been affected by travel plan work and encouraged to reduce their car use through that. In Gloucester, the individualised marketing campaign was considered to have had relatively little effect on education journeys, and officers speculated that this may have been because there had already been considerable work on improving safety around schools in the local area. However, officers in Gloucester clearly felt that in future, integrating personalised travel planning with work on workplace and school travel plans would help to achieve greater results all round.

- **Public and professional acceptance of sustainable transport measures**
There are conflicting views about how far personalised travel planning affects attitudes towards other transport measures. On one hand, Sustrans commented that 'it is intuitive common sense that by establishing the dialogue we do, people will be more likely to become receptive to other measures.' SDG also comment that their work can be an important part of raising the acceptability of sustainable transport policies within local authorities. However, in Gloucester, it was noted that the individualised marketing had not altered the unpopularity of traffic calming. In Nottingham, there could be clear synergies with the Big Wheel travel awareness campaign. However the personalised travel planning work has deliberately 'kept its distance' from this campaign, as it is partially associated with the workplace parking levy, and it was felt that this could affect whether people saw the advice and information that they were being offered as positive and helpful.

5.10 Relationship between spending and impact for personalised travel planning

Overall cost benefit analysis of personalised travel planning has taken place in Australia, including evaluation of both individualised marketing and travel blending (as reported by SDG 2001). In general, these analyses showed extremely favourable ratios (with maximum benefits:costs in the order of 30:1). However, there has been some debate about the methodology used, partly relating to the difficulties of monetarising certain social and economic costs.

In our analysis, we have estimated the cost-impact ratio of two pilot personalised travel planning schemes (Gloucester and Bristol). In addition, we looked at projected cost and impact figures for two proposed large-scale schemes (in Nottingham and London), as we were interested in likely cost-impact ratios once these programmes are scaled up. In all cases, we have only looked at the impacts in terms of car kilometres saved.

For the Gloucester and Bristol schemes, we had case study data on the impact of the intervention, in terms of either car kilometres or car trips saved. In Nottingham, the local authority has suggested a range of plausible impacts of the proposed programme, and we adopted the mid-range estimate. In London, no estimate of likely impact of the proposed large-scale programme has been made. We estimated that it might cut car driver mileage by 10%. (It should be noted that this is a conservative assumption, since it is the mid range of the experience of the London pilots, which showed considerable variation[2]. Moreover, the aim of conducting different trials was to identify what worked best, and apply this information to the larger scale trial. In addition, as highlighted in section 5.2.2, there is some evidence suggesting that larger scale trials tend to be more effective).

In each case, we assumed that the behaviour change achieved in the year following the marketing intervention would be partly maintained in future, decaying by 40% per year.

Expenditure data was drawn from the case studies, with all costs treated as revenue.

Table 5.11 summarises unit costs per person targeted, and per car kilometre saved.

The cost of each car kilometre saved is roughly 3 pence in the pilot projects for which results are available, but may fall to about a penny in large scale programmes. As discussed in section 5.5.2, this difference is partly a consequence of the lower costs of monitoring in large-scale programmes (since monitoring can be carried out on a smaller proportion of the whole population), and also due to economies of scale.

---

[2] As described in section 5.7.2, interim results show a reduction in car driver trips of 11% for the Kingston pilot and a reduction of 16% for the Southwark pilot. In Enfield, combined car driver/passenger trips have fallen by 19%. In Lambeth, there has been a 4% reduction in car driver modal share.

Table 5.11: Calculation of cost-impact ratios for personalised travel planning

	Gloucester pilot	Bristol VIVALDI phase 1	London proposed large-scale scheme	Nottingham proposed large-scale scheme
Number of people targeted	500	2500	120,000 – 150,000	161,800
Impact	Car driver kilometres fell from 21km to 19 km per person per day	Car driver trips fell from 365 to 348 per person per year	Assume car driver mileage falls 10% (from London average of 3457 km per person per year)	Case study mid-range projection: 26255 fewer car trips per day by targeted population
Car kilometres saved per person in year after intervention*	730	238	346	829
Total car kilometres saved per person~	1825	595	868	2073
Cost	£30,000	£50,000	£1.3 million	£2.31 million
Cost per head	£60	£20	£10	£14
Cost per km saved (pence)	3.3	3.4	1.2	0.7

* where impact data is expressed in terms of car driver trips, we assume an average car driver trip length of 14 km, based on national travel data, to calculate car kilometres saved.
~ total car kilometres saved per person based on assumption that behaviour change decays by 40% each year following intervention.

5.11 Future impact of personalised travel planning

The future implementation of personalised travel planning depends on:
- The number of locations in which it is likely to be effective
- Whether there is sufficient organisational capacity to deliver large-scale personalised travel planning programmes
- Whether local authorities can find a way of meeting the cost of personalised travel planning programmes.

5.11.1 Locations where personalised travel planning may be effective

Sustrans suggests that personalised travel planning should be prioritised in those areas where it is most likely to be successful, rather than simply rolled out nationally. They believe that in some cases it will be applicable to whole towns, whereas, in other places, it would only be appropriate for certain neighbourhoods within towns, or along public transport corridors. Case study interviewees suggested that the factors likely to increase the effectiveness of personalised travel planning interventions are:
- A recognition in the community concerned that there are traffic problems.
- A fairly discrete and self-contained community, with reasonable local services and facilities (not just a dormitory or satellite suburb).
- A reasonable level of public transport (and ideally, some recent improvements in services).
- Some excess capacity on public transport.

- A reasonable quality of environment for walking and cycling, including lower speeds and a 'people friendly' street-scene.
- Support from the local authority and other key partners, including public transport operators.

Quedgeley, the area selected for the individualised marketing programme in Gloucester, clearly met some of these criteria. It had good local facilities, including primary and secondary schools, a library and a supermarket, and a good bus service into Gloucester city centre. Nevertheless, local authority officers commented that car use in Quedgeley was relatively unconstrained, with low levels of traffic congestion, and hence that behaviour change might be expected to be more difficult to achieve than in congested inner-city areas. There was a feeling that 'if we can make a difference here, we can do it anywhere'. Officers suggested that it would be appropriate to develop a rolling individualised marketing programme covering the whole of the city of Gloucester over a period of between five and ten years. Frome – the location of the other Sustrans pilot project – was deliberately chosen to assess the feasibility of personalised travel planning in a relatively rural location, and again, showed that reductions could be achieved despite the constraints of the location.

The Bristol case study offers an insight into the effectiveness of personalised travel planning in areas of low car ownership. Bishopsworth and Hartcliffe, the areas selected for the VIVALDI individualised marketing programme, have high levels of social deprivation, relatively low economic participation, and lower than average car ownership. In contrast, Bishopston has high levels of car ownership and good alternatives to the car. In an interview carried out before any results were available, the Bristol interviewees said that they expected that modal shift in Bishopsworth and Hartcliffe might be small. However, preliminary results available shortly after the interview showed a 5% reduction in car driver trips. Whilst initial results from the Bishopston do suggest a bigger shift (a 10% reduction in car driver trips), 5% is still significant, and suggests that personalised travel planning can be effective and worthwhile in areas with low car ownership.

5.11.2 Organisational capacity

Two of the three case study cities had given some thought to the possibility of a large-scale rolling programme of personalised travel planning and London is also currently considering a large-scale programme.

In Gloucester, officers felt that it would, in principle, be feasible to develop a rolling annual programme, covering 10,000 or 20,000 people each year, so that the whole of the city (population 110,000) was covered in about five to ten years. They felt that staffing within the city and county councils would not be a constraint in handling a rolling programme of this size.

As part of considering options for the M1 multi modal study, Nottingham City Council had developed a proposal to apply individualised marketing to five areas within the M1 catchment. The selected areas had a combined population of 161,800 people, equivalent to 25% of the population of the Greater Nottingham LTP area. It was suggested that such a programme could be implemented over a five to ten year period.

Bristol City Council had not considered any further use of individualised marketing beyond the current programme. Interviewees felt that if the programme was to be repeated, to be manageable, it should be at about the same scale as at present, that is, about 5000 people per year. A further project at this scale is now (July 2004) under development.

In London, Transport for London is considering a programme covering 120,000 – 150,000 people per year for three years. If implemented, this would quickly surpass Perth, covering over 350,000 people.

At the time of our interviews, several local authority interviewees felt that the capacity of external consultants to carry out such programmes might be a constraint. Sustrans believed that it would be possible for consultants to 'gear up' to provide personalised travel planning services. In any one location, they commented that programmes would need to be phased, possibly working with no more than 20-30,000 people at one time.

Sustrans also identified ways in which the intervention could be streamlined for larger scale work. Ideas included using door-to-door contact in parallel with phone contact; delivering some information by email; and contracting out the tele-marketing phase to larger call-centres. It might also be possible to integrate large-scale personalised travel planning with the services offered by Traveline and Transport Direct. It should be noted that streamlining should not reduce what are considered to be some of the key success factors of the work – namely direct personal contacts with households, quick response times, a personalised service, a coherent brand identity and an emphasis on information provision.

More recently (July 2004), it has become clear that large-scale projects are developing fast. For example, a large-scale project in Hampshire called 'Infomotion' (involving Socialdata) is aiming to target 286,000 people in four phases between September 2003 and September 2004, including up to 100,000 people per phase. SDG are also extending their 'Stepchange' work in Scotland to cover 10,000 households in the Aberdeen area (in conjunction with two smaller projects involving around 2000 households).

5.11.3 Cost of personalised travel planning

The case study areas had considered several sources of funding for future programmes, including the workplace parking levy (in Nottingham) and developer contributions (in Gloucester).

However, interviewees felt that, whilst such mechanisms could be helpful, lack of funding was a major constraint on scaling up personalised travel planning programmes in their areas. There was a view that personalised travel planning cannot be entirely funded through revenue programmes and should be treated as a capital cost. Interviewees in Gloucester and Nottingham felt that personalised travel planning was more cost-effective than many capital projects, in terms of congestion-relief, and that it was perverse that government funding should be less readily available for projects which were better value for money than many currently-funded capital schemes.

The proposal for a large-scale rolling programme in Nottingham, reaching 161,800 people, was budgeted at £2.31 million (a cost per person of £14 excluding local authority staff time). In Gloucester, the interviewees suggested a rolling programme covering the whole city over five to ten years might cost around £2 million (based on a cost per head of £20). These appear to fall within the range for typical costs of larger scale personalised travel planning initiatives, as discussed in section 5.5.2 (although the Gloucester figure may be a slight over-estimate). It was notable that neither local authority felt that it was feasible to meet this level of expenditure from revenue budgets, under current rules. Both felt that if it was possible to fund personalised travel planning under their local authority's capital programme, the cost:benefit ratio of these programmes would make them an attractive option.

5.12 Key issues for scaling up personalised travel planning

The main constraint to scaling up that emerged from the case studies was the cost of personalised travel programmes, which is too high to be met from local authority revenue budgets. Other issues which emerged from the case studies are described below.

- **Revenue or capital?**

Local authority officers in the three case study areas were doubtful that personalised travel planning would be rolled out after the currently funded programme came to an end, unless it was 'mainstreamed' as part of the Local Transport Plan funding process. Essentially this meant funding via capital programmes.

Interviewees offered two reasons why it might be justifiable to include personalised travel planning in a capital programme:

1. Evidence from other personalised travel programmes carried out abroad suggests that behaviour change is sustained. That is, a one-off intervention delivers an ongoing benefit. Although personalised travel planning programmes might need to be periodically 'topped up', one interviewee commented that it would not be necessary to 'go back two or three years later and do the whole thing again'.
2. In the Bristol case study, personalised travel planning had clearly increased the effectiveness of a capital programme (to improve bus services).

- **Evidence of effectiveness**

Local authority officers in all three case studies reported that there had been (and to some extent still was) scepticism about the effectiveness of personalised travel planning (some aspects of which have been discussed in section 5.7.3). The Nottingham interviewee felt that 'politicians [still] need to recognise its value' and that personalised travel planning is most likely to happen in areas where there is a 'champion'. One Gloucester interviewee felt that it was difficult to 'sell' personalised travel planning to senior officers and councillors because it is so intangible. 'It's a bit like a black box. It's not like any other project where you can show the physical results to people. It's not tangible – it's happening in people's minds.' The Gloucester interviewee suggested that one solution would be to arrange the telemarketing so that politicians could visit and observe it in action. It also seems likely that larger-scale projects, which deliver recordable changes in public transport patronage, may help tackle this problem, and the consolidated information from the 18 pilot projects funded by the Department for Transport and Transport for London should also be helpful.

- **Technical difficulties with information provision**

One case study area reported that they had technical difficulties developing information materials specific to individual bus stops. There may be a need to address this issue nationally, so that local authorities do not need to 'reinvent the wheel' to provide this kind of information.

5.13 Policy implications relating to personalised travel planning

- Greater consideration could be given to ways of funding personalised travel planning, and in particular to whether it may be funded as part of a Local Transport Plan capital programme.
- Local authorities could be encouraged to explore the potential for personalised travel planning to be funded through Section 106 agreements for new residential developments.
- Local authorities could explore the potential for partnerships with public transport operators (who stand to gain commercially from personalised travel planning) and health promotion bodies (who could use personalised travel planning to encourage more healthy lifestyles).
- Wide dissemination of the results from the current programme of pilot projects could be helpful, to assist local authorities in justifying undertaking such interventions locally.
- Further consideration could be given to the issue of monitoring personalised travel planning initiatives. Should all local authorities be encouraged to monitor all the initiatives they undertake (with the associated costs which that incurs), or could national demonstration of effectiveness negate the need for local monitoring? For example, monitoring of planned large-scale projects in Worcester, Darlington and Peterborough as part of the Department for Transport's Sustainable Travel Demonstration Towns project may help to provide more convincing evidence about the effects of such schemes. It is also important that such monitoring is seen to be independent and transparent.

5.14 Acknowledgements

We would like to thank the following people for their help with the case study material:

Individual	Organisation
Adrian Clarke	Gloucester City Council
Paul Hardiman	Gloucestershire County Council
Bruce James	Nottingham City Council
Pete Davis	Bristol City Council
Tim Hapgood	Bristol City Council
James Ryle	Sustrans
Barbara Wilcox	Cambridgeshire County Council
John Ansari	South Yorkshire PTE

Daniel Johnson	City of York Council

In addition to the main case study interviewees, we would like to thank:

Individual	*Organisation*
Patrick Allcorn	Transport for London
Werner Brög	Socialdata
Jeremy Ketley	Department for Transport
Don Nutt	SDG
Peter Stopher	University of Sydney

5.15 References

Allcorn P, Powell A & Hickes C (2003) *Individualised marketing pilot projects in London: Travel options interim report.* Report by Transport for London.

Ampt E, Buchanan L, Chatfield I, Rooney A (1998) *Reducing the impact of the car – creating the conditions for individual change* PTRC European Transport Conference seminar C

Brög W (2002) *The Perth Experience. Reducing the use of cars – the homeopathic way.* Paper presented at a seminar of the London Assembly, Reducing Traffic Congestion in London: policy options other than road pricing

Department for Transport (11/12/02) *Winning bids announced for sustainable travel cash.* News release from DfT

Halcrow (2002) *Multi-modal studies: soft factors likely to affect travel demand.* Final report to Department for Transport

James B (2003a) *Involving local communities in mobility management – the TravelSmart lessons in Perth, Australia* unpublished paper

James B (2003b) *TravelSmart: The individualised marketing story so far…in other places* unpublished powerpoint presentation supplied to the authors

James B (2003c) *Update on the TravelSmart programme in Perth Western Australia* unpublished paper

John G (2002a) Gary John, Manager of Balanced Transport, Department for Planning and Infrastructure, Western Australia. Personal communication with one of the authors

John G (2002b)*The Perth TravelSmart Experience*, paper presented to TravelSmart seminar, London Borough of Camden

Jopson A (undated c1998) *Reducing car use: does the theory of planned behaviour have a role?* Report from the Institute for Transport Studies, University of Leeds.

Perkins A (2003) *The Greenhouse Abatement Potential, in Different Urban Contexts, of Travel Behaviour Change Initiatives,* Report 1 for National Greenhouse Strategy 5.3 Taskforce, Transport SA with Transport West Australia

Roth M, Ker I, James B, Brog W, Ashton-Graham C, Ryle J, Goulias K and Richardson E (2003) *A dialogue on individualised marketing: Addressing misperceptions*. Paper to the 26th Australasian Transport Research Forum.

Sloman L (2003) *Less Traffic where people live: how local transport schemes can help cut traffic.* Report supported by the Royal Commission for the Exhibition of 1851, Transport for Quality of Life and Transport 2000, London.

Socialdata (2003) personal correspondence

Steer Davies Gleave (2001) *A review of the effectiveness of personalised journey planning techniques.* Report to Department for Transport

Stopher PR and Bullock P (2003) *Travel Behaviour Modification: A Critical Appraisal*. Report by the University of Sydney

Stopher PR (2004) *Voluntary travel behaviour change.* Report by the University of Sydney.

Sustrans (2002) *TravelSmart Gloucester pilot project*

Transport Planning Agency South Australia (2004) *Measuring travel behaviour change – the TravelSmart SA Mitcham pilot.*

SDG (2004) personal correspondence with Don Nutt, Steer Davies Gleave

UITP (undated) *Switching to public transport*

6. Public transport information and marketing

6.1 Introduction

In recent years in the UK, bus service improvements have often taken the form of a package – called a quality bus partnership– encompassing improvements to infrastructure and services as well as information and marketing. Quality bus partnerships involve partnership agreements (either formal or informal) between bus operators and local authorities, where both sides agree to implement measures which will contribute to shared objectives. Not surprisingly, the literature reflects this focus on quality bus partnerships, in that analyses of bus improvements tend not to disaggregate the effects of the different measures, but to report overall impacts. In section 6.2, we review the evidence about the overall impact of quality bus partnerships. Subsequent sections look briefly at the marketing of rail services and the impact of public transport ticketing schemes. We also summarise evidence from the literature on what proportion of new public transport trips would have been made by car in the absence of public transport improvements or marketing. Finally, our case studies, and other material gathered during the process of case study selection, offer insights into the specific contribution made by information and marketing measures within a comprehensive package of hard and soft measures.

6.2 Literature evidence on the impact of quality bus partnerships

Three documents give an overview of the success of recent quality bus partnerships: a survey by LEK for the Commission for Integrated Transport, which looked in detail at 11 schemes (LEK / CfIT 2002); a report by the consultancy TAS, which surveyed all the quality partnerships in Britain in 1999, and again in 2000 (TAS 2001); and a report from the Confederation of Passenger Transport (CPT 2002), which includes examples of patronage growth not reported by TAS or LEK. These, and some additional data from reports by Mackie et al (2002), Daugherty et al (1999) and Stagecoach (2002), were in turn summarised by Sloman (2003).

The LEK research examined 11 un-named urban quality partnerships, and found that most schemes (nine out of the 11) delivered increases in patronage of between 7% and 30%. These schemes incorporated a variety of measures: bus lanes, other bus priority measures, low floor buses, more frequent services, real time information, marketing, and higher parking charges. One scheme performed much better than any of the others, with an increase in patronage of over 90%. This was the only scheme to include a guided bus-way, and was also the only one to be associated with a park and ride service. One scheme had much less impact than the others, with patronage rising only about 4%. This was the most limited of all the schemes, involving the introduction of low floor buses and some bus priority measures but no new bus lane.

The TAS research suggests that differences in passenger growth figures are linked to the extent of a quality partnership scheme. It finds that quality partnerships involving only minimal investment in new infrastructure will, on average, deliver revenue and patronage increases of 5%. Where a comprehensive route upgrade is carried out, patronage and revenue can be expected to rise by around 15%, and with very high quality schemes the average increase will be around 30%, with some schemes achieving increases in revenue as high as 45%. However, other factors outside a quality partnership will also affect its impact: for example the level of parking charges or availability of parking; levels of congestion; or competition with other modes such as cycling or light rail. Table 6.1 shows the TAS analysis of the possible range in passenger growth according to these external factors and the extent of the quality partnership itself.

Table 6.1: Expected increases in revenue and patronage for quality bus partnerships

Improvement type	worst case	average	Best case
Minimal infrastructure improvement	-25%	5%	10%
Comprehensive conventional route upgrade	5%	15%	50%
The 'X' factor: something better than a conventional route upgrade	20%	30%	45%

Source: TAS (2001)

Several studies suggest that although some growth in bus use is usually seen quite quickly after improvements are made, passenger numbers typically take up to two years to peak. It takes time for improvements to 'bed in' and for passengers to change their existing travel behaviour and try the new service. For example passenger numbers on Line 33 in the West Midlands increased by a fifth shortly after the quality partnership began, but, 18 months later, bus use had increased by 40%. Similar tendencies for longer term behaviour change to be greater than short term change have been reported from studies analysing responses to altered bus fares, as discussed in section 6.4. Meanwhile, TAS suggests that after two years, patronage increases may level off, or even decline, if no further improvements are made. They argue that in a climate of continually rising consumer expectation, local authorities and bus operators must 'refresh the quality bus product' every five years in order to achieve continuing increases in passenger numbers.

Table 6.2 shows the patronage increases achieved by a variety of quality bus partnerships, as reported by LEK, TAS, CPT and others. Where possible, results have been disaggregated into those about short-term change ('initial' increases, or those occurring in 15 months or less) and medium term increases (those occurring after 18 months or longer, or studies which simply reported the 'overall' effects of schemes).

Table 6.2: Impact of quality partnerships on patronage in individual corridors

Location	Description	Short-term patronage increase[1]	Medium-term patronage increase[2]	Proportion switched from car	Source
Review of 11 bus quality partnerships	Bus lanes, low floor buses, more frequent services, real time information, marketing		Most in range 7 – 30% (guided busway 90%; one scheme only 4%)[3]	Estimate 10%	LEK / CfIT (2002)
Birmingham	Line 33	20%	40%	10%	TAS (2001)
Birmingham	Superline	18%			TAS (2001)
West Midlands	Primeline		5%		TAS (2001)
Birmingham	three Showcase routes			29%	CENTRO, in Mackie et al. (2002)
Cheltenham	Service 2	5%			TAS (2001)
Edinburgh	Greenways schemes		7 – 15%		TAS (2001)
Hertfordshire	Lea Valley Green Route	20%			TAS (2001)
Hertfordshire	Elstree and Borehamwood Network		20%	3%	TAS (2001)
Ipswich	Superoute 66 (guided busways)		75%	33%	First, in CPT (2002)
Leeds	Scott Hall Road (guided busway)		75%	20%	First, in CPT (2002)
London	Route 220 (Harlesden – Wandsworth)		approx 30%[4]		Daugherty et al. (1999)
London	Uxbridge Road		26%[5]		Daugherty et al. (1999)
Nottingham	Cotgrave Connection		10 – 15%		TAS (2001)
Nottingham	Calverton Connection	29%	48%	25%	TAS (2001)
Perth, Scotland	Stagecoach Kickstart pilot		63%		Stagecoach (2002)
Portsmouth	Portsmouth – Leigh Park service	25%			Stagecoach, in CPT (2002)
Rotherham	Rotherham – Maltby services		17%		First, in CPT (2002)
Sheffield	X33 to Bradford		nearly 50%		Arriva, in CPT (2002)
Telford	Redline		46%		Arriva, in CPT (2002)
Telford	Blueline	12%			Arriva, in CPT (2002)
Woking	Route 91		22%		Arriva, in CPT (2002)
AVERAGE		**18%**	**36%**		

Reproduced from Sloman (2003)

[1] Patronage increases are considered short-term where they are described as "initial increases" or are for a period of 15 months or less.
[2] Patronage increases are taken as medium-term if the time period quoted is 18 months or longer, or if it is unspecified.
[3] LEK / CfIT (2002) data are not included in calculation of average patronage increase, since the unnamed schemes analysed by them may duplicate the named examples.
[4] Daugherty et al. quote 'an increase of an average of about 7 to 15% per annum compared to the fleetwide total from about the middle of 1994 until the end of 1996.' Taking a middle figure of 11% per annum over 30 months gives an increase of 30%.
[5] Daugherty et al. quote an increase in patronage of 'almost 30%' compared to a 4% patronage increase on control routes.

The highest performing schemes (patronage +75%), in Leeds and Ipswich, involved construction of dedicated guided bus-ways.

The next highest passenger increase (an increase of 63%, which was around double the average increase) was achieved in Perth, Scotland, where the bus operator doubled bus frequencies, introduced low floor buses, simplified the fares structure and carried out a door-to-door marketing campaign at the same time that the local authority introduced bus priority measures and new bus shelters. This scheme is particularly interesting from the perspective of the current study, as it offers evidence of synergy between soft measures (in this case a marketing campaign) and hard measures. Further information on the Perth experiment was gathered as part of our trawl for in-depth case studies, and is reported later.

Taken together, the listed schemes have increased bus use by an average of more than a third (36%). If the guided bus schemes in Leeds and Ipswich are excluded, the average increase in bus use is slightly lower but still substantial, at 30%. More information would be needed to assess how much of this increase is the result of soft measures. However, we can conclude that the mix of hard and soft together is highly effective in increasing bus use.

6.3 Literature evidence on marketing of rail services

Our literature review primarily focussed on marketing of bus services, but two examples of marketing of rail travel are worthy of mention because of the involvement of public agencies as well as train operators.

First, we looked briefly at 'community rail partnerships', of which there are more than 30, primarily (but not necessarily) in rural areas, and mainly focussed on branch railway lines. These partnerships have sought to increase rail patronage through soft initiatives such as marketing; attractive branding (many lines are given a name reflecting the area through which they pass); changing to a regular clock-face timetable; refurbishing stations; and offering special ticket deals. Some have also increased service frequencies or introduced feeder bus services.

The Bittern Line provides one example of the increase in patronage that may be achieved as a result. This is a rail line between Norwich and Sheringham in Norfolk. After a period of steady decline, a community rail partnership was established for the line in 1996. A combination of effective marketing, upgrading and repair of stations, new signalling, a more frequent (hourly) service, a bus / rail link and other improvements turned the line around, and led to year-on-year growth of over 7% a year, totalling over 40% over five years (Meades 2002). The active involvement of the local community, the county council, and the train operator has been critical to the success of the line. The success of the Bittern Line has prompted other community rail partnerships to be established in the region, including the Wherry Lines between Norwich, Great Yarmouth and Lowestoft, where a partnership established in 2000 is starting to generate growth of between 5% and 7% a year.

Second, information on an awareness campaign launched jointly between the Highways Agency and operator Great Eastern Railways in June 1998 is reported by Crampin (1998). This was aimed at persuading people to use the train rather than the car for trips along the A12 corridor near Chelmsford. The campaign coincided with the introduction of an improved rail timetable. Posters and leaflets were distributed, an ad-van (moving billboard) was driven around the town, and local radio, newspaper and bus side advertisements were also used. Posters included the words 'over 1 hour by car, only 35 minutes by train, what's stopping you!' They carried the logos of both the Highways Agency and First Great Eastern. An evaluation of the campaign by Oscar Faber showed the following:

- awareness of Great Eastern services amongst non-users increased by 11%, and 40% of those surveyed recalled the advertisement used in the campaign.
- Business at Chelmsford Station increased by 12%, there was a 17% increase in the number of standard return ticket sales, and weekly season ticket sales were up by 31% compared to August 1997.

Assessment of the campaign also suggested that there were perceived to be three major positive elements - the campaign was perceived as conveying a strong environmental message; Great Eastern was perceived to be working hard on improving services; and the partnership with the Highways Agency was regarded as positive. (This campaign is also discussed in Chapter 7).

6.4 Literature evidence on the impact of ticketing schemes

The effect of fares on public transport patronage has been subject to a long history of research and analysis. Moreover, as analysed by Dargay and Hanly (1999), longer-term responses to changes in fare levels are typically substantially greater than short-term responses. This finding was recently endorsed in a major review of factors affecting public transport demand undertaken by Balcombe et al (2004). It increases confidence in the findings about short and long term behaviour change in response to quality bus partnerships reported in section 6.2.

As well as interest in specific fare levels, there is also interest in how fares, and associated ticketing, are structured - what we term here 'ticketing schemes'. This refers to initiatives where passengers can buy more than just a single or return ticket for a particular journey, instead buying some kind of pass or card or discounted ticket book, that potentially allows access across different operators or types of public transport and/or is valid for a particular time period or geographical area and/or is transferable between individuals. To some extent, ticketing initiatives are about finding an alternative way of marketing services, and are often discussed in association with, or as part of, public transport information and marketing initiatives. They usually aim to simplify ticketing arrangements in some way, and often reduce the need for passengers to make complex calculations when costing their proposed travel.

Balcombe et al (2004) gave some consideration to different ticketing systems. They state: 'it has often been found that patronage increases, following introduction of [a] travelcard, suggesting that it does stimulate demand'. As one example, they quote a study by Gilbert and Jalilan (1991) about the introduction of travelcards in London, which reported that travelcard introduction led to a 10% increase in the number of underground trips and a 16% increase in bus trips. Balcombe et al also mention patronage increases from the introduction of flat fares in Brighton, as discussed later in this chapter.

Some other commentators have also discussed the impact of ticketing schemes on public transport patronage. FitzRoy and Smith (1994) argue that the introduction of a transferable season ticket, or 'rainbow card' (Regenbogenkarte) was the main factor responsible for stimulating public transport passenger growth in Zürich during the late 1980s. Following a period of relative stability, passenger trips there grew by a third (from 210 million to about 280 million trips a year) between 1985 and 1990. The rainbow card was valid on all modes of public transport, and was transferable to family and friends.

A similar effect was observed in Freiburg, where an 'environmental travel card' (Umweltschutzkarte) was introduced in 1984. In the fifteen years before 1984, public transport demand was roughly constant at about 30 million trips per year. Between 1983 and 1995, public transport patronage increased by an average of 7.5% per year, rising from 27.7 million trips per year to 65.9 million trips per year (FitzRoy and Smith.1998). Over the same period, the population of the region grew by 13% and car ownership grew by 26%. However, car modal share remained constant and the modal share of public transport increased. The environmental travel card was cheaper than the monthly card it replaced, and, as in Zürich, could be used by friends and family members as well as the ticket holder. In the first year of operation of the environment card, an estimated 3000-4000 regular car drivers switched to public transport.

As with quality bus partnerships, it is unclear what proportion of the increase in public transport patronage reported in these cities is due to hard factors (in this case, an effective reduction in the cost of public transport travel), and what proportion is the result of the soft benefits offered by a transferable, multi-mode travel card.

6.5 Literature evidence about transfer from car to public transport

Any increase in public transport patronage (whether due to hard or soft interventions) is likely to be due to a combination of factors, including people making new trips which previously would not have been made; switching from other public transport routes or from walking or cycling; and switching from travelling by car, either as a passenger or as a driver.

Mackie et al. (2002) quote research based on surveys of 2000 travellers which found that 32% of urban bus users were abstracted from the car, and TAS (2002) report that surveys of quality bus partnerships show around 33% of new bus users had previously travelled by car. Data from six of the quality bus partnerships listed earlier (in table 6.1) suggests that typically, somewhere between 10% and 30% of new bus passengers were former car users, with a bias towards the higher end of this range, (although there is one further case where the figure was just 3%).

6.6 Selection of public transport information and marketing case studies

As already discussed, one of the difficulties in evaluating the impact of public transport information and marketing schemes is that they tend to form part of larger packages of measures, including infrastructure and service frequency improvements, rather than being implemented on their own.

It should also be noted that public transport information and marketing is often a significant component of (secondary) school and workplace travel plans; usually takes place as part of personalised travel planning; can form the focus for travel awareness work; and is associated with initiatives such as car clubs. The strong synergies with many of the other soft measures are discussed further in section 6.12.

In drawing up a list of prospective case studies for this chapter, we looked at three types of initiatives:

- Marketing or promotion of a specific route or routes, or of services to a particular destination. In our initial trawl for information, we collected data about a direct marketing campaign in Perth, Scotland, and also data about the marketing of more sustainable ways of accessing the Farnborough Air Show in Hampshire. We also gathered information about route-based promotion as part of one of the Buckinghamshire case studies, and some information on synergy between individualised marketing and bus improvements as part of the personalised travel planning case study in Bristol.
- Personalised marketing of an entire public transport network. One example of personalised area-wide marketing of public transport was examined, namely the Travel Options Planning Service, TOPS, run by South Yorkshire Passenger Transport Executive (SYPTE).
- Area-wide public transport marketing, promotion and re-branding. Here, we considered initiatives in Cambridge, Nottingham, Brighton, Bristol, London and the North York Moors National Park.

The selected case studies were the SYPTE personalised marketing scheme and city-wide public transport promotion in Brighton and Nottingham. Our information about the other schemes (mostly collected in spring 2003) is briefly summarised below, whilst our chosen case studies are described in section 6.7.

6.6.1 Perth, Scotland, direct marketing campaign

Stagecoach ran a marketing campaign to encourage increased bus use on a poor performing, low frequency bus route in Perth with a profile of aged owner-occupiers with high car dependency. Marketing was accompanied by service improvements: frequency doubled, low floor buses were introduced, fares were simplified and the council introduced bus priority measures and new bus shelters. The marketing included launch publicity, door-to-door interviews with potential customers, the offer of free trips, and promotions such as children's competitions and pensioners' lunches. This was followed by a telephone-based direct marketing campaign targeted at non-users.

Passenger growth was 56% over the first two years, and on course to be 63% over three years. There was evidence of modal shift from car to bus. The telephone marketing campaign resulted in conversion to public transport of 7-8% of those non-users contacted. Rosscraig of Stagecoach points out that this is a high figure for direct marketing – the Direct Marketing Association response rate survey 2003 quotes average response rates for comparable telephone campaigns of 4.9% . The people 'converted' to public transport were all ABC1s – that is, people who might be expected to be difficult to convert.

As discussed in section 6.2, the 63% patronage increase is roughly double the average increase for a conventional quality bus partnership, suggesting that a large part of the effect was because of the novel features of this scheme - in particular, the direct marketing.

6.6.2 Farnborough Air Show

Farnborough Air Show takes place in Hampshire every two years, and attracts around 300,000 visitors, including the general public, trade visitors, exhibition staff and others. Associated traffic problems have led to the incremental development of a surface access travel strategy. This has included a number of different components, including, for example, the introduction of shuttle buses from three local rail stations, promotion of rail / shuttlebus and coach options in publicity for the show, new train services for Air Show visitors, promotional work with train operators, better pedestrian and cycle facilities, ending the promotion of free parking and reducing parking at the site and closing local roads. One important element has been the introduction of 'through ticketing' – where visitors can buy a ticket from anywhere in the UK which includes train and bus fares and the show entrance fee. By 2002, 14 train operating companies were offering through ticketing, which is seen as an important element that has encouraged modal shift. Over successive shows, congestion has been reduced to the point where driving times to the show from the nearest motorway exit have dropped from an average of 1.5 hours to only 10 minutes. Shaw (2004) comments that soft factors have had an enormous influence on travel demand, and that traffic congestion for this major event has been eliminated.

6.6.3 Buckinghamshire public transport promotion

In Buckinghamshire, the Travel Choice team which is responsible for workplace travel planning is also involved in public transport promotion and marketing. The Buckinghamshire workplace travel plan case study thus provided useful information about the impact of a recent public transport marketing campaign. Red Route 9 was launched in February 2003, and runs between Aylesbury town centre and Stoke Mandeville Hospital. Red Route 9 buses have a distinctive livery and branding, which includes information about the route and the words 'every 10 minutes' on the side of the bus. The council produced a glossy timetable booklet, which was intended to look aspirational and 'like a Mercedes advert'. This and a personal letter from the council's chairman of transportation was sent to all 5000 people living within 500 metres of the route, encouraging them to try the service. The council was planning to send a one-week free 'trial' ticket to people who had not yet tried the service.

The marketing on Red Route 9 was preceded by a number of infrastructure improvements: a bus lane (or 'red carpet into town') introduced in 2001, which cost £2.5 million; individual signs at bus stops, with a bus stop name, timetable and route map; new shelters and seats; and Kassel kerbs. There have been some problems with the public transport infrastructure - in particular, at the time of the interview, real-time information screens had been out of action for the past two years.

Patronage on Red Route 9 did not significantly increase after the new infrastructure improvements were put in, but in the two months after the marketing work, the number of bus passengers went up by 28%. Figures for December 2003 indicated an overall patronage increase of 42%. As in Perth, this suggests that promotion and marketing can greatly increase the effectiveness of conventional public transport infrastructure improvements.

6.6.4 Bristol VIVALDI project

The Bristol personalised travel planning case study reported on an individualised marketing scheme which took place at about the same time as public transport improvements on a bus 'Showcase' corridor. Monitoring surveys conducted 10 months apart found that the public transport mode share increased from 9% to 11% in a control area which benefited from the public transport improvements but was not targeted by the individualised marketing campaign. However, this change seems to have been due to people switching from walking and travelling as a car passenger, as mode share for both these modes went down. There was little evidence of people switching from car driving to bus travel: car driver mode share in the control area increased from 45% to 46%.

Public transport mode share in the target area (which experienced both the public transport improvements and the individualised marketing), and which was monitored over the same 10 month period, increased by double the amount in the control area: from 9% to 13%. Here, car driver mode share also went down, from 45% to 43%.

This scheme suggests that public transport improvements on their own may have rather little impact on car driver mode share, as the increase in patronage may come mainly from people who previously walked or took lifts as a car passenger. Marketing (in this case individualised marketing) seems both to increase overall public transport patronage, and to attract trips that otherwise would have been made as a car driver.

6.6.5 Cambridge city-wide improvements

In Cambridge, Stagecoach achieved a 25% overall increase in patronage over a period of four months following the re-design of the city's bus network. The company reduced 12 or 13 services to a simpler six service network. Three services became 'turn up and go', with buses every 10 minutes between 7am and 7pm. (At the time of our communication with Stagecoach, in mid 2003, there were plans to increase frequency to every 7-8 minutes on one of the services because it had been so successful.) Other services now run every 30 minutes. The company publicised the service changes with glossy materials, including guides and maps for individual services and pocket-sized timetables. Park and ride buses were coloured blue, red or green depending on which park and ride site they served. 'Megarider' weekly tickets have become very cheap, and the popularity of Megarider and Dayrider tickets has meant that there are few cash-paying passengers, enabling buses to load more quickly.

6.6.6 London bus improvements

Bus use in London increased 31% over the four years to 2004 to 1702 million journeys, the highest number since 1968. The key factor in this has been increased bus mileage of 20% in the same period. A study of bus use by Transport for London found that:

- The number of people who never used a bus fell from 29% three years earlier, to 21% in 2003.
- Half of the additional journeys were made by Londoners who did not use the bus at all three years earlier.
- Half of Londoners who had increased bus usage over the previous three years mentioned 'bus improvements' as a reason for this, with the vast majority agreeing that 'there are more buses about', 'buses are better value for money', 'buses are newer', 'buses are easier to get on / off' and 'travel information has improved'.

As well as the increase in bus mileage, Transport for London points to improvements in four key areas which it feels are likely to have played a major role in increasing bus use, including a number of information, marketing and ticketing initiatives, (Lea 2004). The main areas identified by Transport for London were as follows:

- Simple fares and ticketing: £1 flat fare; single zone bus pass; the Oyster smartcard which has been introduced across a range of ticket products and may be purchased by telephone, on the internet, at tube stations or at ticket outlets; and cashless operation on central London buses which has reduced boarding times.
- Better buses: 91% of the bus fleet is fully accessible; 50% of buses are fitted with CCTV cameras.
- Better information: stop-specific timetables, 'spider maps' at key locations, local area maps, and Countdown real-time information at 2000 stops.
- Perception: customer service satisfaction scores show rising satisfaction with information, cleanliness and condition of buses. The bus service is now the most reliable since figures were first collated in 1977.

6.6.7 The Moorsbus Network

Buses in the North York Moors National Park, run by seven different bus companies, have been given a generic 'Moorsbus' branding, to try and encourage visitor use, with marketing aiming to promote the idea that the bus offers a good alternative to the car. Other features of the marketing and information work include the presence of easily recognisable co-ordinators at key points across the park who can help with information and 'troubleshoot' any service problems; location specific timetables and simplified schematic network maps at every bus stop; discounts for bus users in shops, restaurants and attractions; and 'Moorsbus journey plans' with suggested itineraries for days out. The scheme encompasses over 200 different bus services.

According to Transport 2000 (2001), in 2001, the network was carrying 27,000 passengers a year. A survey undertaken in 2000 suggested that about a third of those who travelled on the Moorsbus had access to a car on the day of their journey.

6.7 Details of chosen public transport case studies

This section describes our chosen case studies in more detail. The public transport initiatives examined in the three case studies are of different types and on different scales, and therefore difficult to compare directly. The South Yorkshire case study was focussed on one aspect of the PTE's information and marketing work, whereas the Nottingham and Brighton case studies looked at those cities' overall information and marketing strategies.

6.7.1 South Yorkshire PTE Travel Options Planning Service

In South Yorkshire, we looked at the PTE's Travel Options Planning Service (TOPS), which provides tailored, personalised travel information to companies, employees and individuals. This is part of a much larger programme of marketing and information provision, but whereas most of SYPTE's information materials are targeted at existing public transport users, TOPS is targeted at non-users of public transport. It was developed in 2001 with some funding from the European Regional Development Fund, and partly has a remit to assist with regeneration. SYPTE also has an agreement with its district local authorities to provide advice and assistance to companies that the planning system requires travel plans from, and TOPS helps with this. The TOPS service has evolved to include a wide range of services and products, such as:

- Personalised journey planners, which are offered to whole organisations, to new employees within client organisations, and to individuals. The service is being extended to job centres for people travelling to interviews, and to children moving up to secondary school.

- Discounted ticket schemes, such as the Flexi Master ticket, that offers 3 days travel in 7 to facilitate part-time working and the Eventmaster, where tickets can be bought in bulk for special events.

- Advice to companies about the production of travel plans and help carrying out travel surveys. At the time of the case study interview, this had been provided to 34 organisations covering about 70,000 employees.

- Area Travel Guides for nearly 400 areas, which are designed to answer the question 'where can I go from this location?', and are a marketing tool aimed at new users of public transport.

- Travel shows, offering face-to-face travel advice at recruitment fairs, company staff meetings and other events.

- Travel awareness training for people with mobility or learning difficulties, and for drivers and operators.

- A dedicated telephone enquiry service for TOPS clients.

- New services. Where TOPS has identified a demand not met by existing public transport, it has worked with bus operators and other partners to develop new services. Examples include the Manvers Shuttle – a service which operates to employment sites on former coalfields and to Dearne Valley College, and which is supported by contributions from local employers.

6.7.2 Public transport marketing and re-branding in Nottingham

In Nottingham, we looked at the re-branding and marketing of bus services by the largest bus operator, Nottingham City Transport, and some broader initiatives to promote public transport use, including the strategy of the city council to 'fill the gaps' between information services provided by individual operators. (The Nottingham public transport case study partly looked at the overarching 'Big Wheel' travel awareness campaign, which is discussed in more detail in chapter 7.)

A review for the city council had found that individual public transport operators provided good information in many different formats, so that once users were 'in the system' they could find the information they needed fairly easily. However, the review found that journeys involving more than one bus operator (20% of journeys), and new customers, were less-well catered for. This led the city council to prioritise actions focussed on interchanges and multi-operator route information, including:

- Development and use of the Big Wheel branding and logo to be used on all public transport information and displays as far as possible, to help with the perception that changes and developments in public transport services are part of a long term transport strategy for the city.

- Multi-operator interchange information. The council has ensured the provision of co-ordinated information at every bus stop on all the major corridors involving more than one bus operator. Bus stops are clustered to form mini bus stations. City centre maps indicating where to change buses are on the back of every bus shelter and on stand-alone panels around the city centre.

- Frequent high quality bus network. The bus network is organised into 18 high quality bus routes, each with a 10 minute frequency. A multi-operator approach is promoted on these routes.

- Sector Guides. The city is split into eight sectors, radiating out from city centre. The council plans to produce journey planning maps for each sector, one of which had been produced at the time of the case study interview.

- Themed maps, showing public transport links to all education sites, larger businesses, health sector sites and leisure and tourist destinations.

- Information provision in a range of formats, including guides for those with physical disability; blind people; those speaking minority languages; people who want to travel late at night; those on concessionary fares etc.

The council is also investigating electronic information provision and new forms of ticketing.

Meanwhile, the main bus operator, Nottingham City Transport, has shifted away from a predominantly engineering-based approach to one which is more customer-focussed, with greater attention given to marketing and promotion, and creation of a simpler, more easily understood network. These changes were partly prompted by falling patronage and concern that Nottingham's new tram system would abstract more passengers from bus services, and partly by the example of NCT's main competitor, Trent and Barton, which has a reputation for good marketing, promotion and branding.

The key changes have been as follows:

- Cross-city services were removed, so all buses now start and terminate in the city centre. This has improved reliability, as 30% of all congestion delays occurred in the city centre, yet only 3% of journeys went beyond the centre.

- Each corridor out of the city centre has been colour-coded, so all buses using that main route are the same colour. All bus stops serving routes along the same corridor are clustered and colour-coded.

- New 'Go2' services on main corridors run every 10 minutes, designed to offer a 'tram-like bus service'. Other less frequent neighbourhood services (rebranded the Nottingham Network) feed into the Go2 services.

The launch of these changes was accompanied by extensive marketing and PR work.

6.7.3 Public transport marketing and information in Brighton

In Brighton, we looked at the long-standing partnership between the city council and the bus company, Brighton and Hove Buses, which aims to make the bus network simple and easy to use. Working together in an informal bus quality partnership, the council and the bus company have developed an approach which involves a mix of hard and soft measures, with hard measures including improvements to services, infrastructure and parking enforcement. There has also been considerable investment in a bus priority information and management system, which now enables the provision of real time information at all major bus stops in the city. The partnership has been successful in increasing bus use by 5% per year for the last decade, very much against the trend of what is happening in other cities.

The soft elements of their approach include:

- 'Metro' branding. The five longest and most-frequent cross-city routes are branded as the Metro service. Other routes feed into this network. There is a tube-style map, and routes are colour-coded.

- A £1 flat fare for any bus trip was introduced in 2002 (increased to £1.20 in May 2003). Prior to the flat fare, fares were typically between 60p and £1.30 for a single journey. The flat fare is felt to have 'completely demystified the use of the bus'. Its introduction was heavily publicised on the sides of buses and through radio advertising. Other ticketing initiatives aimed at attracting bus users are a £2.40 one-day saver ticket and a scheme called 'Bus ID' which enables young people to travel for a 30p flat fare.

- Development of a customer service culture throughout the bus company, including a customer care training programme, at a cost of about £100,000 per year.

- A 'Bus Times' publication, which gives comprehensive information about bus services run by all operators. This is produced by Brighton and Hove Bus Company, but lists Stagecoach, Arriva and council funded services alongside their own.

- Two 'one-stop travel shops' selling tickets and information for all forms of public transport.

- A telephone helpline operated by council staff. It is also possible for travellers to make use of a regional telephone service (Public Transport Information 2000), which the council and the bus company are involved in.

Over and above these specific initiatives, both the local authority and bus company interviewees in Brighton felt that the broader public relations work in support of public transport was important to their success. This has involved developing a good relationship with the local media, so that they talk positively about the idea of public transport and generate a positive role for the bus company in the local community. The bus company interviewee described this sort of work as a 'very soft' factor, and commented: 'Brighton and Hove Buses have taken time to develop a positive culture, which is more than the Metro concept and the flat fare and publicity. It is creating that atmosphere that comes through. People know that they should be using the bus more. It is all part of placing yourself in the community as part of the fabric of the city'.

Some information was also provided about the 'Breeze Up to the Downs' initiative, a new network of three bus routes fanning out from the centre of Brighton and Hove to popular countryside destinations. Promotion work has included carefully targeted radio advertising; advertising on other bus services; the production of individual route guides and advertising in association with rail marketing. Use of services is included in the one-day city saver ticket and real time information about services is available at most city bus stops. As part of encouraging use, vintage, open-top buses are used on the routes, as well as modern, low floor vehicles.

6.8 Staffing and budgets for public transport information and marketing

Table 6.3 summarises the staffing and budgets dedicated to public transport information and marketing in the three case study areas.

Table 6.3: Staff time and resources allocated to public transport information and marketing (summer 2003)

	SYPTE (TOPS)	Nottingham	Brighton+
Staff time in local authority / PTE	7^	2.7~	1
Staff time in bus company	Not relevant	10#	1
Local authority / PTE revenue budget in most recent year (including staff costs)	£176,000	£85,000	£60,000*
Local authority capital spending in most recent year	Not relevant	Average £220,000 per year over last 2 years	Not relevant
Bus company spending in most recent year	Not relevant	£250,000	£225,000

+ Funding for specific initiatives, such as the Breeze up to the Downs project, Public Transport Information 2000, services for Sussex University and the bus priority and information management system are not included.
* This assumes an average staff cost of £25,000 per post.
^ This only includes staff dedicated to TOPS, as opposed to those in the wider information team.
~ Staff working on the Big Wheel campaign are not included, as this is a wider initiative.
# Call centre staff answering telephones in the Travelcentre are not included. Nor is the member of staff in this department who deals with software development for integrating schedules and rotas.

At the time of the interview, SYPTE was employing seven full-time staff to run the Travel Options Planning Service. This was an increase on the original four full-time posts dedicated to TOPS when the service was launched, and, at the time of the interview, included a bursary post funded by the Department for Transport. The Information and Development Team within which TOPS is located were also employing a further four staff responsible for other parts of their information service, such as producing in-house marketing, new timetable and leaflet products, databases and electronic information systems. The budget for TOPS was £176,000 in 2002/03, which is about 5% of the total budget for information and promotion within SYPTE, and about 0.2% of the PTE's overall budget. This figure includes staff costs.

In Nottingham, the city council was employing the equivalent of 2.7 full-time staff to promote public transport. Two appointments had been made within the last 18 months, and before this the council had no staff dedicated to promotional work. The council's promotional work had involved capital expenditure of about £440,000 over the past two years (on information panels, information 'drums' at bus stops, departure boards, and real-time information). Revenue expenditure in 2002/03 was £35,000 (for maps, timetables and other promotional material), plus about £50,000 staff costs.

Nottingham City Transport was employing about 10 staff on marketing and communications, not including travel centre staff. The budget for marketing activities was £250,000 in each of the last two years. This has covered production of timetables and bus stop information, Go2 advertising, radio adverts, poster campaigns, and various other activities. This was somewhat less than 1% of the company's budget.

In Brighton, there was one full-time post dedicated to information and marketing within the public transport team, which had 3.7 fte posts overall. The staffing level had been the same since the authority was formed in 1997. The council's public transport publicity budget was £35,000 a year in 2002/3 (not including staff costs, estimated at £25,000). This does not include payments for particular services from Sussex University, or from the Countryside Agency for the Breeze Up to the Downs initiative, or for specific initiatives such as Public Transport Information 2000 or the bus priority information and management system.

Brighton and Hove Buses had one full-time post dedicated to marketing and promotion, and this had been unchanged for many years. The company were allocating about £225,000 per year to publicity and marketing, which was about 1% of its budget.

6.9 The scale of public transport information and marketing work

The branding, marketing and information in Nottingham and Brighton is aimed at the whole population of each city, comprising 270,000 people and 250,000 people respectively. Both cities are also net 'importers' of large numbers of commuters, and also attract visitors. In Brighton, an estimated 8 million people visit every year.

The SYPTE TOPS service bears more similarity to travel planning or personalised travel planning, in that it is targeted at specific employers and individuals.

Between 2001 and 2003, TOPS worked with a total of 225 different organisations, including four local authorities, 13 organisations from the health sector and seven organisations from the education sector. Table 6.4 shows the scale of various activities carried out by TOPS between 2001 and 2003.

Table 6.4: Scale of various activities carried out by TOPS

Type of Measure	Number of organisations^
Staff travel surveys and reports	34
Management presentations	153
Travel issues consultation	183
Travel awareness roadshows	48
Tailored promotions	5
Ticketing information provision	220
Timetable leaflets	153
Ticketing agency	34
Park and ride deals/ discounts	8
Organisation specific travel guides	101
Organisations offering Personalised Journey Planners for staff / new starters	33
Dedicated phone service to Traveline*	9
Modifications to existing services	12
Dedicated shuttle bus services	13
Company travel plans~	17
Special ticketing products	32
Restricted parking/ car park charges	7
Improved pedestrian routes	1

^ Figures are for the combined number of organisations receiving the service in 2001/02 and 2002/03.
* This is a hash number on the company phone or a single button press that links the caller direct to Traveline.
~ Companies that have produced travel plans as a result of TOPS assistance.

Travel surveys have been carried out in 34 organisations covering 70,000 staff. This represents 14% of the workforce in South Yorkshire, and provides baseline information about initial travel habits.

Over 1300 personalised journey plans have been provided for staff in the organisations SYPTE is working with. About three-quarters of these have been for staff in nine organisations that fund personalised journey plans for their staff on a subscription basis. In other cases, plans are provided to individual staff on a one-off basis, frequently free of charge. Table 6.5 shows the breakdown by employment sector.

Table 6.5: Number of employees receiving personalised journey planners

Type of organisation	Number of personalised journey plans*
Hospitals (3)	635
Sheffield Hallam University	35
Local authorities (2)	90
Private sector companies (3)	269
Individuals	335
Total	1364

*Figures are the combined total for 2001/02 and 2002/03. In addition to figures in this table, Meadowhall gave employees (and visitors) internet access to SYPTE's Journey Planner. At the time of the case study interview, Sheffield University was putting its travel plan in place and had not yet taken up the personalised journey planning service.

The TOPS service has mainly concentrated on the journey to work and on large organisations. Small and medium sized businesses have proved difficult to reach. TOPS has also had a focus on newly developing centres of employment. There are plans to target the journey to school, people seeking or starting employment and people with mobility difficulties.

6.10 Public transport information and marketing impacts on car use

6.10.1 Increases in public transport patronage

All three case studies reported increased public transport patronage. The main results are summarised in table 6.6, along with results from other areas.

Table 6.6: Effect of marketing and information improvements on public transport patronage

SYPTE TOPS	Follow-up monitoring of 750 people who had received personalised journey planners suggested the initative had delivered significant increases in public transport use, as follows: • 18% increase in bus use (the frequency of using this mode) • 10% increase in train use • 12% increase in tram use. At Meadowhall, TOPS led to a 19% shift from car to bus amongst 250 management staff. One bus service which was promoted to companies along the route saw a 23% increase in patronage and subsequently had its frequency increased. New services such as the Manvers shuttle have generated 4000 entirely new public trips per week, mainly to call centres (which have ample car parking). (It should be noted that these changes are taking place in the context of a much bigger picture. Bus use across the whole of South Yorkshire is declining, although there is some evidence that the rate of decline is slowing).
Nottingham	Re-branding, marketing and better information have reversed a previous long-term decline in bus use. Previously, bus patronage was declining about 1% a year. Now passenger journeys are increasing at about 1.8% a year, or 1.3 million journeys per year. If re-branding and other initiatives had not taken place, we infer that public transport use would have continued to decline by about 1%, or 0.7 million trips per year. Thus, one year after the intervention, the local authority and bus company actions were responsible for about an extra 2 million trips.
Brighton	Bus passenger journeys increased by 45% between 1993 and 2002. Growth has been in fits and starts: for example patronage increased by almost 9% in 1999, but was static the previous year. The average growth is about 5% per year. In the year to June 2003, patronage increased by 4.6%, or 1.45 million bus passenger trips.

Perth, Scotland	A package of service improvements coupled with direct marketing delivered passenger growth of 63% over three years, roughly double the average increase for a conventional quality bus partnership. The people 'converted' to public transport were all ABC1s – that is, people who might be expected to be difficult to convert.
Buckinghamshire	Service improvements on one bus route (Red Route 9) delivered no significant increase in use. These were followed by a marketing campaign, which increased patronage by 28% within two months, and 42% after 10 months.
Bristol	Public transport improvements in a bus 'Showcase' corridor led to an increase in public transport mode share from 9% to 11% among a control group of people who did not receive targeted marketing, mostly due to a shift away from walking and travel as a car passenger. Among a separate group which received targeted marketing materials as part of an individualised marketing campaign, there was double the shift to public transport, from 9% mode share to 13%. Car driver mode share in the control group rose from 45% to 46%, whereas it fell in the target group, from 45% to 43%.
Cambridge	Simplification of the city's bus network, better information materials and simpler ticketing delivered a patronage increase of 25% over a four-month period.
London	Bus patronage increased by 31% over four years, with half the additional travel made by people who previously did not use buses at all. Although 'hard' measures played an important role, 'soft' measures, particularly the introduction of a simple flat fare, are also felt to have been important.

The experience summarised in table 6.6 points to the following conclusions:

- Where a bus service is improved or is of reasonable quality, it is possible to achieve substantial increases in patronage over only a few months through targeted marketing, re-branding, better information materials and simpler ticketing products. Evidence from Perth and Buckinghamshire suggests the patronage increases resulting from marketing-led schemes may be substantially higher than those observed with conventional quality bus partnerships: for example 40-60% on targeted routes.

- Targeted marketing may be particularly effective in attracting former car drivers, whereas general increases in public transport quality that are not accompanied by marketing may mainly influence existing public transport users, or replace journeys previously made on foot or as a car passenger. For example, TOPS personalised journey planning in South Yorkshire achieved a 19% shift from car to bus amongst staff at Meadowhall; the marketing campaign in Perth was particularly effective amongst ABC1s, who are more likely to already have access to a car; and individualised marketing along the bus Showcase corridor in Bristol led to reduced car driver mode share, which was not achieved by the Showcase improvements on their own.

- Marketing and information may increase public transport patronage even in circumstances where it has been declining, as in Nottingham.

- Attention to soft marketing and information interventions may help achieve sustained patronage growth over periods of a decade or (possibly) more, as demonstrated in Brighton.

For most of the interventions we examined, soft marketing and information initiatives were accompanied by hard public transport improvements such as new services, increased frequencies, bus shelter improvements and bus priority schemes, or other measures likely to favour public transport, such as parking restraint. It is difficult to assess what proportion of new passenger trips may be directly attributed to the soft interventions. However, the Brighton and Hove Buses interviewee suggested that good promotion and marketing of a package of service improvements is at least as important as the improvements themselves: that is, promotion could account for as much as 50% of the resulting patronage increase. Although, in practice, promotional and marketing activity is indivisible from service improvements, this implies that as much as half the annual increase in bus patronage in Brighton, or 726,000 passenger trips per year, could be attributed to soft factors.

This conclusion is consistent with experience in Bristol, Perth and Buckinghamshire. In Bristol, hard service improvements on their own delivered a 2%-point increase in public transport mode share, whereas hard improvements coupled with individualised marketing delivered a 4%-point increase. In Perth, the increase in public transport patronage achieved by hard improvements and a marketing campaign was roughly double what might be expected from an average quality bus partnership. In Buckinghamshire, the contribution of the soft marketing campaign appears to have been even more significant. There, hard improvements two years earlier had failed to increase bus patronage, while the marketing campaign has increased bus use by 42% in under a year.

6.10.2 Modal shift from car to bus travel

The case studies provided relatively little information on what proportion of any increase in public transport patronage might be attributed to journeys that were previously made by car. The available evidence was as follows:

- In Brighton, no data on modal shift was collected, but the bus company believed about 10% of the increase in bus patronage was due to mode shift from the car. The city council put the figure much higher at 50%. Traffic leaving and entering Brighton city centre fell (by 12%) between 2000 and 2003. This is consistent with some of the increase in bus patronage coming from former or 'would be' car drivers.
- In Bristol, mode share data suggests that roughly half the increase in bus mode share may have come from trips previously made as a car driver.

There was some data from public transport initiatives aimed at leisure journeys, indicating alternative travel options for customers, as follows:

- In a survey of the Breeze up to the Downs initiative, 36% of passengers said that they would have come by car if the bus had not been an option.
- In the Moorsbus survey, about a third of passengers said that they had access to a car on the day of their journey.

Alongside this should be set the results from the literature reported in section 6.5, which indicate that about a third of new public transport trips generated by a conventional quality partnership may replace car trips.

As discussed in section 6.10.1, there is some evidence that public transport enhancements may be more effective at attracting former car drivers if they include a substantial marketing element, (though clearly this will depend upon how the marketing is targeted.)

6.10.3 Types of journeys affected

In Brighton, the city council interviewee felt that the greatest growth in bus use was occurring in the middle of the day, although there has also been considerable success in attracting users for new express commuter bus services. The introduction of the flat fare has encouraged longer journeys, whilst the all day saver ticket has meant that people are making more optional journeys by bus (including, presumably, relatively short trips).

In Nottingham, the greatest growth in bus use has been during the peak period, but most routes are also busy throughout the day.

TOPS has mainly focused on commuting trips, given its remit. However, it has included considerable work with hospitals and call centres, where many employees work shifts and weekends, and therefore travel at off-peak times.

In general, therefore, it seems that public transport information and marketing can potentially affect all types of trips.

6.11 Other effects of public transport information and marketing

The following additional benefits of public transport information and marketing were identified by case study interviewees:

- **Reduced social exclusion**
Marketing of public transport services can reduce social exclusion, by increasing awareness of what services are available amongst people who are on low incomes, elderly or otherwise potentially socially excluded. TOPS has a specific remit to aid with regeneration, and has developed products for school leavers, job seekers, the mobility impaired, single parents, asylum seekers and the probation service. One of its targets between 2002 and 2004 has been to achieve a 5% reduction in those seeking employment citing lack of transport as a barrier to accessing work. In Brighton, the interviewee also commented on the potential social inclusion benefits of information and marketing work, highlighting the elderly as one group who might not be fully informed or aware of their options. In Nottingham, the council is about to embark on specific initiatives aimed at job seekers, and at improving information for accessing hospital trusts.

- **Improved relationships between bus companies and the business community**

Innovative promotional work improves relationships between bus companies and the business community, which in turn gives the bus company greater influence in local economic partnerships and business forums. For example, the bus company interviewee in Brighton commented: 'being seen to invest means that your voice will be respected and listened to'.

- **Improved retail vitality**

Public transport improvements and associated marketing are perceived to have contributed to retail vitality in Nottingham.

- **Increased revenue for operators**

Successful marketing generates increased revenue for the public transport operator.

6.12 Synergies between public transport information and marketing and other policies

The case study interviewees identified various examples of synergy between public transport information and marketing and other policies.

First, there is clearly strong synergy between marketing and public transport service improvements. This works in two ways. In Nottingham and Brighton, interviewees saw information and marketing as crucial to increasing the impact of new or better services. In South Yorkshire, the interviewee felt that TOPS has helped identify areas with unmet demand for public transport, leading to some new services being developed.

Parking enforcement, on-street parking charges and parking charges implemented through workplace travel plans were perceived as tipping the balance in favour of public transport in Brighton and South Yorkshire. There was also a feeling in South Yorkshire that TOPS had smoothed the path for implementation of residents' parking schemes around Sheffield University and Royal Hallamshire hospital.

Public transport information and marketing initiatives are often complementary with a wide range of other soft measures. In Nottingham, the bus company felt that the city council's workplace travel planning (and especially its Commuter Planners Club) was complementary to the bus company's own initiatives to promote bus services to commuters. In Buckinghamshire, providing organisations with public transport information (and persuading them to display it) is seen as a good way of starting a dialogue about workplace travel planning with an organisation without scaring them off. In SYPTE, TOPS is already clearly integrated with workplace travel planning, as described earlier.

Public transport information and marketing has formed an important element of some secondary school travel plans. For example, in early work at Sandringham School in Hertfordshire to encourage modal shift from car to bus, timetables were branded in an 'X-files' style, to capitalise on association with the popular TV series, using the slogan 'S-files: the truth about travel to Sandringham school', (Davies and Gardner 2000). Interviewees in Nottingham and South Yorkshire both mentioned potential benefits from working with schools. For example, TOPS was involved in a pilot project with Willowgarth School in Barnsley, where children undertaking Trident work experience were encouraged to use the bus, via provision of personalised journey planners and discounted tickets.

As discussed in Chapter 5, personalised travel planning initiatives either rely on good quality public transport information or stimulate its production, and TOPS already makes considerable use of personalised travel planning techniques.

Public transport information and marketing is also associated with travel awareness work. More information about Nottingham's city wide Big Wheel campaign is reported in Chapter 7, whilst in South Yorkshire, Travelwise was mentioned as generating a useful forum and network for discussing issues relating to public transport information and marketing. Chapter 7 also reports on a travel awareness experiment in Denmark (called 'BikeBus'ters) which involved joint promotion of cycling and public transport.

Car clubs often involve arrangements for members with public transport service providers, and encouraging people to perceive public transport services as good quality often plays an important role in persuading them to forego personal car ownership. Indeed, improving perceptions about public transport is an important element of any initiative which is potentially encouraging people to adopt a less car dependent lifestyle.

Finally, the bus company in Brighton pointed to the positive effect of city centre regeneration policies which had boosted bus travel into the centre. Conversely, TOPS has a specific remit to contribute to regeneration objectives.

6.13 Relationship between spending and impact for public transport information and marketing

The evidence provided for Brighton and Nottingham enabled some assessment of the relationship between spending on public transport information and marketing, and the impact on car use. In calculating this relationship, we have assumed that:

- Around half the increase in public transport patronage in Brighton and Nottingham is the result of promotion and marketing, with the remainder due to physical service improvements. This is inevitably a judgement (rather than a clear conclusion from research evidence). It is derived from an estimate made by the Brighton and Hove Buses interviewee, supported by evidence from Perth, Bristol and Buckinghamshire.
- Around 30% of new bus trips would otherwise have been made by car (and in line with average car occupancy levels, we assume 19% would formerly have been car driver trips and 11% car passenger trips).
- We assume an average car trip length of 13.9 kilometres to convert from car driver trips to car driver mileage (based on National Travel Survey data on the average length of car driver trips).
- In Nottingham, we take account of the change from long term decline in bus use prior to 2000 (about 1% a year) to year-on-year increases of about 1.8%, and infer

the local authority and bus company interventions are responsible for an increase in passenger journeys of about 2.8% in one year, or 2 million passenger journeys.

- We assume the behaviour change in the current year will be partly sustained in future years, decaying by 40% per year.
- We assume that investment in marketing and promotion by the bus company at least pays for itself in increased ticket revenue, which presumably provides their justification for spending it. Money spent by the bus company is therefore not taken into account in calculating net costs. (As discussed below, information from SYPTE provides some further evidence in support of this general assumption).
- The cost of achieving the increased patronage in the current year is taken as the total of revenue and capital in the current year only, with capital costs annualised at 3.5%. No account is taken of spending in previous years.

We were unable to draw any general conclusions about the cost-impact ratio of the TOPS service in South Yorkshire, as there has so far been only limited monitoring. However, there is evidence that TOPS almost pays for itself in terms of additional revenue generated from ticket sales. The SYPTE interviewee said that season ticket sales of at least £150,000 per annum could be directly attributed to TOPS. This is a conservative estimate, as it only includes sales through organisations that are agents or are receiving special discounts. It does not include tickets purchased independently by people who have received information from TOPS. Given that the overall cost of TOPS is some £176,000 per year, this means that the maximum net annual cost of the initiative is just £26,000, and, in reality, it is probably considerably less. Meanwhile, via this funding, TOPS has undertaken work with 225 organisations, including production of between 550 and 800 personalised journey plans per year.

Table 6.7 summarises our calculations of cost-impact ratios for marketing and promotion of city-wide services in Brighton and Nottingham.

These calculations suggest that the public sector costs for marketing of city-wide bus services are about 2 pence per car kilometre saved. As discussed earlier, this takes no account of bus company investment, on the assumption that this investment at least pays for itself in terms of increased ticket sales. In reality, it may more than pay for itself, generating additional revenue for the operating company, which could be balanced against the public sector investment to reduce the overall cost per car kilometre saved. Even without this effect, it appears that once a public transport service exists, additional money spent upon its promotion represents excellent value per car kilometre reduced.

Table 6.7: Calculation of cost-impact ratios for public transport information and marketing

	Brighton	Nottingham
Annual increase in bus passenger trips	1.45 million	2.0 million
Increase in bus passenger trips in current year attributed to soft factors	0.73 million	1.0 million
Reduction in car driver trips in current year*	139,000	190,000
Reduction in car driver distance in current year (km)~	1.93 million	2.64 million
Total car driver distance transferred to bus (kilometres)#	3.87 million	5.28 million
Local authority revenue spend in current year^	£60,000	£85,000
Local authority capital spend in current year^	Not relevant	£220,000
Total local authority spend in most recent year, with capital costs annualised +	£60,000	£92,700
Cost per car kilometre saved (pence)**	1.6	1.8

* Reduction in car driver trips in current year = 0.19 x (increase in bus passenger trips in current year attributed to soft factors)
~ Reduction in car driver distance in current year = (reduction in car driver trips in current year) x (average mileage of a car trip). Average mileage of a car trip is 13.9 km (derived from NTS 1999/01)
# Total car driver distance transferred to bus is calculated by assuming that a proportion of new bus passengers in the current year will continue to use the bus in future years, with a decay rate of 40% per year.
+ Capital costs are annualised at 3.5%.
^ Costs are taken from table 6.3.

6.14 Future impact of public transport information and marketing

Interviewees in Nottingham and Brighton felt that it would be possible to sustain current levels of public transport patronage growth, although in Brighton there was an awareness that sooner or later the existing market might be saturated, and further growth would depend on aiming at new markets. They identified commuter travel as one such market. Interviewees also felt that higher growth rates would be difficult to achieve, and that increasing current spending on marketing and information would not necessarily be the top priority to generate the desired growth. Current levels of spending in these areas were felt to be about right.

The one exception to this was that interviewees in both cities felt that real-time information (at roadside information points, on the web, and to support electronic personalised journey planning) would be an important tool to help penetrate new markets. One of the Brighton interviewees commented that the next group they aim to target is 'wedded to the internet' and not the sort of people who would pick up a copy of Bus Times.

The main constraints on further public transport growth were felt to be congestion on the existing road network (which could be tackled through better enforcement of bus lanes, and congestion charging); gaps in the public transport network (which require investment in extra services); and difficulties with staff recruitment due to poor pay and conditions.

Although the Brighton and Nottingham interviewees all felt that their current spending on information and marketing was about right, the bus company interviewee in Brighton commented that elsewhere in the country some bus companies are spending very little on marketing, and that they had the potential to achieve a significant increase in patronage through investing in this field.

The Brighton interviewee also felt that it would be possible to make a substantially greater difference using very intensive, personal and individualised marketing, but that this would involve highly unrealistic levels of budgeting and staffing. Interestingly, in this 'fantasy' scenario, he felt that there would still be a subsection of society who would not be interested in public transport, but this would only be about 10-20% of the total population.

In South Yorkshire, the TOPS scheme was expected to remain at about the same level of staffing and resources, although there was some uncertainty about this because of the withdrawal of DfT bursary funding coupled with internal budgetary pressures. If resources were not a constraint, the interviewee judged that the main limit on future impact would be the level of interest from client organisations. Small and medium organisations were felt to be difficult to reach. However, if additional resources could be dedicated to working with specific target sectors (such as hospitals, universities and job centres), it was felt that a doubling of resources would enable TOPS to easily more than double ticket sales, but that increasing staffing and budgets above this level would not be worthwhile. In other words, the interviewee felt that there is the potential for TOPS to achieve rather more than double its current impact. In the short term, one TOPS target is to increase by the number of client organisations using any of the products on offer by 20 per year.

6.15 Key issues for scaling up public transport information and marketing

Most of the obstacles to increasing public transport patronage in future were felt to relate to difficulties providing a good service that was worth marketing, rather than to the marketing and information process itself.

- **Staff recruitment and retention**
Bus company interviewees in Nottingham and Brighton both mentioned their difficulties recruiting and retaining drivers. One commented that the shortage of drivers is related partly to the low status of the job, and also to the fact that people can obtain comparable wages in jobs where they are less exposed to the perceived dangers and anti-social behaviour encountered by bus drivers.

- **Revenue support for public transport services**
One of the Brighton interviewees commented that 'the best way to promote public transport is for there to be more of it'. Local authorities' revenue budgets for supporting bus services were felt to be inadequate.

- **Tackling congestion**
Bus operators said that local authorities had to be prepared to take tough action in installing bus priority at pinch points. Powers for more effective bus lane enforcement

were needed. Nationally, interviewees felt stronger government support for congestion charging would be helpful.

- **Better co-ordination**

The SYPTE interviewee said that the PTE's lack of control over bus operators' was a difficulty, as frequent timetable and service changes made information provision problematic. He felt legislative change was needed to enable the provision of 'sensible' ticketing arrangements. In South Yorkshire, the lack of a zonal ticketing system was also seen as an obstacle to marketing efforts.

- **Relative cost of motoring and public transport**

The Brighton interviewee suggested that there were problems with public misperceptions about the relative cost of travel by car and public transport. Real-terms increases in fares in recent years, coupled with the fall in the real cost of motoring, had made this even more of a problem, and the interviewee thought that government action was necessary to address the growing disparity.

- **Lack of incentive for employers to become involved**

The Brighton interviewee suggested that tax changes to encourage local employers to take more responsibility to promote transport efficiency would be helpful. In South Yorkshire, the interviewee commented that it was frustrating that the planning process tended to concentrate on the development of travel plans, with little monitoring of outcomes, or enforcement of implementation.

6.16 Policy implications relating to public transport information and marketing

- Increased revenue support for bus services is likely to be a necessary condition for the growth in bus patronage, both to meet the rising cost of attracting enough staff, and to enable provision of more, and more frequent, services.
- If traffic congestion increases, it will be difficult to deliver better bus reliability. Local action (re-allocating road capacity, and restraining parking) and national action (in support of congestion charging and other restraint mechanisms, including fuel duty) could therefore be important if the potential increase in bus patronage is to be achieved.
- The lack of directive powers for local authorities and PTEs to set the framework for the services to be provided by public transport operators (for example, defining a zonal ticketing system) can be an obstacle to the creation of good public transport services, and associated information and marketing activities.
- OFT constraints are sometimes perceived to inhibit cooperative arrangements on joint information, ticketing and timetabling arrangements between operators. National clarification that this is encouraged could be helpful.
- Notwithstanding the constraints on providing a public transport network that is worth marketing, there are likely to be many places where better promotion could lead to patronage growth on existing services.

6.17 Acknowledgements

We would like to thank the following people for their help with the public transport information and marketing case studies:

Individual	Organisation
Paul Crowther	Brighton and Hove City Council
Roger French	Brighton and Hove Buses
Andy Gibbons	Nottingham City Council
Nicola Tidy	Nottingham City Transport
Lynn Hanna	Nottingham Development Enterprise
John Ansari	South Yorkshire PTE

In addition to the main case study interviewees, we would like to thank:

Individual	Organisation
Stefan Dimic	Buckinghamshire County Council
Elaine Rosscraig	Stagecoach
Steve Loveridge	Stagecoach
Chris Shaw	Consultant
Pete Davis	Bristol City Council
Tim Hapgood	Bristol City Council
James Ryle	Sustrans
Helen Lea	Transport for London Surface Transport

6.18 References

Balcombe R (ed) et al (2004) *The demand for public transport: a practical guide.* TRL report 593, Crowthorne.

Confederation of Passenger Transport (2002) *Better buses: a manifesto* CPT, London.

Crampin J (1998) *HA and Railtrack seeking mutual benefits through co-operation.* Local Transport Today 5/11/98 pp10-11

Dargay JM & Hanly M (1999) *Bus fare elasticities.* Report to the Department of the Environment, Transport and the Regions

Daugherty GG, Balcombe RJ and Astrop AJ (1999) *A comparative assessment of major bus priority schemes in Great Britain.* Transport Research Laboratory Report 409

Davies D & Gardner D (2000) *Providing for journeys on foot.* IHT, London.

Fitzroy F and Smith I (1994) The demand for public transport: some estimates from Zurich *International Journal of Transport Economics* 21(2) 197-207

FitzRoy F and Smith I (1998) Public transport demand in Freiburg: why did patronage double in a decade? *Transport Policy* 5(3) 163-173

Gilbert CL and Jalilian H (1991) *The demand for travel and for travelcards on London Regional Transport.* Journal of Transport Economics and Policy, 25 (1), pp3-29

Lea H (2004) Personal communication with Helen Lea, Transport for London Surface Transport.

LEK / Commission for Integrated Transport (2002) *Obtaining best value for public subsidy for the bus industry*

Mackie PJ, Bristow AL, Shires J, Whelan G, Preston J and Huang B (2002) *Achieving best value for public support of the bus industry Part 1: Summary report on the modelling and assessment of seven corridors*, in LEK / Commission for Integrated Transport (2002) Obtaining best value for public subsidy for the bus industry

Meades P (2002). Personal communication with Anglia Railways.

Rosscraig E (2004) Personal communication with Elaine Rosscraig, Stagecoach.

Shaw C (2004) Personal communication with Chris Shaw, consultant and agent to Hampshire County Council.

Sloman L (2003) *Less Traffic where people live: how local transport schemes can help cut traffic.* Report supported by the Royal Commission for the Exhibition of 1851, Transport for Quality of Life and Transport 2000, London.

Stagecoach (2002) *Kickstart: better value, better bus services* Stagecoach Group Ltd, Perth.

TAS Partnership (2001) *Quality Bus Partnerships Good Practice Guide,* TAS Partnership, Preston.

TAS Partnership (2002) *Monitoring quality bus partnerships volume 1: the evidence.* TAS Partnership, Preston.

Transport 2000 (2001) *Tourism without traffic: a good practice guide.* Transport 2000 Trust, London.

7. Travel awareness campaigns

7.1 Introduction

Travel awareness campaigns, such as 'Travelwise' and 'In Town Without My Car', use a wide range of media aimed at improving general public understanding of problems resulting from transport choices, and what can be done to solve these problems including changing their own behaviour. The campaigns stem from experience of much bigger and longer established use of campaigns applied to road safety (notably drink-driving and seat belts); other social problems such as smoking, drinking, suicide, domestic violence and security; and positive issues such as literacy, health and citizenship. Those involved in travel awareness campaigns frequently refer to the need to counter the effects of even bigger commercial advertising campaigns, especially by car manufacturers, which are aimed primarily at selling cars, but which can also often encourage their wider use.

As well as focusing on local environmental and health impacts, travel awareness campaigns also aim to improve informed knowledge of the facilities available for walking, cycling and public transport use. Where this information is expressed at a rather general level it is usually described as a travel awareness campaign, and where it is aimed at specific local conditions and individual journeys it is closer to personalised travel planning, as discussed in chapter 5, but there is no sharp dividing line between them. Similarly, there can be considerable overlap between travel awareness campaigns and public transport marketing as discussed in chapter 6.

The instruments used in travel awareness campaigns include posters, leaflets, advertising on press, local radio and television, high profile events aimed to focus attention ('carrots, sticks *and tambourines'*), activities in schools and neighbourhoods, provision of factual information on websites or at local travel centres, and interactive experiments encouraging self-monitoring and awareness.

There has been much discussion on whether travel awareness campaigns have a life and independent role of their own, or are best thought of as an attachment to other initiatives which make improvements to travel services. Their independent role is justified by psychological theories that better awareness of the alternatives is a precursor to changing behaviour; by empirical studies showing that people often do not have full and objective information or understanding of transport choices; and also by an expectation that if the public had better understanding, people would more easily support local authorities who are pursuing policies such as reducing car use. On the other hand, their role as an attachment to other policies is emphasised by the argument that it is unrealistic to expect people to change their behaviour unless better alternatives are open to them: in this case the tangible effects expected are that a campaign may accelerate and maximise the response to these other changes.

It is much more common for the 'success' of travel awareness campaigns to be monitored using indicators drawn from commercial market research, such as how many people have noticed the campaign, and what they remember from it, than to attempt to measure specific changes in travel behaviour, which are difficult to isolate.

This chapter reviews the available evidence about travel awareness work, including literature evidence from the UK and overseas. Later sections of the chapter draw on detailed interviews in York – our chosen case study for this topic.

7.2 Overview of the literature

There is an extensive literature on the impacts of campaigns such as voting patterns in the USA, health promotion, etc, and some examples of evidence that these have affected behaviour even without changes in other underlying conditions (eg Etzersdorfer & Sonneck (1998) report substantial effects on suicide rates in Austria following a change in the way suicides were reported in the media).

Fergusson et al (1999) drew on lessons from the health promotion sector and the transport literature to conclude that there was a substantial potential to achieve change by this means. In particular, they highlighted a report undertaken the RAC (Goodwin et al 1995), which suggested that around 20% of car trips are not car-dependent, in the sense that the trips were either very marginal, or could easily be undertaken by other means. This work also suggested that perhaps another 20% were only weakly car-dependent, and could be attracted by improvements in other modes or alternatives. They also highlighted the suggestion by Cairns et al (1998) that the appearance of relatively stable traffic patterns at aggregate level may conceal very considerable variation in individual choices, and that this dynamism in individual behaviour means that changing people's travel behaviour may not be as intractable as is traditionally perceived.

There have recently been a number of European projects, investigating travel awareness theory and practice, notably including INPHORMM (Hamer, 1997-1999), CAMPARIE (Papaioannou, 1997-1999) and TAPESTRY (2000-2003). PORTAL (Pressl and Reiter, 2003) summarised and reviewed these and other related EU projects together with a helpful key to their acronyms or purpose[1].

Many of these projects have overlapping membership and results, and have used websites as their main dissemination medium, actively updating reports while the project is 'live' but then tending to fall into disuse. This is unsurprising, given that they are purely funded by EU project funds, which have a finite life, and has led to more recent projects (such as TAPESTRY) choosing to produce a CD ROM of results. The EU projects tend to be very much stronger on the elaboration of general frameworks and generic advice than detailed quantitative results of local research. Pressl and Reiter (2003) summarise the summaries, the key concept being that travel awareness activities, like other soft policies, can be used together with hard policies

---

[1] CAMPARIE (Campaigns for Awareness using Media and Publicity to assess the responses of individuals); COSMOS (Development of a Training Course for Mobility Consultants); EDITION, a learning CD-Rom for children; ELMO a legal frame for company mobility plans; ICARO (Increase of Car Occupancy through innovative measures and technical instruments); IMPACT (Information packages for energy-efficient mobility); INPHORMM (Information and publicity helping the objective of reducing motorised mobility); MOBILE a demonstration project; MOMENTUM (Mobility management for the urban environment); MOSAIC linked with Momentum; MOST (Mobility Management Strategies for the Next Decades); PROSITrans (Products and Services to increase the use of the sustainable transport modes in irregular transport flows); TAPESTRY (Travel Awareness Publicity And Education Supporting A Sustainable Transport Strategy In Europe); TOMY a computer based tool for mobility advisers; TOOLBOX (Toolbox for Mobility Management in companies).

like infrastructure investment in order to 'maximise the benefits of investment'. However, Tyler (2004) reports that whether campaigns simply support or maximise the benefits of investment in other (hard) areas, or whether they can work in their own right to influence travel behaviour, is a hotly debated topic amongst experts in the field, with a number of subscribers to the latter view.

TAPESTRY (2003 a, b, c) reviewed the results of the earlier EU projects and collated 18 local research project reports from across Europe[2]. It also focused on models of change in travel behaviour, and guidelines for setting up and monitoring the effects of communication programmes. It found most useful a model of behaviour change developed as part of the INPHORMM project, in which five stages were identified, namely Awareness, Acceptance, Attitudes, Action and Assimilation, though these stages were 'not necessarily linear as people can move back and forth between the various model stages'. (INPHORMM's model was, in turn, based on the 'Transtheoretical model of behavioural change', which Ferguson et al (1999) also identified as the most useful pyschological model of behavioural change, most commonly used in the health promotion sector). TAPESTRY drew on elements of this, and other models, to develop and test a new model, the 'Seven Stage Model of Change'. This is now being used by both members of the TAPESTRY consortium, and others, to plan and assess campaigns, (Tyler 2004).

In general, all of the European work on travel awareness campaigns highlights the importance of identifying a target audience, and that people with different existing travel habits may be motivated to adopt or continue more sustainable travel behaviour by different messages. The INPHORMM project also concluded that positive messages were more likely to be motivating than negative or 'guilt-inspiring' messages, and many travel awareness campaigns are now specifically focusing on the positive health benefits that can result from walking and cycling. TAPESTRY further highlighted that behaviour change is usually a long term process, such that campaigns should not be seen as 'quick fix' solutions, but can help to provide the changes in attitudes and perceptions which may be an essential precursor to alterations in actual travel behaviour.

7.3 Insights from transport campaigns on road safety

The longest standing experience of campaigns in the field of transport has related to road safety. DETR (1998) describes a sequence of four media campaigns that were run between 1995 and 1998 aimed at improving children's safety. These were:
- 'Wonderful Cross', a 30 second TV commercial shown in March 1995 and January/February 1996 costing £500,000. This was aimed at 7-12-year-olds, particularly boys, to highlight the dangers of playing in or around roads. Spontaneous awareness amongst the target audience was 55%, whilst prompted awareness was 76%.
- 'Peter Pan' and 'Doctor', two radio commercials which ran in March 1996 at a cost of £300,000. These were aimed primarily at parent drivers and children (7-10) and

---

[2] Although many of these local project reports did provide some quantitative evidence about the impacts of travel awareness style projects, the majority are not reviewed here, since, for this project, many of these initiatives would more naturally be considered in other chapters, since they involved work in schools, workplaces and/or individualised travel planning initiatives.

teenagers (11-14) as a secondary audience. They were designed to reinforce the importance of wearing rear seat belts.

- 'Hedgehogs', a TV commercial run in January/February 1997 at a cost of £500,000. This commercial aimed at 8-11-year-olds and encouraged safer road crossing. In post campaign research, the campaign was spontaneously recalled by 71% of 7-14 year olds.
- 'King of the Road', a 40 second TV commercial run in January 1998 at a cost of £600,000. This advert basically aimed to reinforce the previous hedgehogs advert and was also run in cinemas and on a selection of children's video rental releases.

These adverts were generally evaluated in terms of recall amongst target groups, but not in terms of behaviour change.

The most significant example of a case where impact has been measured in relation to targeted behaviour is probably the work done on drink driving (DETR, 1997 and Masurel 2003). There is widespread acceptance that public attitudes towards drink driving have changed, partly as a response to extensive media work. A widely noted sign of this is that the offer 'one for the road', once seen as a symbol of hospitality, has nearly disappeared. However, at the same time, there has been a substantial increase in breath testing and associated police work discouraging drink-driving.

A brief description of the work illustrates the difficulties of assessing the effects of awareness raising work. Breath testing and the (anti) Drink Drive campaign were both introduced in 1967, following drink-drive legislation, and the percentage of accidents where drink was a factor reduced from 25% to 15%. However, the level of publicity was not maintained, and the percentage of drink-related accidents increased back to 35% by 1975. It is not clear what happened in terms of breath testing over this period. Drink Drive advertising recommenced in the run up to Christmas 1976, and continued as an annual campaign from then on. From 1976-1987, campaigns focused on the tragic consequences, and also the personal inconvenience of getting caught (including the probability of being caught, the inconvenience of not owning a license and the difficulties of obtaining insurance after a conviction). In addition, work in the early 1980s focused on educating people about the alcohol content of drinks, as this was identified as something people were not aware of. From 1987 to 1996, the campaign focused around the slogan 'drinking and driving wrecks lives', and from 1992, the Christmas campaigns were supplemented with a summertime campaign. The 1997 campaign altered to the slogan 'have none for the road', to try and encourage recognition that drink can be dangerous even if someone is not drunk.

In terms of effects, between 1979 and 1991, the proportion of drink-related accidents reduced from 32% to 19%, and the absolute numbers fell from 19,470 to 11,690. Since then, there has not been a clear decline, although there has been some fluctuation around that level. Figure 7.1 shows the trends in drink-drive related deaths, and associated changes in breath testing.

Assessing the significance of the awareness raising work (in isolation) is difficult. Clearly, the biggest changes were achieved in the 1980s, via both awareness raising and police reinforcement. Arguably, this work was particularly effective since it was a period of altering people's *knowledge* about the effects of drinking on driving capability and the consequences (both in terms of personal inconvenience and injury to selves and others). Since then, it is often argued that people are familiar with these arguments and that the remaining drink-driving accidents represent a 'hard-core' of drivers, who are aware of these messages but remain unaffected. However, hypothetically at least, it can be argued that there might be an alternative focus for the campaigns that could impact further.

Figure 7.1 Changes in drink-drive deaths, and breath testing

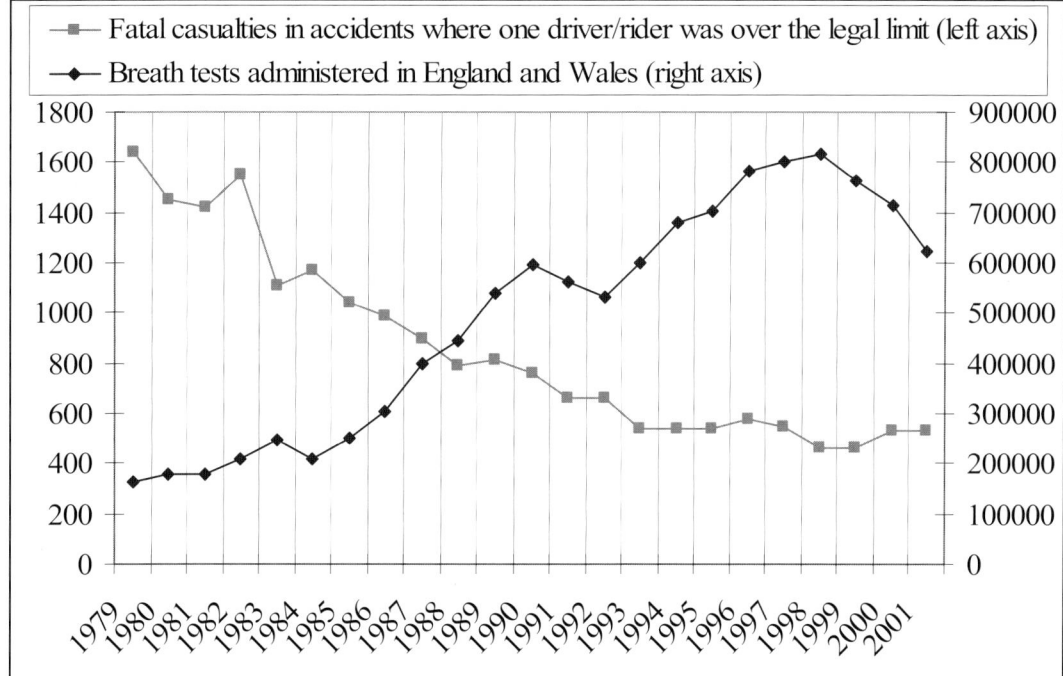

Source: Data used from the Home Office annual statistical bulletins on 'Offences relating to motor vehicles in England & Wales' and 'Statistics of breath tests in England and Wales', and from Masurel (c. 2003)

7.4 UK national campaigns aiming to affect car use

Early work on travel awareness in the UK was pioneered in the early 1990s by Hampshire, with its 'Headstart' campaign, and Hertfordshire, with its 'TravelWise' campaign. Subsequently, the National TravelWise® Association (NTWA), has evolved as a partnership of local authorities and other organisations working together to promote sustainable transport, who share resources including travel awareness campaign materials, and who use 'TravelWise' as a common brand. In 2002, membership included over 120 local authorities, health authorities and/or passenger transport executives (Sykes, 2002).

In 1998, the DfT launched a national campaign entitled 'Are you doing your bit?', (DEFRA, c.1999). This was intended to encourage small but important behavioural changes in everyday actions to benefit the local and global environment. The first year of activity focused on energy saving, transport and air quality issues, and achieved measurable consumer recognition on a budget of £2 million, using national women's press and consumer interest magazines. In 1999/2000, the campaign focused on TV, using well-known celebrities carrying out small, environmentally-friendly actions in slightly incongruous situations. The TV campaigns were also reinforced with a smaller range of radio commercials.

In addition to this generic campaign, there have also been a number of national travel awareness campaigns aimed at specific aspects of travel.

In Town Without My Car

This campaign, often labelled with an exclamation mark 'In Town, Without My Car!' (ITWMC), is based on the concept of closing town centre streets to cars and other traffic in order for people to enjoy walking, cycling, street theatre, live music, dancing, public art and children's play areas. Early events date back to the mid 1990s, and include a street party event in Bath (UK) and an 'en ville sans ma voiture' day in La Rochelle (France). In 1998, France were the first to have an official national ITWMC day. The event expanded across most countries in the European Union by 2000, and in 2001/02, it spread further, across most of Eastern Europe and beyond. ITWMC now forms part of European Mobility Week. In 2002, 1400 towns and cities participated from 38 countries. There were 43 events in the UK, which was twice as many as in 2001. In 2003, according to the website of the European co-ordinating centre, Energie-Cites (2004), the campaign affected over 111 million inhabitants in 1035 participating cities and 428 supporting cities. In the UK, the event is now supported by the Department for Transport, having previously been promoted by the Environmental Transport Association, (Department for Transport, 7/11/03; Tyler 2004).

Bike Week

Bike Week was started by the Cyclists Touring Club in 1923. In the past three years, it has been developed to appeal to all cycle owners rather than just cycling enthusiasts. From 14-22 June 2003, 1,220 local cycling events and rides were promoted, involving an estimated 116,385 participants. In response to a request from the Department of Transport, 94% of events were promoted to 'new or occasional' cyclists. Consequently, two-thirds of participants were not members of any cycling organisation, club, campaigning group or Sustrans. The biggest registered event was the York Cycle Show, a two-day event attracting more than 10,000 visitors. The most popular type of event to promote was 'Bike2Work' which was promoted by more than 90 employers and workplace bicycle user groups. No data are available about the costs. Bike Week 2004 is planned to be a bigger event, including free cycle safety checks to an estimated 10 million 'lapsed' cyclists, and group members are seeking a total funding of £100,000. The cycle industry has already announced £25,000 funding, and a further £75,000 is being sought from government, (Harvey, 2003).

Walk to school week

Walk to School events began to take place nationally in the UK in 1994. Starting as 'walk to school day', the campaign extended to become 'walk to school week', which took place in May. The campaign has now extended to constitute two weeks, one in May and one in October. Other countries also launched walking campaigns, including the USA in 1997, Canada in 1998 and Ireland in 1999. In 2000, these countries made formal links to launch a fully co-ordinated international effort. October 2003 saw the first international walk to school week. In May 2003, more than 2 million children and their carers were estimated to take part in the UK walk to school week. In October 2003, it was expected that more than 3 million pupils would be walking to school as part of events, from 30 different countries ranging from Argentina to Zambia, (Living Streets 2003).

7.5 UK local campaigns aiming to affect car use

At local authority level, there has been a pattern for general travel awareness campaigns to evolve into more targeted initiatives. This section summarises experience from six areas, namely Hampshire, Hertfordshire, Cambridgshire, Chelmsford, Glasgow, and Nottingham. (The Chelmsford experience is also discussed in Chapter 6). The following sections report on our main case study on travel awareness, York.

Hertfordshire – Travelwise

Sykes (2002) describes the development of Travelwise in Hertfordshire, from 'raising awareness through mass media campaign' to 'a more central strategy to support sustainable transport policy'. He also describes a number of ways in which the work had become more targeted by 2002. These included:

- *Walk to school week:* The number of schools participating had increased from 130 in 1994 to 201 in 2001, with a much larger increase in the number of pupils participating, from 18,000 to 52,330
- *Theatre in education programmes:* since 1997, a Travelwise theatre production had visited over 70 secondary schools, involving over 3000 students. From 2001, a new play for primary schools about Travelwise and road safety was being launched, with plans to visit 30 schools in 2002.
- *Curriculum support materials:* by 2002, 260 (Key Stage 1/2) and 100 (Key Stage 3/4) transport packs and 200 literacy packs had been distributed to schools within the authority
- *Community work:* over time, advertising had become more targeted (based on research about effectiveness) leading to targeted, selective use of bus backs, posters, press releases, newsletters, web sites, promotional events and exhibitions.
- *Involvement in regional and national events:* the council was involved in Green Transport Week, Bike Week, Car Free Day, Festival of Cycling and the DTLR "Are you doing your bit?" Roadshow. Hertfordshire County Council designed and developed the sustainability roadshow which subsequently secured DTLR sponsorship to become the national roadshow. The council also provides annual grants of £100 for local groups to promote cycling alongside business and County Hall events that promote Bike 2 Work Day.
- *Promotion work to accompany other transport initiatives:* the Travelwise messages have been promoted alongside the implementation of transport schemes and through publications such as bus timetables.

As part of the Travelwise programme, Sykes also reported on the work of the council on school and workplace travel plans, including the development of a Business Travelwise partnership.

In terms of staffing and resources, in 2001/02, the Travelwise officer time to support the programme was described as a workload equivalent to one full-time member of staff split across three officers. In addition, a full-time post to develop school travel plans was in place. The Travelwise budget was £70,000, with the expectation of spending £25,000 on education, £25,000 on business and £20,000 on community initiatives. The campaigns took place throughout Hertfordshire, which has approximately 420,000 households and 805,000 residents.

Over time, the proportion of people saying that they had heard of the Travelwise campaign increased from 9% in 1994 to 17% in 2000. Initially, respondents were mainly aware that the campaign promoted public transport. Over time, people have become aware that it is associated with a wider range of messages, including the promotion of modal shift, public transport, discounted travel and park and ride.

Hertfordshire's walk to school week

Hertfordshire have been involved in the TAPESTRY EU project, which included an assessment of their Walk to School week campaign, as carried out in May 2002 (Tapestry 2003)[3]. This campaign cost £14,800, and, together with countywide advertising, it was delivered into 147 separate schools reaching almost 60,000 schoolchildren and their parents. Evaluation was conducted at 11 schools which received the campaign and two control schools. The schools receiving the campaign this year had also done so last year, whilst the control schools had never participated in Walk to School week. Analysis was conducted via a before and after survey. In total, about 1000 completed surveys were received from campaign schools, with a further 200 from control schools.

The evaluation survey adopted a seven stage model of behaviour change. It found that the campaign made little difference to people's awareness of traffic problems or their sense of responsibility for them, which is probably because high levels of awareness had already been achieved. However, it did have some impact on how they perceived and evaluated different options, and whether they were prepared to increase the amount that they walked. Specific results were as follows:

- Respondents were asked whether they agreed with 11 positive statements about walking. The percentage agreeing or strongly agreeing with 10 of those statements increased in the campaign schools after Walk to School week.
- Respondents were asked whether they agreed with 11 positive statements about car use. The percentage of respondents at campaign schools agreeing or strongly agreeing decreased for seven statements after Walk to School week (whilst this was the case for only three of the statements at the control schools). In particular, the percentage agreeing or strongly agreeing that the car doesn't cost much declined from 21% to 16% in the campaign schools after Walk to School week.
- The proportion of parents in campaign schools strongly agreeing that "I intend for my child to walk to school for his/her next journey" rose from 48% to 54% (with growth from 64% to 66% in the proportion agreeing or strongly agreeing overall). A similar growth was seen in control schools.
- There was a small (1.3%) increase in the proportion of children walking to school at least once a week in the campaign schools compared with a small (1.3%) decline in the proportion at control schools.
- Before Walk to School week took place, respondents were asked how often their child walked to school compared with the same time the previous year. At campaign schools, 15% of respondents said their child walked more often now, and 10% of respondents said the same at control schools. After Walk to School week, these percentages rose slightly (by about 1%-point in both cases).

In general, these results suggest Walk to School week is having a positive effect, and that schools which receive the campaign receive more of the benefits. Some of the

---

[3] A brief summary of this work is also given in Chapter 4.

parallel changes that occurred at the control schools suggest that it may also be having a knock-on effect in schools which do not participate directly. Hertfordshire County Council now intends to extend the advertising and marketing work associated with walk to school week, to become a year round campaign, targeting it at the types of parents who seemed most receptive to the messages.

Hampshire's promotion of rural buses

Hampshire's involvement in the TAPESTRY project involved an interactive marketing experiment in ten satellite villages in East Hampshire (TAPESTRY 2003), where residents were involved in the development and promotion of public transport marketing materials. All ten villages received at least one bus service per week, however the area is typified by small populations, high car ownership and use, and a decline in local rural services. During the project, before and after questionnaires were conducted with approximately 40 stakeholders (42 in the before survey and 36 in the after survey) and about 1000 residents (1115 in the before survey and 956 in the after survey). Some beneficial effects were seen, despite the fact that the private bus operator cut services during the work. Specifically:

- After the project, there were increases in the proportion of stakeholders considering that the bus routes were good (25% increasing to 44%), the proportion considering that stops were conveniently located (55% rising to 72%) and the proportion considering the provision of bus information to be good (45% rising to 56%).

- After the project, there were increases in the proportion of residents considering the bus services to be enjoyable (increasing from 19% to 22%), cheap (increasing from 6% to 11%), reliable (increasing from 8% to 11%) and 'a means of travel with a good image' (increasing from 8% to 12%).

- The number of people who said that they travelled frequently by car reduced from 87% to 85%.

- More residents said that they had started travelling by bus. (This is according to the executive summary – it was not apparent from the evaluation report).

Cambridgeshire's walk to school week

Cambridgeshire has carried out an evaluation of its walk to school week campaigns in 2002[4], (Cambridgeshire County Council, 2002a and 2002b). Pupils were asked to record how they travelled to school each day for a period of 9 days – 2 days in a week that was two weeks before walk to school week, the five days of walk to school week, and 2 days in a week a few weeks after walk to school week. Data were only analysed for pupils who completed records for all 9 days.

May 2002 walk to school week involved 67 schools and 14,200 pupils. 500 classroom packs were distributed. 3074 pupils provided completed records that could be analysed. These showed that car use fell by 27% during walk to school week, and remained 11% lower three weeks later.

October 2002 walk to school week involved 33 schools and 7000 children. 250 classroom resource packs were distributed. 2,222 pupils provided completed records that could be analysed. These showed that car use was 22% lower during walk to school week and remained 2% lower a fortnight later.

---

[4] This has also been briefly discussed in Chapter 4.

Chelmsford - promotion of rail services by the Highways Agency and rail operator

Crampin (1998) reports on an awareness campaign launched jointly between the Highways Agency and operator Great Eastern Railways in June 1998. This was aimed at persuading people to use the train rather than the car for trips along the A12 corridor near Chelmsford. The campaign coincided with the introduction of an improved rail timetable. Posters and leaflets were distributed, an ad-van (moving billboard) was driven around the town, and local radio, newspaper and bus side advertisement were also used. Posters included the words: "over 1 hour by car, only 35 mins by train, what's stopping you!". They also carried the logos of both the Highways Agency and First Great Eastern. An evaluation of the campaign by Oscar Faber showed the following:

- Awareness of Great Eastern services amongst non-users increased by 11%, and 40% of those surveyed recalled the advertisement used in the campaign.
- Business at Chelmsford Station increased by 12%, there was a 17% increase in the number of standard return ticket sales, and weekly season ticket sales were up by 31% compared to August 1997.

Assessment of the campaign also suggested there were perceived to be three major positive elements - the campaign was perceived as conveying a strong environmental message; Great Eastern was perceived to be working hard on improving services; and the partnership with the Highways Agency was regarded as positive. (This campaign is also discussed in Chapter 6).

Glasgow - Walk in to work out

Mutrie et al (1999) report on the initial evaluation of the 'Walk in to work out' education campaign. 295 employees from 3 Glasgow workplaces who were thinking about walking or cycling to work (i.e. 'actively' commuting) were randomly assigned to an intervention group (145 people) or control group (150 people). Both groups completed questionnaires about physical activity, motivations and perceptions of health at the start of the project, after six months and after 12 months. The intervention group received an education pack immediately after the start of the project whilst the control group received their pack six months later. The intervention pack was based on the 'Transtheoretical model' of behavioural change, aimed at 'contemplators' (those thinking about actively commuting) and 'preparers' (those already doing some irregular active commuting). The cost of full design, development, pre-testing and printing of the pack for use in the study was £13,000. The results were as follows:

- a significantly larger percentage of the intervention group (49%) progressed to a higher stage of 'active commuting' behaviour than the control group (31%) after six months
- six months after the start of the project, for those who were not previously walking to work, members of the intervention group were typically spending 125 minutes per week walking to work compared to 65 minutes for members of the control group. In other words, after six months, the intervention group were nearly twice as likely to increase walking to work as the control group
- the intervention was not successful in increasing cycling to and from work
- there were no seasonal, gender or age influences on the probability that a person increasing their walking to work
- after six months, individuals in the intervention group improved their mental and physical health functioning scores significantly more than individuals in the

control group. In particular, their scores were statistically better in relation to general health, vitality and mental health.

- 12 months after receiving their intervention pack, 25% (n=36) of the intervention group were still regularly actively commuting to work

The researchers highlight that the intervention compares well with other interventions, for example, quoting a study on smoking where only 2% of smokers both successfully quit and had not relapsed one year after receiving personal advice on how to stop.

Nottingham – Big Wheel

Nottingham was chosen as a case study area for examining experience of public transport information and marketing (as discussed in chapter 6). In the process of conducting the interview, we also obtained information about their experience of more general travel awareness campaigning. A campaign called 'The Big Wheel', managed by the Nottingham Development Enterprise, was set up for three years to Oct 2004, and will probably be extended. Its aim has been to articulate a transport vision for the city and to raise awareness of the measures contained in the Local Transport Plan (LTP). It has been aimed at both the general public and the business community, partly to encourage confidence within the business community that some of the radical transport policy developments occurring in the city are part of a coherent, long term vision. There are approximately 650,000 residents in the LTP area covered by the campaign.

The first phase of the project involved awareness raising via general promotional products. Later phases have included the production of factual information, and establishment of a Big Wheel brand. This brand is used on timetables, area travel guides, school travel plan packs, workplace travel plan information, brochures, posters, postcards, etc.. The brand uses a bright, technicolour style with straightforward imagery of the various elements in the city's transport network. For the business sector, a more sober sub-brand has been developed. This sub-brand is used on a specially developed business magazine called 'Freewheel', and on inserts that are placed in the business pages of the local press.

Specific versions of the public campaign have used themes such as:
- A radical change in transport that people can join– 'Join The Revolution'
- The vital impact of your mode of transport on personal health - 'Better for Everybody'
- Air quality, pollution and the environment – 'Can you do without it for a day?'
- Bus travel is a better option to car travel during the congested festive season - the 'Christmas Carol' campaign

Associated promotions have included sponsored discounted bus travel, and cut price admission to local attractions at times that should help to ease rush hour congestion, ('twilight leisure offers'). Nottingham City Transport have worked closely with the Big Wheel.

The Big Wheel involves a core staff of 2 full-time people. Between October 2001 and March 2004, it received a total of £629,623 (including funds allocated to it for this period at the time of the interview in July 2003). This equates to approximately £250,000 per year.

Early in 2003, the Big Wheel carried out a 'familiarity study' with 1200 residents and a random sample of 299 businesses. The results were compared with a similar survey in 2001 to assess the success of the campaign, (TTR, 2003). Changes noted were as follows:

- In 2003, businesses were implementing more environmental measures (such as staff travel plans and using public transport for business travel).
- Since 2001, members of the public have become much more aware of the LTP – a 27% increase, but business awareness appears not to have changed.
- Members of the public were much more aware of the Big Wheel campaign than businesses. 67% of City of Nottingham residents and 52% of residents in a wide travel-to-work area, including Hucknall and Long Eaton, were aware of the Big Wheel. This was only 6 months after its launch.
- In 2003, most businesses and members of the public found out about the Big Wheel in the local newspaper. This was the same for familiarisation with the LTP in 2001.
- Most members of the public interpreted the Big Wheel pictures as encouraging them to walk or use public transport more.

The City judges that the promotional work has eased the path of the construction phase of the tram and the workplace parking levy, and has helped to promote the overall vision of integrated transport.

7.6 Additional overseas evidence

In addition to national work, we were expecting a considerable amount of evidence from international experience. As discussed in section 7.2, although there has been a considerable amount of European work on the topic, travel awareness work with monitoring of changes in travel behaviour is rare. The following section provides some insights from travel awareness work which has involved relatively interactive and intensive campaigning. Both examples go further than the more conventional travel awareness work, and it is interesting that both are reporting some impressive results.

7.6.1 Education work with young adults

Cairns & Okamura (2003) undertook a travel awareness experiment, investigating the effects of educating 17-18-year-old students about the costs of different transport options, to see what effect this had on their attitudes about the desirability of car ownership and use, and whether it could increase the attractiveness of alternative modes of travel, safer driving and smaller, more environmentally friendly cars. An experiment was undertaken, comparing the responses of 38 Japanese students who received the education materials with 40 Japanese students who did not. Following the intervention:

- when asked how they might make six hypothetical journeys, in all cases, less of the intervention group thought that they would choose to drive
- when asked to indicate their degree of agreement or disagreement with 30 statements relating to cost and mode choice, for 25 of the 30 statements, there was a difference between the intervention group and the control group as predicted. Namely, the intervention group saw cost as more important, were less likely to

consider car ownership and use as desirable, reported that they were more likely to drive safely due to high insurance premiums following an accident and that they were more likely to consider buying an environmentally friendly, 660cc car.

It was also notable that for 29 of the 30 statements, there was more variation in the answers of the intervention group, suggesting that the intervention has had more effect on some students than others, with some remaining unaffected.

Work of this nature has since been expanded in experiments undertaken by Fujii & Takasu (2003). In 2001, they recruited 178 non drivers in their first year at Kyoto University. The students were assigned at random to one of five groups, including a control group and four groups which received different types of information about negative aspects of car use. They were then surveyed about their attitudes towards car use. 18 months later, the same participants were re-surveyed about their attitudes to car use and whether they had obtained a driving license, with responses received from 160 of the original group. At the time of the second survey, 225 other second year students from Kyoto University were also asked whether they possessed a drivers licence, to provide a much larger control group for comparison.

The four types of information that the groups received were about: the costs of car use; the dangers of driving a car; the stress that car drivers report due to traffic congestion; and information about all three of these issues together.

Comparing the responses of the (first) control group and experimental groups, there were no differences in how safe any of the groups perceived car use to be. However the 'cost' group and the 'all information' group perceived car use to be more expensive than any of the other groups in the first and second surveys. In terms of perceptions about the 'enjoyability' or 'essentialness' of car use, there were no significant differences between the groups in the first survey. However, by the second survey, all of the intervention groups (except the 'all information' group) were giving a slightly lower rating to the enjoyability of car use than the control group, and the 'cost' and 'stress' groups also saw car use as less essential. In other words, by the time of the second survey, at least one belief or attitude of every experimental group differed from that of the control group.

These findings become particularly significant given that these changes in attitude appear to have had a dramatic effect on students' decisions to obtain a driving licence. The results are given in the table below.

Table 7.1: License holding by different groups

Group	Size	Number with licences	% with licences
Cost group	36	18	50.0%
Danger group	26	9	34.6%
Stress group	34	10	29.4%
'All information' group	34	16	47.1%
Total 'experimental' group	*130*	*53*	*40.8%*
Original control group	30	20	66.7%
New control group	225	140	62.2%

Averaged overall, the interventions appear to have reduced the proportion of students choosing to obtain driving licences from over 60% to 41%. Fujii & Takasu also note that, although the biggest differences in attitudes between the control group and the intervention groups were in relation to transport costs, perceptions of the enjoyability of car driving appear to have had more impact on whether students have chosen to obtain licences.

Preliminary results from similar experiments in Tokyo appear to be showing the same effects as the experiments in Kyoto (Fujii, 2004).

7.6.2 Bike Bus'ters in Aarhus

Another important travel awareness experiment was the Bike Bus'ters project in Aarhus in Denmark. This took place between April 1995 and 1996. It is reported by Overgaard-Mansen et al (undated), with some supplementary information from Bunde (1997). The municipality of Aarhus is Denmark's second largest municipality. Approximately 275,000 people live in the area and over 100,000 commute into the centre of Aarhus each day. The Bike Bus'ter project was designed as an interactive travel awareness campaign (i.e. to be more than an information campaign). However, at the same time, restrictive measures to discourage car use were not considered. The project was explicitly designed around the "carrot principle". The aim of the project was to encourage habitual car users to use other means of transport, by giving them major incentives to use buses and/or bikes. 1700 people volunteered to participate in the project and 175 were selected. These were all daily users of the car, and they lived 2-8 km from their workplace, which was located in the centre of Aarhus.

Participants received:
- the new bicycle of their choice (maximum value 5000 DKK), a child seat (if desired), unlimited free servicing and the option to buy the bicycle at the end of the year for 1000 DKK
- a one-year pass for public transport in the municipality (worth about 5000 DKK), and free timetables
- rain gear, an umbrella, gloves and a towel
- optional information meetings and a bimonthly newsletter (giving advice and enabling participants to exchange experience)
- an optional health check

In return, participants had to sign a 'contract' promising to try and take the bicycle and bus as much as possible, and to participate in regular surveys. The project, including the evaluation, cost a total of 3 million DKK, provided in equal parts by the Danish Environmental Protection Agency, the Danish Transport Council and the Municipality.

The results of the project are shown in the following figures.

Figure 7.2: Modal split before, during and after the BikeBus'ter project for all trips and trips between home and work specifically.

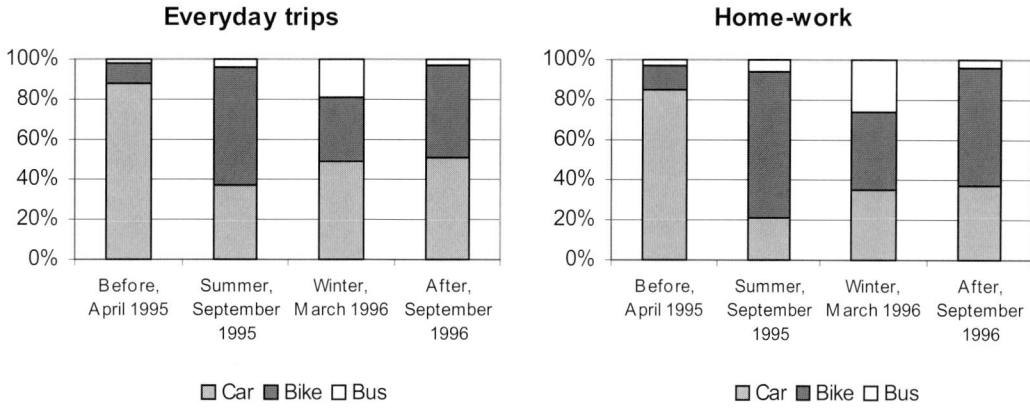

Source: Overgaard-Mansen et al (undated)

Figure 7.3: Average number of weekly trips by bus per BikeBus'ter compared with the average number of weekly kilometres travelled by bike.

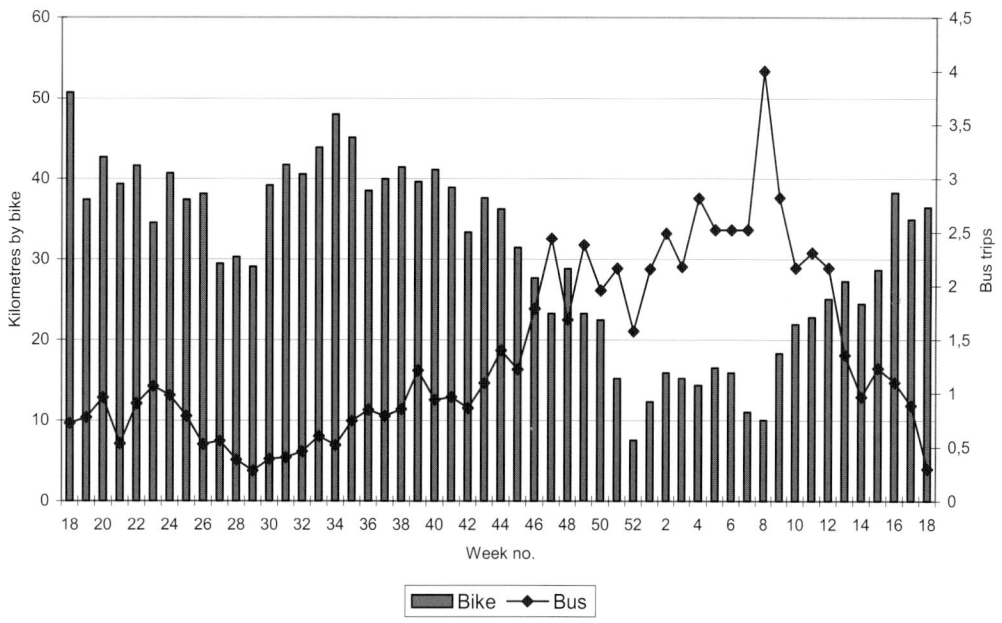

Source: Overgaard-Mansen et al (undated)

In general, the results show that the project was remarkably successful in achieving its aims. The data suggest that the proportion of all trips made by car fell from about 80%[5] to 48% in the winter and was still only 45% of all journeys four months after the project ended. The impact on work journeys was particularly dramatic, where the proportion of trips made by car fell to less than 40%. The researchers noted that this was despite particularly unpleasant weather in the winter of 1995-96. They also note that during the winter months, cycling declined whilst bus use increased.

---

[5] There is some apparent inconsistency in definitions in the source document. The graphs show the proportion of trips being made by car is greater than 80% for both all trips and home-work trips. However, the text reports that the initial percentage of trips being made by car is 78%.

Other findings were that the transfer from car to bike/bus was most significant on trips characterised by a high degree of regularity in time and space (with the greatest change seen in work and shopping trips), whilst the impact was lowest on 'diffuse' trips, including recreational activities, business travel and visits to relatives or friends. Modal shift was also most evident for trips made within the city limits.

Participants appeared to be most motivated by the possibility of more exercise and better health, whilst less motivated to save money or reduce environmental problems, with implications for campaign messages. The researchers also noted that 17 of the participants were involved in self-reported accidents, with seven sustaining personal injuries and two receiving severe injuries. They suggested that bike promotion campaigns should be complemented by measures to improve safety for cyclists.

7.7 Selection of travel awareness case study

So far, reported material has primarily been based on available literature. We also wanted to undertake a more detailed assessment of local authority work on travel awareness. In selecting a case studies of travel awareness campaigns, we originally considered:

- Hampshire County Council
- Hertfordshire County Council
- North Yorkshire County Council
- City of York Council

Hampshire and Hertfordshire both have long-term reputations for undertaking travel awareness work. At the time of our selection procedure, both were involved in the EU TAPESTRY project, undertaking and evaluating particular travel awareness initiatives. Given that these were already written up for the TAPESTRY project, it did not seem appropriate to undertake case study interviews with them. Their results have already been reported in the literature review.

North Yorkshire County Council was investigated because it had recently undertaken a high-profile poster campaign for TravelWise, together with an evaluation of that campaign. However, although the work has been evaluated in terms of the best received messages, at the time of selecting our case studies, there did not seem to have been an evaluation of the effects on travel behaviour.

Consequently, York City Council, which has been undertaking a range of travel awareness campaigns and evaluating their effects was chosen as the main case study for this chapter.

In addition, the interview about public transport information and marketing conducted with Nottingham City Council also provided some useful information about their 'Big Wheel' travel awareness campaign, which has already been reported in section 7.5

7.8 Details of York case study

The City of York has been involved in work on marketing travel awareness since December 1998. Promotional campaigns for travel awareness have been led by the Mobility Management team in the local authority's Transport Planning Unit.

The council's approach is to run sustained campaigns rather than the short bursts of events such as 'bike to work' day that are commonly run by other authorities. Their rationale is that it takes time to reinforce a message, but that, by using different sources, it is possible to build up a message over a long period and achieve sustained modal shift.

Campaigns are based on media space that car drivers will see: for example, on the back of buses, on the back of city centre parking tickets and at the motor show. There have been advertisements on the local radio station – because car drivers frequently tune into this - and at out-of-town cinemas. More recently, the Mobility Management team have produced coasters and beer mats that can be distributed to local pubs and employers. The campaigns are not focused on a specific geographical area, but cover the whole of York.

Using these media, the council has run the following specific campaigns:

- 2001: a walking campaign using eight different images. The main message was that walking is healthy, but there were other subsequent messages about congestion and climate change. The main target was car drivers. Pictures showed shoes with strap-lines such as: 'Enhance your business credentials…. Arrive in comfort and style by walking to work' and 'With sporty looks and powerful pavement handling… Walking is the healthiest way to travel'.

- 2001/02: a cycling campaign using the slogan 'How far will you go?' was designed to make cycling exciting to a younger audience. It set out to evoke a sense of freedom and the idea that cycling and using the cycling network could offer a better quality of life. It showed images of couples on the cycling network and strap-lines such as 'How far will you go.. for a fitter body?' and 'How far will you go… to get closer to nature?'. The target group was 18-25 year olds.

- 2003 (ongoing): a campaign with the two slogans: 'Walk on by' and 'Ride on by' is designed to encourage both walking and cycling, and is aimed at young professionals going to work. It has emphasised the health message, with straplines such as 'Walk on by… bypass the traffic with a healthy way to travel… choose walking'. This is the first campaign to make use of coasters and beer mats in local pubs.

The council has gone on to develop the cycling side of this campaign and now has a new cycling road show which is being used around town, at fairs, events and businesses. There has also been a recent focus on trying to identify drivers who are 'time poor', since there is evidence that people generally feel that there is pressure on their time and that congestion wastes their time, (ICM Observer Precious Time Poll, 2003).

One feature of the council's current approach is that, because the Travelwise budget comes from capital funding from the local transport plan, campaigns are linked to specific infrastructure improvements. For example, the 'How far will you go?' campaign was linked to the opening of a specific cycle route, from the urban area to a rural village, while the 'Walk on by' campaign was linked to the walking route between the station and the city centre. The new version of the cycle route map was launched in conjunction with the opening of an important piece of the cycle network, contributing to a route across the city. Making these links has been necessary to satisfy the district auditor.

7.9 Scale of travel awareness work

Assessing the scale of travel awareness campaigns in the UK is problematic. Given the national 'Are you doing your bit' campaign, Walk to school week campaigns (2 million children affected in 2003), Bike Week (aiming to affect 10 million people in 2004) and In town without my car ! (43 towns and cities involved in events in 2002), it could be argued that the majority of the country has been touched in one way or another. In a review for the Department for Environment, Transport and the Regions undertaken in 2001, SDG found that 31% of local authorities regularly took part in travel awareness activities and 37% took part sometimes. In York, the travel awareness campaign potentially aimed to affect the whole city, although the target audience was somewhat smaller. Similarly, campaigns reported for Hertfordshire and Nottingham potentially aim to affect the whole county, but with specific elements aimed at smaller target segments. This highlights that, for travel awareness campaigns, the key issue is not whether they take place, but their scale, targetting and intensity. This issue is discussed further in section 7.15.

7.10 Staffing and budgets for travel awareness work

In York, in the initial stages of the work, general campaigns to promote travel awareness took up around a third of one officer's time, the other two thirds being spent on workplace and school travel plans. There is now one full time member of staff dedicated to marketing travel awareness. This is similar to Hertfordshire's Travelwise staffing in 2002 (reported to be the equivalent of one full time person spread across three posts), and not that dissimilar to Nottingham's staffing (2 full time staff), given that Nottingham's campaign is aimed at a considerably larger number of people (since Big Wheel is for the local transport plan area, not simply the City).

Initially, in York, approximately £7000 was spent on travel awareness work (including salary costs). By 2002/03, the Travelwise budget was £66,000, described as '1% of the budget allocated to the integrated transport plan', top-sliced from the transport capital budget. The officer's salary was additional to the 1%, giving a total budget of £88,000 plus salary overheads.

This can be compared with budgets for other travel awareness campaigns as shown in Table 7.2.

Table 7.2: Budgets for travel awareness work

Campaign	Budget	Target audience	Implied cost per head
Annual road safety TV and/or radio adverts	£300,000-600,000	Typically, 3 year bands of children (approx 2 million)	15-30p per child
Are you doing your bit ?	£2 million	National campaign (approx 25 million households)	8p per household
Bike Week 2004	£100,000	>10 million lapsed cyclists	1p per cyclist
Hertfordshire Walk to School week 2002	£14,800	60,000 pupils and their parents	25p per pupil
Walk in to work out	£13,000	290 participants involved in pilot, and future recipients	£45 per pilot participant
Bike Bus'ters in Aarhus	3million DKK (@ £270,000)	175 volunteers	£1543 per volunteer
Hertfordshire Travelwise 2001/02	£70,000	All in Hertfordshire (approx 420,000 households and 805000 people)	17p per household, or 9p per person
Nottingham's Big Wheel	£250,000	650,000 residents	38p per resident
York	£88,000	181,094 residents	49p per resident

These results suggest that spending on travel awareness campaigns is typically in the order of 10p to 50p per target group member, with York's spending being towards the top end of this range. Of the two campaigns with significantly higher spending per person, both were pilot projects. In the case of 'Walk in to work out', the expectation was that the materials developed would subsequently be distributed to a considerably wider audience. In the case of Bike Bus'ters, the project was significantly more interactive and intensive than most travel awareness campaigns (and appears to have produced very substantial behaviour change).

It is notable that, with a few exceptions, the budgets allocated to travel awareness campaigns have so far been relatively small by comparison, for example, with marketing budgets used in the motor industry. The figures almost certainly reflect shortage of funds rather than a calculated assessment of best value for money. No clear guidance is available about an optimal level of spending. The case of York is interesting in citing a guideline of 1% of integrated transport capital expenditure (based on the rationale that campaigns are focused on getting maximum benefit out of 'hard' improvements paid for from the capital budget). In cases where the campaigns are related to both revenue and capital budgets, it would make sense to apply such a percentage to the whole transport budget, not just one component of it. Arguably, overall spend will affect both the levels of awareness and behaviour change that are achieved, with intensive campaigns potentially producing more substantial results.

It is worth noting that for some authorities, spending 1% of their transport capital budget on travel awareness campaigns at their *current* rate of expenditure on soft measures overall would seem a distortion. Increasing spending for travel awareness campaigns should therefore probably be seen in the context of an expansion of soft activities generally.

7.11 Awareness of campaigns

In York, one of the council's targets is for 50% of residents to be aware of the Travelwise campaign by 2006. This seems realistic from surveys carried out so far, showing 10% awareness in 1999, 18% awareness in 2000, and 32% awareness in February 2002 following the walking campaign.

More detailed surveys were carried out in February 2002 to assess the impact of the walking campaign. There were interviews with 500 York residents aged 16 and over, carried out on the street at eight different locations around the city. The evaluation found that:

- About one third of those surveyed recalled seeing at least one of the eight posters produced as part of the campaign.
- Respondents from households with a car (35%) were more likely to recall the posters than those without (21%), demonstrating that the campaign's aim of targetting car drivers was successful.
- There was a high level of support for the council's involvement in promoting walking, cycling and public transport: 47% 'strongly supporting' and 41% 'tending to support'. Only 2% of respondents opposed the council's involvement in this activity.

York's results can be compared with those of other studies as shown in Table 7.3.

Table 7.3 Awareness of transport campaigns

Campaign	Level of awareness
'Wonderful Cross' road safety campaign 1996	55% spontaneous recall, 76% prompted recall amongst target audience
'Hedgehogs' road safety campaign 1997	71% spontaneous recall amongst 7-14 year olds
Hertfordshire Travelwise 2000	17% of residents had heard of Travelwise
Chelmsford rail promotion 1998	40% of respondents recalled the campaign
Nottingham's Big Wheel 2003	67% of Nottingham residents and 52% of residents in the wider area were aware of the campaign, including 27% greater awareness of the LTP since 2001.
York's walking campaign	About a third of residents recalled seeing posters of the campaign, including 35% of car drivers

In brief, these suggest that some campaigns (notably the road safety TV campaigns, which were relatively high budget and high profile) can reach awareness levels of 70% or more amongst their target audience. However, it is more common for 20-40% of residents (or 20-40% more residents) to become aware of travel awareness campaigns and their messages when they take place.

7.12 Effects of travel awareness campaigns on car use

In York, the assessment of the walking campaign asked 500 residents a series of questions about whether people had, or would, change their behaviour, (York, 2002). With caveats about interpretation of such statements, the report states:

"Very pleasingly, 45% of respondents said that they walk places more now than they did say a year ago. However, one in three respondents said this wasn't the case and as many as one in four felt unable to give a view either way. As to whether this positive finding can be attributed in any way to the walking campaign, the problems with this kind of 'cause and effect' analysis have already been highlighted. But, for the record, the survey found no difference between those who recalled seeing the posters and those who did not: in both instances the same proportion of people (45%) said they now walked more.

"The issue of the limits of publicity is further highlighted by the fact that only a minority of respondents, though a fairly sizeable one (34%), believed that all the publicity about the effects of cars has made them try to use their car less. As many as half the respondents disagreed with this proposition. (But that is not to say that it hasn't had an effect on them, but rather that they choose not to think it has.) Interestingly, analysis by social group found that AB respondents, a target audience for this campaign, were the group most likely to say that publicity had made them try to use their car less (44%)."

Also of interest, in terms of the effect of the campaign on its target group, is that there was extra analysis of changes amongst car users (about 200 of the total sample), of whom about a third recalled the campaign. Although subsequent breakdowns lead to small sample sizes, making conclusions relatively tentative, it is interesting that car users who recalled the campaign were more likely to report that they walked more than previously, and that they were using cars less. Specifically, 38% of car users who recalled the campaign agreed with the statement that "all the publicity about the effects of cars has made me try to use my car less", compared with 28% of car users who did not recall the campaign.

Meanwhile, the main supporting evidence is provided by traffic and related data about whether there were observable changes in behaviour over the period. York has carried out an extensive series of traffic counts and surveys which do demonstrate significant changes in travel behaviour over the period, though it must be emphasised that these relate to the combined effects of many initiatives and policies of which travel awareness campaigns can only be a small proportion.

In summary, walking has increased substantially: from 10.9% in 2000 to 14.1% in 2002 (12 hour day) and from 12.5% in 2000 to 18.3% in 2002 (morning peak). There has been a slight decrease in car use, from 46.2% to 43.7% and from 42.6% to 37.0% respectively.

The City's Mobility Management team believes that the travel awareness campaign is *contributing* to reductions in traffic but is certainly not the sole cause: for reasons of policy and funding arrangements, the campaigns are in any case linked to specific 'hard' measures, such as a new cycle route or pedestrian improvements, and to other policies, such as parking restraint, the public transport strategy and effective land use planning (to ensure that travelling distances are realistic for walking and cycling). So the possibility of separating the effects is limited.

The results from York are compared with the findings from other studies in table 7.4.

Table 7.4: Impacts of travel awareness work

Campaign	Impacts
York 2001	• 34% of all respondents said they were using cars less (regardless of whether they recalled the campaign) • a third of car drivers recalled the campaign, and 38% of those had reduced their car use, implying potentially about 12% of all car drivers have reduced their car use as a result of the campaign. • in terms of saying that they had reduced their car use, approximately 10% more car drivers who recalled the campaign said that they had, compared with those who did not recall it - ie. about 3.3% of all car drivers. • car use has fallen by 5.4% overall and 13.1% in the morning peak
Hertfordshire 'Walk to School' week. May 2002	At campaign schools, 15% of parents said their children walked to school more often than last year, compared with 10% of parents at control schools.
Hampshire's promotion of rural buses, 2002 (check)	• After the project, a further 3% to 5% of all respondents were likely to rate services positively on various criteria. • 2% of respondents said they were no longer travelling frequently by car.
Cambridgeshire 'Walk to School' weeks in 2002	• In May 2002, car use was 27% lower during walk to school week, and remained 11% lower a few weeks later • In October 2002, car use was 22% lower during walk to school week and remained 2% lower a few weeks later
Chelmsford rail promotion 1998	• 40% of respondents recalled the campaign, with 11% of non-users saying it had increased their awareness of rail services • standard return ticket sales from Chelmsford increased by 17% and weekly season ticket sales were 31% higher than the previous year
Walk in to work out	Six months after an intervention to promote active commuting amongst car users • 31% of a control group and 49% of the intervention group had progressed to a higher level of behaviour change (according to the Transtheoretical model of behavioural change) • the intervention group were spending 125 minutes walking to work per week compared to 61 minutes for the control group
Japanese education work with young adults	License holding amongst an intervention group of students was 41% compared with over 60% for a control group
Bike Bus'ters	The proportion of trips made by car by participants fell from about 80% to 45%, whilst the proportion of commuter trips made by car fell to below 40%. This represents reductions in car use of 45% and >50%.

As highlighted in section 7.11, travel awareness campaigns typically affect 20-40% of the target group (people, trips etc.). Given a level of awareness, both surveys and traffic counts indicate that well-judged campaigns can have an effect on the attitudes and intentions of those targeted, and that car use, walking, cycling and public transport use can change in locations where, often, both travel awareness campaigns and other initiatives have been pursued. One unresolved question is whether the campaigns have accelerated responses that, in time, might have happened anyway, or magnified them, or have been a necessary condition for them.

In the case of campaigns which have been evaluated with 'control' and 'experimental' groups, it is clear that there are often changes in control groups. One explanation is that both groups are responding to other measures taking place in the area that could encourage the observed behaviour. An alternative explanation is that there are 'spill over' effects. For example, in Hertfordshire, there had been general publicity about walk to school week as well as specific publicity in participating schools, which could have affected the control schools. In the 'Walk in to work out' promotion of active commuting, members of the control and experimental groups were working in the same locations and could potentially have influenced each other. Often, both processes are occuring, and it is impossible to distinguish between these effects.

Third, these results suggest that the amount of behaviour change achieved is variable, depending on degree of targetting, intensiveness and the nature of the intervention. It can tentatively be suggested that our campaigns fall into two groups, as follows:

- One group consists of travel awareness campaigns that are closely targeted and intensively implemented, where behaviour changes in the order of 20% are recorded, potentially rising to as high as 50%. These include the week of Walk to school week in Cambridgeshire[6] (changes of 22% and 27%); Walk in to work out (18% of the intervention group at a higher level of behaviour change and walking twice as much); the Japanese education work (19% of students persuaded not to obtain driving licenses) and BikeBus'ters (car drivers persuaded to reduce their car use by 45% or more)

- The second group consists of more general travel awareness campaigns, where untangling the effects is more complex, and where behaviour changes tend to be smaller, up to about 10%. Examples include Hampshire's promotion of rural buses (2% no longer travelling frequently by car); the effects of Cambridgeshire's walk to school week on general car use[5] (reductions of 11% in summer and 2% in the autumn); Hertfordshire's walk to school week on whether children generally walk more (5-15% of parents affected) and York's walking campaign (3% of car drivers almost certainly affected, with potential impacts on a further 30%, and recorded reductions in car use from a range of policies of 5% overall and 13% in the peak).

---

[6] It should be noted that the two sets of Cambridgeshire results are from the same campaign. However, we have included them in both groups since there are results from both the intensive phase of the campaign (during 'Walk to school' week), and the significantly less intensive period after the campaign.

7.13 Synergy between travel awareness campaigns and other policies

Travel awareness work was seen as synergistic with the majority of both hard and soft initiatives aiming to promote more sustainable travel. For example, national campaigns such as 'Walk to school week' contribute to school travel work. Moreover, there is considerable overlap between travel awareness work, personalised travel planning, and public transport information and marketing initiatives, as discussed in the introduction.

In York, the council is working on a considerable range of 'soft' measures besides the travel awareness campaign. The Mobility Management team says that it is valuable to get the sustainable travel message across from different sources. Some synergies are more specific. For example, the Travelwise Officer is producing materials for use with companies developing travel plans, and a guide on cycling for parents that can be used by the school travel plan co-ordinator. Given the focus of their most recent campaign on professionals going to work, there is a clear synergy with workplace travel plans anyway

A number of commentators have also highlighted the value of travel awareness work for increasing the palatability of potentially unpopular measures. As highlighted in section 7.5, Nottingham's work has primarily been aimed at reassuring businesses that transport developments such as the workplace parking levy are part of a long term vision and strategy for improving the city.

It was notable that in many of our other soft factor interviews, the need for some kind of national travel awareness work was raised, as something which would 'smooth the path' of other initiatives, with a desire for high profile television and radio advertising. Partly, it was felt that people do not understand the nature or viability of an alternative, more sustainable transport future, or the fact that they can and should contribute to bringing it about. In other cases, it was felt that national backing is needed, to make it clear that local authorities who pursue more sustainable transport policies are following mainstream advice and that such an approach is expected to be socially beneficial. It was interesting that in Cambridgeshire, one of the interviewees (discussing workplace travel plans) highlighted the quality of an 'Are you doing your bit' campaign advertisement (showing Chris Evans offering someone a lift), but commented that public service advertising often takes place at unsociable times (such as late at night) when it will have less impact. Another interviewee commented that travel awareness work has received considerably less national support than road safety campaigning. In York, it was argued that 'to get the real impact of a message across', a big national campaign was needed to complement local travel awareness initiatives.

Finally, it is clear that health promotion is often an important feature of current travel awareness work, and offers the potential for synergy with initiatives taking place in the health sector not simply the transport sector.

In York, the Primary Care Trust co-fund campaigns. Partly as a result of their work, officers believe that they have seen a shift in the attitudes of the leisure industry. Where there was previously a culture among the profession that people don't want to cycle and walk, there is now more openness to working with the council on promoting this kind of activity. Marketing cycling and walking for their health benefits is also seen as helping to address social exclusion problems in York. This is because poor communities tend to have poorer health and less access to gyms. Walking, in contrast, is free.

Significantly, the Government's Chief Medical Officer has recently argued that the easiest way for people to get fit is by incorporating changes into everyday life such as walking and cycling instead of driving, and this advice now forms part of the Government's Obesity Strategy, (LTT 2004).

7.14 Relationship between travel awareness campaigns spending and impact

While it is not possible to derive an empirical relationship between spending on travel awareness campaigns and their impact on car use from the evidence so far available, the York experience does provide a means of testing orders of magnitude.

Broadly, we can say that, as a minimum, approximately 3.3% of car drivers were probably affected by the campaign. An over-optimistic assumption would be that as many were affected as recalled the campaign or said that they were driving less (about a third of both drivers and non drivers). A more realistic (but still potentially optimistic interpretation) would be to suggest that the 12% of drivers who said they recalled the campaign and had reduced their car use were, to some extent, affected by it. Hence, 3.3% to 12% of drivers can be taken as the credible range of those who potentially altered their behaviour as a result. We assume that those who reported a reduction are telling the truth, and that this reduction would not have been less than 5% (or they would not have noticed it) nor more than 20% (as a conservative estimate of maximum change). This gives a possible range for the population as a whole of a 0.17% to 2.4% reduction in car use. This compares with an actual reduction in car traffic in the city, from all reasons, of 5.4%, and a reduction in work traffic of 13.1%. Spread over the average car use for both owners and non-owners of 5400 km (according to 1999/01 National Travel Survey data), gives a range of roundly 9km to 130km a year per person attributable to the campaign. In line with our other cost-impact assessments, we assume that the effects of the campaign decay at a rate of 40% per year, which implies total savings of 18 to 260 km per person.

The cost of the campaign was £88,000, or 49 pence per York resident. This implies a cost impact ratio in the range 0.2 – 2.7 pence per car km reduced.

While these figures are clearly very tentative, the interesting thing about this range is how similar it is the range of costs and impacts from other soft measures. This implies that, at the margin, expenditure on travel awareness campaigns has a similar level of productivity in influencing behaviour, ie car kilometres reduced per £ spent, as the more targeted measures which they support, albeit with a caveat that it would not, in general, be plausible to expect such campaigns to have an independent existence without the other measures.

7.15 Future impact of travel awareness campaigns, and key issues for scaling up

As highlighted in section 7.7, it is very difficult to assess the future scale of travel awareness work, since it depends on its nature and intensity, which can be highly variable.

York was planning to continue with their '1% of the integrated transport budget' approach, and considered that with this funding, they could achieve awareness levels of 50% by 2006, and contribute to achieving a car use level of 40.1% (compared with 46.2% in 2000). However, the officers considered that, given double the budget, they could more than double the impacts of their work, partly because campaigns could become more carefully refined and targetted to have a bigger effect. As already mentioned, they also highlighted that their work would be considerably enhanced by reinforcement with a national travel awareness campaign. They also felt that they had relatively good quality walking, cycling and bus infrastructure to promote, whereas conditions might be less favourable in other areas.

Currently, many authorities undertake only limited awareness campaigning, with some undertaking no activity in this area. One issue will clearly be the need for a source of funding to create a base level from which future expansion can take place. The York experience is innovative and helpful in this: by relating the campaign budget to the transport infrastructure allocation (*not* to a notional 'soft measures' budget), both the flexibility and allocation of expenditure are improved. This approach also has the advantage of being consistent with the view of most authorities involved in travel awareness campaigns that they should be seen as supportive of, and related to, other specific measures and policies.

In addition to general funding, it is clear that some authorities believe an underpinning national campaign could help to support and enhance the effectiveness of local work.

A final issue relates to the generic evaluation of traffic reduction. Bike Bus'ters clearly achieved a high level of traffic reduction but at relatively high level of input to relatively few participants. For some authorities, there may be social equity issues about trying to achieve a large impact with a small group, compared to a smaller impact with a larger group. National values attached to 'removing a car kilometre from the road network' may be helpful in enabling local authorities to make clearer judgements about appropriate investment decisions. Current values are discussed further in section 5 of Chapter 13.

7.16 Policy implications relating to travel awareness campaigns

From York, and the literature as a whole, the following policy issues seem to be the most commonly noted.
- Travel awareness work is seen as a synergetic policy to complement other transport policy initiatives, which can be usefully undertaken at both local and national level.

- Health promotion is an increasingly significant part of many travel awareness campaigns - the physical activity benefits of walking and cycling could be usefully promoted more at national level.

- Advertising and marketing work seems to be most successful when linked with real improvements in transport options, or when there is a perception mismatch between the options on offer and their actual strengths. Local authorities could be encouraged to undertake work on travel awareness in these situations.

- Until more detailed evidence arises, topslicing as in the York approach of 1% of the transport capital budget may be a useful source, and indicative scale, for this type of activity.

- More travel awareness projects, with explicit monitoring of impacts, could usefully contribute to knowledge about this area.

- Many travel awareness programmes have gradually evolved into more targeted initiatives, such as personalised travel planning programmes and school travel work. However, it seems that there can be benefits from undertaking generic awareness raising to complement these specific initiatives, and many of those interviewed feel that a national campaign could be valuable.

7.17 Acknowledgements

We would like to thank the following people for their help with the case studies that addressed travel awareness:

Individual	Organisation
Daniel Johnson	City of York Council
Anne Skelton	City of York Council
Andy Gibbons	Nottingham City Council
Nicola Tidy	Nottingham City Transport
Lynn Hanna	Nottingham Development Enterprise

We would also like to thank:

Individual	Organisation
Sophie Tyler	University of Westminster
Adrian Davis	Adrian Davis Associates
Kirsty Gilliland	Cambridgeshire County Council
John Sykes	Hertfordshire County Council

7.18 References

Bunde J (1997) "The BikeBus'ters from Aarhus, Denmark: 'we'll park our cars for 200 years...'" reported in Tolley R ed. (1997) *The greening of urban transport*. John Wiley and sons, Chichester, UK, pp373-378

Cairns S., Hass-Klau C & Goodwin PB (1998) *Traffic impact of highway capacity reductions*, Landor publishing, London.

Cairns S. & Okamura K. (2003) Costs and choices: the effects of educating young adults about transport prices. *Journal of Infrastructure Planning and Management,* JSCE 737/IV-60, pp101-113

Cambridgeshire County Council (2002a) *Walk to school week, May 2002. A report of the findings of walk to school week in Cambridgeshire*, Environment Programme Team, August 2002, Cambridgeshire County Council.

Cambridgeshire County Council (2002b) *Walk to school week, October 2002. A report of the findings of walk to school week in Cambridgeshire*, Environment Programme Team, December 2002, Cambridgeshire County Council.

Crampin J (1998) HA and Railtrack seeking mutual benefits through co-operation. *Local Transport Today* 5/11/98 pp10-11

Department of the Environment, Transport and the Regions (1997) *Drink Driving Campaign 1997*. Report downloaded from the DETR web site on 08/11/98

Department of the Environment, Transport and the Regions (1998) *Child Road Safety: a campaign history*. Report downloaded from the DETR web site on 08/11/98

DEFRA (undated c.1999) *Sustainable Development Factsheet: are you doing your bit?* Factsheet downloaded from www.sustainable-development.gov.uk 24/3/04

Department for Transport (2003) *What is 'In Town, Without My Car!' ? Also available (as of 7.11.2002)* from DfT website. Replaced by DfT (2003, 2004).

Department for Transport (2003, 2004) In town without my car! - Good practice guide 2003 (DfT website http://www.dft.gov.uk/intradoc-cgi/nph-idc_cgi?qckQuery=In+town+without+my+car&IdcService notes that this was modified 19.3.2004, modification not specified).

Energie-cites (2004) Promoting sustainable energy policy through local action. (International dissemination by website http://www.22september.org/ not paper, but see DfT (2003) who are supporting the event in the UK)

Etserdorfer E & Sonneck G (1998) Preventing suicide by influencing mass-media reporting. The Viennese experience 1980-1996. *Archives of Suicide Research 4*, pp67-74

Fergusson M, Davis A & Skinner I (1999) *Delivering changes in travel behaviour: lessons from health promotion.* Institute for European Environmental Policy, London.

Fujii S & Takasu Y (2003) *Communication with non drivers promotes wise decisions regarding possession of a drivers licence.* Publication pending.

Fujii S (2004) personal communication.

Goodwin PB (editor) (1995) *Car Dependence.* Report for the RAC Foundation for motoring and the environment, London.

Hamer L, project leader (1997-99) *Information and Publicity Helping the Objective of Reducing Motorised Mobility*, University of Westminster, London.

Harvey N (8/8/03) *Bike week 2003 exceeded expectations.* Press release issued for the Bike Week 2003 Steering Group, www.bikeweek.org.uk

Living streets (15/5/03) *Four million feet step it out for walk to school week.* And (2/10/03) Walkers of the world unite, on the way to and from school! Press releases produced by Living Streets, London, www.livingstreets.org.uk

Local Transport Today (6/5/04) *Tackling obesity epidemic requires change in travel habits says medical chief.* News report p1, Landor Publishing, London.

Masurel P (undated c.2003) 'Drinking and driving'. Chapter 2 of an unidentifiable document downloaded from the Department for Transport website 24/3/04.

Mutrie N et al (1999) *Walk in to work out: A randomised controlled trial of a cognitive behavioural intervention aimed at increasing active commuting in a workplace setting.* Report to the Chief Scientists Office by the University of Glasgow, Glasgow.

Pressl R and Reiter K (2003) Mobility management and travel awareness, Austrian Mobility Research (AMOR), Graz, Austria, and on http://www.eu-portal.net

Overgaard-Madsen JC, Lohmann-Hansen A & Lahrmann H (undated) *BikeBus'ters - From car to bike and buses in Aarhus.* Report from the Transport Research Group, Aalborg University, Denmark.

Papaioannou P, project leader (1997-99) *Campaigns for Awareness using Media and Publicity to Assess Responses of Individuals in the Europe*, University of Thessaloniki, Greece.

SDG (2001) *Take up and effectiveness of travel plans and travel awareness campaigns.* Report to the Department for Environment, Transport and the Regions.

Sykes J (2002) *Travelwise policies - publicity, education and promotion.* Report to the Environment Scrutiny Committee, Hertfordshire County Council, 22/01/02.

TAPESTRY (2003a) *State of the Art Review*, Deliverable 2, Transport and Travel Research Ltd, UK

TAPESTRY (2003b) *Tapestry National Reports*, Deliverable 2 Annex B Transport and Travel Research Ltd, UK

TAPESTRY (2003c) Collected Papers published as The TAPESTRY CD, TTR, Nottingham and University of Westminster, London.

TTR (2003) *Measuring the Success of Marketing the Greater Nottingham Local Transport Plan – Phase 2.* Final report to Nottingham Development Enterprise.

Tyler S (2004) Personal communication

York (2002a) *Policies into Action, Local Transport Plan Second Annual Progress Report* and Annexes, City of York Council, York

York (2002b) Walking Campaign: Evaluation Survey, together with Car Users Additional Analysis City of York Council Marketing and Communications Group (paper reports provided by the council).

8. Car clubs

8.1 Introduction

The basic idea of a car club is that people can have access to a car in their neighbourhood without having to own it. Typically, car club members pay an annual membership fee to an operator (in the order of £100-£200) who provides and maintains a range of vehicles in their neighbourhood. Members then pay by the hour and mile when they use a vehicle. Some operators prefer to charge a higher hourly rate and do not ask for a membership or mileage fee. The combined costs of membership and use are intended to be cheaper than personal car ownership, for car owners who do not do a high mileage, and to encourage the adoption of relatively diverse personal transport strategies. The idea was imported from mainland Europe in the late 1990s.

In June 2004, Carplus, the umbrella organisation for UK car clubs, was aware of at least 25 car clubs in the UK with a reported combined membership of 1165 (Kirkbride 2004). Clubs range from city-wide schemes run in conjunction with local authorities (e.g. Bristol) to independent clubs with only a few cars based in villages and market towns (e.g. Moorcar in Ashburton, Devon). Some clubs have particular features. For example, Hour Car at Hebden Bridge in West Yorkshire uses vehicles that run on bio-diesel; Rusty CarPool in Leicester involves renovation of older vehicles and a scheme set up in a low income area of Manchester forms part of a Local Exchange Trading Scheme, so that vehicles are available to people with little cash. In terms of mainstream schemes, key operators in the UK at the moment are Smart Moves, Urbigo and EasyCar. Details of many of the clubs can be found on the Carplus website www.carclubs.org.uk.

Most UK clubs have been developed from the bottom up: that is, projects have emerged from local interest. Usually, vehicles are distributed around the local neighbourhood in convenient locations, members are attracted by advertising and word-of-mouth, new cars are added to the scheme as membership grows sufficiently to support them, and there is a sense of belonging to a 'community club'. In 2003, the vehicle rental firm EasyCar decided to trial their own version of a car club, by introducing 27 vehicles at one site near Edgware Road in central London. They then invited 3000 people to join, who were regular customers of their conventional car rental service who always returned their cars on time, in good condition. To some extent, this stretches the definition of 'car club', being more akin to a rental depot loyalty scheme (LTT 2003, Meaton 2003).

The potential for car clubs in the UK was reviewed by Bonsall (2002) in a report commissioned by DTLR and the Motorists' Forum. The report was deliberately cautious in nature, avoiding drawing many conclusions, with the author highlighting that "the literature on car clubs is limited in nature. Much of the documentation issued in recent years is produced by those with interest in the field and is poorly referenced. There is little academic work on the subject of car clubs and it has not been possible to examine and substantiate all the claims that have been made for the success of car clubs." However, whilst the report itself avoided many definitive statements, the

Motorists' Forum (2002) subsequently produced a summary report with more specific conclusions. In particular, they argued:

> "Our view is that car clubs are most likely to succeed organically in dense urban areas where there is good public transport provision and parking constraints... However, we do not believe that the perceived benefits of car clubs are presently sufficient to warrant a significant injection of public money to support individual projects without further research."

In their response to the report, the government essentially accepted this view and has not provided mainstream support for individual car clubs, although they continue to support the umbrella organisation, Carplus.

Although the support for Carplus is welcomed, the car clubs community has expressed disappointment at the general conclusions, with a formal rejoinder by Kirkbride 2003. This emphasised the reported benefits from car clubs, their potential to be a complementary element of a sustainable transport policy and argued that they are likely to be appropriate in more locations than the Motorists' Forum believes. In particular, Kirkbride highlighted ongoing work between the Countryside Agency and Carplus to introduce 13 pilot car clubs in rural areas, of which five are now operational. He states that membership growth in these pilot rural clubs (in terms of new members per year per car) is typically higher than in many urban clubs. According to Carplus (forthcoming), currently, in the UK, on average 4.5 members are joining per car per year in urban areas, whilst 8.2 members are joining per car per year in rural areas.

In the remainder of this chapter, Sections 8.2-8.4 primarily explore the international evidence that is available about the scale and impacts of car clubs. The subsequent sections report on our detailed examination of experience in Edinburgh and Bristol, together with some available material from other UK car clubs.

8.2 Literature evidence on growth of car clubs

Car club membership in Switzerland has been growing rapidly since the mid-1990s. Membership growth has been helped by the various car clubs joining forces to form a national organisation, Mobility CarSharing Switzerland, and by initiatives such as a combined season ticket marketed with Swiss Railways. In 1990 the number of members of car clubs in Switzerland stood at about 500 (similar to numbers in the UK in 2002). By 1997 it had increased to more than twenty times this figure, and by 2003 it had grown more than a hundred-fold to 58,000 members.

Growth has also been rapid in Germany, although there the pattern has been slightly different, with a number of car clubs in existence. The German umbrella association for car clubs reported a total membership of 55,200 in 2001, following growth of over 20% a year for several years. Membership is conservatively estimated to reach over 200,000 people by 2010, (Bundesverband CarSharing 2002). Although there are many car clubs operating in Germany, the trend is towards consolidation and merging, so that around 65% of German car club members are served by companies with over 2000 members, and only 13% are served by companies with less than 500 members (Traue 2001).

Data was also obtained for growth of car club membership in one city in Germany, Bremen, (Glotz-Richter 2003). The car club in Bremen was launched in 1990, with three cars and 28 members. Initial growth was slow, increasing to 500 members by 1994 and 1200 members by 1998. This was followed by a membership surge (to 1900 members in 1999) and then growth of about 200 – 250 members per year, reaching 2900 members in September 2003.

Car clubs in North America took off in the late 1990s, and Shaheen et al. (2002) report that by mid-2002 US car clubs had between them approximately 11,500 members, and Canadian car clubs reported a total of 5065 members. By winter 2003/04, the Carplus newsletter reports that US car clubs in 8 cities served by the three main players (Zipcar, Flexcar and City Carshare) had over 30,000 members. Communauto in Québec (Canada) has grown to over 3000 members in 7 years, and Zipcar in Boston attracted an impressive 4000 members in its first 3 years.

In both Germany and North America, most of the growth in membership has been a consequence of established car clubs getting larger or expanding to new cities, rather than new organisations being set up. For example, there are 14 car clubs in the US, but 92% of US car club members belong to the three main players, City CarShare, Flexcar or Zipcar, all of which operate in several cities (Shaheen et al 2002). In Germany, the largest 13 car clubs (out of 66 belonging to the German car club association) serve 85% of all members, but these are spread right across the country with almost all cities of over 200,000 people now having a car club, (Bundesverband Carsharing 2002). In Switzerland, the national car club Mobility claims a presence in 390 communities, (Mobility 2002).

It is noteworthy that car clubs have been promoted in different ways in different countries. For example, in Germany, they have been targeted at the environmentally aware. In contrast, for example, in Boston, they have been marketed as a smart feature of city living.

Figure 8.1 shows that the growth in number of UK car club members is comparable to the early years of the Mobility club in Switzerland. The inset suggests that the rate of growth of UK clubs is falling behind that of Switzerland; this is mainly due to the members lost between the collapse and re-launch of the Edinburgh car club. The UK data do not include members of the Easy Car initiative in London.

Figure 8.1: Car club membership growth in the UK compared with Switzerland

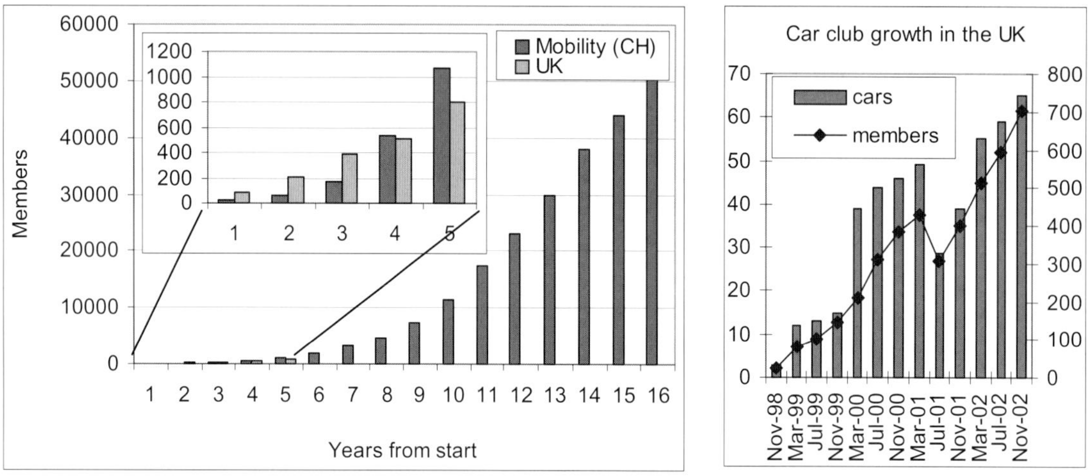

Source: Kirkbride 2003. Figures exclude members of the EasyCar scheme

8.3 Literature evidence on the target market for car clubs

In Switzerland, Muheim (1998) estimates that approximately 9% of the population are potential car club members. This is based on an evaluation of the number of people whose personal circumstances mean they could benefit from a car club, combined with survey data which found 36% of potential users were very or fairly interested in the idea.

In the US, Sperling et al. (2000) found that 15% of an experimental group in an area well-suited to a car club became members of car club, CarLink, after receiving targeted information and personal contact. She postulates that intense marketing of car-clubs to a carefully selected target population can elicit up to 15% participation.

Both these estimates of the potential for car clubs are broad-brush, but they are in line with estimates from a more detailed Austrian study (Steininger et al. 1996). Steininger surveyed 198 members of Austrian car clubs to identify the characteristics of "pioneer" car club members, or early adopters, and from this developed a profile for people most likely to join a car club:

- Age 25-43
- Highly educated (university degree or university entry level)
- Own at least one car, but not in a high price bracket
- Yearly car mileage for one car below 15000 km
- Less than 33% of trips currently made by car (based on car modal share for car club members *after* joining)
- Currently involved in environment-protective action.

He then surveyed 350 non-car-club members in two urban residential areas of Graz, and found that in one area, deemed an "average" urban residential area, 8.8% of residents had the right profile to be car club early adopters. In the second area, with a high academic population, the figure was 16.0%. Steininger argues these figures are probably an underestimate. Some residents in the areas surveyed were excluded because they made more than a third of trips by car, and yet their car modal share could be expected to fall once they joined a car club. Taking account of these extra

194

people, the pioneer potential in the first residential area rose to 17.7% and in the second area to 37.6%. Steininger further argues that this is not the absolute upper limit for car clubs: once it becomes a familiar concept it may expand to other groups and social segments, and its attractiveness will also grow if the "complementary good" of public transport becomes better.

Carplus (2004) provide data on their website for a sample of car club members in the UK, who belonged to clubs using cars sourced through the partnership between Carplus and Vauxhall Motors Ltd. 258 members were surveyed in August 2002. The social profile that emerged was remarkably similar to that shown in the Austrian study. In particular:

- 77% of members were aged 23-49 (including 12% aged 23-29; 38% aged 30-39 and 27% aged 40-49), and
- 86% of members were in professional and managerial jobs (55% recording themselves as professional, 22% as managers and administrators and 9% as associate professional and technical)

However, again, it should be noted that this is the profile of existing UK car club members, who, by definition, can be defined as city-based 'early adopters', since car clubs are relatively new in the UK and have largely been developed in cities. Carplus (forthcoming) report on a survey of 36 rural car club members (who were surveyed on joining one of five clubs between October 2003 and March 2004). Although only a small sample, it suggests that rural car club members tend to be slightly older, and from a much broader range of social classes, including more housewives and retired people. In particular, about only 60% report that they are in professional jobs (and no managers have yet joined).

In brief then, international literature suggests that perhaps 9% of the population might be attracted to car clubs, rising to as high as 38% in certain areas. UK data of car club member profiles suggest that the UK experience of city car clubs is similar to elsewhere, although car clubs in rural areas may appeal to a slightly different social profile.

8.4 Literature evidence on the effect of car club membership on car use

Several studies have evaluated "before" and "after" levels of car use amongst people who join car clubs. Briefly, these studies demonstrate that members who give up their car on joining a car club are able to reduce their car mileage by 60 – 70%. Car club members who do *not* give up a car (either because they never had one or because they are treating car club membership like a second household car) seem not to significantly alter their travel patterns. The main studies are Muheim (1998) and Meijkamp et al. (1997), and their findings are summarised in table 8.1.

Table 8.1: Distance travelled by car before and after joining a car club

Average annual km of….		Muheim (1998)	Meijkamp et al. (1997)
Members who give up a car on joining the scheme	before	9300	13380
	after	2600	4730
Change in km driven		-72%	-65%
Non car owners	before~	3100	5360
	after	3100*	3820
Change in km driven		little change	-29%
Members who keep their car on joining the scheme	before		21700
	after		22386
Change in km driven			+3%
The average car club member	before		8450
	after		5660
Change in km driven			**-33%**

* Car mileage of non-car owners after joining car club is inferred. Muheim (1998) reports this group only slightly changed their travel behaviour on joining the club.
~ This includes getting lifts and borrowing vehicles from friends and family

Muheim (1998) analysed the travel patterns of 511 car club members and 340 potential members in Switzerland, and found that members who gave up their own car were able to reduce their car mileage by an average of 72%, from 9300 km per year to 2600 km per year. This brought their level of car use into line with non-car owners, who, despite not owning cars, still travelled about 3100 km a year by car (for example getting lifts or borrowing vehicles from friends or family). Muheim reports that people who did not own a car before joining a car club, or who used a car club in addition to their own car, only slightly changed their travel behaviour.

Meijkamp et al. (1997) undertook a similar analysis of reported mileage before and after joining a car club, amongst 337 members of Dutch car clubs. For car club members taken overall, the *average* reduction in distance driven was 33% or 2790 km (from 8450 to 5660 km per year). However, this masked substantial differences according to whether or not people had owned a car before joining, and whether they kept it once they were members. People who gave up their car on joining the car club ("substituters") reduced their car mileage by 65%. Those who used the car club in addition to their own car slightly increased their overall mileage by 3%. Surprisingly, Meijkamp et al. found that car club members who had previously been without a car ("new car drivers") *reduced* their car mileage by 29% on joining. (One plausible explanation for this apparently counter-intuitive result may be that car club membership encourages more conscious choice of mode and increases knowledge of the actual cost of driving a car. This seems to be borne out by an attitudinal survey of the people in Meijkamp's study.)

Reports for the EU MOSES research project (Traue (2001) and MOSES / UITP (2002)) quote several figures for reductions in car mileage: a reduction from 13000 car driver km per year before joining to 3000 km per year afterwards, representing a reduction of 77% and 10,000km (Munich); a decrease in car driver mileage of 71% (cambioAachen); a decrease of 57% (Swiss study); and a decrease of 50% (German study). While these broadly corroborate the studies by Muheim and Meijkamp, it is not clear whether these figures refer to the average change for all car club members, or the change for members who have given up a personal car. Carplus (2004) report that, in Berlin, the average mileage per car club member dropped from 5425 miles to 2560 miles, a reduction of 53% or 4,600km; and that in Bremen, the mileage of the average car club member has fallen by 3,500 miles (5,600km).

Given the substantial differences in car mileage between those people who give up their personal car and those who do not, it becomes important to know what proportion of car club members fall into each category. This issue is explored by Meijkamp and by several other German studies, summarised in Sperling et al. (2000) and listed in table 8.2.

Table 8.2: Vehicle ownership patterns before and after joining a car club

	Wagner (1990)	Hauke (1993)	Baum and Pesch (1994)	Meijkamp et al. (1997)
Would never buy a car (%)	37	36	13	71
Gave up car independent of car club (%)	31		30	
Foregone planned car purchase due to car club (%)		16	32	
Gave up private car because of car club (%)	26	42	23	21
Continue to own private car (%)	6	6	3	9

Adapted from Sperling et al. (2000)

Although there is a lot of variation in the figures, it seems that:
- Between 35% and 71% of car club members previously did not own a car: either they had never owned one, or they had sold it some time earlier. Although the evidence from Meijkamp's study suggests this group might reduce their car mileage, it seems safer to assume that they will *not* do so.
- A much smaller percentage, 3 – 9%, continued to own a car after joining a car club. From the evidence presented by both Muheim and Meijkamp it seems likely their car mileage will go up a little, but they make up such a small proportion of car club members that this will have little impact on total "after" mileage.
- The remainder, between 21% and 58%, either gave up a car when they joined a car club, or chose car club membership instead of buying a car. For this group, it seems reasonable to assume a substantial reduction in car mileage, of the order of two-thirds, compared to what would have happened if a car club had not been available.

In summary, it seems reasonable to expect somewhere between a fifth and a half of car club members will give up their cars as a direct result of joining a car club, and as a consequence of this will reduce their car mileage by a substantial margin of around two-thirds. Car club members who do not give up a personal car will not change their travel patterns very much on joining a car club.

8.5 Selection of car club case studies

Car clubs are still in their infancy in the UK. The most substantial and longest established is the Edinburgh car club, which was therefore a clear case study choice. The Edinburgh club began in March 1999, received a substantial blow when Budget, the car rental company, dropped out in March 2001 (due to international financial problems) and has since re-established itself as a partnership between the council and the company Smart Moves.

Other clubs that were looked at as potential case studies for this project were based in Bristol, Bath, Oxford and London. In the end, Bristol was chosen, given that it is reasonably well established (having been launched in July 2000), and we were interested in the potential synergy with other initiatives taking place in Bristol. The main drawback of this decision was the similarities between the Edinburgh and Bristol schemes, as both operate in conjunction with Smart Moves. The other main national players are Avis car hire, who are involved in schemes in Oxford and London using the brand name Urbigo, and EasyCar, with their new model of car club, (as described in the introduction). Both of these organisations may also play an important role in how car clubs expand in the UK.

During the course of the case study work, it emerged that Cambridge may be considering a car club for one of its residential areas in the future, and that the Milton Keynes car share scheme was originally set up with a car club element (although this proved unsuccessful - largely, according to the organisers, because the hire cars were available close to people's workplaces rather than their homes).

In summary, the main case studies for car clubs were:
- Bristol City Car Club
- Edinburgh City Car Club.

From the other case studies, there was some information from:
- Cambridge
- Milton Keynes.

As part of the shortlisting process, we collected limited information from:
- the Bath car club, run by Envolve, a local environmental charity
- Urbigo car club in Oxford, involving Avis
- Urbigo car clubs in Sutton and Southwark, involving Avis
- London City Car club, involving Smart Moves, with sites in Camden, Kensington and Chelsea, Islington, Lambeth, Merton, Ealing and Brent.

There was also some available information about car clubs registered on the Carplus website, and we received some material from their forthcoming report about their pilot work on rural car clubs, being undertaken with the Countryside Agency.

8.6 Details of chosen car club case studies

Edinburgh: The Edinburgh City Car Club was the first major car club in the UK. It was launched in March 1999, with financial support totalling £253,000 from the city council, Scottish Office and DETR. Initially it was operated by Budget Rent a Car, who over a period of two years grew the operation to 170 members, 22 vehicles and 23 sites. However, Budget abandoned the car club in March 2001. In October 2001, the Car Club was re-launched by Smart Moves with a development grant of about £40,000 from Edinburgh City Council, and considerable work was needed to regain members. At the time of the case study interview (July / August 2003) the club had 215 members and 17 cars at 15 sites around the city. By April / May 2004 there were 317 members and 19 cars.

Bristol: The Bristol car club originated through a partnership between a voluntary group (Bristol Community Car Club Association) and Bristol City Council. It was launched as BEST (Bristol Environmentally Sustainable Transport) in 2000. and renamed Bristol City Car Club in 2001, when Smart Moves took on a more instrumental role in its operation. The council agreed a four-year funding package, starting in 2002, totalling £160,000. At the time of the case study interview (July 2003) it had 92 members and six cars. By April 2004, there were 160 members and 11 cars. Members of the scheme are entitled to a 10% discount on tickets on First Bus.

8.7 Staffing and budgets for car clubs

Table 8.3 compares the staffing and budgets for the Edinburgh and Bristol car clubs.

Table 8.3: Comparison of staffing and budgets for car clubs

	Edinburgh	Bristol
Length of time scheme has been running	2 years*	3 years
Number of car-club members registered~	215	92
Number of regular users ~	Not known	60
Staff time at local authority once scheme established	Very low	Very low
Staff time at car club operator ~	2 fte	1.5 fte
Start-up grant	£48,000 invested in Budget scheme#, plus £39,750 grant to Smart Moves scheme	£50,000 grant so far, with another £110,000 committed
Other annual costs to local authority +	£6000	No costs apart from core grant
Total cost to date	£99,750	£50,000

* Current scheme operated by Smart Moves
~ Figures are for time of case study interview (July 2003)
# Funding for feasibility study and parking infrastructure
+ Note that the cost of designating car parking bays was not separately identified by the case study local authorities, but other local authorities have identified this as a significant cost, at least in the initial stages of establishing a car club.

Both clubs have rather low staff time requirements within their respective local authorities, as day-to-day management is carried out by Smart Moves staff. The main roles of council officers are involvement in steering groups; liaison between the car club and other parts of the local authority; and arrangement of traffic orders and signing for car club parking spaces.

The car clubs themselves each have a full-time co-ordinator, and in Edinburgh there is also a part-time assistant. Both clubs receive some support from the Smart Moves head office in Coventry, including call-centre support.

The current car club in Edinburgh has benefited from the research and investment that led to formation of the previous car club, operated by Budget. This totalled £253,000, of which £150,000 covered initial set-up costs, £55,000 was for monitoring and evaluation, and £48,000 (in kind) was for a feasibility study and the cost of parking infrastructure at car club stations. In addition, over £200,000 was spent on promotional activities while Budget was operating the car club. It is difficult to estimate the value of this investment to the current car club. Key benefits were that the current club inherited 60 members from the Budget car club, and that car parking bays were already designated. However, Smart Moves were not able to use the original Budget technology, and had to invest in new technology themselves – highlighting that equipping each car with the relevant technology typically costs £1000. They also had to overcome the reputation of the previous scheme of being unreliable. We therefore tentatively assume that the £48,000 spent on feasibility work and parking infrastructure might reasonably be considered to have been of direct benefit to the current car club, but that other investment in the Budget scheme has not resulted in any particular benefit to Smart Moves.

City of Edinburgh Council subsequently provided Smart Moves with a grant of £39,750 to cover operating deficits in the first two years (from May 2001). The business plan at that time forecast that the club would be able to operate without financial support after two years, and would move into profit in 2003/04. Membership growth has been slower than forecast in the business plan, and, at the time of our case study interview, the club was intending to seek further development funding from the city council. However, it expected to reach break-even point (around 500 members, representing about 7% of current car owners) by the end of 2004. In addition to the grant of £39,750, the city council contributes about £6000 per year towards promotional costs such as printing leaflets. Some costs are also associated with preparation of traffic orders for parking spaces. These are met from the parking budget.

In Bristol, there is also financial support from the local authority, but it is at a higher level and spread over a slightly more generous timescale: £50,000 a year for two years, then £30,000 a year for two years, totalling £160,000 over four years. A quarter of this grant is from the European VIVALDI programme. Funding is linked to a target of achieving 1000 members by the end of the funding period. As in Edinburgh, there is an expectation that the club will become self-funding and then move into profit.

It is too early to say at what point the Edinburgh and Bristol car clubs will reach the number of members required to break even, and the timing will depend on a number of factors, both within and outside the clubs' control, which are discussed below. However, it is noteworthy that car clubs should not require ongoing public funding. In this, they differ from most other soft measures, potentially offering 'traffic reduction for free' to the local authority once break-even point is reached. This makes them a potentially attractive investment prospect for influencing travel behaviour.

In addition to the information from the two main case studies, it should be noted that Bath car club started with a £30,000 grant from the council (for effectively one year) although further funding may be sought. The Oxford scheme expected to be loss-making for the first three years. For the London City Car Club run by Smart Moves, Transport for London provided an initial grant.

Meanwhile, the economics for rural car clubs may be substantially different, where they use a different operational model. Carplus (forthcoming) provides anonymous data for two existing rural clubs, which suggests that they may be able to break even with considerably fewer members than urban car clubs, following smaller start-up subsidies in the order of £60,000. Carplus believe that this is due to two reasons. First, members of rural car clubs typically drive much further in the vehicles, so the incoming money to the club is greater. Second, rural car clubs' overheads tend to be much lower. For all car clubs, overheads typically comprise the salary costs of management, and lease charges (including insurance). In the case of rural car clubs, ventures are typically being run as independent community initiatives, involving a local part-time person, less technology, and are not part of the more formal, official schemes promoted by the main players. Consequently, their overheads are much lower, and break-even point can be reached much more quickly.

To some extent, it is perhaps inevitable that small, rural clubs can run on a much more informal, lower-overhead basis, than larger urban clubs. Presumably, in the case of the smaller rural clubs, there is much more scope for personal arrangements and trust, which obviates the need for some of the more formal, hi-tech booking systems and arrangements of the larger, urban clubs. Urban clubs, by nature of their size, must tend to be more anonymous and therefore, conversely, presumably require these arrangements. However, this is a hypothesis only, and it remains to be seen how the different models evolve.

Finally, it should be noted that public subsidy elsewhere for car clubs has often been considerably more substantial. Enoch (2002) reports that City CarShare in San Francisco benefitted from a federal grant of $750,000 (currently equivalent to £430,000), and the free provision of off-street parking bays. Carplus (spring 2003) report that the Italian government has put 10 million euros into setting up clubs in 16 cities (equivalent to about £420,000 per city)

8.8 Comparison of case study findings on scale of implementation

The Carplus website lists all car club schemes that they are aware of in the UK. This shows that, in the UK, the number of car clubs appears to be growing over time. Specifically, Carplus list 4 schemes that launched in 2002, 7 that launched in 2003 and 12 that have launched in 2004.

They also provide data about the size of the clubs, and the number of vehicles. This information (for all clubs except our case studies), is given in Table 8.4

Table 8.4 Scale of UK car clubs (as of May 2004)

Club	Launch date	Cars	Members	Ratio of members to cars
London City Car Club, London	Mar-03	15	159	11
Urbigo, Oxford	Summer-00	6	60	10
Manchester Airport	2000	n/a	60	n/a
Campus Cars, Cranfield	1996	4	58	15
Urbigo, Sutton & Southwark, London	Sep-01	8	40	5
City-Wheels, Swansea	Jan-01	5	40	8
Your Car, Bath	May-01	2	36	18
Moorcar, Devon	Sep-02	4	27	7
Stroud Valleys Car Club, Stroud	Jun-03	3	26	9
Brighton & Hove City Car Club, Brighton	Sep-03	3	23	8
Rusty Car Pool, Leicester	1990	6	20	3
OurCarYourCar, West Yorkshire	Mar-03	4	19	5
Car Share Lewes, Sussex	1994	1	18	18
A2B, Wiltshire	Nov-02	3	16	5
Co-Drive, Leeds	1998	1	15	15
Hulme, Manchester	May-02	1	10	10
Hour Car, West Yorkshire	Jan-04	2	8	4
Exe Car Club, near Exeter	Jan-04	1	4	4
Woodgate Car Club, Leicester	Jul-00	1	3	3
Clay Wheels, Cornwall	Mar-03	1	2	2
Hour cars, Salisbury	Jul-03	3	2	1
Media Centre Car Club, Huddersfield	Jan-04	1	13	13

Source: Carplus website, accessed May 2004.

The table gives a mixed picture. It shows that most of the recent car clubs are still relatively small, although there are now at least 16 with more than 10 members (in addition to the EasyCar scheme and our two case studies). The Edinburgh interviewee stated that 15 to 20 people per car is seen as optimum in the initial phase of development, based on European experience, and there are four clubs with this ratio. Generally, the bigger clubs are getting at least 8 members per car, and this is also the rate reported for the newly emerging rural car clubs, as highlighted in section 8.1.

In addition to this information, we had more detailed insights from our case studies, which can be compared with international experience. Table 8.5 and Table 8.6 summarise data on the scale of the Edinburgh and Bristol car clubs, in comparison with international data. Meanwhile, Figure 8.2 shows the growth rates of the UK schemes.

Table 8.5: Scale of case study car clubs compared to international schemes

	Start date	Duration	Latest data		Historical data
			No. of cars	No. of members	
Edinburgh (Budget scheme)	Mar 99	24 months	22*	170*	Started with 35 members and 6 cars. 95 members by end of year 1.
Edinburgh (Smart Moves scheme)	Oct 01	30 months	19	317	Restarted with 60 members (40 from the old club) and 10 cars. 95 members and 10 cars by March 02, 131 members and 13 cars by July 02, 156 members and 15 cars by Nov 02, 170 members and 15 cars by March 03 and 203 members and 17 cars by July 03.
Bristol	July 00	46 months	11	160	In the first year, there were 20 members sharing 2 cars. By July 03, 92 members and 6 cars (including 60 regular users).
Mobility Switzerland	1987	17 years	1700	58000	Started with 28 members and 2 cars. 23000 members and 1050 cars (1998); 44,000 members and 1650 cars (2001).
Bremen (Germany)	1990	14 years	About 100	2900	Started with 28 members and 3 cars. 500 members (1994); 1200 members (1998); 1900 members (1999).

* Figures for Edinburgh (Budget scheme) are for 2001, when the company pulled out.

Table 8.6 Key indicators for case study car clubs compared with international clubs

	Edinburgh (Budget)	Edinburgh (Smart Moves)	Bristol	Mobility Switzerland	Bremen, Germany
Starting membership	35	60	20	28	28
Ratio of members to cars in the first year	5.8	6	10	14	9.3
Average annual 'starting' growth*	75	147	68	174	125
Current ratio of members to cars	7.7	16.7	14.5	34	28

* For Edinburgh (Budget), this is the figure for the last year of the scheme. For Edinburgh (Smart Moves), it is the growth between March 03 and April 04. For Bristol, it is the growth between Jul 03 and April 04. For Mobility Switzerland, it is the average growth between 1987 and 1990. For Bremen, it is the averaged growth between 1990 and 1994.

Figure 8.2: Membership growth in Edinburgh and Bristol car clubs

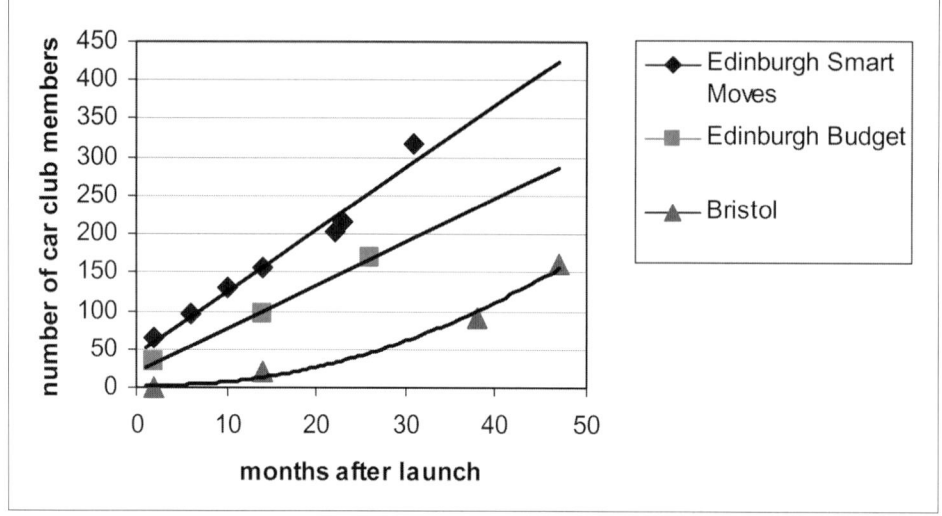

The following conclusions emerge:

- The Edinburgh interviewee suggested that at the current stage of development in the UK, 15 to 20 people per car is seen as optimum, based on European experience. However, it is rare for schemes to have this ratio when they start. Both Bristol and Edinburgh started with considerably fewer members per car than this, but are now reaching the lower end of the range. Meanwhile, evidence from Switzerland suggests that as schemes become very large (over about 20,000 members), this figure rises to about 20 people per car, and continue rising to over 30.

- Growth rates of the case study schemes seem broadly comparable - somewhere in the order of 70-150 members a year, providing that car availability is increased in parallel. It may be that this growth only occurs after an initial period when schemes become established. For example, it took about a year before the Bristol club started to grow steadily. For comparison, the Bremen scheme grew at just over 100 members per year in its first four years of operation, with more rapid growth later on.

In summary then, there are an increasing number of car clubs setting up in the UK. Meanwhile, the ratios of members to cars, and the rates of growth, of the case studies, which are some of the oldest clubs in existence in the UK, appear comparable with the early years of European experience.

As well as membership figures, which clubs consider to be an important indicator of their success, they are also concerned about the use of car club vehicles, since this partly determines how much money they make, and their financial viability. Smart Moves estimates car club vehicles must be used for 40% of their chargeable time (6.4 of the 16 hours between 7.30 am and 11.30 pm) in order to be self financing.

The Bristol scheme was reporting average utilisation rates of 39% in July 2003 (15.3 members per car). Edinburgh has reported utilisation rates of 37% in March 2002 (9.5 people per car), 42% in July 2002 (10.1 people per car), 35% in November 2002 (10.4 people per car) and 40% in March 2003 (11.3 people per car). The Edinburgh interviewee commented that the scheme has attracted fewer members than expected, but higher usage per member than expected, such that the financial viability of the scheme looks reasonably healthy. These figures take into account that five vehicles are not available to members during the day, as they are used by Edinburgh City Council as a car pool. However, being able to lease the vehicles to the council has clearly increased the viability of the scheme. In Bath, leasing car club vehicles to local businesses and the council during the working day is being investigated as a strategy to help sustain the club. The Edinburgh interviewee also commented that as new car club sites (or 'stations') are added, average usage drops until the new site becomes established.

In conclusion, both Edinburgh and Bristol car clubs seem to be achieving the level of use required to achieve financial viability, despite the relatively low ratio of people to cars in Edinburgh (in the order of 10 people per car). In addition, the Edinburgh club's viability is helped by leasing the car club vehicles as local authority pool vehicles during the day.

8.9 Comparison of findings on effects on car use

There is relatively scant data from the UK about how car club membership has affected the car use of its members. Table 8.7 summarises what is available.

Table 8.7: Effects of car clubs on car use

Edinburgh (Budget)	Members were seen as being divided into two groups: • Non car owners, who joined to gain access to a vehicle for journeys that were difficult or expensive by other means - e.g. the trip to IKEA - which were previously made by day car hire or borrowing a friend's car • Ex car owners who had already minimised their driving, who had old cars that were due for replacement, and who viewed the car club as an experiment or a point of transition between vehicles. A Scottish Executive report (Hope 2001) concluded that 'the increased car use by the non car owners appears to have matched the reduced use made by those who joined when they gave up a car'. A survey of 38 members found that 12 had disposed of a car as a result of joining the car club – i.e. about a third of the sample.
Edinburgh (Smart Moves)	In terms of use, the cars are not used for commuting, however they are used for business trips, trips to IKEA, shopping, garden centres, meetings, weekend and day trips, and taking children to school. The interviewee estimated that one car club vehicles typically replaces five cars, although the main impact is an alleviation of parking problems rather than a reduction in traffic. In terms of car ownership, the interviewee's opinion is that: • Very few members are using the car club for a second vehicle • The majority of members were previously non car owners • Those that have given up a car tend to be giving up an older vehicle. She also commented that car club members use the vehicles more than they think that they will. Each car club vehicle averages 16,100 kilometres per year.

Bristol	Of the 60 regular users (with 92 members in total), 30 are thought to have got rid of a car (often a 'horrible old car'), and another five are considered to have joined the club rather than buying a car. One example was given of a family generally using cars less as a result of changing from private ownership to car club membership. In terms of journey purposes, the vehicles are not used for work or very short local trips (e.g. going to the corner shop), but possibly divided into two types: • People living close to a car station use the cars for short journeys and specific purposes • People living further from the car station use the cars for longer journeys (day trips, weekend trips) and/or for chained journey purposes. Each car club vehicle averages 19,300 kilometres per year.
Bath	A survey was carried out with 22 respondents in 2003. This showed that 7 (32%) only use the vehicles for business, 4 (18%) only use the vehicles for personal use, and 11 (50%) use the vehicles for both. In terms of car ownership: • 11 (50%) were non car owners before joining although four mentioned that they had access to another car belonging to friend, family member or employer • 4 (18%) owned a car before joining the club, which they have kept • 7 (32%) either gave up their car, or joined the club instead of buying a car. (Of these, 1 gave up the car sometime before joining the club, 2 gave up the car on joining the club, 1 joined the club instead of buying a car, and 3 joined the club instead of buying a second family car).
Rural car clubs	Carplus (spring 2004) report that in their recent survey of 36 rural car club members: • 6% would otherwise have bought a car • 23% are expecting to get rid of a car as a result of joining

This evidence suggests the following:
- Car club vehicles often replace older, more polluting vehicles.
- Car club vehicles are rarely used for commuting, although they are used for business trips. They tend to be used for journeys that would be awkward by other means (e.g. to visit IKEA), for journeys that are not made regularly, and for day or weekend leisure trips.
- About 30-40% of members gave up a privately-owned car when they joined the car club or joined the club as an alternative to plans to buy one.
- The rest (60-70%) either did not previously own a car, or kept their own car when they joined the car club.

The high proportion of car club members who previously did not own a car is within the range reported in the literature (section 8.4). Some commentators have expressed concern that car clubs may encourage car use in this group. The opposing argument is that a car club enables a household to continue without owning a private vehicle, whereas otherwise they might have purchased one at some point in the future, with a far more substantial impact on their travel behaviour.

The simplest way to calculate the impact of a car club on its members' overall car mileage would be to find out the distance travelled by a sample of car club members before and after joining the scheme. Unfortunately, this data were not available for any of the UK schemes. We therefore looked at the available data on the average distance travelled per car club vehicle, and the car ownership and use profile of club members for our case studies. In summary, our approach was to estimate how many privately-owned vehicles are replaced by each car club vehicle, and how many former non car owners use each car club vehicle. The calculation is shown in table 8.8.

Table 8.8 Calculation of effect of car clubs on annual car mileage of all members

		Edinburgh Smart Moves	Bristol
A	Number of privately-owned vehicles given up, per car club vehicle	5	5.8*
B	Number of members who previously did not own a car, per car club vehicle	7.6~	4.2#
C	Average annual car kilometres before joining club, for members who gave up their car+	12580	12580
D	Average annual car kilometres before joining club, for non car owners+	225	225
E	Average annual car kilometres per car club vehicle	16100	19300
F	Number of vehicles in car club fleet	17	6
	Net distance saved in most recent year (km) **	824670	327654

* 35 people gave up a car, or did not buy a car, on joining the Bristol club, and it had 6 vehicles.
~ In July 2003 there were 17 cars and 215 members. The case study interviewee estimated each car club vehicle replaced five private cars, implying 85 members had given up a car. At the maximum, this leaves 130 members who previously did not own a car, or 7.6 per vehicle.
# In July 2003 there were 6 cars and 92 members, of whom 60 were active users. 35 active users had given up a private car, or not bought one. At the maximum, this leaves 25 active users who previously did not own a car, or 4.2 per vehicle.
+ Average annual car kilometres from National Travel Survey 1999/2001
** Net distance saved in most recent year = (E – [A x C] – [B x D]) x F

It suggests that the Edinburgh car club saved roughly 825,000 car kilometres per year in 2003, and the Bristol car club roughly 328,000 kilometres. These figures do not take account of any car club members who keep their car on joining the club. However, assuming that this group is small in size, is unlikely to substantially increase their personal car mileage after joining the car club and may even use the car club vehicle more and their personal car less, the effect of incorporating them into the calculation is likely to be relatively neutral.

In terms of kilometres saved per member, the figures work out at approximately 3,800 for Edinburgh and 3,600 for Bristol. This is a bit higher, but the same order of magnitude, as the figure of 2,790 quoted by Meijkamp et al (1997), and is lower than all the figures quoted in the MOSES and Carplus reports.

A final point in relation to the effects of car clubs is that, perhaps counter-intuitively, their impact mainly tends to be on the types of journeys that they are not used for. Typically, their impact is most likely to be to reduce car use for regular trips and those where alternatives are most readily available, (such as commuting, school escort trips and shopping and other personal business purposes). The rationale is that car club membership enables people to drive for journeys which are heavily car-reliant, such as transporting a heavy load or escorting an elderly relative. This then reduces the overall need to own a car and leads to other journeys to be made by non-car modes. A number of car clubs in Europe and the USA have specific arrangements with the local public transport operator, and, for example, Carplus (2004) report that there has been a 28% increase in walking and cycling, and a 35% increase in public transport use amongst car club members in Berlin. Some UK car clubs have started to develop arrangements with public transport operators, as discussed in section 8.11.

8.10 Other effects of car clubs

In terms of other effects, the following are reported:

- **Greater choice, less hassle and reduced financial costs to the individual**

Much car club publicity highlights the benefits of not having to personally tax, service and repair a vehicle, and of potentially being able to have access to different types of vehicles for different occasions. Urbigo estimate that the owner of a 1.4 litre Astra who drives 5000 miles a year would typically save £2,255 over three years by joining a car club, and Bonsall (2002) reports on literature evidence that membership of a car club will be cheaper than car ownership for people whose annual mileage is less than 8000 miles. However, in his conclusions, Bonsall argues that this will not necessarily be so for people who buy and run old vehicles over a long period of time, given that depreciation of such vehicles is minimal.

- **Increased sense of community and communal responsibility**

This benefit was reported in both the Edinburgh and Bristol case studies. Specifically, the Bristol interviewee commented that the car club provides a sense of shared ownership and communal responsibility, as well as acting as a social focus in the community, encouraging a sense of civic and community pride.

- **Impacts on social inclusion**

In Edinburgh, it was noted that the scheme has not currently increased social inclusion, because the initial phase of establishing the club has mainly focused on relatively wealthy, inner-city areas of Edinburgh, and both the cost of membership and insurance approval have potentially limited its accessibility. However, there are plans to work with job centres and the unemployed, and to obtain vehicles for the mobility impaired. In Bristol, the aim of increasing mobility for those who cannot afford a car was also mentioned as a potential future benefit of the club.

However, there are other schemes where there have been clearer social inclusion benefits. Kirkbride (2003) highlights that a significant number of members of the Co-Drive scheme in Leeds come from lower-income estates, whilst the Carplus website features 'City-Wheels' in Swansea, a scheme specifically set up to serve social housing residents. Carplus (2004) identifies the people most likely to benefit from car clubs as lower income households with no car, or struggling to run a car; households where the only car is used for the daily commute, leaving others with no access to a car; less mobile or less active people, e.g. elderly or disabled people; people setting up a small business, and those seeking employment.

In contrast, Carplus also highlight that plans to introduce a car club in Northwest County Durham partly failed because poverty is so serious that a car club was still felt to be out of reach of many people. Bonsall (2002) highlights that car clubs do offer the potential to reduce social exclusion for some groups of people but that there may be problems introducing them in relevant areas (such as high insurance costs, vandalism and difficulties for poorer people in raising the membership fee).

8.11 Synergies between car clubs and other transport policies

The following synergistic (or non synergistic) effects were noted:

- **Interaction between car clubs, parking policy and road user charging**
Both Bristol and Edinburgh mentioned that dedicated spaces for club vehicles and shortage of parking are key factors in the success of car clubs. The Edinburgh interviewee also thought that the club could potentially have been used to mitigate some of the criticisms of the council's parking strategy, although this had not been done. In Edinburgh, the issue of road user charging was also raised. The interviewee felt that exempting members from the charge might increase the popularity of membership, and, conversely, aid the acceptability of charging. These issues are discussed further in section 8.14.

- **Value of the car club for winning support for other transport policies**
In the case of Bristol, the interviewee noted that 'a car club sidelines the idea of a binary split between private car and public transport', and that this could help to encourage people to re-evaluate their travel choices. In Edinburgh, the club was considered useful because 'it is a pro-car initiative'. This was felt to be useful in a climate where some people saw the council's transport strategy as anti-car.

- **Interaction with workplace travel plans and fleet management**
As discussed in section 8.8, leasing car club vehicles to employers during the day, to form part of a car pool, is one way of considerably increasing the viability of car clubs. This is turn could work well with workplace travel plans, where providing a vehicle for journeys during the course of work can help to reduce the need for the individual to commute by car.

- **Interaction with transport publicity and personalised travel planning**
In Edinburgh, inclusion of the car club in the council's general 'On route' campaign, that publicises the local transport strategy, is seen as benefiting the club. In Poole, Western Challenge Housing Association have worked in partnership with the council to put together a residential travel plan for a new development. A car club is seen as underpinning a raft of other measures including individualised travel planning, a travel information pack, discounted bus tickets, secure cycle storage, broadband installation and an electric car recharging point, (Carplus spring 2004).

- **Synergy benefits from reduced car ownership**
The Bristol interviewee commented: "By providing a good quality alternative to owning a car, the car club makes it possible for marginal car users - those who need a car from time to time - to avoid having to buy a car, or keep a second car. This in turn

encourages people to look at alternative modes of transport when planning journeys, rather than immediately using the car. It is hoped that this will lead to more thoughtful and sustainable car use."

- **Interaction with public transport**

Bonsall (2002) notes that there is usually "considerable mutual advantage from co-operation between public transport operators and car club organisers". There are a number of examples where car clubs work in partnership with public transport operators to get benefits for their members, who are, in turn, expected to use public transport more. Specifically, First Bus in Bristol offers a 10% discount on tickets to car club members. In Edinburgh, Lothian buses provide Daysavers packs (7 Daysavers worth £2.50 each) to new car club members. Deals on bus and train passes are being negotiated. In the Edinburgh interview, Smart Moves reported that West Yorkshire Metro were interested in being involved in a Leeds car club, and they have also worked with Brighton buses and Thameslink in London (who provide a £50 discount on season tickets for London car club members). The Bristol interviewee notes that availability of good public transport will be one of the factors that encourages people to join a car club.

- **Potential negative effects on other soft measures**

It was noted that a car club has the potential to undermine other soft measures, for example where car club vehicles are used to transport children to school.

8.12 Relationship between spending on car clubs and impact

In evaluating the relationship between cost and impact for the Edinburgh and Bristol car clubs, we estimated the total car mileage saved over the period each scheme has been running, based on the assumption that impact increased linearly, from zero in the first year to the levels recorded in the interviews. Even if no more money were to be spent, we assume there would be some impact in subsequent years, but that this would decline at the rate of 40% a year. We treat all spending as revenue. Table 8.9 shows the calculation.

Table 8.9: Calculation of relationship between cost and impact for car clubs

	Edinburgh Smart Moves	Bristol
Net distance saved in most recent year (km) *	824670	327654
Total car distance saved ~ (km)	2061675	982962
Total cost to date	£99,750	£50,000
Cost per km saved (pence)	4.8	5.1

* See calculation in table 8.6
~ 'Total car distance saved' assumes linear behaviour change in car kilometres saved, from zero in year 1 to current year figure, plus some behaviour change in future years, declining by 40% per year after current year if no further money is spent.

The cost-impact figures suggest that so far, car clubs are costing about 5 pence per car kilometre taken off the road. As the car clubs expand, this figure will fall. Eventually, both the Edinburgh and Bristol car clubs aim to become self-financing. If they are successful in reaching this stage, previous grants from their local authorities might be considered as one-off capital funding, and the cost-impact ratio will effectively become zero – i.e. a reduced volume of traffic at no cost to the local authority.

This logic should also apply to rural car clubs once they break even, although the economics for the period before this happens may be significantly different (as discussed in section 8.7). We did not have enough data for rural clubs to enable the calculation of alternative cost-impact assessments.

8.13 Future impact of car clubs

The future impact of car clubs depends on:
- The rate at which existing (and new) car clubs grow.
- The rate at which new car clubs are successfully established.
- The maximum size of the target market.

The case studies provide information on the rate at which existing and future car clubs may grow, and this is evaluated below. They also provide some useful information on the likely target market. They do not help assess the rate at which new car clubs may be established, or the maximum size of the target market. We use data from national car club umbrella organisation Carplus and material examined during the course of the literature review to evaluate these factors.

8.13.1 Future rate of growth of existing car clubs

The Edinburgh and Bristol car clubs have both set themselves ambitious growth targets. In Edinburgh, the car club had 203 members at the time of the case study interview (July 2003), and aimed to reach 450-500 (the break even point at which the club will be financially self-supporting) by the end of 2004. The original business plan projected another doubling of membership in 2005, and again in 2006. The latest estimate (received from Ball, 2004) is that the club will have 700 members by October 2005.

To reach these targets will require a higher growth rate than the club has achieved so far, or than was achieved by Budget in the original scheme. This will depend on overcoming some barriers to expansion, which are discussed below. The club is also hoping for some planning-led support through developers, and assumes that there will be some additional revenue from a large corporate user. If these barriers are not overcome, or the anticipated additional support does not materialise, the club may continue to grow at its current rate of just over 80 members per year, taking until 2006 to reach 500 members and become financially self-supporting.

The Bristol car club had 92 members at the time of the case study interview (July 2003), which had risen to 160 members by April 2004. At the time of the interview, it had a target to reach 1000 members by 2006. The most recent growth projection is for 750 members by the end of 2005 (Ball, 2004). Again, these are ambitious goals, and those running the scheme argue that they partly rely on overcoming problems with parking supply. The current rate of growth is about 90 members per year, and at this rate, the club would only have about 400 members by 2006.

In the longer term, the Edinburgh interviewee felt that the market for car clubs might reach 4,000 by 2010 although the potential number of people who could eventually become members was much more. The Bristol interviewee suggested that as many as 5,000 people might become members in the longer term.

We conclude that UK car clubs feel considerable pressure to set ambitious targets in order to demonstrate their credibility in the face of some scepticism. They also face pressure to reach financial viability over short timescales, with local authority start-up funding under threat of withdrawal if high growth rates are not achieved in the first year (as has happened in London).

However, the current growth rates in Edinburgh and Bristol are respectable and bear comparison with growth rates achieved in the early days of individual car clubs in Switzerland and Germany. The size of the long term potential market in both Edinburgh and Bristol is also clearly perceived to be considerable. The expansion of car club membership in other European countries has been a product of two things: steady growth (rather than 'exponential' growth) at individual locations, coupled with an expansion of the number of towns with car clubs. For example, the Bremen car club (as reported in section 8.8) achieved growth rates of just over 100 people per year in its first four years.

It should be noted that a steady rate of growth within a club is partly to be expected, given that the decision to join the car club may be dictated by the pace of other things happening in people's lives. Specifically, for example, the recent research on rural car clubs has shown that 77% of joiners had undergone some sort of life change that influenced their decision to join. These included moving house (25%), selling a car (19%) and changing job (14%), (Carplus, spring 2004). In Edinburgh, the interviewee commented that there are a few members who join for a short period of time to coincide with a stay in the city, whilst there are some who leave the club because they move away, or get a company car, or have children.

Meanwhile, as highlighted in section 8.8, the number of car clubs starting in the UK seems to be growing. Moreover, there is starting to be synergy between them. Carplus (winter 2003/04) report that members of Smart Moves car clubs in Edinburgh, London, Bristol, Brighton, Bradford-on-Avon or Stroud can all book vehicles from each other clubs. Carplus (spring 2004) report that members from all other UK car clubs can now book a vehicle from Clay Wheels car club in St Austell, Cornwall. This might apply, for example, should car club members happen to be on holiday in Cornwall.

8.13.2 Target market

To judge the potential for car clubs it is important to know what types of people are attracted to them, and the size of the target market.

- **Type of people**
As discussed in section 8.3, there is a certain type of person who typically joins a city car club – aged 25-45, from a managerial or professional occupation, undertaking relatively low car use and with some degree of environmental awareness. The type of people joining car clubs in Edinburgh and Bristol is similar.

In Edinburgh, members of the Budget scheme were typically 'young professional households with lower than average car ownership and higher than average incomes'. Similar, the profile of the Edinburgh Smart Moves members is middle class, professional, with higher than average educational attainment, and high levels of environmental awareness. There is a wide spread of ages, from 21 to 75. A few foreign or temporary visitors to the city have joined. As mentioned earlier, it was also noted that there is the degree of churn, with people leaving as well as joining. It should be noted that the Edinburgh scheme was partly initially targeted at people unable to afford a car, although this group does not seem to have constituted a high proportion of the resulting membership (as discussed in section 8.10).

In Bristol, car club members similarly have higher than average incomes, liberal attitudes and above average educational attainment.

Environmentally-aware, middle-class, well-educated households may be the social group most likely to join car clubs at present, but this does not mean that car clubs will always be confined to this group. Other factors, such as the proportion of households that would gain financially from car club membership, are also likely to be important in determining the maximum potential of car clubs, and the profiles of those attracted to car clubs may be different in different areas (as discussed in section 8.3).

- **Types of location**

Locational factors such as parking shortage or availability of other means of transport may affect the success of a car club. In Edinburgh, areas of low housing density with plenty of parking are not regarded as fertile territory, whereas the city centre (which is compact and densely populated with a shortage of resident parking) is more promising. In Milton Keynes, the provision of a car club in the central area (associated with a car sharing scheme) was considered a failure, because of the lack of residential land use in the centre, such that the car club vehicles were only in reach of people's work places, rather than their homes.

New residential developments are seen as opportunities to set up car clubs in Cambridge and elsewhere. Bonsall (2002) commented that "the potential for incorporating car clubs into new low-car developments is particularly attractive". In London, Urbigo has established a scheme on a housing development in Deptford. In addition, Smart Moves is working with a developer at three locations in Brent. They operate a car club in associated with BedZED (Beddington Zero Energy Development) in Sutton, and, at a new development in North Ealing, they secured Section 106 funding to provide a car club of eight vehicles (at Grand Union Village). However, surprisingly, Edinburgh's car club vehicle stationed in the UK's first car free residential area (Slateford Green) has not proved very attractive to residents.

Both Edinburgh and Bristol partly attributed the success of their car club to the fact that the cities are relatively environmentally aware, and progressive in terms of transport policy.

In addition to city centre and low-car housing locations, Carplus also believe that car clubs can be feasible in rural areas, as discussed in the introduction, and there are now five clubs operating which they expect to break even within a relatively short space of time. Meanwhile, it is interesting that their pilot work has also identified some areas where car clubs are not feasible. Specifically, in Windermere, in the Lake District, serious interest was mainly from young residents for whom securing insurance would be difficult. In Holbeach, the planning of the club was overtaken by the introduction of a demand responsive bus. Third, as already mentioned, in North-west County Durham, widespread poverty, the fact that the local area operates on a cash-based economy and a desire to prioritise other transport options have all meant that the car club is not seen as appropriate.

8.14 Key issues for scaling up car clubs

Both car clubs reported constraints which were making it difficult to expand their membership, potentially jeopardising targets to become self-supporting. In addition, Enoch (2002) provided a worldwide review of mechanisms for supporting car clubs. The following issues emerged as key factors determining the success of car clubs:

- **Designation of car park bays**

In the UK, it appears that the biggest constraint on car club expansion in cities is the length of time it takes to designate parking bays to be car club stations. In Bristol, it took more than two years to designate the first six dedicated parking bays (although this was partly because a major increase in streetworks caused a backlog in the Traffic Regulation Orders process). Another 12 parking bays are needed as part of the club's expansion plans, but because of delays, expansion into new areas was not being actively pursued at the time of the case study interview.

In Edinburgh, it takes about nine months to get new parking bays opened. One of the Edinburgh interviewees explained the difficulty: putting cars in a new locality before members are recruited is expensive, so interest in the car club must first be gauged and potential members recruited. However, the time lag can sabotage marketing efforts – by the time the cars finally arrive, potential members may have lost interest.

It is also clearly important that the car parking bays are in appropriate locations. Some bays in Edinburgh are not considered to be in viable locations, and, as previously mentioned, an attempt to set up a car club in association with the car sharing scheme in Milton Keynes was a failure because people could not access the vehicles from their homes. The Bristol interviewee commented that it is important to choose locations where there are unlikely to be major objections during the consultation period, as this can result in delays to the designation of spaces. Enoch (2004) comments that it is important not to spread the distribution of car club cars too thinly – if there is only one car located in a neighbourhood, people may be concerned about its likely availability, whereas more concentrated provision may provide reassurance. He argues that car club operators should work with councils to set up a rolling programme of traffic regulation orders for car club spaces radiating out from centres of existing car club membership. These could be initially suspended, but then quickly be brought into use when needed.

- **Car supply**

In the UK, there have also been delays obtaining cars. At the time of our interviews, both case study car clubs used vehicles provided by Vauxhall under a leasing arrangement organised via Carplus. Interviewees said that in the past the supply of cars had been unreliable, although the agreement between Vauxhall and Carplus was being renegotiated and this was expected to resolve the problem. Sources of vehicles for the biggest car club operator, Smart Moves, have broadened since the case study interviews: as of July 2004, Smart Moves leases only a quarter of its fleet from Vauxhall, with the rest coming from three other contract hire sources. In Bristol, the interviewee noted that it would be useful to have a depot, to enable better management of the fleet.

- **Time profile of car club use**

Members' use of car club vehicles is mainly at evenings and weekends, and the lack of use during the day can make cars uneconomic. In Edinburgh the council has helped solve this issue by block-booking five vehicles during weekdays as a car pool for its staff. The car club is hoping to enter a similar arrangement with the university, and is also interested in the small business sector. In Bristol, the car club is working with North Bristol NHS Trust, although this initiative has experienced delays.

- **Planning guidance for new developments**

In both case study cities, there is potential to develop car clubs as part of new housing developments. In Edinburgh the council feels there are many new developments in the pipeline where this would be appropriate. However, it is not automatic that car clubs will be considered. Interviewees felt stronger planning guidance to encourage incorporation of car clubs into residential developments would be helpful. As previously mentioned, Smart Moves is expecting to access Section 106 funding to provide a car club in North Ealing, London. Meanwhile, the London Borough of Islington has Supplementary Planning Guidance on 'car-free and car-reduced housing' within its Unitary Development Plan. They aim to develop such housing in all suitable areas, and their design guidance states that at larger sites, developers may be asked to provide or contribute towards a car club, (Carplus 2004).

- **Fiscal incentives for car club members**

Interviewees also felt the government could help car clubs develop more quickly by looking at fiscal incentives. For example, tax or duty exemptions for car club vehicles would help increase financial viability. Exempting car club members from future road user charges in Edinburgh is seen as one way of making the scheme more attractive. In Southwark, car club members are exempt from the congestion charge. The pricing regime of the scheme – that is, the balance between fixed costs of membership and the cost per unit of use – may also affect its attractiveness, and, in Edinburgh, there are plans to evaluate the current regime. Enoch (2002) reports that the car club in Portland has benefitted from a system of tax credits from the Energy Conservation Bill, which encourages managers of parking lots to add spaces for the club.

- **Initial budget and staffing constraints**

Both case study car clubs operate on small budgets and low staffing levels, probably because the perception that car clubs are unproven makes it difficult to secure more start-up funding. The expectation placed on the clubs to deliver rapid expansion in a short timescale on a low budget seems very challenging. However, both clubs have proved that they can successfully grow their membership, and targeted increases in public funding might now enable them to reach break-even point more quickly. However, the Bristol interviewee commented that the success of the scheme is critically dependent on Smart Moves, which is a small company, and therefore vulnerable to short-term changes. She also argued that the club might scale up far more quickly if it was possible to 'flood the market' with car club vehicles - for example, by having three stationed in every neighbourhood - and that this would change the public and political dynamic of the scheme.

- **Importance of a local presence**

Both car clubs feel that a local presence is important, and that it would be more difficult to resolve problems and recruit new members without a local base.

- **Importance of a 'green' culture**

In both cities, it was noted that environmental awareness among some social groups is quite high, and that this has helped provide the initial supply of car club members. As mentioned in section 8.3, high levels of environmental awareness were also found to be a characteristic of early car club members in Austria. However, this may partly relate to how schemes are marketed. As mentioned in 8.2, European clubs have often been marketed at the environmentally aware, whereas, in the USA, they are often marketed as a smart feature of city living. Enoch (2004) argues that the US model of promotion may also prove effective in the UK.

- **Importance of avoiding customer dissatisfaction**

Member satisfaction is important, both to retain existing members and to attract new ones by word of mouth. In Edinburgh there was a high level of dissatisfaction with the original scheme run by Budget, partly because of technical problems. Smart Moves has greatly reduced the number of customer complaints. Increasing the range of cars available is seen as a future step to increase customer satisfaction.

- **Importance of publicity, local authority and national commitment**

Both the Bristol and the Edinburgh interviewees highlighted the importance of publicity for the car club to attract new members, and to increase the acceptability of on street parking spaces being designated for the club. They also felt it would be useful if government provided a national lead on this issue. In Edinburgh, the £6000 per year provided by the council for publicity material is seen as very useful. In Edinburgh, it was also notable that the club feels it would be valuable to advertise the benefits of the club to members of the council, to local politicians and to council staff. Enoch (2002, 2004) also highlights the importance of political support, publicity and marketing. He highlights that clubs could consider putting more marketing material onto the vehicles themselves (to help identify that they are car club cars), and making the on-street changes relating to the car club spaces a more visible reminder of the scheme. He argues that car clubs need a national symbol, and reports that Carplus are working on this.

8.15 Policy implications relating to car clubs

- Once 'break-even' point is reached, car clubs offer the potential to sustain reduced traffic levels at no cost to the local authority.
- Explicit support from national government for car clubs, highlighting that they can contribute to a sustainable transport strategy, could help to gain local political support and acceptance for schemes.

- The process of preparing traffic orders for car club parking spaces could be fast-tracked, which would help to reduce the long time gap between canvassing potential car club members in a new locality and providing a car. National guidance on this might help.
- Tax and duty exemptions for car club vehicles would increase financial viability and could enable clubs to reach break-even point more quickly. In London, exemption from the congestion charge is seen as one way of making car club membership more attractive, and such exemptions could also be incorporated in road pricing schemes elsewhere.
- Local authorities could be given greater encouragement to consider making car clubs a condition of planning permission through S106 agreements in new residential developments.
- Greater availability of start-up funding, for a realistic period of time, could help many more schemes to become established. It is not helpful if funding bodies set or expect unrealistically high growth targets in the early stages of car clubs.
- Encouraging employers (particularly in local authorities and the health sector) to consider the use of car club vehicles as pool cars during the day could help to make car clubs more viable. Inclusion of this issue in guidance on workplace travel plans might be helpful.
- A national symbol for car clubs might be helpful.

8.16 Acknowledgements

We would like to thank the following people for their help with the car club case studies:

Individual	Organisation
Matthew Barrett	Bristol City Council
Iris Eiting	Bristol City Car Club
Laetitia Jan	Edinburgh City Car Club
Brian Torrance	Edinburgh City Council
Chas Ball	Smart Moves

We would also like to thank:

Individual	Organisation
Judy Ballard	Carplus
Clive Brown	Edinburgh City Council
Barry Maunder	Envolve
Menna Martens	Smart Moves
Sarah Stables	Smart Moves
Graham Cookson	Smart Moves
David Williams	Urbigo
Sarah Holt	PhD student, Germany
Antonia Roberts	Carplus
Marcus Enoch	University of Loughborough

8.17 References

Ball C (2004) personal correspondence

Baum H and Pesch S (1994) *Untersuchung der Eignung von Car-Sharing im Hinblick auf die Reduzierung von Stadtverkehrsproblemen.* Bonn, Germany, Bundesministerium fuer Verkehr

Bonsall P (2002) *Car share and car clubs: potential impacts.* Report by the Institute for Transport Studies, University of Leeds.

Bundesverband CarSharing (2002) German CarSharing Federal Association, at www.carsharing.de, accessed December 2002

Carplus (various) *Update newsletters* Spring 04, winter 03/04, autumn 03, spring 03, summer 02, produced by Carplus, Leeds

Carplus (2004) Material downloaded from website www.carclubs.org.uk, accessed May 2004. Carplus, Leeds, and personal correspondence with Antonia Roberts, Carplus.

Carplus (forthcoming) *National Rural Transport Partnership: Rural car clubs. Year 3 (final) annual report 2003/2004*, Carplus, Leeds.

Enoch M (2002) *Supporting car share clubs: a worldwide review.* Report by the Open University for the EU MOSES project.

Enoch M (2004) personal correspondence.

Glotz-Richter (2003) personal communication with one of the authors

Hauke U (1993) *Carsharing – Eine Empirische Zielgruppenanalyse unter Einbeziehung Sozialpsychologischer Aspekte zur Ableitung einer Marketing-Konzeption.* Bremen, Germany.

Hope S (2001) *Monitoring and evaluation of the Edinburgh City Car Club,* Scottish Executive Central Research Unit

Kirkbride A (2003) *Car clubs in the UK: Status report and future scenario briefing,* Carplus briefing note, Carplus, Leeds.

Local Transport Today (16/10/03) *Car rental sector looks to add 'car club' brands to product range.* Landor Publishing, London.

Meaton J, Starkey S & Williams S (2003) Stelios – the accidental environmentalist? The potential impacts of the Easycar Club in the UK. *World Transport Policy & Practice* 9 (1), pp31-36

Meijkamp R and Aarts H (1997) *Breaking through habitual behaviour: is car sharing an instrument for reducing car use?* PTRC 25th European Transport Forum Seminar C

Mobility (2002) website of Mobility CarSharing Switzerland at www.mobility.ch, accessed December 2002

MOSES / UITP (2002) *Bremen paper: Public transport and car-sharing: together for the better.*

Motorists' Forum (2002) *Car clubs / car sharing research project: Motorists' Forum Conclusions and Recommendations*. Motorists' Forum, Commission for Integrated Transport, London.

Muheim P (1998) *CarSharing – the key to combined mobility*. Report for Swiss Federal Office of Energy, at www.mobility.ch, accessed December 2002

Shaheen SA and Meyn MA (2002) *Shared use vehicle services: a survey of North American market developments* at http://www.gocarlink.com/pdf/shaheen_meyn.pdf, accessed December 2002

Sperling D, Shaheen S and Wagner C (2000) *Carsharing and mobility services: an updated overview*, at http://www.calstart.org/resources/papers/car_sharing.html, accessed December 2002

Steininger K, Vogl C and Zettl R (1996) *Car-sharing organisations. The size of the market segment and revealed change in mobility behaviour* Transport Policy 3(4) 177-185

Traue R (2001) *MOSES State of the Art Report*. Report of the EU MOSES project.

Wagner C (1990) ATG-Umfrage 1990. Stans, Switzerland, ATG AutoTeilet Genossenschaft

9. Car sharing schemes

9.1 Introduction

Car sharing schemes aim to encourage individuals to share private vehicles for particular journeys[1]. They include a range of different initiatives, including informal encouragement for arrangements for sharing trips which, to some extent, happen spontaneously anyway, between individuals at neighbourhood, workplace and even household level; formal schemes with elaborate arrangements for trip matching, often focused on commuting journey; and organised linking with an ethos somewhat similar to hitch-hiking, often aimed at encouraging sharing for longer-distance leisure journeys. Some schemes are open to all and usually operate via internet based sites, whilst others involve initiatives confined to members of particular organisations and often combine websites with a more explicit management element. This chapter in principle includes all these activities, though the case studies focus mainly on schemes promoting car sharing for journeys to work.

There are many active schemes in the UK, and a number of major companies who offer car sharing software and support. For example, Intrinsica and JamBusters provide software which requires administrative support. In contrast, Liftshare and Share-a-journey provide Internet based software systems which do not require day-to-day management. Local authorities often choose to buy in to one of these types of scheme, which can then be locally organised and branded, although some have chosen to develop their own. Some local authorities have primarily developed car sharing as a component of their work on company travel plans, including the City of York Council and Cambridgeshire County Council.

There are also schemes run for business parks, and numerous schemes run by individual organisations for their employees - schemes run by Egg Financial Services in Derby, and by Marks & Spencer's Financial Services in Chester were highlighted as particularly successful initiatives in recent work on travel plans, (Cairns et al, 2002).

There has also been some interest in encouraging car sharing for the journey to school, with reports of success at promoting car sharing for travel to independent schools from Buckinghamshire, Cambridgeshire and Camden Council.

In some instances, the boundary between car sharing and public transport use becomes blurred. For example, the company Vipre promotes a concept they call 'Driveshare', where they provide a vehicle for a group of up to 8 employees, who then travel to work together, with employers sometimes contributing to the cost of the vehicle and the fuel. Some school travel plans involve the use of minibuses driven by parents (who sometimes take it in turns to drive). In other situations, the relationship between car sharers and public transport use is specific - with, for example, ticket discounts for car sharers on public transport.

---

[1] It is often more common to use the term 'car pooling' or 'ride sharing' in other countries, with car sharing often being used as the term for car clubs (as defined in Chapter 8).

The next sections of this chapter review the available literature about car sharing. Subsequent sections then describe the findings from our main case studies – Bucks Carshare and CARSHAREMK – as reported to us during interviews in summer 2003, together with some other data gleaned in the course of the project relating to specific schemes and the opinions of car share scheme providers.

9.2 Overview of car sharing literature

There is a very long tradition of observations that the average occupancy of cars is rather low, typically in the range 1-2, this being one of the reasons for their disproportionate effects on congestion. Smeed and Wardop (1964) calculated that for small and medium sized towns, the potential use of fully occupied small cars could approach standards of efficiency of road space normally only associated with buses.

Policy interest in car sharing was particularly apparent following the fuel price increases in the early and mid-1970s, and schemes were initiated in a number of countries, with results that were becoming apparent towards the end of the decade: work published at that stage rather tended to conclude that success was limited and complex, and interest declined for a period (especially as fuel costs also declined in real terms) except for the rather special focus on HOV lanes in the USA, where this instrument tended to attract the attention shared among a much wider range of policy instruments in European countries.

UK work on car sharing in the late 1970s and early 1980s was rather downbeat about the potential for car sharing. For example, Bonsall (1980) drew a conclusion which is typical of the rather low-key assessments on car sharing generally: namely, that *'car-sharing schemes are unlikely to have more than a marginal effect on congestion, parking requirements or energy use'*.

His own calculations suggested, in the absence of special incentives and fixed transport costs, a typical organised car sharing scheme would attract 8% of city centre workers, with a disproportionate number of those having longer than average journeys to work, and only about a third being those who would share driving (as opposed to giving or receiving lifts). Allowing for the fact that it would not be possible to match all applications, he then estimated that a scheme based on 21,000 city centre workers might lead to 1.5% of them becoming car sharers, resulting in an overall reduction in peak period vehicle kilometres of 0.3%. He further estimated that a scheme based on longer-distance commuters might lead to 5% becoming sharers, and a reduction in peak period vehicle kilometres of just over 1%. He argued that free parking near work would increase participation, and that major increases in fuel prices and public transport fares could potentially lead to a doubling of impacts.

Bonsall's work also drew attention to a problematic finding that up to half the number of future car-sharers might be abstracted from public transport, although in an earlier study (Bonsall 1979), he highlighted that this could be beneficial if public transport was over capacity at peak times.

Dix et al (1983), using social research methods based on qualitative interviewing, suggested that another potentially negative effect could be greater use, by other household members, of cars that had been left at home due to car-sharing for journeys to work. However, whilst this is clearly a potential risk, earlier work by Vincent and Wood (1979) seems to suggest that the scale of effect is relatively small.

Specifically, they analysed 1975/76 National Travel Survey data. This showed that only about 3% of car drivers travelling to work are typically taking it in turns with other drivers (what they termed 'car-pooling'), with the majority of car passengers being unable to drive themselves. However, this was still estimated to be saving over 10 billion vehicle kilometres per annum. Vincent and Wood also showed that the families of car poolers made limited use of the pool car on those days when it was left behind for off-peak use, with additional travel being only an extra 10km per week, on average. They also highlighted that there could be significant gains from, say, a 10% increase in car occupancy, but argued that perceived motoring costs might need to double in order to achieve this.

Meanwhile, Ab Rahman (1993), has reviewed corresponding experience in the USA. He also highlights that, although car sharing was first introduced in the mid 1960s, it only became of mainstream interest during with the 1973 oil crisis. This led to the the enactment of the Emergency Highway Energy Conservation Act in January 1974, which aimed to

> '... *conserve fuel, decrease traffic congestion during rush hours and enhance the use of existing highways and parking facilities...*' and to '*.... encourage the use of car pools in urban areas by means of programmes which included funding of car pool demonstration projects, and the encouragement of local authorities to establish schemes by various means including dissemination of information and technical guidance*'.

Federal grants and other supporting measures were subsequently initiated.

From subsequent experience, Ab Rahman concludes the following:

> "*The United States experience suggests that ridesharing will only increase significantly if there exist clear incentives for the participants. The most important incentives to ride-sharing appear, in practice, to be reserved road space and parking space, and the absence of a convenient alternative mode e.g. where there are no public transport services. The reservation of road space for high occupancy vehicles is therefore essential...*"

He also identified a number of other factors that would need to be in place for car sharing to be attractive to commuters. These included increases in the price of petrol; incentives such as preferential parking spaces; efficient management of the scheme; and promotion by the employer. He noted that 'the personal touch is an important element in any car sharing matching service' and 'efforts for ride sharing should be concentrated within recognized groups, rather than spread across the community. New pools are largely formed when participants have a clear affinity with each other'. Ab Rahman also highlighted that spontaneous formation of a car sharing group could be equally as important as sharing achieved via an official matching service, and that loss of flexibility for individuals is the most significant drawback of car sharing.

A recent European assessment was carried out by the project ICARO (Increasing Car Occupancy Through Innovative Measures And Technical Instruments). Its final conference report, ICARO (1999) drew conclusions from demonstration projects in ten locations (4 in Switzerland, and in Graz, Rotterdam, Pilsen, Brussels, Salzburg and Leeds). Its tone, like the earlier work, was rather cautious. Conclusions were as follows:

> *'It could be said that the potential of car-pooling to dramatically change current mobility patterns and traffic conditions seems to be, at best, limited. But it is worth [introducing] as a complementary and inexpensive measure, especially for some specific conditions: rather big affected areas with high numbers of daily commuters, and significant concentration of working places in some central areas'. (Monzón and Aparicio, in ICARO 1999)*

There was also some quantitative assessment of the magnitude of potential impact:

> *'The existing modal split shows a car occupancy rate in Europe of between 1.14 and 1.2....The potential of car-pooling is quite respectable' (The potential was described as an increase in car occupancy of 13%, for home to work journeys). 'It should be mentioned that about one-fifth of this potential could be a shift from public transport' (Samner, in ICARO 1999)*

The only ICARO project in the UK involved the trial of an urban high occupancy vehicle lane in Leeds, primarily for buses, coaches and cars carrying 2 or more people, (as reported by Leeds City Council 1999a,b and 2002, and LTT 1999). The lane was introduced in two sections in May 1998, over a stretch of about 2 kilometres, on a major dual carriageway into central Leeds from the north west of the city (the A647). A partnership with the police was developed, to ensure enforcement. The scheme was made permanent in November 1999.

At about the same time (October 1998), as part of the EU INTERCEPT project, a trial HOV lane was introduced on the A4174, a two-lane dual carriageway. It is located on the westbound stretch between Bromley Heath roundabout and the Bristol Road (B4427). It forms part of the Avon ring road, located in the northern fringe of Bristol. This HOV lane was also subsequently made permanent by South Gloucestershire Council.

With the Leeds HOV lane, during the trial period, the effects of the lane were extensively monitored over an area of $15km^2$. Results showed that there was a significant initial reduction in traffic on the A647, and a small decrease across the whole of the area during the first few months of the scheme. However, a year after introduction, traffic had returned to above pre-scheme levels. This was partly because of improved traffic signal efficiency, which returned additional capacity to general traffic. Journey times for both HOV and non HOV traffic improved, with gains being 4 minutes and 1.5 minutes respectively for the 5km trip from the Leeds Outer Ring Road to the Inner Ring Road. Monitoring across a cordon of 4 inbound routes showed that vehicle occupancy was virtually unchanged, although there had been some redistribution of vehicles between the routes, with more HOVs using the A647 and choosing to travel at peak time. Specifically, the average car occupancy rate on the A647 increased from 1.35 (before the scheme) to 1.43 in June 1999. Meanwhile, bus operators had increased the number of morning peak hour services using the route from 20 (in 1997) to 33 (in 1999), and were reporting some increases in patronage.

A results update will be published by Leeds shortly, based on their 2002 survey results. These are expected to show that whilst morning peak car occupancy remains at 1.43 on the A647, bus occupancy has risen by approximately 20% since June 1999. Unfortunately, journey times have also risen, caused in part by a 9% traffic increase on the A647 since opening. However, HOV journey times remain 2½ minutes faster than non-HOV times for the 5km journey (Dixon 2004).

The scheme continues to be considered successful because of the maintained journey time improvements for bus users and car sharers.

Since that project, there has been relatively little interest in high occupancy vehicle lanes in the UK, although this appears to be changing. The DfT are expected to publish a local authority guidance note on HOV lanes soon. Leeds (and partners[2]) are about to conclude what promises to be a successful research project into the detection of car occupancy by camera. Moreover, in early July 2004, it was reported that the Government is considering introducing HOV lanes on several motorways during rush hours, with the M1 and M3 being identified as potential candidates (BBC News 4/7/04).

In addition to the renewed interest in HOV lanes, there has been considerable development of car sharing schemes by individual employers, and some literature evidence about this is reviewed in the next section.

Meanwhile, the general potential for car sharing was reviewed again by Bonsall in 2002 for the Department of Transport, Local Government and the Regions and the Motorists Forum. This work included literature review (with the conclusion that there was relatively little useful literature), interviews with experts, and surveys of public attitudes and experiences. This time, Bonsall's conclusions were more optimistic, including statements that:
- *"Car sharing can make a useful contribution towards reduction in traffic levels*
- *Car sharing can potentially offer a more cost-effective method of providing mobility to certain communities than is possible with conventional public transport,*
- *Car sharing can make a useful contribution towards reducing the need for parking spaces at places of employment, and*
- *Potential exists for an increase in the number of organised car sharing schemes".*

Bonsall also highlighted that the amount of informal sharing is always likely to be greater than that of organised sharing, and reiterated the concern that formal schemes may abstract revenue from conventional public transport.

---

[2] The HOV MONitoring project (HOVMON) is funded by the UK Department for Transport and involves a collaboration between Golden River Traffic, Laser Optical Engineering, Leeds City Council, Photonics Consultancy and the University of Sussex.

Like Ab Rahman, (and despite experience in Leeds), Bonsall argued that car sharing is likely to be encouraged by priority measures for high occupancy vehicles. Bonsall also identified the value of demand management measures as a stimulus for car sharing – namely, the introduction of workplace parking levies and road-user charging. He also suggested that 'good practice' for introducing organised car sharing schemes was already relatively well established.

9.3 Literature evidence about car sharing in the context of workplace travel plans

As highlighted earlier, employer-led car sharing schemes represent only a small subset of car sharing schemes. However, there has been considerable interest and development of such initiatives in the UK, with impressive levels of resulting increases in car sharing being reported. Cairns (2000) reviewed 10 schemes introduced by employers to encourage car sharing on the commuting journey. This study was later extended to examine experience at 20 organisations, and reported as part of a wider Department for Transport study of workplace travel plans (Cairns et al, 2002). The results are shown in table 9.1

In terms of effects on modal shift, the report concludes:

> *"The available data show that, of the 14 companies with schemes that enable them to identify formally registered, active sharers, on average, 14% of staff have become active sharers. Schemes asking people to car share on an irregular basis have achieved the highest levels of take-up – and the two reported here (Marks and Spencers Financial Services and Computer Associates) have persuaded about a third of their staff to become active sharers."*

For organisations where *overall* levels of car sharing (including formal and informal sharing) have been measured, on average, an additional 3% of staff had been encouraged to start car sharing. This is a small absolute number, although given the previously low levels of car sharing in the organisations represented here, it is still a 23% increase over previous levels. Six of the 10 organisations that had been most successful in encouraging people to actively share through formal schemes were, of necessity, excluded from the analysis, as they did not have data about overall levels of car sharing by their staff. Consequently, the average figure of 3% is thought to provide a very conservative measure of the potential for achievable change. Finally, it is notable that one of the organisations – Orange at Temple Point – had recorded a drop in overall levels of car sharing. This is because staff relocated from an out-of-town site to a town centre site, where the range of public transport options, cycling and walking opportunities were significantly greater. Hence, the drop in car sharing should probably be interpreted as a success, since it had been replaced by an increase in staff using other, more sustainable modes.

Table 9.1: Monitored levels of car sharing for commuting

Organisation	Overall % of staff car sharing		%-point change	Active car- sharers in formal scheme
	Before	After		
Computer Associates	6	12	6	34*
Marks and Spencer Financial Services	--	--	--	31*
Egg	20	26	6	26
Pfizer	18	20	2	20
AstraZeneca	--	--	--	18
Addenbrooke's NHS Trust	--	16	--	16
Government Office for the East Midlands	--	10	--	10
Boots	--	--	--	8
Plymouth Hospitals NHS Trust	--	--	--	7
University of Bristol	12	14	2	6
Vodafone	8	--	--	6
Agilent Technologies	26	26	0	4
Wycombe District Council	15	17	2	2
Buckinghamshire County Council	16	18	2	1
Nottingham City Hospital NHS Trust	2	11	9	--
Orange (Almondsbury Park)	6	14	8	--
Bluewater	20	24	4	--
Oxford Radcliffe Hospitals NHS Trust (JR site)	17	18	1	--
BP	4	4	0	--
Orange (Temple Point)	14	8	-6	--
Stockley Park	--	--	--	--
Average	13	16	3	14
National travel survey comparison	22			

Notes:
- For the organisations with *, this is the proportion of staff who have registered to car share one or more days per week.
- -- means that the information was not available, or that it would not be appropriate.
- From staff travel surveys, overall levels of car sharing have sometimes been calculated by doubling the number of car-passengers (since each must arrive with a driver), and including them in addition to staff who officially identify themselves as car sharers. An alternative approach would have been to try and get comparable proportions of car-passengers for each organisation. The former approach was adopted for ease of comparison with proportions of staff in formal schemes (where there are usually few measures of car sharer occupancy rates), and because some staff travel surveys do not ask about car passengers, but only about car sharers and single occupancy vehicle drivers.
- The number of sharers in a formal scheme may be significantly lower than the total proportion of staff arriving at the site in a shared vehicle, if many do not join the official scheme.

There were also various other insights from the report:
- The ratio of registered sharers to active sharers ranged from 11:1 to 48:31 - a very substantial difference. A low ratio was assumed to be due to software problems with matching people, or lack of critical mass, or a lack of incentives for existing car sharers are to join.
- It was common for car sharing to encourage more than two people to share a car, with one scheme specifically targeting 3+ sharers
- Most schemes reported growth over time- from 2% to 8% of staff in one case, and from 5% to 18% in another. However, it was also noted that the length of time a scheme had been running for did not seem to be a particularly important determinant of its overall success.

- It was difficult to assess how car sharing interacts with other modal choices for commuting. There are some arguments that it may undercut more sustainable modal choices, and opposing arguments that it may encourage people to make a transition away from the car, eventually resulting in more use of other sustainable modal choices. It was hard to identify evidence on this topic from the organisations studied.

In terms of determining how many people registered to car share, the study suggested that the following were the most important factors:

- **Specific incentive payments and/or direct relief from parking charges.**
  The success of Egg was particularly notable in this respect, since car sharers have been exempt from paying a 75p a day parking charge, and this has been the only motivation provided to encourage car sharing. (Note that they did not have any kind of scheme to match up potential partners). Computer Associates and Marks and Spencer were providing substantial financial payments to car sharers (approx £300-400 p.a., and £100 p.a. respectively)

- **Events to encourage car sharers to meet, particularly major launch events**
  Both Computer Associates and AstraZeneca held a major launch event in the cafeteria at lunch time. Computer Associates matched people at time, using a large plasma display screen which helped to encourage others to follow suit. In addition to their initial launch, Astra Zeneca held a 'Happy birthday car share' event, a year into the scheme, which helped to boost use.

- **Dedicated parking spaces in the most attractive spots**
  Various organisations mentioned that when implemented during the scheme, dedicated spaces had helped to promote sharing, and to provide a visible reminder of the scheme.

In addition to key success factors, many organisations highlighted a few other factors which they felt were important to be in place to encourage people to join, although they were unlikely to guarantee success by themselves. These were:
- a guaranteed ride home
- a small gift such as a voucher for registering
- publicity

In terms of the costs of offering car sharing, companies reported the following:
- cost of setting up a database - £3000-£10,000, but typically £5000.
- cost of guaranteed ride home - maximum quoted £700 per annum
- demarcating dedicated parking - £200 for 12 spaces per annum
- staff time once the scheme was operating - 0.5 days per week
- incentive payments to staff, ranging from approx £100-£1000 p.a. per car sharer.

Most other costs, such as publicity, were being absorbed within the general travel plans budgets.

In addition to the general work on employer car sharing schemes by Cairns et al (2002), there has also been more specific research into the issue of vanpooling by

Enoch (2003). He defines vanpooling as being the situation where a group of 7-15 people commute together on a regular basis in a minibus, driven by a voluntary driver from the group, with expenses shared amongst the group and/or sometimes partially paid for by their employer. Enoch reports that such schemes are considered to be very successful in the US and are starting to take off in the Netherlands. However, he expresses reservations about their suitability for the UK, because:

- A special license is required to drive a van carrying more than 8 passengers (compared with 14 in the US).
- Employer supported van pools would be taxed as a benefit-in-kind, and the main driver would have been considered, for tax purposes, to have been allocated a company car (and would therefore have to pay tax accordingly).
- Insurance companies seem reluctant to back schemes, (although their accident record is generally good).
- Both the public, and policy makers, are relatively uninformed about the concept.
- Vanpools in the US appear to work best where employees for the same company live relatively close to each other but more than 25km from their workplace, and it is unclear how often this situation would apply in the UK.

Nonetheless, despite these issues, Enoch argues that Vipre's 'Driveshare' concept (mentioned in the introduction) which is based on the idea of lift sharing in smaller vehicles, should have some potential in the UK, and that many of the institutional issues could be addressed.

9.4 Selection of car sharing case studies

In selecting case studies for this project, we were keen to look at schemes that were not for the members of only one organisation, and where some sort of monitoring data were available about use and effects on trip-making.

The following locations were considered in spring 2003:
- Bucks CarShare, a scheme covering the whole county of Buckinghamshire, run by the county council
- CARSHAREMK, a scheme focused on Central Milton Keynes
- a scheme for Park Royal, an industrial estate in northwest London
- Liftshare, the national site (which also operates branded websites for other organisations and areas),
- CarShareDevon, a scheme run by Liftshare for Devon County Council
- Airport Carshare, a scheme run by Vipre for BAA airports, and
- Share-a-journey, which also offers services for member organisations

Availability of data about the effects of schemes on car sharing behaviour favoured the first two mentioned, the schemes run by Buckinghamshire County Council and Milton Keynes Council, as the primary case studies.

During the course of interviews for other case studies in Cambridgeshire and York, we also received information about;
- CamShare, a county wide scheme for employees in Cambridgeshire
- CarShareYork, a City of York scheme, which has been primarily marketed for journeys to work, but can be used for any journey.

In our final selection, we ended up with managed schemes, that have primarily focused on work trips. This is partly because data about the effects of schemes largely relies on scheme management – internet based schemes where people make their own arrangements do not usually yield data about subsequent trip matching. So far, managed schemes have probably tended to focus on the journey to work because of the way in which they have historically developed, and, in some cases, because there is a belief that the national internet-based sites will 'take care' of other types of trip[3].

During the course of the project, there has also been further communication with company representatives from Intrinsica and Liftshare, (Gibson 2003 and Clabburn 2004 respectively), which has yielded additional useful information about their activities.

The following sections summarise the information gathered about the schemes that were not our main case studies. Section 9.5 then describes our chosen case studies in more detail.

9.4.1 Liftshare

Liftshare, at Liftshare.com, was established in 1997, and reported over 53,000 members by May 2004, with over 6.6 million journeys registered on their website for the coming twelve months[4]. Their website enables the arrangement of specific lifts on-line, including click-on national and local maps of where members are based, though the density of members in a specific locality may be low.

As well as the national scheme, Liftshare also provides separately branded car-sharing schemes to about 300 businesses and communities, including locally branded Internet sites for many local authorities and national sub-sites aimed at the school run, students, those in London and those based in rural communities. Within locally branded sites, some then offer further sub-sites with restricted access for secure private groups. For example, within a local authority site, it is possible to have a subsite which can only be accessed by employees from the same business park, who can choose to only show their details to each other.

Where communities contain individuals who do not have internet access, it is possible for schemes to have a local administrator (who can manually input the members journey details and search for matches on their behalf), or scheme organisers can purchase a call centre licence from Liftshare, who perform the same service. Clabburn (2004) notes that the enthusiasm, marketing and project management skills of those running the local schemes can often be a key factor in determining their success.

Liftshare believe that their approach of creating sites that are part of one network, rather than a series of stand-alone schemes, is also an important part of achieving success, in that it can help to gain critical mass faster, provides a common user

---

[3] Note that this belief seems rather out of keeping with opinions expressed elsewhere about the importance of publicity and complementary parking regimes. It may reflect the fact that car sharing is also at a relatively early stage of development in the UK at the moment.
[4] It should be noted that many of these are regular, repeat trips, such as the journey to work, since the average number of registered journeys per member is 125.

interface in different location, enables synchronous updating of shared information pages and can generate economies of scale in terms of costs.

Liftshare's website (accessed May 2004) reports that approximately 34% of all journeys registered result in successful matches, with a higher rate – 43% - for branded liftshare schemes for specific communities. Their site also reports an estimate that they are saving about 18 million miles of car travel a year. They plan a promotional event under the name 'National Liftshare Day' on 14th June 2004.

In terms of costs, Clabburn (2004) highlights that schemes are largely designed to run themselves so the administrator only needs to use them to monitor uptake, although they can play a more direct role in accessing the data if they require. 'Typical' set up costs are reported as follows:

- Schools start from £20 per year
- Small businesses: £400 set up and £200 running costs per year
- Medium sized businesses: £600 set up and £300 running costs per year
- Large businesses: £1000 set up and £500 running costs per year
- Branded schemes start from £3000 set up and £1000 running costs per year

The most expensive scheme they have set up was for a group of 13 London boroughs (www.gatewaytoshare.com) and cost around £22,000 (including the cost of a five year licence). It should be noted that these figures do not include marketing costs, which Clabburn highlights can be highly variable and, in his experience, do not always directly relate to take up. In general, he comments that:

> *"The cost of setting up an automated liftshare scheme varies from £400 - £8,000 depending upon the specification and each scheme must pay an annual licence of around 25% of the set up cost.*
>
> *The liftshare journey matching facility is fully automated. Therefore once the scheme has been set up, no further input is required by the group administrator. However most administrators typically spend a day a month monitoring their schemes and dealing with questions from their members.*
>
> *Effective marketing is usually the key to the success of a scheme and we advise companies to budget on £5 per employee for marketing and incentives".*

Finally, Clabburn (2004) notes that one of their fastest growing schemes has been 2carshare.com, a South Gloucestershire branded scheme, which now has 1800 members. This scheme is particularly notable since it has included promotion work above the HOV lane on the A4171 (described in section 9.2). It has also involved the launch of a 'Park and Share' car park at Longwell Green, on the outskirts of Bristol, which has 200 car parking spaces and cycle stands.

9.4.2 CarShareDevon

CarShareDevon was launched in March 2003. It is provided by Liftshare for Devon County Council, and covers the whole of Devon. It includes public access sub-sites for those based in and around Torbay, Plymouth and the rest of Devon, and for those planning to attend the North Devon Walking Festival. It also provides the portal into specific sites for Devon County Council, Plymouth City Council, Torbay Council, Royal Devon and Exeter Health Care, Plymouth University, and a cluster of organisations called '4 Front North Devon' (including Barnstaple Civic Centre, North Devon College and Devon District Hospital).

It was extensively marketed, including 40 temporary road signs on regular commuting routes; 'saucy' radio adverts; 116 bus back adverts; adverts on the back of car park tickets; 5000 leaflets sent out with NHS Trust wage slips; leaflets sent to all staff at Plymouth University; contact with 511 larger employers with more than 50 staff; publicity on all outgoing council franked mail; displays at the Devon County Show and in large libraries; and a message from the Chief Executive of Devon County Council placed on the bottom of wage slips for all 24,000 staff.

By May 2003, 388 members were registered. This was seen as being rapid take-up, partly attributed to the marketing work. Most of those registering seemed to be interested in finding matches for regular trips to work and further education. The Travelwise officer reported that it was one of the most effective things she had done, and that she feels car sharing is particularly appropriate for large rural local authorities such as Devon. By June 2004, 1673 members had registered, (Smith 2004).

9.4.3 CamShare

As part of the work of the Cambridgeshire Travel for Work Partnership (which is focused around workplace travel planning), a countywide car sharing facility has been established in collaboration with Liftshare. This was launched in summer 2002 with the involvement of five pilot employers, representing a total of 13,000 employees. It cost £15,000 to set up. Employers pay to register, and also pay a yearly licence fee to use the scheme. It is up to employers to promote the scheme at their workplace, to provide a guaranteed ride home, and to consider marking out dedicated parking spaces (which some are doing). One perceived weakness with the system is that there are not countywide incentives for using it.

By summer 2003, about 350 potential sharers had registered, and 230 were considered to be live members. However, between the end of November 2002, and mid January 2003, 161 searches were made but only two e-mails were sent seeking fellow car sharers. It is believed that some people may be using the system to find potential sharers and then making their own arrangements. It is also felt that some time will be needed to build up a critical mass. At the time of our interview, the system was being expanded so that employees are not limited to only finding matches with other employees at the same organisation (as they were at the time).

9.4.4 CarShareYork

City of York Council have funded a Liftshare-based car sharing scheme, which was launched in March 2003. It was being particularly promoted to staff at the hospital, the University of York, the College of St John and the council itself, but was also available city-wide. The site was mainly dealing with journeys to work but could be used for any journey. In the first three months, 150 people registered through the site, but, at the time of our interview, there were no figures on the level of active use.

9.4.5 Intrinsica

Intrinsica supply software to organisations who want to introduce car share schemes, primarily in the UK, Europe and the USA. Their software requires that each scheme is managed, and their belief is that managed schemes are more expensive, but generate higher levels of car sharing.

In the UK, they work closely with the company Vipre, who are implementors of car share schemes. In the last three to five years, Intrinsica has seen a 3-4 times growth in their number of customers, and suggest that companies are encouraged to invest in schemes such as car sharing during times of growth, site changes, or economic prosperity.

They believe that financial incentives, co-operative company cultures, good consultation processes and appropriate parking regimes are all important to the success of car sharing schemes, and that schemes take 2-3 years to establish. The Director of Intrinsica (Gibson, 2004) commented that they have had particular success working with the Benelux countries, which he partly attributes to a greater sense of employer responsibility towards their employees. In the UK, it is felt that many companies spend too much money writing travel plan documents, and not enough money on introducing appropriate measures.

9.4.6 Airport Carshare (BAA)

In 2000, the BAA Heathrow travel plan was (re)launched, and this was followed by the launch of 'Airport Carshare' in April 2001, a scheme run by Vipre. Potentially, 60,000 members of staff at Heathrow were eligible to join and offered small incentives (such as Boots vouchers and sun visors) to do so. By November 2001, there were 1034 registered members (representing 88 companies) at Heathrow, and 268 car pools had formed (involving 587 people), as reported by McInroy (2001).

Data from the website (www.airportcarshare.co.uk), in Spring 2003, suggested that there were 2100 members, representing 120 companies, and that more than 60% of members were actively sharing for an average of 3 days a week.

Latest data from the website (accessed May 2004) shows that the scheme has subsequently been extended to employees at Gatwick, Stansted, Southampton, Glasgow, Edinburgh and Aberdeen. There are also clearer incentives as all members are now offered priority parking bays in BAA managed car parks, an emergency ride home and a range of discounts from local companies (including motoring organisations, shops and various theme parks). There are also (undated) reports of over 80 members of the Aberdeen scheme, almost 90 members of the Southampton scheme, over 100 members of the Edinburgh scheme and 200 carshare groups at Gatwick.

9.4.7 Park Royal CarShare Scheme

Park Royal is a 600ha industrial estate in north west London. In spring 2003, there were 35,000 people there, working for 1,800 companies. A car share scheme was introduced for the whole estate, operated by Vipre on behalf of the Park Royal Partnership. By spring 2003, 300 people had registered and 80-100 were regularly car sharing. However, there were reported problems with funding marketing of the scheme, and there were felt to be problems incentivising the scheme to the same extent that would be possible for an individual company.

9.4.8 Share-a-journey

Share-a-journey was set up in 2000. It promotes its services to members, and member organisations then encourage staff or visitors to register on the site. In spring 2003, there were 12 member organisations (mostly public sector clients), and 1500 individuals had registered. Most were registering for a regular trip (principally commuting) although about 5% were registering for occasional journeys. Most were registering, on average, 1 or 2 journeys, although a few had registered up to 10[5]. The scheme does not generate data about whether this leads to shared journeys. Share-a-journey has been involved in developing a scheme for 15-20,000 regular visitors to the Eden project ('passport holders' who live within 50-60 miles), and a lift-sharing scheme for the school run for private schools in Cambridgeshire, in collaboration with Cambridgeshire County Council.

The Director of Share-a-journey (Cutler 2003) feels that the growth of car sharing will be slow unless the government does more to promote it, and that there is a danger that companies are joining schemes in order to 'tick a box' for workplace travel planning. Specifically, he argues that national government could aid the growth of car sharing by the use of preferential parking; prioritising the use of road space including the development of more HOV lanes in areas with car share schemes; inclusion of passenger numbers in the pricing of congestion or road user charging schemes; and large scale promotion of the concept of car sharing by campaigns "on a level equivalent to the current 'Think!' speed reduction campaign". Cutler believes that a cultural shift is needed, such that solo driving starts to be seen as something to feel guilty about. He also feels that concerns about car sharing competing with public transport are overstated since, in many situations, there are no public transport alternatives, and because the majority of commuter travel is currently done by car, such that achieving a major growth in car sharing would inevitably impact on car users.

9.5 Details of chosen car sharing case studies

Information on our chosen car sharing case studies was collected in summer 2003, and is as follows.

---

[5] It should be noted that repeat trips are only counted once. For example, someone logging a work trip would only register 'one journey'. Meanwhile, the number of trips removed per year would relate to how often they subsequently car share.

9.5.1 Buckinghamshire County Council

Buckinghamshire County Council began researching the potential for car-sharing in 1998, in parallel with the development of the county's own workplace travel plan. Their car-sharing scheme, Bucks CarShare, was launched in March 2000, based on Intrinsica software.
Although originally launched as part of the county council's travel plan for its own employees, Bucks CarShare is open to anyone in Buckinghamshire. The scheme aims to match people for regular trips rather than 'one-off' trips – generally for the journey to work although recently the council has started promoting Bucks CarShare for school trips. Publicity for car-sharing emphasises the financial benefits to car-sharers – if you car-share, you can save enough money for a 'free' holiday or slap-up meal. Buckinghamshire Business Watch, an organisation representing the interests of local businesses, is responsible for scheme administration. Buckinghamshire Economic Partnership has helped to promote the scheme.

County council staff may be attracted to join Bucks CarShare because the council provides a few dedicated, parking spaces for sharers in the multi-storey car park adjacent to County Hall (although only certain staff are eligible to park there, and all parking for those staff is free). For employees of other organisations, the incentives to join are fairly limited: there is a free prize draw every year but no other benefit. However, the council is currently discussing with Aylesbury Vale district council the possibility of offering car-sharers half-price parking in local authority car parks.

The key issue for Bucks CarShare has been to try to get a critical mass of people registered on the database. With the current number of registrees, matching of journeys is difficult. To increase the number of people registered, the Travel Choice team has started automatically entering people's names into the car-sharing database unless they specifically choose to opt out, when they sign up to schemes associated with Buckinghamshire's general workplace travel planning.

9.5.2 Milton Keynes Council

CARSHAREMK was originally set up and managed by MK Sustainable Transport Ltd. This company was a partnership between Milton Keynes Council and English Partnerships. The scheme was launched in 2002, on the same day as a major expansion of parking charges across the town centre. It was established using Intrinsica software.

The scheme has been primarily targeted at commuters, and was launched with substantial publicity. Initially it was funded from planning obligations obtained from a new retail and leisure development in the city centre (Xscape). In summer 2003, future funding was expected to come from the central area parking revenue.

Members can park free in central Milton Keynes, if they car share. To qualify, two registered sharers must display their individual but linked permits together in the windscreen of the vehicle. There are designated car sharer parking bays distributed around the town centre in prime sites, and sharers can also park free in the standard bays. In comparion, central parking charges for non-sharers are about 20p per hour in standard bays or 80p per hour in premium bays. Sharers also receive discounts on the bus services (typical fares of over £1 are reduced to 55p). There is a 'Gold card' which gives extra benefits for heavy users.

There were plans to expand the scheme to a wider initiative involving Bedfordshire and Northamptonshire[6].

9.6 Staffing and budgets for car sharing

Budgets for individual employer schemes have been discussed in section 9.3. The set up and running costs for area wide schemes can be different.

The car sharing schemes in Buckinghamshire and Milton Keynes have developed in different ways: one scheme has been very much 'hands-on' as far as the local authority is concerned, while the other has been 'arms length'.

In Buckinghamshire, initial research to develop the scheme took place in-house. Project co-ordination is still carried out mainly by local authority officers, as a small part of their wider workplace travel planning responsibilities, although an outside organisation, Buckinghamshire Business Watch, is contracted to run the journey-matching software.

In Milton Keynes, initial research and development work was contracted out to a consultancy rather than being done in-house. The scheme is now co-ordinated by an independent organisation, Milton Keynes Sustainable Transport Ltd, which receives half its funding via the council and half via the regeneration agency English Partnerships. Apart from providing funding and managing the contract with the project co-ordinator, the local authority has little hands-on responsibility.

The cost (in money and time) of setting the schemes up has also been markedly different. Table 9.2 compares the staffing and budgets for the two schemes.

Buckinghamshire spent £15,000 on setting up their scheme, mainly on purchasing software. Staff time researching how the scheme might work took up an estimated 5% of one person's time for about 18 months. Milton Keynes spent considerably more, including funding for a consultant to research how the scheme might operate. We estimate that set up costs were approximately £35,000. There were no significant in-house staff costs in the local authority.

---

[6] Since our interviews, we have been informed that the council took over MK Sustainable Transport in April 2004, and that CarShareMK is now funded through Central Milton Keynes parking revenue (Harper 2004). Meanwhile, Clabburn (2004) reports that the CarShareMK scheme is not being expanded, and that, instead, in March 2004, Liftshare were awarded a contract to set up car sharing services for Milton Keynes, Northamptonshire and Bedfordshire, to provide schemes that cover all individuals, 50 businesses and 150 schools.

Table 9.2: Comparison of budgets and staffing for car sharing schemes in Milton Keynes and Buckinghamshire (summer 2003)

	Milton Keynes	Buckinghamshire
Length of time scheme has been running	1 year	3 years
Staff time in local authority once scheme established	0	0.2 fte
Staff time in outside agencies, once scheme established	1 fte	<0.1 fte
Start-up costs	£35,000~	£15,000
Annual running cost, including salaries^	£69,500	£12,500
Annual running cost to local authority	£34,730#	£12,500
Annual equivalent of start-up plus running costs*	£70,725	£13,025
Cost to date	£104,859	£41,250
Cost to date, with start-up costs annualised*	£71,084	£26,775

~ In the first 7 months, £75,917 were spent. Given a running cost in the subsequent year of £69,500, or £5,800 a month, this implies that initial set up costs were about £35,000.
^ Salary costs are based on the assumption of an average salary of £25,000. In the case of Milton Keynes, 0.43% of this figure has been added (i.e. £10.750) to the annual budget of £58,711. In the case of Buckinghamshire, 0.2% of this figure has been added (i.e. £5000) to the annual budget of £7,500 a year.
# Based on the information that half of the costs for the scheme come via the local authority.
* Calculated assuming that start-up costs are annualised at 3.5%

There have also been differences in budget and staffing in terms of operating schemes. In Buckinghamshire, running costs were reported to be £7,500 a year (much of which was being spent on promotion), plus local authority staff time which was reported to be equivalent to one day a week, (although shared between two people). We estimate the total cost to be in the order of £12,500 a year.

In Milton Keynes, running costs were reported to be £58,711, plus part of the co-ordinator's salary. We estimate the total cost to be about £69,500. The scheme was being managed by Graham Simpkins at MK Sustainable Transport Ltd with a part time assistant, adding up to one full-time equivalent member of staff. Their roles were described as: enrolling members; publicising the scheme; dealing with day-to-day problems; negotiating deals (e.g. with transport operators); and assessing and reviewing the location of reserved parking bays. Gibson (2003) commented that some of the costs of the scheme related to time spent involving the retail sector, and generating personalised materials for the scheme (such as the cards that go on the windscreen). He felt that these have contributed to the success of the scheme. However, the website developed for the scheme was relatively expensive, and it has been questioned whether there were substantial benefits from it.

These figures can be compared with the earlier information reported from Clabburn (2004) in section 9.4.1. This suggested that set-up costs were in the order of £400-£8,000.

Once set up, Clabburn highlighted that the annual license would be 25% of this (ie. £100-£2000), and that administrator time spent is typically one day per month. Assuming an average salary cost of £25,000, and an average of 240 working days per year, this would imply a total running cost of £1,400-£3,300. This is dramatically cheaper than the annual running costs of the schemes in Buckinghamshire and Milton Keynes. However, it does not include funding for marketing.

Clabburn also recommended a marketing and incentives budget of £5 per employee. In the case of Buckinghamshire, this would justify a further spending of £10,500 on County Hall staff alone, and in the case of Milton Keynes, it would justify spending of £50,250 in order to target all car drivers entering the central area during the AM peak hour. Combined with the previous information about software and administrator costs, this would result in figures which are still lower, but not that dissimilar to the actual budgets reported for the schemes.

It is not clear whether the spending in Buckinghamshire and Milton Keynes has been distributed in this fashion or not. Given that, at the time of our interview, they were both 'managed' schemes, it would be expected that their running costs would be higher anyway. Moreover, Intrinsica's comments highlight that there may be other costs, particularly when establishing schemes, such as securing the involvement of key sectors of the local community.

Significantly, these discrepancies highlight that those wishing to introduce car sharing need to think carefully about the different elements of the scheme. The 'operations' part of the scheme will undoubtedly be an essential component, but the associated marketing and promotion activities are likely to represent a considerably bigger expenditure of time and money[7].

9.7 The scale of car sharing schemes

According to the 1999/01 National Travel Survey, out of 1019 trips per person per year, 407 are made as a car driver and 231 are made as a car passenger. In other words, approximately a third of car use is passenger travel. Notably, passenger journeys are also, on average, slightly longer (8.8km as compared with 8.7) although the difference is fairly minimal.

We also obtained more specific statistics about travel for work. National Travel Survey data indicates that 82 cars are used for every 100 people travelling to work by car. Of these 100 people, 69 drive alone, 13 are drivers with at least one passenger, and 18 are passengers. In other words, 31% of those travelling to work by car are sharing a vehicle, and average car occupancy amongst commuters who already car share is 2.4 people per vehicle.

As highlighted by Vincent and Wood (1979), very few of these arrangements may represent the situation where drivers take it in turns to drive (and therefore clearly

---

[7] It should be noted, however, that software operations are not always smooth, even with schemes provided by the major providers. Both Camshare and Bucks Carshare have reported issues which needed resolution with the providers, and it is important that technical hitches do not nullify the effects of publicity and marketing work.

remove a vehicle from the road). However, arguably, if they were unable to share, one option for at least some of these people might be to acquire and drive their own vehicle. The effects of car sharing on car use are discussed further in the next section. Meanwhile, these figures highlight that sharing (of some sort) is already a widely established practice adopted by millions of people every day.

It is also significant to establish how successful formal car sharing schemes have been at attracting members. Table 9.3 gives an indication of the scale of some of the car sharing schemes operating in the UK.

Table 9.3: Scale of car sharing schemes in the UK

	Start date	Duration (months)*	Most recent data about registrees (and possible market)
Bucks CarShare	Mar 00	39	407 (All in Buckinghamshire eligible to register. Strong promotion to 2100 council staff)
CARSHAREMK	Aug 03	10	1200 (Commuters working in central Milton Keynes targeted. Pre-scheme 11,658 car drivers and passengers entering central Milton Keynes in the peak hour)
CamShare	Aug 02	11	350 (5 employers representing 13,000 staff initially involved)
CarShareYork	Mar 03	4	150 (All in York eligible to register. Mainly promoted to 4 organisations)
Park Royal CarShare			300 (35,000 people working in 1800 companies)
Airport Carshare	Apr 01	23	At Heathrow, 2100 representing 120 companies. (60,000 staff at Heathrow). At least 650 further members from related BAA schemes.
CarShareDevon	Mar 03	15	1673 (Everyone in Devon)
Liftshare	1997	72+	> 53,000 members and 6.6 million journeys. (All of the UK – approx 48 million adults)
2CarShare.com	n/a	n/a	1800 (Everyone in South Gloucestershire)
Share-a-Journey	2000	36	1500 (from 12 member organisations, potential target market unspecified)

* Duration refers to the approximate length of time that the scheme had been running at the time for which we have monitoring data (which is different for different organisations). The most recent data about registrees is then given in the following column.

These figures demonstrate, that in terms of getting people interested:
- There is no clear relationship between the length of time scheme has been running and the number of members. For example, the Milton Keynes scheme has over three times the number of members of the Cambridge scheme, despite running for a similar length of time, and drawing on a similar pool of people. CarShareDevon

reported that they were particularly pleased with their initial take-up (388 members in 2 months), compared to experience from a similar scheme in Norfolk, which Devon attributed to their own, substantial publicity.

- There does not seem to be a clear relationship between the potential pool of members that the scheme can draw on and the number who actually register.

A number of the schemes have provided some insight into growth over time. In particular, Figure 9.1 is taken from Liftshare's website, whilst Figure 9.2 gives information about growth rates in Buckinghamshire and Milton Keynes.
This graph is taken from Liftshare's website.

Figure 9.1 Information from Liftshare's website

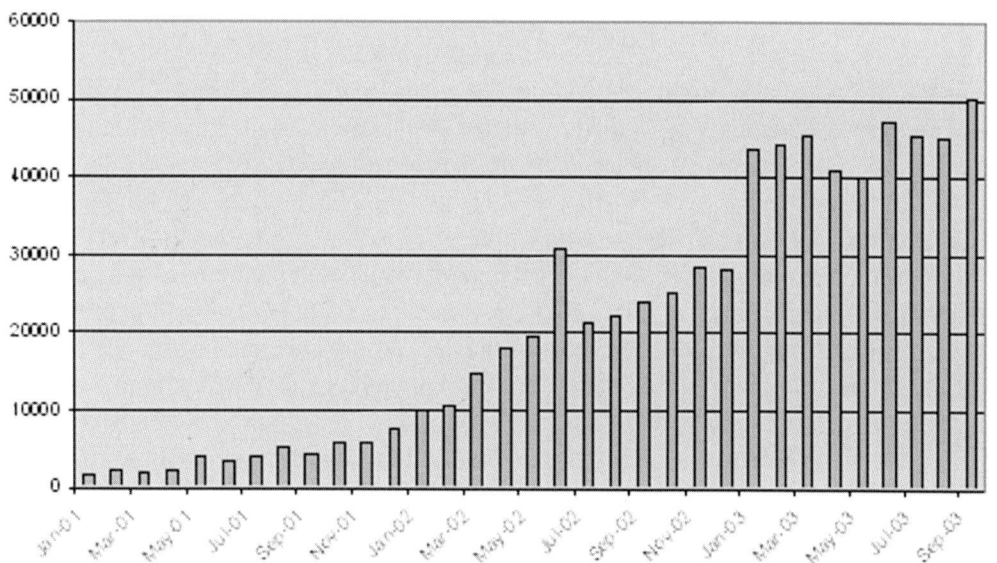

Figure 9.2: Comparative growth rates of the Milton Keynes and Buckinghamshire schemes (as of summer 2003)

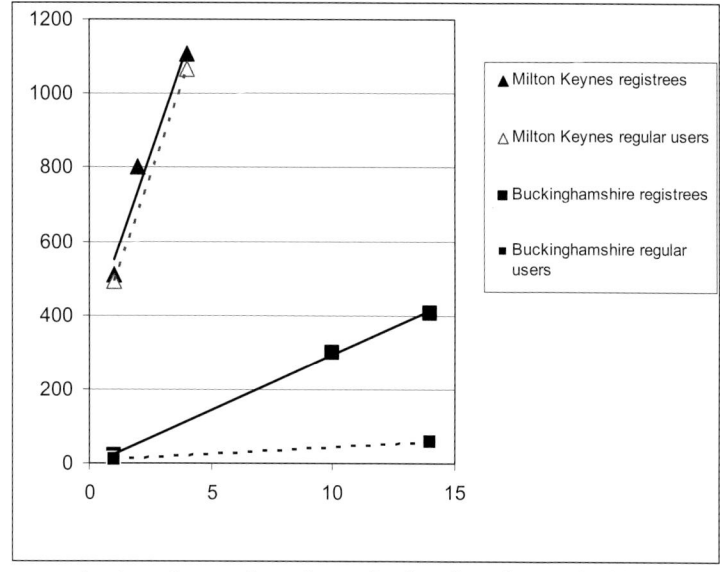

Note: x axis gives the number of months that the schemes had been running.

Taken together, these graphs demonstrate that schemes usually show growth, but the speed of that growth varies dramatically. Moreover, it is not always linear, and people drop out, as well as joining schemes.

In summary, this section indicates that formal car sharing schemes differ substantially in terms of the numbers of members they attract. This has also been indicated in earlier work – as discussed in section 9.3 in relation to car sharing schemes put in place by individual employers. Given that the duration of a scheme, and the total number of potential members, do not appear to account for the number of members that car share schemes attract, it is important to identify the other factors which generally account for success or failure. These are discussed further in section 9.12.

9.8 Effects of car sharing on car use

Data about the effectiveness of car share schemes is often relatively limited. This is partly because some schemes simply offer a web based matching facility, which does not enable the operator to identify whether matches result or not.

A recurrent problem in interpretation of the impact of car sharing is the (often unknown) degree of car-sharing that has been taking place informally before a scheme is initiated, and would continue to happen in the absence of a scheme, or is prompted to take place but does not get recorded in the scheme. Where schemes offer few incentives, it is probable that publicity may encourage sharing although sharers may not necessarily be prompted to join an official scheme. Where there are incentives to join (other than to find a fellow sharer), it is probable that many existing informal sharers will join in order to capitalise on the benefits.

It is also often difficult to get information about whether there are any non car drivers in car share schemes, and how many people are typically sharing per car share car. Formal car sharing schemes and car sharing publicity may also lead to the perpetuation of 'good' travel habits – e.g. non purchase of a household car or the continuation of sharing arrangements which might otherwise have lapsed. Again, assessment of such effects is problematic.

A further issue is the relationship between car sharing and other modes, and that promoting car sharing may undercut the market for more sustainable means of travel. As highlighted in the literature review, there are arguments which endorse this as a legitimate concern, and counter arguments which suggest that car sharing may facilitate the transition towards more sustainable travel, and provide a useful strand in a general sustainable travel options package. It is very difficult to draw evidence about this from the case studies, although it is notable that, in the case of Milton Keynes, car sharers have been offered reduced fares on the buses, with typical discounts of 45%, and increases in bus use were being reported.

The information that we do have is given in the following table.

Table 9.4 Information about the impacts of car sharing on car use

Buckinghamshire	Of the 407 members reported in summer 2003, 60 people had matches and were sharing regularly. Thirty were working for the

	Council and 30 were from a range of other businesses. The scheme administrator estimated that, of all members, no more than 20 people were informally car sharing before they joined the scheme. 41% of those joining had not provided a car registration number, suggesting they may have been non-car owners or did not wish to drive. Average car occupancy amongst those sharing is not estimated to be much above 2. The interviewee commented that car sharing was tending to be a more attractive option for people who live further away from work, and was mainly been undertaken for commuting. He also commented that car sharing tends to encourage people to leave work on time, therefore reducing the potential for evening peak spreading. According to the county council's own travel plan surveys, overall car sharing within the county council has risen by a greater amount than those officially sharing via the scheme. Specifically, in June 2003, 153 people classified themselves as car passengers and 210 described themselves as 'car sharers', with an implied increase of about 110 people (+3.7%) sharing vehicles compared with August 1998. Moreover, this is against a county trend of decreasing car sharing for commuting.
Milton Keynes	Of the 1200 members registered in summer 2003, over 90% were routinely using the scheme, and one count suggested that 8% of central parking was official car sharers, which would represent the majority of the membership. Members were coming from a broad social and economic spectrum, involving a full range of car types. Average car occupancy amongst those sharing was 2.25. The majority of share journeys were for commuting, but there was also some use for other purposes at weekends. Some non drivers were known to have joined the scheme as a way of reducing transport costs. Some people were car sharing in one direction, as part of making their transport options more flexible.
CamShare	Of the 350 members reported in spring 2003, 230 were considered to be live members. However, in a recent three month period shortly after the start of the scheme, only 2 e-mails had been sent seeking fellow sharers, although 161 searches were made. Those running the scheme commented that people are potentially making arrangements off-line.
Park Royal Carshare	Of the 300 members registered in spring 2003, 80-100 were reported to be regularly sharing.
Airport Carshare	Of the 2100 members reported for the Heathrow scheme in spring 2003, more than 60% of members were reported to be sharing regularly, on average for three days per week. Earlier data (from November 2001) suggested that the average size of a car pool was 2.2 people.
Liftshare	In May 2004, 34% of all journeys registered were resulting in successful matches, with 43% for branded Liftshare schemes for specific communities.
Share-a-journey	In spring 2003, about 95% of people were registering for a regular trip (mainly a commute trip), although about 5% were registering for occasional journey.

In addition to the information above, Intrinsica (Gibson, 2004, personal communication) consulted four of their clients about the degree of informal sharing that was probably occurring before official car share schemes were put in place. The results were as follows:

- the Meteorological Office in Bracknell employs 400 people. Before the official car share scheme was introduced, they had 15 dedicated car park spaces for sharers. It was very rare for these places to be fully used.
- At Bristol Airport, the car share manager estimated that maybe 3-4% staff were informally sharing before the introduction of the car share scheme.
- EDF Energy (previously London Electricity) has sites at both Soton Park in Exeter and Aztec West in Bristol. They reported that informal sharing was very low before the introduction of the Intrinsica based scheme.
- BAA estimated that 4% staff were previously sharing before the introduction of a formal car share scheme.

(It should be noted that these results all presumably relate to levels of sharing with other employees from the same site).

Combined with the information from the literature, the following conclusions emerge:

- Schemes vary hugely in the ratio of members to active sharers. This is presumably a result of how schemes are set up. For example, in Milton Keynes, it is probable that many existing sharers will have registered to get the incentives. In the case of Cambridgeshire, it is probable that people will only register if they are actually looking for a match, which is why the number of resulting car share matches is much lower. Liftshare's information highlights that matches are likely to be higher where schemes are focused on a particular community.
- Almost all interviewees were clear that it is important to have a critical mass of members registered on any car share scheme in order to increase the probability of being able to make a match.
- The relationship between formal and informal sharing is complex. For example, in both Buckinghamshire and Cambridgeshire, the scheme has probably increased the amount of informal sharing, even though such matches have not been officially sanctioned through the scheme. Meanwhile, national statistics (as reported in section 9.7) highlight that per-scheme levels of some kind of sharing must usually be higher than scheme operators perceive, although it is plausible that much of this sharing is not between people employed in the same place. Instead, one obvious type of sharing would be between different household members, where one drops the other one off at work on the way to their own employment. Given this, it is plausible that the levels of sharing reported by individual organisations amongst their employees may indeed by 'new' sharing, although this conclusion becomes less likely for schemes covering a wider area.
- Sharing seems to be most common for work journeys, although there is also some evidence of its being used for occasional trips or non work travel.
- People who car share often do not do so every single day, with an average frequency of three times a week being reported from experience at Heathrow.
- It is probable that car sharing schemes for commuters will reduce their ability to travel at non peak times (on the days that they share), and, on those days, it also seems likely that they will be less inclined to chain their work trip with other journey purposes.
- Car sharers may often be travelling relatively long distances to work.

- Schemes can attract non drivers, and the way which schemes are set up may help to determine whether they are complementary or competitive in relation to other sustainable modes. Formal arrangements giving car sharers discounts on public transport may be beneficial, based on Milton Keynes experience.

9.9 Other effects of car sharing

In terms of other effects, the following were reported from the case studies, and are broadly endorsed by the literature:

- **Improved access to work, improved flexibility of travel options and reduced social exclusion**

In Buckinghamshire, in at least one instance, a new employee has been able to accept a job due to the car share scheme, as they lived in a rural area, and would not have been able to get to work without it. The interviewee also mentioned that there was the potential to encourage car sharing for shopping trips from surrounding villages, thereby increasing transport options for some residents. In Milton Keynes, some non drivers who had joined the scheme reported that it had improved their options. Bonsall's work has highlighted that car sharing may be a particularly cost effective way of providing mobility to certain types of community that are difficult to serve with conventional public transport. Liftshare's website highlights the potential social inclusion benefits offered by car sharing.

- **Financial savings for the organisation**

Buckinghamshire Council has saved money from the reduction in car parking spaces, which they estimated as being a saving of £25,000 a year due to car sharing.

- **Financial benefits for the individual**

Both Buckinghamshire and Milton Keynes reported that individuals were saving money as a result of the car sharing schemes, and this is likely to be particularly true for sharers making longer than average journeys.

- **Improved work-life balance**

In Buckinghamshire, it was reported that car sharers are more likely to adopt the discipline of leaving the office on time, which is presumed to result in an improved work-life balance.

- **Improved sociability**

Car sharing is potentially associated with increased sociability for members, and the Liftshare website (accessed spring 2003) reported that at least one marriage had resulted from the scheme. In contrast, the Buckinghamshire interviewee highlighted that people are concerned about their own space, and that car sharing promotion needs to address this issue. The work reported in section 9.3 highlights that events where car sharers can meet informally, before signing up to official arrangements, may help to allay concerns about the nature of potential car share partners, and allow people to make more personally suitable arrangements.

9.10 Synergies between car sharing and other policies and issues

In terms of synergistic effects, the following were noted:

-
- **Improved ability to sell other transport policies**
Both Milton Keynes and Buckinghamshire commented that the car share scheme benefitted from being a transport policy which could help to cut traffic but was not seen as 'anti car'. Hence, people were less likely to be antagonistic towards it, and it might also help to provide a bridge for selling other sustainable transport policies. It is notable that car sharing in Milton Keynes was launched on the same day as an expansion of parking charges, because the two were seen as synergistic.

- **Synergy with school and workplace travel plans**
Car share schemes are often seen as an explicit part of workplace travel plans, and are starting to become an explicit component of school travel plans. For example, Bucks CarShare was publicised to schools in October 2002, and, as a result, one independent school set up its own car-sharing scheme and three schools asked for more information. At the time of the interview, the council had recently been publicising car-sharing to sixth-formers. Camden and Cambridgeshire have also reported success at promoting car sharing amongst pupils travelling to independent schools, and Liftshare and Share-a-journey both operate sites aimed at the school run.

- **Synergy with other soft measures**
As well as synergy with school and workplace travel plans, car sharing may be seen as a generally important component of a package of soft measures. In Devon, the scheme was being done by the TravelWise officer, who said that she felt it was one of the most effective thing she had done in the last five years. However, there are also concerns about the relationship with public transport as discussed earlier, with discounts on public transport for car sharers potentially helping to ensure that schemes are complementary.

- **Synergy with other hard measures**
As highlighted previously, dedicated and/or free parking, petrol pricing, priority road space and other demand management measures may all help to encourage car sharing. This is discussed further in section 9.12.2.

9.11 Relationship between car sharing spending and impact

In evaluating the relationship between cost and impact for the Milton Keynes and Buckinghamshire car sharing schemes, we estimated the total car mileage saved over the period each scheme had been running, based on the assumption that impact increased linearly, from zero in the first year to current levels. Even if no more money were to be spent, we assumed there would be some impact in subsequent years, but that this would decline at the rate of 40% a year.

Some of the costs associated with car sharing schemes are clearly one-off costs, and these were treated as capital and annualised at 3.5%, with a cumulated total calculated for the length of time that the schemes had been running. (These were largely small-scale costs, covering items such as computer software). All other costs were treated as revenue. Cost figures take account of total expenditure over the period each programme has been running. (They have been previously defined in section 9.6).

Table 9.5 sets out the calculation.

Table 9.5 Calculation of relationship between cost and impact for car sharing schemes (summer 2003)

	Milton Keynes	Buckinghamshire
Active car sharing members (current year)	1080~	60
Net distance saved in current year* (km)	4929100	273800
Car distance saved since scheme set up~ (km)	9858200	821500
Total cost to date #	£71084	£26775
Cost per km saved (pence)	0.7	3.3

~ Calculated as 90% of sharers currently registered.

* We assume conservatively that a car sharers journey-to-work distance is in line with the national average distance of a car driver commuter journey. This is 16.3km according to the 1999/01 National Travel Survey. At 240 working days per year, and a car occupancy rate of 2.4 (in line with national average car occupancy for commuters who car share), annual distance saved is 4564 kilometres per car sharer.

~ 'Car distance saved since scheme set up' assumes linear behaviour change in car kilometres saved, from zero in year 1 to current year figure, plus some behaviour change in future years, declining by 40% per year after current year if no further money is spent.

Total cost to date includes start-up costs annualised at 3.5% and running costs. It is based on the information given in section 9.6.

The cost per kilometre saved is slightly under 1 penny in Milton Keynes, and about 3 pence in Buckinghamshire. These figures may be overestimates, since there is qualitative data suggesting that people who have longer than average journeys are more attracted to car sharing, though this may well be balanced by the fact that some car sharers will not share every day. The issue of informal sharing also complicates matters – in Buckinghamshire, inclusion of the stimulation of informal sharing would reduce the average cost per kilometre saved, whilst in Milton Keynes, the fact that at least some people in the scheme were probably previously sharing would increase the average cost per kilometre saved.

The cost-effectiveness of the Buckinghamshire scheme is also lower because active users make up a rather small proportion of those registered on the car sharing scheme. If about two thirds of those registered on the scheme were active, the cost per vehicle kilometre would fall to the same level as in Milton Keynes. This may partly be related to the issue of critical mass (which has limited the amount of potential sharing), which, in turn, may be partly due to the lack of incentives offered.

As discussed in section 9.6, it is not entirely clear why the set-up costs and running costs in Milton Keynes were so much greater than in Buckinghamshire. Although there is a case for increased spending in Buckinghamshire in order to promote the scheme, it is not clear that the extra spending in Milton Keynes has been used in this fashion. Intrinsica also commented that both the Buckinghamshire and the Milton Keynes scheme might reach more people if potential members were able to register on line as well as via paper registration (the system in place at the time of the interviews). Consequently, it may be possible to set up successful schemes that operate more cheaply than in Milton Keynes, or that operate for the same cost but have an even greater impact, although we cannot conclude this with any certainty.

9.12 Future impact of car-sharing

The future impact of car sharing depends on three factors:
- The speed with which local authorities or others can expand existing schemes, and set up new schemes.
- Implementing measures which make schemes effective
- The number of places where car sharing schemes could be suitable.

These issues are discussed in turn in the following sections.

9.12.1 Potential expansion of existing schemes

In summer 2003, the Buckinghamshire and Milton Keynes interviewees both felt that growth of their own schemes was likely to be steady, and at a similar rate to growth so far.

Buckinghamshire: In Buckinghamshire, it was felt that a larger publicity budget and greater levels of staffing would result in higher levels of take-up, although there were no plans for this. If spending in Buckinghamshire remained at existing levels, with no major additional incentives, the interviewees felt that it was realistic that the scheme might have 800 members by 2006 and 1600 by 2011. Assuming linear growth, this implies 1960 members by 2015. The maximum size of the target market was put by the Buckinghamshire interviewee at 20% of people driving to work (assuming that car-sharing continues to be mainly targeted at this journey purpose). In Buckinghamshire 153,811 people usually drove to work in 2001. If the scheme grew at the predicted rate, it would involve just over 1% of car drivers by 2015, well under this estimate of the maximum number of people likely to share. This suggests that the growth rate in Buckinghamshire is not constrained by a lack of potential car sharers.

Milton Keynes: In Milton Keynes, it was suggested that a major increase in the budget would enable effective marketing of the scheme to larger employers, which would probably more than double the number of people registered. However, there were no plans to increase resources to enable this. If growth is linear, the scheme would have 4700 members by 2010 and 7700 members by 2015. In Milton Keynes, 67,986 people usually drove to work in 2001. If the scheme grew at current rates, it would involve about 11% of former car drivers by 2015. Although this sounds ambitious, it may not be unrealistic if the parking incentives are maintained. It should also be noted that it would represent a very high proportion of those driving into Central Milton Keynes, and therefore presumes some expansion of the scheme into other areas, as was being considered at the time of the interview.

9.12.2 Key factors determining the scale of schemes

As discussed in section 9.7, there do not seem to be any 'inherent' determinants of how effective car sharing schemes are. Instead, it seems that the details of the scheme act as a key determinant on its success. Particular factors that seem to determine the success of schemes are as follows:

- **Parking, financial incentives and road priority**

The most important success factor in Milton Keynes seemed to be the parking/financial benefits of using the scheme - car sharers could park free, saving up to £5 per day or 80p per hour. In contrast, in Buckinghamshire, only a small number of county council employees are eligible for dedicated parking spaces if they are car sharing (whereas the scheme was targeted countywide) and there are no financial savings. At the time of the interview, the council was hoping that recently introduced parking arrangements would make a difference to interest in the scheme, and they were discussing further changes to parking payment regimes that could encourage sharing. Cambridgeshire and Park Royal both commented that they felt unable to incentivise car sharing appropriately ('in the way that an individual company might be able to') and that this was limiting the effectiveness of schemes. Meanwhile, the success of the South Gloucestershire scheme (as reported in section 9.4.1) may partly reflect their decision to develop a dedicated 'Park and Share' car park, as a location where people can meet to combine their journey. Several interviewees also mentioned that high occupancy vehicle lanes might help to encourage car sharing.

- **Publicity**

Both CarShareDevon and Milton Keynes highlighted the importance of publicity in promoting their schemes. Clabburn (2004) also emphasised the importance of enthusiasm and marketing skills of scheme promoters, whilst Cutler (2004) argues that national awareness raising is needed to create a climate that is conducive to car sharing. Buckinghamshire and Park Royal both commented that lack of budget for publicity was a problem for their schemes. CarShareDevon has been particularly proactive, as described in section 9.4.2. The work on schemes run by individual organisations (as reported in section 9.3) has highlighted the particular importance of launch events.

- **Critical mass**

If schemes are to promote new matches between people, it is clearly important that they have enough people on the system to make finding a match possible. In some cases, this has meant adjusting software so that it can match for 'pass by' trips as well as trips from the same origin. Buckinghamshire also highlighted that, on materials associated with their general workplace travel plans scheme, they ask participants to opt out of being registered for car sharing, as opposed to asking them to opt in.

- **A committed organisation**

The Share-a-journey interviewee commented that some organisations joined the scheme to be able to 'tick the box' as part of developing a travel plan, and saw this as an easy option. In these circumstances, he felt the schemes were unlikely to be successful. In Milton Keynes, the substantial budget and the links between the car sharing scheme and other areas of transport policy, may reflect that it is given a high priority, and help to explain the success of the scheme. In general, small incentives and offering employees a guaranteed ride home are associated with successful car sharing schemes in individual organisations, partly as a way of showing that the organisation recognises and supports car sharing.

- **Identity**

It is clear that car sharing schemes can work when people are not all employed by the same organisation. However, it seems plausible that schemes are more successful where their identity is one which people can more closely relate to. Liftshare's experience highlights that it is easier to find matches where schemes are for a specific community, and Ab Rahman reported that experience from the USA had found this to be the case.

9.12.3 Where schemes might, or might not work

In Milton Keynes, at the time of the interview, there were plans to extend the current scheme to Milton Keynes General Hospital, as part of their travel plan, and to the area around the railway station (aiming to affect people commuting into London). It was also felt that a scheme covering several counties could be valuable, (see the footnote in section 9.5.2 about recent developments).

The Milton Keynes interviewee suggested that car sharing works best in medium-sized towns with significant numbers of town-based employees and a traditional 'hub and spoke' structure. In towns smaller than Milton Keynes, he suggested commute distances and parking might not be such important issues, and hence car sharing schemes might not be implemented (although this is not borne out by Bucks CarShare, many of whose members work in the small town of Aylesbury). In larger towns and cities, he suggested that public transport might obviate the need for car sharing schemes.

The Buckinghamshire interviewee suggested that car sharing works best where people are travelling relatively long distances. The Devon interviewee commented that car sharing was particularly appropriate in large rural areas.

It is notable that both of our case study areas have relatively high levels of car ownership and use. Buckinghamshire has one of the highest proportion of households owning 2 or more cars in the country, and the development of Milton Keynes was based around facilitating car-based accessibility. This implies that car sharing may be particularly appropriate in areas where there are currently high levels of car dependency.

9.13 Key issues for scaling up car sharing

In addition to the issues discussed in section 9.12.2, the interviewees identified the following factors as potentially helping to promote car sharing:

- **A stronger steer from government that this is an important area of policy interest.**

It was felt that future guidance on local transport plans could highlight the value of car sharing, and the parking regimes and road space prioritisation which give benefits to sharers. Cutler (2004) further argues that those introducing congestion or road user charging schemes should be encouraged to include passenger numbers in their pricing, such that solo drivers pay more.

- **A national advertising scheme**

It was felt that a national advertising scheme to promote car sharing could be helpful, particularly if it was aimed at businesses with the message that car sharing can help cut parking costs and individual petrol costs. Cutler (2004) argues that such advertising needs to be "on a level equivalent to the current 'Think!' speed reduction campaign" and should aim to form part of a cultural shift, whereby solo driving becomes less socially acceptable.

To these points we add a further strategic consideration. There are a number of different models of schemes to promote car sharing. As well as differences in incentive regimes, there are a number of different ways in which schemes can be organised. These include at least three types: (a) schemes which have a tight local catchment, whose members have a high degree of awareness and knowledge of each other, with minimum management resource; (b) web-based schemes where there is also minimum management, but for reasons of software rather than knowledge; and (c) organised schemes involving professional managers and substantial publicity budgets which may operate for small communities or over considerably larger areas. These models may correspond better with different types of area, but the costs and impacts may both be different, with major implications for estimating value for money.

9.14 Policy implications relating to car sharing

In terms of national steps to promote car sharing, the following emerge as potential suggestions:

- More national guidance (for example in local transport plan guidance) could be provided about car sharing, including appropriate parking regimes and other complementary measures that can be put in place to ensure that it forms part of the general sustainable transport package.
- Advertising, particularly to businesses, about the benefits of car sharing could be undertaken in association with other publicity and marketing about workplace travel plans, or as part of more general travel awareness work.

9.15 Acknowledgements:

We would like to thank the following people for their help with the car sharing case studies:

Individual	*Organisation*
Graham Simkins	MK Sustainable Transport Ltd
Graham Walter	Milton Keynes Council
John Harper	Milton Keynes Council
Stefan Dimic	Buckinghamshire County Council
Rosemary Bryant	Buckinghamshire County Council

In addition to the main case study interviewees, we would like to thank:

Individual	*Organisation*
Ali Clabburn	Liftshare

Nick Gibson	Intrinsica
Lesley Smith	Devon County Council
Paul Cutler	Share-a-journey
Daniel Johnson	City of York Council
Barbara Wilcox	Cambridgeshire County Council
Simon Jay	Park Royal Regeneration Agency
Tim Dixon	Leeds City Council
Marcus Enoch	University of Loughborough
Stuart Mitchell	JamBusters

9.16 References

Ab Rahman, A (1993), *Behavioral and Institutional Factors Influencing Car Ownership and Usage in Kuala Lumpur*, Ph.D Dissertation, Texas A&M University,Texas, 1993.

BBC News (4/7/04) Plan for 'car-share fast lanes', report on the website news.bbc.co.uk

Bonsall, P.W (1979), *Car Pooling in the USA: A British Perspective*, TRRL Supplementary Report 516.

Bonsall P W (1980) *Predicted performance of organised car-sharing schemes, Supplementary Report* , TRRL Crowthorne.

Bonsall, P, 2002, *Car Share and Car Clubs: potential impacts*, DTLR and Motorists' Forum Final Report, Institute of Transport Studies, University of Leeds, Leeds.

Cairns S (2000) *Current experience in car sharing schemes*, Working Paper 2000/11, ESRC Transport Studies Unit, University College London

Cairns S, Davis A, Newson C & Swiderska C (2002) *Making travel plans work: Research report.* Department for Transport, London.

Clabburn A (2004) Managing Director of Liftshare.com Ltd. Personal communication

Cutler P (2003) Managing Director of Share-a-journey. Personal communication

Dix M C et al (1983) *Car Use: A Social and Economic Study*, Gower, Oxford
Gibson N (2003) Managing Director of Intrinsica Technology Ltd. Personal communication

Dixon T (2004) Leeds City Council. Personal communication

Enoch M (2003) 'Pooling together: why the vanpool works in the US and the Netherlands'. *Traffic Engineering + Control*, January, pp12-14.

Harper J (2004) Transport Policy Manager, Milton Keynes Council. Personal communication.

ICARO (1999) *Implementation Guidelines for Increasing Car Occupancy Directorate General for Transport* DGVII, Brussels

Leeds City Council (1999) *A647 High Occupancy Vehicle Lane Demonstration.* Report to the Director of Highways and Transportation, plus technical appendix.

Leeds City Council (1999) *HOV Lane Information Sheet – Issue 5* (November)

Leeds City Council (2002) *HOV Lane Information Sheet – Issue 6* (June)

Local Transport Today (19/11/99) *Leeds HOV lane to be made permanent after data show journey time savings.* Landor Publishing, London.

McInroy H (2001) Travel planning at Heathrow. Presentation at a Travel Plans seminar, convened by the Energy Efficiency Best Practice Programme, 28/11/01, London.

Smeed R J & Wardop J (1964) *An exploratory comparison of the advantages of cars and buses for travel in urban areas*, Institute of Transport Journal, March

Smith L (2004) TravelWise Officer for Devon County Council. Personal communication.

Vincent, R.A. and Wood K. (1979), *Car Sharing and Car Pooling in Great Britain: The Recent Situation and Potential*, TRRL Laboratory Report 893.

10. Teleworking

10.1 Introduction

Working practices have traditionally been viewed as something which the public sector does not get involved in, unless there is a need to protect employees (e.g. health and safety legislation), or in relation to financial issues (e.g. taxation and accounting). However, over the last ten years or more, government has increasingly aimed to work in partnership with private industry in relation to a range of corporate, social and environmental responsibility issues. Moreover, as a major employer, the public sector, of course, has a major opportunity to influence the work and business travel of its own employees. Company travel plans were discussed in Chapter 3, whilst Chapter 11 concentrates on the opportunities for teleconferencing to influence business mileage. This chapter focuses on teleworking – where employers encourage employees to adopt a range of remote working practices (i.e. more flexible practices than simply commuting to a fixed workplace every day), including working at home or in a closer location than their main workplace, for some or all of the time.

There are various reasons why teleworking is a relevant issue for government to consider. It is, of course, undoubtedly the case that many of those who undertake teleworking do so as a result of private business initiatives, which are rarely undertaken for transport motivations (alone) or as a result of public sector stimulation. However, local authorities have got involved in both adopting and promoting teleworking, via a range of initiatives. It is interesting that their motivation is also rarely transport alone, and more commonly related to a desire to increase economic competitiveness and/or social inclusion (both of economically deprived groups and geographically remote areas). Initiatives include:

- The provision of remote access to government services and information. For example, the LINNET terminals developed by Lincolnshire County Council placed in libraries across the county are one example (McInroy, 1999). Another is the Cambridge Online City project, established to increase access to public information through the use of the Internet, (www.colc.co.uk).
- Information and advice for companies wishing to develop electronically advanced facilities. For example, Cambridgeshire County Council developed a 'teleworking toolkit', in association with the East of England Development Agency, for companies that wanted to introduce teleworking (cf. Cambridgeshire workplace travel plans case study). In the East Midlands, EMNET exists as an independent, not for profit organisation (supported by the local authorities) to give advice to SMEs with limited resources about how to make best use of the Internet, (www.emnet.co.uk).
- Pilot projects to trial teleworking amongst local authority staff.
- The provision of 'telecentres' which provide a range of services for those who wish to work from home or satellite location close to their homes.

The extent and nature of available local authority experience to assess teleworking is discussed later in this chapter (in section 10.6). Meanwhile, the first part reviews the available literature about the topic.

There is an extensive literature on teleworking, including surveys of changes in travel behaviour comparing people who telework and those who do not, and also before-and-after surveys of new teleworkers. This material is supplemented with papers of comment, analysis and re-working of the experimental data to develop a theoretical framework for the behaviour changes that occur.

Research on the impact of teleworking on travel behaviour was comprehensively reviewed for DTLR by HOP Associates and the Transport Research Group at University of Southampton (DTLR 2002), and their report and database of reviewed research provided a valuable source for the summary presented here. Since that report was published, HOP Associates have continued to update their summary of published reports on the impacts of ICT (information and communication technologies) on travel behaviour. The online version (at www.virtual-mobility.com) includes summaries of more than 126 reports (website accessed 16 April 2004). Telework is also the subject of ongoing European research, via projects such as TARGET and SUSTEL[1].

In this literature review, we concentrate primarily on papers which present experimental results about the effects of teleworking, and do not attempt to summarise the many papers which re-work this data. In reviewing the literature, we were particularly interested in evidence to answer the following questions:

- Does teleworking cut car travel, and if so by how much? What evidence is there for second-order effects off-setting the car miles saved by teleworking?
- What proportion of the workforce teleworks now, and how many might do so in future?
- What are the travel characteristics of teleworkers?
- What estimates exist of the potential future impact of teleworking?

10.2 Literature evidence about whether teleworking cuts car travel

10.2.1 Overview of literature evidence about the traffic impacts of teleworking

Intuitively it seems likely that if someone works at home or at a nearby telecentre rather than driving to the office, their car mileage will fall. However, the debate about the potential contribution of teleworking to reducing travel demand is not quite as simple as this. If an employee starts teleworking all or (more likely) some of the time, the following second-round changes in household travel patterns may result:

- The employee may make other journeys by car during the day (for example to take the children to school or to visit the shops). These journeys might have been made as part of a linked trip if she or he had been driving to work.

---

[1] TARGET (Travel Awareness Regional Groups for Environmental Transport) 1 and 2 projects are being led by Metro (the West Yorkshire Passenger Transport Executive), www.eu-target.net
SUSTEL (Sustainable Teleworking) is being led by Prof Peter James, at the SustainIT unit of the UK Centre for Economic and Environmental Development in Peterborough, www.sustel.org

- Another family member may take advantage of the fact the car is available, for example to drive to work when he or she would previously have taken the bus.
- In the longer term, teleworking could encourage people to live further from their work. The benefit of reduced travel time on teleworking days would be offset (in part or even in whole) by increased travel on days when the employee travelled to work.

Much of the extensive US literature on teleworking has tended to suggest that these effects either balance or outweigh the first-round travel benefits of not driving to work. However, this seems to be largely based on speculation rather than empirical evidence, and the DTLR (2002) researchers concluded that:

> *"Literature that looks at the wider effects of teleworking and other online activities and their relationship to personal travel (mainly in the US) have tended to suggest that travel substitution effects are balanced or outweighed by new trip generation. The studies, however, do not persuasively show anything beyond the observation that both traffic and telecommunications use are growing.*
>
> *An influential school of thought in the US (Ben Akiva, Mokhtarian, Niles) seem to have formed the view that while the direct effects of teleworking may be to reduce travel, the wider effect of telework and other ICT use is to generate a sufficient number of new trips to eliminate the benefit (which is seen as marginal in any case) or even to increase traffic levels…*
>
> *The problem is, however, that the evidence for the traffic-generation effects of teleworking is partly anecdotal, partly speculative modelling, but mostly repeated assertion by experts. We have not found any compelling evidence (or much evidence at all) in empirical studies for the speculated generative effects. This is not to say that there are no such effects, as common sense would indicate that there are likely to be. But they have not as yet been measured."*

The results of some of the main experimental studies are summarised below. A few summaries are based on information provided in the HOP Associates database, and have not been independently reviewed. These are indicated in the reference list.

10.2.2 Empirical studies of the traffic impacts of teleworking

State of California Telecommuting Pilot Project
A detailed travel diary study of 40 participants in the State of California Telecommuting Pilot Project found that on average, telecommuters made 27% fewer trips in total on days when they worked at home, made up of a reduction in car trips to work and an increase in car trips for other purposes. They travelled 77% fewer miles by car (down from 44.8 miles to 10.2 miles) on teleworking days, compared to their behaviour before they began telecommuting (Koenig et al. 1996). Interestingly, although non-work trips increased, non-work mileage *fell*: that is, the teleworkers made shorter but slightly more frequent non-work car trips on teleworking days. The mileage reduction was the sum of fewer miles driven to work (a saving of 29.3 miles) and fewer miles driven for other trips (a saving of 5.3 miles).

The results of this study are similar to an earlier survey as part of the California Telecommuting Pilot Project, which studied 219 people and found average total mileage reductions on telecommuting days of 75% (Pendyala et al. 1991). Pendyala et al. also found evidence that teleworkers chose non-work destinations that were closer to home, exhibiting "contracted action spaces".

California Residential Area-Based Offices Project
Other Californian studies have evaluated the impacts of telecentre-based commuting, where the worker travels to a neighbourhood telecentre (Balepur et al 1998; Mokhtarian et al. 1998). These studies found slightly lower but still significant reductions in car mileage on teleworking days, of between 53% (reported by Mokhtarian et al.) and 65% (reported by Balepur et al.). Workers generated additional car mileage by driving home in the middle of the day for lunch and back to the telecentre in the afternoon. However, the number of non-commuting trips on teleworking days either fell or remained constant. Balepur et al. calculated that when the reduction in car mileage was weighted by the frequency of teleworking, the overall reduction in car mileage was 17% of total weekday commuting travel. Mokhtarian et al. (1998), with a slightly larger evidence base, concluded that the reduction in car commuting mileage was 11.5% over the week (on average teleworkers used a telecentre about 1¼ days per five day working week).

Teleworking in the Washington Metropolitan Area
The Washington Metropolitan Telework Demonstration Project involved eight organisations in the Washington metropolitan area who were provided with help to expand or start formal telework schemes. Six were private sector organisations, one was a government body, and one was a non-profit organisation. Most of the teleworkers worked at home one or two days a week, although one site's teleworkers worked at home full-time (Metropolitan Washington Council of Governments 1999).

The study gathered evidence on the effect of teleworking on vehicle use and vehicle miles travelled. It asked about non-commute trips that were eliminated (e.g. not going out for lunch) and non-commute trips that were made (e.g. going shopping after work). The interviewees were also asked if any other household member had used their vehicle on their most recent telework day. Amongst 100 employees surveyed, the average number of vehicle trips per day fell by 0.6, and average vehicle miles per day fell by 16, per teleworker.

The study also looked for evidence of people adapting to teleworking by moving further away from work. Amongst 22 people involved in the survey who had moved or were planning to move, it found the move was equally likely to be closer to work or further away.

Teleworking in the Netherlands
Hamer et al. (1991) analysed travel diaries of 30 employees of the Dutch Ministry of Transport who spent between 20 and 60% of their time teleworking. The study also surveyed the travel activity of members of the teleworkers' households. For the teleworkers, they found that:
- The overall number of trips made fell by 17% (compared to the number of trips made before teleworking began)
- Peak-hour trips fell by 19%, and peak hour distance travelled fell by 26%

- Trips as a car driver fell by 19%, and distance travelled as a car driver also fell by 19%
- Peak hour car trips fell by 26% and peak hour car mileage by 34%.

For other household members, the study found:
- The overall number of trips fell by 9%; most of the decrease was for non-work related travel
- The estimated distance travelled by household members showed hardly any significant change.

The study found that the decrease in number of trips was more immediate for the teleworkers, whereas household members only gradually started to travel less. The reduction in trips made by household members was unexpected, and despite a further qualitative survey the researchers were unsure of the explanation for this.

Teleworking in Greater Münich

This study (Glogger et al. 2003) examined the travel behaviour of teleworkers in eight large organisations in Greater Münich, using travel diaries before and after teleworking was introduced. Before and after travel diaries were completed by 37 teleworkers and 29 members of their households. The study found that people who began teleworking reduced their total number of trips (for all purposes, not just for work) by 19%. The number of trips made by other household members also fell. Taking the household as a whole, the total number of trips for all purposes fell by 14%. The study suggested that in the absence of teleworking, traffic in the Greater Münich Area would be 2% greater.

Teleworking in Denmark

This study (Jensen et al. 2003) involved a questionnaire to a panel of 946 Internet users in Denmark who telework some of the time. People who always worked at home were excluded from the survey. It compared the travel behaviour of teleworkers on days when they worked at home with their travel behaviour on commuting days. The total amount of time spent travelling in the teleworkers' own cars was 48.6% lower on days when they worked at home. Travel time for all other modes apart from walking (that is, cycling, bus, train, and travel in someone else's car) also fell by between 21.0% and 74.8%. The survey did not ask about travel patterns amongst other household members.

The survey examined whether working at home had affected choice of where to live, or might do so in future. 4% of respondents said teleworking had influenced their choice of where to live, with equal numbers saying it had led them to move closer to, and further away from, work. 7% said that in future, the opportunity to work at home would have considerable influence on their choice of where to live; while 21% said it would have some influence. The number who said they would be likely to move further away was approximately the same as the number who said they would move closer to work.

Just over 3% of respondents had changed where they worked because they wanted the opportunity to telework. Equal numbers had moved to a workplace that was closer to, and further away from, their home. Six per cent said they were considering changing their workplace in order to be able to telework, and again half said the distance between home and work would increase and half said it would decrease.

The study's authors concluded that the opportunity to telework will potentially affect long-term decisions about place of residence and place of work; that it is impossible to say whether the result will be a spatially more or less dispersed pattern; but that at present it seems that teleworking will have limited effect on these choices.

Teleworking in the UK

Hopkinson and James (2003) report the results of the European SUSTEL study on sustainable teleworking, including surveys of teleworking staff at BT and BAA. Information from the BT survey is reported in more detail, from section 10.7 onwards. Meanwhile, the following information is given about BAA. In the main administrative building for BAA at West Point, 64 out of 250 employees telework. The SUSTEL survey was completed by 20 staff, all of whom reported their commuting had decreased since becoming a teleworker, with mean reductions of 61 miles per week. This was partially offset by additional trips, mainly for shopping and child escort. Across the whole sample, this resulted in additional weekly travel of 16 miles per person, giving net weekly travel reductions of 45 miles per person. It was notable that the initiative has also led to reduced space requirements, estimated to be resulting in savings of £400,000 per annum.

The research by HOP Associates and the University of Southampton reports a study by Hopkinson et al. (2001) which looked at the changed travel patterns of 103 AA call-centre staff who moved to home-based working. Before the shift to working at home, 88% of commuting trips were by car, and journey length was on average 9 miles. By almost completely eliminating commuting trips, 3680 vehicle miles were saved per employee per year. This was offset by occasional employee visits to the office and home visits by managers, which came to about 30-40% of the miles saved. Of 29 employees who gave information about their non-work travel, most said that this had also reduced but nine said they now made longer or more frequent journeys.

An earlier study (Mitchell and Trodd 1994) examined the travel behaviour of a small sample of existing UK teleworkers. It found an average reduction in travel of 113 miles per week (after allowing for remaining travel to work and additional non-work trips). Half the sample reported no extra non-work trips. The journeys of this sample of teleworkers were significantly longer than the average journey to work – 21 miles compared to the national average at the time of 8.3 miles. On the assumption that long distance commuters might be more likely to find telework attractive, the study estimated a saving in car use nationally of 5 – 12%.

Travel plans literature (Hop Associates 2001) also gives reports from four private sector companies as follows:

- IBM introduced a 'Smart' project, which was a scheme mixing home-based working and shared office touchdown points. This resulted in a 13% reduction in travel time, a 36% increase in time spent with customers and a total space-saving of 30%.
- RM Consulting, an internal consultancy for the Post Office, began a 'location independent working' pilot project in 1995. Within two years, the 145 employees involved had reduced their mileage by around 500,000 km, with 10% of them

travelling half the distance that they had at the start of the project. In the following two years, the target was to double the number of employees involved.

- ADAS Consulting Limited adopted ICT based working practices about five years ago. Since then, it has reduced its number of office sites from 90 to 26, and more than 500 of the staff now work from home. Travel savings for each of these employees is estimated to be around 2000 miles a year.
- Yorkshire Water introduced a mobile working pilot project for its engineers. This resulted in annual mileage savings of up to 20%, mainly by eliminating daily visits to the team office.

There has been a more recent study by National Opinion Polls, as reported by Geraghty (2004) and Fogarty (2004). It involved interviews with 1,600 Internet users in December 2003. The sample was weighted to match Financial Research Survey[2] generated profiles of Internet users, and selected from 17,931 GB adults (who were screened for Internet usage in the previous 12 months using the FRS and NOP's two Omnibus Vehicles). Of the 1,600 Internet users who worked from home for some or all of the time, the average mileage of the round trip saved was 16.3 miles. 56% made non-work related car journeys whilst working from home of an average length of 4 miles. Consequently, the net effect, per teleworker, was 12.3 miles saved per day (an overall reduction in commuting mileage of approximately 75%).

10.2.3 Summary of findings about the impacts of teleworking on car use

The evidence from these various studies points to the following conclusions about the impact of teleworking on car use:

Teleworking does reduce the car mileage travelled by teleworkers, even allowing for some extra non-work car trips.
Estimates of the effects of teleworking are reported in a variety of ways, but all point in the same direction. Studies which compare distance travelled by teleworkers on teleworking days with that on non-telework days find reductions in mileage of between 48% and 77% (Balepur et al. 1998; Jensen et al. 2003; Koenig et al. 1996; Mokhtarian et al. 1998; Pendyala et al. 1991; Geraghty 2004 and Fogarty 2004). Reported overall reductions in mileage or trips (measured across both teleworking and non-teleworking days) range from 11% to 19% (Balepur et al. 1998; Glogger et al. 2003; Hamer et al. 1991; Mokhtarian et al. 1998). There is some evidence that teleworkers exhibit 'contracted action spaces': that is, that they begin to choose non-work destinations which are closer to home (Koenig et al. 1996; Pendyala et al. 1991).

There is rather little evidence about the impact of teleworking on other household members. However, the evidence that is available points towards their travel remaining the same or perhaps even falling slightly, rather than increasing.
Glogger et al. (2003) found that both teleworkers and other household members made fewer trips after teleworking began. Average trips per household fell by 14%. Hamer et al. (1991) found that the number of trips made by other household members fell by 9% after teleworking began, and that distance travelled showed little change. Hamer

---

[2] This is one of the most respected surveys of consumer behaviour in relation to the personal financial services sector, designed to give a representative picture of the UK.

et al. also noted that the behaviour change was more gradual for other members of teleworking households: whereas the decrease in trips for teleworkers was immediate, other household members only gradually started to travel less.

There is little evidence about the impact of teleworking on people's choice of where to live. What there is, points towards teleworking being of rather little importance in choice of home location, although there are links between teleworking and trip distance that may indicate long run effects, as yet not understood.

Two studies explicitly sought information about whether the opportunity to telework might lead people to move further away from their work, increasing commuting distances on non-telework days. The MWCOG (1999) study included 22 teleworkers who had recently moved or were planning to move. The direction of their move was equally likely to be closer to work or further away from work. Similarly, Jensen et al. (2003) found that amongst people who said teleworking influenced their choice of where to live (or would do so in future), the move was as likely to be closer to work as further away. There is also some evidence suggesting teleworkers may have longer commute journeys than the national average, reported in 10.4 below. This might be explained by teleworkers moving further away, or might indicate that employees who live further away have a greater incentive to telework, or even that both are associated with some other cause, such as income. The long run effects of this kind are, as yet, unknown.

Further comparisons of the various studies are given in section 10.10.

10.3 What proportion of the workforce teleworks, or might do so?

The proportion of the working population that is teleworking is growing fast. In 1993 it was estimated that about 0.5% of the workforce in Britain (130,000 people) sometimes teleworked (DTI 2002). By 2001, data from the Labour Force Survey showed that 2.2 million people in the UK (7.4% of the labour force) worked from home at least one day a week using a telephone and computer. Since 1997 the number of teleworkers in the UK has increased by on average 13% a year, giving an overall increase between 1997 and 2001 of 65%.

The same report (DTI 2002) also defined a subcategory of teleworker, as being people who could not perform their job *without* the use of both a computer and telephone. In 2001, there were reported to be 1.8 million of these (approximately 6% of the labour force). The 'essentialness' of telecommunications equipment is not of particular interest in transport terms. However, this subcategory is of interest, because there are later figures available from the Labour Force Survey. Specifically, as reported on content.equaltelework.org (a site run by the Telework Association), the 2003 Labour Force Survey showed that this subcategory had grown to 2.1 million in 2003, with a growth rate of 12% in the last year.

If growth rates of 12-13% p.a. continue for about 10 years, this would result in approximately 30% of the UK workforce teleworking for at least some of the time by the end of the period.

Clearly not everyone works in a job where teleworking is possible, which might mean that some kind of 'ceiling' could be reached, in terms of the proportion of the population who are able to telework. The same report (DTI 2002) provides some insights into this issue. In particular, it gives the number of teleworkers in two sets of occupational classification systems. These can be compared with the total numbers of employees that fall into these classifications, as shown in Tables 10.1 and 10.2.

Table 10.1 Breakdown of employment by occupation (figures for Spring 2001)

	% of employees in each employment category	% of teleworkers in each employment category	% of those in each employment category who are tele workers
Managers and senior officials	13.7	23	13
Professional occupations	11.9	25	16
Associate professional and technical	13.3	20	12
Administration and secretarial	13.4	9	5
Skilled trades	12.0	15	9
Personal services	7.2	3	3
Sales and customer services	7.8	2	2
Process, plant and machine operatives	8.6	2	2
Elementary occupations	12.2	1	1
Total	100	100	n/a

Sources: Figures for general employment taken from the ONS Labour Force survey reports on the ONS website, Spring 2001. Data are for all in employment. Telework data read from graphs in DTI 2001 (hence figures in second two columns only given to one or two significant figures). Both data sets coded according to the 2000 Standard Occupational Classification.

Table 10.2 Breakdown of employment by industry sector (figures for Spring 2001)

	SIC category	% of employees in each employment category	% of teleworkers in each employment category	% of those in each employment category who are tele workers
Agriculture, forestry and fishing	a,b	1.2	2	13
Energy and water	c,e	0.7	0	5
Manufacturing	d	15.0	12	6
Construction	f	4.7	14	24
Wholesale, retail and motor trade	g	17.6	9	4
Hotels and restaurants	h	6.6	1	2
Transport, storage and communications	i	6.3	5	6
Banking, finance and insurance	j	4.2	4	8
Real estate, renting and business activities	k	14.6	24	13
Public administration and defence	l	5.5	4	6
Education	m	8.4	10	10
Health and social work	n	10.2	6	5
Other community, social and personal	o-q	5.0	8	14
		100	100	--

Sources: Figures for general employment taken from National Statistics (2002) Annual Abstract of Statistics, TSO: London. Telework data read from graphs in DTI 2001 (hence figures in second two columns only given to one or two significant figures). Both data sets coded according to the 1992 Standard Industrial Classication (SIC).

Table 10.1 shows that the majority of teleworkers currently, and the highest incidence of teleworking, occur in managerial, professional, administrative (including secretarial) and skilled occupations, in each of which between 5% and 16% of the workforce currently telework. These groups make up 64% of the total workforce. The remaining one-third of the workforce currently has a quite small incidence of teleworking, at around 2%. However, all occupational groups have some degree of telecommuting already.

This is further illustrated by table 10.2, which uses the standard industry classification, where there are significant proportions of employees in every industry who are teleworkers - even including industries which rely heavily on personal contact, such as 10% in education, 13% in real estate and 5% in health and social work.

Hence, this initial analysis suggests that there is no clearly defined 'ceiling' in terms of the proportion of the population who might telework. Moreover, there are several trends which suggest that the growth of teleworking may continue to increase. The 'naturally' high teleworking occupations are also those which have, in recent years, been a growing proportion of the economy. There is a growth in the incidence of teleworking within those jobs most suitable for it. There has been the development of new techniques of work styles which apply telecommunications to those tasks previously thought unsuitable (such as medical diagnoses, further education teaching, estate agency, personal advice, and production control). Improving technologies have made it easier to work remotely. Moreover, occupations not presently seen as appropriate for teleworking may involve a proportion of tasks which could be carried out away from the main workplace relatively easily, and, as telework becomes more widespread, attitudes to working at home in these occupations may change. The growth of telesales, decline of traditional travel agencies, and changes in the music business all indicate that the pace of change can be rapid.

There have been a few other studies which have attempted to assess the potential scale of teleworking in the UK. These are as follows:

Institute of Employment Studies

DTI (2002) quotes research by the Institute of Employment Studies (Huws et al, 2001). This analysed the proportion of particular occupations in the total workforce. They are said to have included "for example managers, computer professionals, teaching professionals, writers and creative performing artists, and administrative associate professionals." Their study suggested that 22.6% of the UK workforce could potentially telework. (It is perhaps interesting that, in the same report, the DTI (2002) quoted a study from the United States in 2001, which suggested that 21% of the labour force were already teleworking.)

HOP Associates

A study for DTLR by HOP Associates (Lake et al. 1997) gives an insight into the potential for teleworking in occupations where it is currently low. Lake et al. looked at the "teleworkability" of tasks carried out by 2300 employees of Cambridgeshire County Council, and concluded that, of the tasks carried out by different types of employee:

- 5-20% of tasks carried out by support staff were location-independent
- 30-60% of tasks by service delivery staff, including field workers, were location-independent
- 30-50% of tasks by managers were location-independent.

Given that, as discussed below, some data suggest that teleworkers only tend to work from home for an average of about 30% of the time, this implies that some degree of teleworking may actually be feasible for the majority of staff. In particular, these figures show that occupations which are not presently seen to have much teleworking potential (such as support roles and service delivery) involve a significant proportion of tasks which could be carried out away from the workplace.

Motors or Modems

Dodgson et al (2000) quote US findings (reported by Fouracre and Hill, 1998) which suggest that 50% of the workforce are 'information workers' and 80% might telecommute, leading to a saturation level of 40% of the workforce. In their own scenario building, Dodgson et al estimate that 15% of the workforce might be teleworking by 2010 on any one day.

National Opinion Polls survey

As reported in section 10.2.2, a recent National Opinion Polls survey (reported by Geraghty 2004 and Fogarty 2004) involved interviews with 1,600 Internet users in December 2003. These were selected from 17,931 GB adults (aged 15+), who were screened for Internet usage in the preceding 12 months.

The NOP survey showed that, of internet-using employees, 25% were working from home some or all of the time. (It also showed that the proportion of broadband users sometimes working from home was higher – namely 31%). From the initial selection procedure, NOP concluded that 24.9 million GB adults were Internet users, and 66% of these were in employment – i.c. approximately 16.4 million people. Given that 25% of those in employment were working from home some or all of the time, this implies a total of 4.1million (14.4% of the labour force[3]). This is considerably higher than the figure quoted from the earlier Labour Force Survey (c.f. DTI 2002). This may partly reflect higher growth rates for home working than previously, and/or may reflect different definitions of teleworking. Given the high proportion (25%) of Internet users who were working from home, the results also imply that, as Internet penetration increases, it is possible that teleworking will increase.

Meanwhile, for those Internet users who are in employment but don't currently work from home (estimated to be 12 million employees), the NOP survey suggested that 77% do not want to telework, 17% want to but would not be allowed to and only 7% want to and would be allowed to. Consequently, Fogarty (2004) and Geraghty (2004) argue that the potential for growth in teleworking amongst this group may be relatively small.

---

[3] This assumes that there are currently 28.2 million people in employment, as given in the April 2004 Labour Force Survey Quarterly Supplement produced by National Statistics.

10.4 Characteristics of teleworking

Frequency of working from home amongst teleworkers
The DTLR (2002) review of published literature concludes that on average teleworkers work about 1½ days a week away from the main office. Dodgson et al (2000) quote research by Fouracre and Hill (1998) which estimates that tele-workers typically work from home for 25% of their time (ie. just under one and a half days). The Cambridgeshire County Council study by Lake et al. quoted above indicates that amongst the managers and service delivery staff they studied, there was the *potential* to work at home between 1½ and 3 days per week: in other words 1½ days telework per week would represent the lower limit of the amount of time that is actually spent on location-independent tasks. The National Opinion Polls survey suggested that, for those working at home in their survey, the average frequency was 3.1 days per week, (Geraghty, 2004). Their results are shown in Figure 10.1.

Figure 10.1: NOP results about the frequency of teleworking by those in their study (Geraghty 2004)

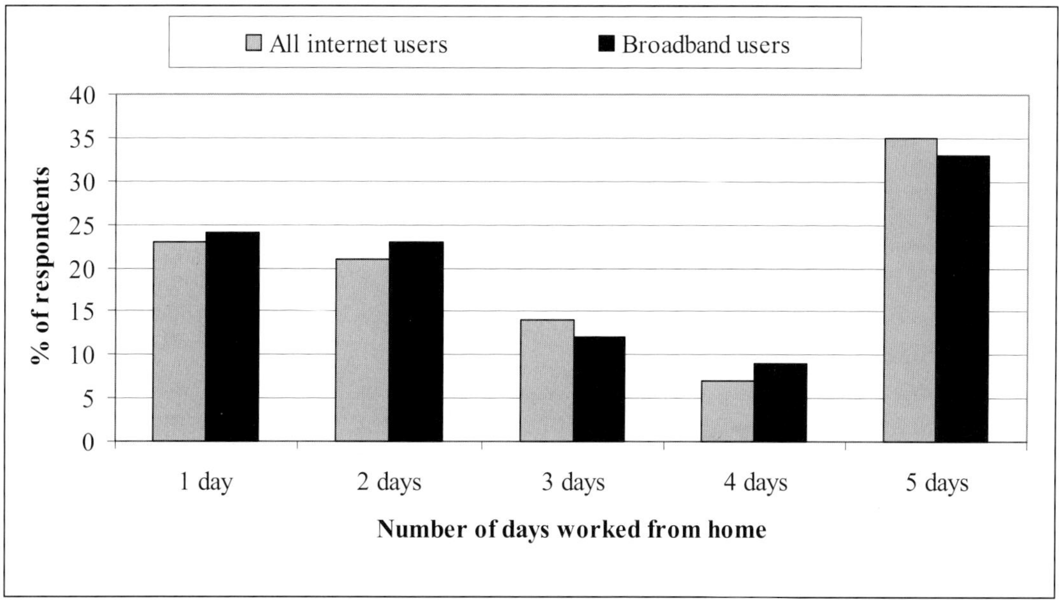

Journey to work distance of current teleworkers
There is some evidence suggesting teleworkers may have longer commute journeys than the national average. Mitchell et al. (1994) found teleworkers had average commute journeys of 21 miles compared to the national average at the time of 8.3 miles. DTLR (2002) concluded from their review of the published literature that 'generally teleworkers record longer (substituted) commute journeys than the average national commute journey.' As discussed in section 10.2, the cause and effect of this observation is ambiguous.

Information about the profile of people who currently telework (from DTI 2002) also suggests teleworkers might be more intensive car users than the national average. Two thirds of teleworkers in the UK are male; and they are concentrated in managerial and professional roles and hence likely to be on higher than average incomes.

10.5 Literature evidence about the future potential traffic impact of teleworking

Several studies have attempted to forecast the potential future impact of teleworking on car travel demand. A report by HOP Associates (2003), based on their review of the literature for DfT, argues that these forecasts follow a common pattern: working from data on current levels of teleworking, making projections of future uptake, calibrating through case study information, and making some reductions for expected compensatory trips. The earlier report by the same authors (DTLR 2002) concluded that this type of approach was generally unconvincing, and that more work was needed to gather the base data for this type of exercise.

Nevertheless, for comparative purposes, the forecasts of future demand which have been made by various studies are recorded below and summarised in table 10.3.

- Dodson et al (2000) estimated teleworking could lead to a reduction in car commuting traffic of 10% by 2005 and 15% by 2010. (This would be equivalent to a reduction in traffic for all trip purposes of about 2.5% in 2005 and 4% in 2010.) It is notable that they have revised their estimates slightly upwards from their original 1997 report, on the basis that teleworking is becoming easier due to technological development

- Lake et al. (1997) suggested from their study of Cambridgeshire County Council that if teleworking was adopted for suitable tasks, total traffic could be cut by 4-8%, with greater reductions in the morning and evening peaks.

- Illegems et al. (2002) looked at a range of scenarios for the growth of teleworking in Belgium. If teleworking increased at 5% a year, they predicted a car commuting reduction of 2.4% by 2011. If it increased at 20% a year, they predicted a reduction of 8.4% by 2011.

- Martens et al. (1999) used a model called Scenario-Explorer to assess the impact of second-order effects, including induced travel because of newly freed capacity. The model concluded that second-order effects would almost completely nullify the impacts of teleworking in substituting for travel. Recreational and business trips would increase because of the new highway capacity released by teleworkers. Allowing for these second-order effects, the authors concluded that teleworking would reduce the overall number of trips in the Netherlands by 1% at most, although the effect was higher for commuter trips at about 5%. A further second-order effect predicted by the model was reduced car ownership, as households had less need for a second car because of teleworking. Effects were greatest in urban areas (the Randstad) due to higher congestion levels, a higher education level and a high share of information-related employment, although a breakdown to show the difference in impact in urban and rural areas was not given.

- TfL (2003) highlight that London has the highest level of telework of all of the regions and estimate that, by 2016, 17-26% of London's workforce might telework for some of the time, resulting in a reduction of am peak commuter journeys of between 4.5% and 8.3%.

Table 10.3 Estimates of the future potential of telework

Source	Estimate
Dodson et al 2000	National commuting traffic reduction of 10% by 2005 and 15% by 2010. Total traffic reduction of 2.5% by 2005 and 4% by 2010
Lake et al 1997	4-8% reduction in total traffic
Illegems et al 2002	2.4-8.4% reduction in car commuting trips in Belgium by 2011
Martens et al 1999	5% of commuter trips in the Netherlands. Up to 1% of all trips
TfL 2003	4.5-8.3% of am peak commuter journeys.

10.6 Selection of telework case studies

For more detailed consideration in this study, we looked at a number of potential case studies from local authorities. These included:

- Hertfordshire's Trading Standards department (65+ staff) introduced 'flexible working', with part of the motivation being described as the Council's Travelwise scheme (HOP Associates, 2000-2003). This included the introduction of localised workstations called 'Oases', to reduce the number of journeys made to headquarters. In-work mileage (reimbursed) was reduced by 7% - a total saving of 9000 miles, representing a 5-8% reduction in travel costs. Personal miles were also reduced, although no figures were given.

- Sefton Metropolitan Borough Council undertook a pilot where 19 employees were offered telework as an alternative to conventional working over a twelve-month period, (SustainIT, 2002). Over the period, a total of 294 days was spent working from home and employees kept travelogues detailing their travel patterns and how they were affected by teleworking. Almost 22,000 km of car travel was saved. Since the successful pilot, the personnel department has appointed a senior manager to continue developing and promoting teleworking as an integral part of the Council's approach to flexible working.

- In 1997, Surrey County Council launched a five-year programme (called 'Surrey Workstyle') aimed at 3500 staff (SustainIT undated, Bibby 2000). The key motivation was to save office space, including a 33% reduction in floorspace and rationalisation from 74 buildings to 20. Initiatives include hot desking, teleworking, development of ICT infrastructure and intensive staff training in ICT skills. Costs were quoted at £6.7 million but savings were expected to include £11 million capital and £1 million revenue p.a. There is no information available about the effects of the strategy.

- As part of the EU 'Target' project, Wakefield Metropolitan district council began a pilot project in 1999 with 23 volunteers, who agreed to work from home once a week, from across a wide spectrum of the organisation, (Target 2001, Coles 2002). There are plans to extend the initiative to 9,500 staff within the authority. However, there is currently no information about the effects of the pilot initiative.

- York City Council is running a trial of teleworking with its own staff, (c.f. York travel awareness, marketing and campaigns case study).

- Nottinghamshire County Council and Buckinghamshire County Council have both developed remote tele-centres for both their own staff, and use by others in the local areas where the centres are established, (c.f. Chapter 11).

There were also a number of potential private sector schemes that we considered, including BAA and British Telecom, which have both been part of the SUSTEL project.

In the end, the British Telecom experience was chosen as the case study, because it has been far more extensively monitored than the majority of other cases, and is also operating on a larger scale than the majority of local authority schemes. Much of the information reported in the BT case study is drawn from the published research of the European SUSTEL programme, a two year research project financed by the European Commission which has been looking into the economic, environmental and social impacts of teleworking.

10.7 Details of chosen telework case study

BT began investigating teleworking in 1990. In 1997/98 promotion of teleworking was formalised through the Workstyle 2000 (then Options 2000) programme, which was renamed Workabout in 2002. The company itself rarely uses the term teleworking, seeing this as just one part of a broader commitment to flexible working. Part of the motivation for the company is to use office space more efficiently, and teleworking has gone hand in hand with re-organisation and re-location of office space, including development of several 'Workstyle' buildings which incorporate Internet cafes, meeting rooms and hotdesk space for workers. Flexible working is also seen as a way of enhancing staff morale, addressing work-life balance issues, and as a positive selling point when recruiting.

Employees who are part of the Workabout scheme are provided with the following help:
- phone and email support helpdesk (involving five dedicated staff)
- computer (sometimes the office computer re-deployed to the home office with new equipment such as a modem as appropriate)
- dedicated phone line (ADSL since 2002 with upgrade programme for others)
- furniture budget of up to £650
- option to work some of the time at a local telework office (if appropriate).

BT are also involved with teleworking as a commercial service for other businesses.

10.8 Staffing and budgets for telework

Our study was not able to collect full data on the cost of BT's teleworking programme, as the information was commercially confidential. However, we estimated that costs per employee might be about £750 (on the basis that staff who begin teleworking are offered a furniture budget of £650, and there may be some other costs, such as installing a modem). In addition, the team of five people assigned to support BT staff might cost an estimated £100,000 per year. (Although some of the time of this team is spent on commercial work for other organisations wishing to develop teleworking.)

Against these costs, BT explicitly recognise offsetting financial benefits in terms of lower office space requirements, improved staff retention and increased staff performance. These benefits are outlined further in section 10.11.

10.9 Case study evidence about the scale of teleworking

At the time of the interview (July 2003), over 7500 staff were registered with the Workabout scheme, out of a total workforce of 108,000 (7% of the workforce). Notably, this is approximately the same proportion of people who were working from home at least one day a week in 2001 nationally.

At BT, growth has exceeded targets, increasing from 5128 staff in March 2002. The number of staff registered with Workabout is growing at about 200 per month. These figures imply a growth rate of approximately 2% of the workforce each year, which may be gradually accelerating. (This is slightly higher than the national growth rate).

Staff registered with Workabout have a very wide range of work patterns. About a third work mainly at home with occasional days or half-days at BT offices, while a quarter have mixed work locations, split between home and multiple BT offices. Hence, the average frequency of teleworking is clearly higher than 1.5 days a week, although difficult to precisely calculate. A reasonable estimate might be an average of about 3 days per week. Table 10.4 gives the findings of research by Hopkinson et al. (2002), which indicates the complexity of different flexible working patterns, and that there is no one type of teleworker.

Table 10.4: Different types of teleworker at BT

Category of teleworker	Number	%
a Primarily work in a main BT office but regularly spend days/ half days working at home. Relatively small amount of in-work travel.	16	0.9%
b Mixed working locations split between home and main BT office (on average more than one day a week in each of the two different locations). Relatively **small** amount of in-work travel.	63	3.4%
c Mixed working locations split between home and main BT office (on average more than one day a week in each of the two different locations). Relatively **large** amount of in-work travel.	79	4.3%
d Mixed working locations split between home and multiple BT offices (i.e. no main BT office).	460	25.1%
e Mixed working locations split between home, BT offices and customers premises	350	19.1%
F Home working at start and finish of most working days, on the road during the day routinely visiting customers and clients. One day or less on average in BT offices	226	12.3%
g Primarily work at home with occasional days/half days in BT offices for team meetings, training etc	576	31.4%
h None of the above - I do not consider myself to be a teleworker.	4	0.2%
i None of the above for other reasons -	59	3.2%
TOTAL	1833	100.0%

Source: Hopkinson et al. (2002)

The onset of active encouragement for teleworking in the late 1990s coincided with a change in culture of the engineering workforce who work in the field. More than half of these now base themselves at home, picking up their work schedules and reporting remotely.

Uptake of teleworking was particularly high for staff who had previously worked in London.

10.10 Effects of teleworking on car use

There have been a number of surveys of the effects of teleworking on the travel behaviour of BT staff.

Hopkinson and James (2001) analysed self-completion questionnaires from BT employees who were about to register with the BT Options 2000 teleworking programme. Some employees were already working at home an average of 1.9 days per week and, taken overall, respondents anticipated that in future they would work from home an average of 3.6 days per week. The average car mileage 'saved' by pre-existing teleworking was 95 miles per week per teleworker. If future increases in employees' frequency of teleworking were in line with their predictions, the authors estimated further savings of 76 miles per week car commuting per teleworker, suggesting a potential future saving of 171 miles per week altogether.

Hopkinson et al. (2002) refers to a second survey of BT staff, which found mileage savings of 186 miles per week for teleworkers who travelled by car.

As part of the SUSTEL programme, a third survey was emailed to all 5128 BT staff registered with Workabout in March 2002. This received responses from 1874 employees (a response rate of 37%). It reported an average reduction in commuting of 178 miles per week for car users (Hopkinson et al. 2002).

A further SUSTEL survey was sent to 814 BT staff registered with Workabout in October 2002 (Hopkinson and James 2003). This received 199 responses (a response rate of 24%). It found that about 90% of Workabout registrees had reduced their commuting travel, with nearly 80% describing the reduction as 'considerable'. The mean commute mileage reduction per respondent was 253 miles per week, although there is no data on whether these journeys involved passengers or car sharing. There were also offset effects:

- some people (20% of the sample) said they now used the car more for other trips. For these, the increase in car use was 77 miles per week.
- some people (47% of the sample) made replacement journeys for tasks that would previously have been part of a chained commute (for example to go shopping, or to escort children). For these, the increase in car use was 34 miles per week.
- business travel also increased for some staff, although this was balanced by other staff who said it had decreased.

There is no information on whether teleworking has resulted in participants living further from the workplace, nor whether it has affected the time of day that they make their replacement journeys.

Taking account of the offsetting effects, Hopkinson and James (2003) suggest the net effect was to reduce travel by 193 miles per week per teleworker.

Thus the four surveys of BT staff have found net reductions in car mileage of between 95 miles and 193 miles per week per teleworker. The lower figure is based on a survey of staff who were teleworking to a limited extent and were about to increase the amount of time spent working from home. The other three surveys suggest rather similar figures of 178 – 193 miles per week.

Meanwhile, separate data provided by BT suggests that, between 1998/99 and 2002/03, the total distance travelled by company cars, private vehicles and the BT fleet, for which expenses claims were made, fell from 852 million kilometres to 760 million kilometres, a reduction of 11%.

Table 10.5 compares the case study findings on car use at BT with findings from the literature review (section 10.2) and from the review of potential local authority case studies (section 10.6). Meanwhile, table 10.6 is an attempt to standardise some of the results given in table 10.5 as average weekly reductions in car mileage. In practice, standardising these different figures proved almost impossible, as they are from different countries and some are net car mileage savings (allowing for greater car use for other trips) while others only refer to the effect on commuting trips. In addition, some report on studies of people who work from home full time, whilst others report on studies for people who only work from home part-time. Some quote figures for 'tele-work days', whilst others quote for weekly travel, which will sometimes be an average of days when normal commuting took place (although this is clearly not the case where people are full time teleworkers). In a number of cases, it is not actually clear what is being quoted. However, despite this confusion, the findings do consistently back up the conclusion from the BT case study that teleworking delivers reduction in car mileage, even allowing for offsetting effects, and that these reductions can be substantial.

Table 10.5: Key results about impacts on car use

Study	Target group	Impacts on car use
BT	BT staff about to register with Options 2000 programme. Existing average if teleworking 1.9 days per week. Intended future teleworking of 3.6 days per week	Pre-existing teleworking reducing car mileage by 95 miles per week. Intended future teleworking predicted to reduce car commuting by 171 miles per week (given increased frequency).
BT	BT staff	Average car commuting mileage reduced by 186 miles per week. No further details.
BT	1874 staff registered with Workabout	Average car commuting mileage reduced by 178 miles per week. No information on offsetting mileage for other trips.
BT	199 staff registered with Workabout	Average car commuting mileage reduced by 253 miles per week.

		Net effect after allowing for more non-work car trips was 193 fewer car miles per week.
BT	Expenses claims	11% reduction in business mileage
State of California Telecommuting Pilot Project	40 tele-commuters	27% fewer trips and 77% less mileage on telework days. (Non work trips made more often, but less far)
	219 tele-commuters	75% less mileage on telework days. Shorter non-work trips
California Residential Area-Based Offices Project	People using neighbourhood tele-centres (on av., 1.25 days per week).	53-65% less mileage on tele-centre days. 11.5-17% less mileage per week. (No increase in numbers of non-work trips on tele-centre days)
Washington Metropolitan Area study	100 employees from organisations offering telework. Most teleworking 1-2 days per week.	0.6 vehicle trips and 16 vehicle miles less per day (including use of vehicles by other household members). Those moving house equally likely to move closer or further.
Dutch Ministry of Transport	30 employees who spend 20-60% time teleworking.	19% reduction in car driver trips and mileage. Greater than overall trip reduction. Bigger reductions in peak hour travel. Other household members reduced trips by 9%, with no change in travel distance.
Greater Munich	37 teleworkers and 29 household members	14% reduction in trips overall
Denmark	946 Internet users who sometimes telework (excluding full time teleworkers)	48.6% less time in own car on telework days. Those moving house equally likely to move closer or further.
AA call centre	103 call centre staff who switched to working at home	3680 vehicle miles saved per employee per year with 30-40% offset – i.e. net saving of 2200-2600 miles. Inconclusive results about non-work travel
BAA	64 employees teleworking	Average weekly reductions of 45 miles per week, made up of an average reduction of 61 commuting miles and an average increase of 16 new trip miles.
Mitchell & Trodd	'small' sample of UK teleworkers	Average reduction of 113 miles per week per person
IBM	Staff home working for part of the time	13% reduction in travel time

RM Consulting	145 employees involved in a 'location independent working' pilot	Reduction of 500,000km
ADAS Consulting	500 staff work from home	2000 miles per year less per employee
Yorkshire Water	Daily visits to team office reduced	20% reduction in annual mileage
Hertfordshire's Trading Standards department	65 staff using tele-centres	Total business mileage reduced by 7%, or 9000 miles.
Sefton MBC	19 employees, working from home an average of 15 days per year each	22000 km of car travel saved in 12 months.

Table 10.6 Standardising the vehicle mileage savings

Study	Mileage savings per person
BT	178 - 193 miles per week
BAA	45 miles per week
Washington Metropolitan Area study	16 miles *per day* for part-time home-workers
AA call centre	48-57 miles per week (full time home-workers)
Mitchell & Trodd	113 miles per week
RM Consulting	47 miles per week
ADAS Consulting	43 miles per week (full time home workers)
Hertfordshire's Trading Standards department	3 miles per week for in-work mileage
Sefton MBC	15 miles per week per person 46 miles per telework day

Yearly totals converted to weekly totals assuming 46 weeks worked per year.

10.11 Other effects of teleworking

There are a number of other benefits that are typically identified for teleworking. These are outlined as follows, with illustrative data from BT.

- **Improved performance.**
81% of BT respondents reported improved performance from teleworking, including higher productivity, better quality of work, higher total output and more creative work. Employees reported this was due to less disruption while working, and more time spent working instead of travelling.

- **Lower levels of absenteeism.**
BT estimate that Workabout employees only take 25-30% the amount of sick leave of BT employees overall.

- **Higher staff retention rates, and higher rates of return to work after maternity leave.**

93-96% of BT employees return to work after maternity leave, which is considerably higher than the national average

- **Employees who would not be able to do office-based work are able to continue in employment.**

10% of BT Workabout employees said that they would be unable to undertake their current job if they could not telework. People affected include staff with responsibilities for child care, or who need to care for ill or disabled family members, or who are themselves disabled or recovering from an illness.

- **A positive effect on quality of life and a better balance between working life and personal life.**

90.3% of BT respondents reported that teleworking was having a positive effect on their quality of life, and high proportions reported beneficial effects for their partner and/or children. In addition, a small but significant minority were reporting increased involvement in the community (with 14% finding it easier to engage in community activities, and 6% spending more time on such activities).

- **Individual financial savings**

55.9% of respondents felt that they had experienced personal financial benefits from teleworking, with many individuals reporting savings of over £1000 p.a., (although it should be noted that 15.6% felt that they had been negatively affected).

- **Lower office costs.**

Teleworking was felt to have contributed to BT's space savings of £180 million per year, although it was not possible to disaggregate telework savings and savings arising from other re-organisation.

There were also a few negative effects reported. In particular, many BT respondents (75.7%) reported that they were working longer hours. 37.2% believed that they were slightly or considerably more isolated from work colleagues that previously and that this effect was negative, although only 10.9% of respondents felt this to be true for contact with non-work colleagues (with the majority feeling less isolated). In addition, 25.8% of BT respondents reported increases in domestic conflict, whilst 17.8% reported a reduction in such conflict.

10.12 Synergies between teleworking and other policies and issues

The promotion of teleworking is often associated with other business benefits, such as 'improved work life balance' and reducing office space requirements. Hence, it is synergistic with a range of other initiatives that may take place within organisations for non transport reasons. In some cases, it has also been promoted as an important element of workplace travel plans.

Where teleworking gives employees greater flexibility to organise their day, it could also be seen as synergistic with school travel plans, since it may make it easier for full-time workers to not drive their children to school. Where teleworking reduces the need to own a car and/or encourages greater participation in the locality, it may also be synergetic with car club membership.

In addition to its teleworking programme, BT encourages the use of tele-conferencing by its staff, as discussed in Chapter 11. It seems plausible that the ready availability of tele-conferencing technology within the company makes it easier for staff to work from remote locations, and thus helps make teleworking viable. At the same time, staff who are relatively 'technology literate' from teleworking may be more willing and able to get involved in teleconferencing initiatives.

10.13 Relationship between telework spending and impact

In evaluating the relationship between cost and impact for BT's teleworking programme, we assumed that an average teleworking employee had reduced their car mileage by about 185 miles per week (a mid-range figure based on the two most recent SUSTEL surveys of staff registered with Workabout). We estimated the total car mileage saved over the period the scheme has been running, assuming that impact increased linearly from zero in the first year to current levels. Even if no more money were to be spent, we assumed there would be some impact in subsequent years, but that this would decline at the rate of 40% a year.

We assumed a cost in the current year of £750 per employee registered with Workabout, plus £100,000 for staff costs. Total costs of the programme were estimated on the assumption that each employee registered with Workabout had received a single payment of £750 when they began teleworking, with other staff costs growing linearly from zero in 1997, when the Options 2000 programme was launched, to £100,000. We were not able to take account of cost savings arising from the programme, so our estimate of cost per car kilometre saved is an upper figure. Given the cost savings due to office space released by teleworking, increased productivity, and better staff retention, it is possible – and even likely – that the Workabout programme has delivered net cost savings to BT.

The cost per kilometre saved is not a public cost, but a private one. However, it gives some indication of what might be the public cost of a programme to support teleworking, for example if a local authority offered grant funding to businesses to enable them to establish telework programmes.

Table 10.7 sets out the calculation.

Table 10.7 Calculation of relationship between cost and impact for teleworking

	BT
number of teleworkers in current year	7500
net distance saved in current year (km)	107,177,341
total car distance saved (from 1997 to 2003, plus future) (km)	482,298,037
cost of furniture and other resources (£)	5,625,000
cost of staff support team in current year (£)	100,000
total cost to date (estimated) (£)	5,925,000
cost per km saved (pence)	1.2

The cost is about 1 penny per kilometre saved, though again we emphasise that this is an upper estimate that does not allow for offsetting cost savings.

10.14 Future impact of teleworking

The future impact of teleworking depends upon:

- What proportion of the workforce is able to telework some of the time
- The average frequency of teleworking

Future levels of teleworking
Growth in teleworking over the next ten years will depend upon both the development of technology and a continuing shift in society's practices of work and work / life balance. Organisations such as BT have embraced the idea that their employees can work productively from home, and have developed effective management techniques to support this. For other organisations, a cultural shift may be necessary.

Some jobs do not lend themselves to teleworking: nurses, primary school teachers, shop workers and office reception staff, for example, are unlikely to be able to work from home. However, analysis of current patterns of teleworking suggest that considerable growth seems possible before 'natural limits' are reached, with 64% of the workforce in occupations where 5% or more already telework. There are also various trends which may cause growth to accelerate, as technologies become cheaper and more widespread, the employment structure alters etc..

At BT, the case study interviewee reported accelerating growth in the proportion of staff teleworking, and suggested that up to 65% of the BT workforce might ultimately take part in some form of telework. Research by Lake et al. (1997) suggests that the majority of staff in a local authority might be able to work from home at least one day a week. Evidence from the US suggests that, by 2001, 21% of the workforce was already teleworking (DTI 2002), and that 40% of the workforce were 'information' workers who should be able to telework relatively easily (Fouracre & Hill, 2000). An Institute of Employment Studies report (Huws et al 2001) suggested that 22.6% of the UK workforce might telework. A recent National Opinion Polls survey suggests that 25% of Internet users are already working from home at least some of the time (although their figures suggest that the potential for further growth amongst this group may be small).

If current growth rates continue, around 30% of the workforce would be teleworking in ten years time. Although there are some estimates which are lower than this, the majority of evidence seems to suggest that such growth may occur, and may even be exceeded.

Average frequency of teleworking
The BT case study revealed a wide range of types of teleworking (table 10.2 in section 10.9). Taken overall, it seems that a reasonable estimate is that an average teleworker at BT works from home about three days a week. The Lake et al. (1997) study suggested an upper limit of 3 days per week (or 60% of the time of a full-time worker) for local authority workers. The NOP results (Geraghty, 2004) suggested an

average frequency of 3.1 days per week for the teleworkers in their study. As reported in the literature review, other estimates suggest that the average teleworker currently spends about 1½ days a week away from the main office, or 30% of the time of a full-time worker. Thus we have a range of estimates of how often, on average, teleworkers work from home in current circumstances, from about 1½ days per week to about 3 days per week.

10.15 Key issues for scaling up telework

The case study suggests that teleworking is likely to continue to grow steadily within BT. In other organisations, it was suggested that teleworking would be likely to grow more rapidly in areas where congestion charging or a workplace parking levy were brought in. It was also suggested that legislation to encourage flexible working would increase levels of teleworking, and that a higher public profile for teleworking could also encourage take-up. Some commentators have further highlighted that companies perceive teleworking to mean 'working from home five days a week' and that a greater awareness of the potential for part-time teleworking might help to increase participation.

When considering the impact of teleworking on the number of work trips, it is also important to remember that a small number of employees who telework all or most of the time, will have a larger effect than a greater number who only telework occasionally, and therefore scaling up the effects will be more sensitive to the size of the former group.

10.16 Policy implications relating to telework

- Teleworking has the potential to deliver substantial reductions in car travel at peak hours.
- Demand management policies for car use, such as road pricing, fuel duties, workplace parking levy and congestion charging, are all likely to encourage more sustainable commuter travel.
- Requiring employers to take more responsibility about how their employees get to work could help to facilitate more sustainable commuter travel (including, probably, helping to stimulate telework).
- Information and advice about teleworking could be included as part of any initiative aiming to influence commuter travel, including the literature relating to travel plans.
- More education and guidance about what constitutes telework could be of benefit. Currently, it is often taken to mean people working at home five days a week. However, many organisations with successful telework strategies offer employees a more flexible range of options, for example, the chance to work at home one-day a week or to use satellite offices on occasion.
- The social benefits of teleworking (greater participation of those with disabilities; better work life balance) could be more widely disseminated.
- Local authorities could be encouraged to lead by example – perhaps by enabling their employees to sometimes use satellite offices. Occasional use of district council facilities by county council employees was given as one successful form of teleworking.

- Local authorities could potentially be encouraged to set up local office facilities that can be used, on occasion, by employees from a range of companies (including small and medium enterprises) to reduce their commuting distances.

- Either government or local authorities could potentially encourage teleworking through grants to businesses, to help meet the initial costs of establishing a teleworking programme, perhaps as part of workplace travel plan programmes. There may also be a role for tax breaks – for example enhanced capital allowances to establish telecentres.

10.17 Acknowledgements

We are very grateful for the help of the following people with the main case study:

Individual	*Organisation*
Ian Wood	BT Social Policy Unit
Peter James	University of Bradford

In addition to the main case study interviewees, we would like to thank:

Individual	*Organisation*
Alan Denbigh	Telework Association
Andy Lake	HOP Associates
Barry Fogarty	BT Wholesale

10.18 References

Balepur, P.N., Varma, K.V., Mokhtarian, P.L. (1998) The transportation impacts of center-based telecommuting: interim findings from the neighbourhood telecenters project *Transportation* 25(3) 287-306

Bibby A (2000) *Surrey County Council pioneers new ways of working.* Article published in 'Flexible Working 2000'.

Coles M (14/9/02) Battle to survive on the home front. *The Guardian*

Department of Trade and Industry (2002) *Teleworking in the UK, Labour Market Trends* June 2002

Dodgson J, Pacey J & Begg M (2000) *Motors and modems revisited: the role of technology in reducing travel demands and traffic congestion.* Report by NERA for the RAC Foundation and the Motorists Forum.

DTLR (2002) *The impact of information and communications technologies on travel and freight distribution patterns: review and assessment of literature.* Report by HOP Associates and Transport Research Group, University of Southampton

Fogarty B (2004) *A role for teleworking: the BT experience.* BT Seltrans presentation.

Fouracre & Hill (1998) *Report for the Highways Agency research programme on understanding travel behaviour*, produced by TRL, as quoted in Dodgson et al (2000).

Geraghty C (2004) How the Internet can help ease traffic congestion. Presentation at 'Alternative Approaches to Congestion' conference convened by BT, 26/1/02.

Glogger, A.F., Zängler, T.W. and Karg, G. (2003) *The impact of telecommuting on households' travel behaviour, expenditures and emissions*. Proceedings of the TRIP research conference, Hillerod, Denmark, February 2003

Hamer, R., Kroes, E., Van Ooststroom, H. (1991) Teleworking in the Netherlands: an evaluation of changes in travel behaviour *Transportation* 18 365-382

Hills, S., Hopkinson, P., James, P (2002?) *SUSTEL Case Study UK-2, BT Workabout.*

HOP Associates (2001) *Travel plans: new business opportunities for suppliers of information and communication technology.* Report produced by the Energy Efficiency Best Practice Programme. General report 80.

HOP Associates (2003) *Virtual mobility research monitoring 2002-3 report* (unpublished report for DfT)

HOP Associates (2000-2003) *Case study on flexible work: Miles better – Hertfordshire County Council Trading Standards.* Report downloaded from www.flexibility.co.uk

Hopkinson, P., James, P. (2001) *The BT Options 2000 – a pilot study of its environmental and social impacts.*

Hopkinson, P., James, P., Mayurama, T., Selwyn, J. (2001) *The impacts of teleworking – a study of AA employees.* As summarised on the HOP Associates database at www.virtual-mobility.com.

Hopkinson, P., James, P., Maruyama, T. (2002) *Teleworking at BT – the economic, environmental and social impacts of its Workabout scheme.* Report on survey results 14/10/2002. Report as part of SUSTEL programme.

Hopkinson, P., James , P. (2003) *UK report on national SUSTEL fieldwork.*

Huws H, Jagger N & Bates P (2001) *Where the butterfly alights, the global location of e-work.* Institute of Employment Studies, Report 378, as quoted in DTI (2002).

Illegems, V., Verbeke, A. and S'Jegers, R. (2002) Telecommuting / teleworking: a virtual commuting possibility – the cases of Belgium and Brussels. In: Stern, E., Salomon, I. and Bovy, P.H.L. (editors): *Travel behaviour: spatial patterns, congestion and modelling (*2002). As summarised on the HOP Associates database at www.virtual-mobility.com.

Jensen, L.M., Jensen-Butler, C., Madsen, B., Millard, J. and Schmidt, L. (2003) *A web-based study of the propensity to telework, based on socio-economic, work organisation and spatial factors.* Proceedings of the TRIP research conference, Hillerod, Denmark, February 2003

Koenig, B.E., Henderson, D.K., Mokhtarian, P.L. (1996) The travel and emissions impacts of telecommuting for the State of California telecommuting pilot project. *Transpn. Res.-C* 4, 13-32

Lake, A.S., van Vuren, T. (1997) Assessing the impact of advanced telecommunications on work-related travel. Summarised at www.hop.co.uk/ict2002

McInroy R (1999) *Linnet Locals in Lincolnshire – electronic provision in a rural setting.* Article by the Operations Manager for Library Support Services, Lincolnshire County Council, produced by South Bank University

Martens, M.J., Wilmink, I.R., Korver, W., Heijma, A.O.J., van Katwijk, R.T., Harrell, L. (1999) The mobility impact of the electronic highway. A technology forecast and assessment using a scenario approach. TNO Inro report: Inro-transport/2003-05, The Netherlands.

Metropolitan Washington Council of Governments (1999) Commuter Connections: Washington Metropolitan Telework Demonstration Project August 1997 – April 1999

Mitchell, H. and Trodd, E. (1994) An introductory study of telework based transport – telecommunications substitution. Research project for the Department of Transport. As summarised on the HOP Associates database at www.virtual-mobility.com.

Mokhtarian, P.I., Varma, K.V (1998) The trade-off between trips and distance travelled in analyzing the emissions impacts of center-based telecommuting *Transpn. Res.-D* 3(6) 419-428

Pendyala, R.M., Goulias, K.G., Kitamura, R. (1991) Impact of telecommuting on spatial and temporal patterns of household travel *Transportation* 18, 383-409

SustainIT (undated) '*Surrey Workstyle: Surrey County Council*'. Case study report downloaded from www.sustainit.org

SustainIT (2002) '*eWell-Being Awards – 2002 winners. Commended: Sefton Metropolitan Borough Council*'. Report downloaded from www.sustainit.org

TARGET (2001) Flexible working: teleworking pilot. News release dated 2/5/01, downloaded from www.eu-target.net on 28/5/03.

Transport for London (2003) *Soft options: review of studies*. Report produced by and for Transport for London

11. Teleconferencing

11.1 Introduction

Teleconferencing can be defined as the use of telecommunications to facilitate contacts that might otherwise have involved business travel – such as meetings, training sessions, interviews or information provision. It typically involves two or more people in a multi-way phone conversation or video link or web link[1]. There are a range of ways in which teleconferencing can be provided, including private facilities, public facilities, special rooms fitted with equipment, facilities available via individual PCs etc.

In common with teleworking, teleconferencing has not often been seen as an appropriate focus for public sector attention. However, local authorities have been involved in developing a range of related initiatives. Their motivation has rarely been transport alone, and more commonly related to a desire to increase participation and social inclusion (both of economically deprived groups and geographically remote areas), and to improve local business competitiveness. Initiatives include:

- the provision of remote access to government services and information. The LINNET terminals developed by Lincolnshire County Council placed in libraries across the county are one example (McInroy 1999). Another is the Cambridge Online City project, established to increase access to public information through the use of the internet, (www.colc.co.uk).
- Information and advice for companies wishing to develop electronically advanced facilities. For example, Cambridgeshire County Council developed a 'tele working toolkit', in association with the East of England Development Agency, for companies that wanted to introduce teleworking, (c.f. Cambridgeshire workplace travel plans case study). In the East Midlands, EMNET exists as an independent, not for profit organisation (supported by the local authorities) to give advice to SMEs with limited resources about how to make best use of the Internet, (www.emnet.co.uk).
- Pilot projects to trial teleworking or teleconferencing amongst local authority staff.
- The provision of 'tele centres' which provide a range of services for those who wish to work from home or satellite location close to their homes.

However, information about, and monitoring of, these initiatives is rare - particularly, any information about their transport impacts. Moreover, there are a number of other ways that the public sector could get involved in promoting teleconferencing, as discussed in section 11.12.

In terms of literature on teleconferencing, papers on the subject date back to the mid 1970s (although Bennison, 1988, comments that HG Wells speculated on the

---

[1] Although it is not theoretically appropriate to exclude one-to-one telephone conversations from a definition of teleconferencing, we do so on the belief that these are already exploited to the full, and that it is other forms of teleconferencing that have the potential to impact on business travel in the future.

importance of teleconferencing as early as 1902). However, the amount of empirical work remains remarkably sparse, particularly in contrast to the large literature on teleworking. Moreover, different studies have taken place at different times - when the technology available for teleconferencing will have been significantly different.

As a common characteristic, the majority of papers (covering a period of nearly 30 years) highlight the technical and cost issues associated with teleconferencing, and that both technical problems and financial costs are likely to reduce in 'the future', providing a stimulus to increased use.

Many of the papers also share a number of undesirable characteristics. In particular, there is a tendency to use the terms teleconferencing and videoconferencing interchangeably, even when it is clear that the authors recognise that there are different forms of teleconferencing.

Another issue with the literature is a range of complexity. Specifically, some papers estimate the amount of business travel that could convert to teleconferencing, and assume that this is the likely potential effect. Others highlight that the issue is more complicated - specifically, teleconferencing may generate meetings that might otherwise not have taken place; in some cases it may foster contacts which lead to more face to face meetings; and in some cases it may generate alternative trips to videoconferencing facilities. There is also a tendency for papers to begin with empirical evidence and then make theoretical estimations about the implications of that evidence for total business travel, or, in some cases particular types of business travel (with particular interest in the implications for air traffic), without being clear about the transition from evidence to estimates. In this chapter, we try to present the results as unambiguously as possible.

The following section summarises the available literature. Subsequent sections describe our main case study for teleconferencing – British Telecom – and compare BTs experience with the findings reported in the literature.

11.2 Literature evidence on teleconferencing

11.2.1 Early studies

Salomon (1985) describes some of the earliest work on the subject undertaken by Pye (1976), Goddard & Morris (1976) and Goddard & Pye (1977). This was focused on exploring the potential to decentralise office activities from London. Based on detailed communications diaries, they concluded that 34% of the meetings recorded could have been performed by audioconferencing and that an additional 10% would have been possible by videoconferencing - in other words that 44% of the meetings could have been replaced by teleconferencing.

Twelve years later, Bennison (1988) reports on an evaluation of a British Telecom 'videoconferencing' trial, which partly drew on this earlier work. The trial took place between 1983 and 1986. 14 companies were involved, and were provided with videoconferencing facilities in two or more locations. There were some technical problems, and some organisations were not connected until the last four months of the trial. The majority (11) actually made very little use of the facilities they had been given, after an initial period of experimentation. When asked why, the reason given by most respondents was that the facilities were "not strongly promoted". The three companies where videoconferencing was used regularly came from 3 different industrial sectors - banking, toiletries, and oil and chemicals. However, Bennison comments that they shared some characteristics, namely a large number of intra-organisational contacts between people based on different sites (each of which was supplied with a videoconferencing facility) and had a culture of calling meetings at relatively short notice to undertake routine activities.

In terms of the characteristics of videoconferencing (sample of 47 meetings):
- 71% were booked with less than seven days notice
- 76% involved 4-6 people
- 92% lasted two hours or less
- the main purposes of the videoconferences were to discuss ideas, exchange information and make decisions. However, some of them also included report presentation, negotiation, and conflict, and the only activity which was seen as being confined to face-to-face meetings was "forming impressions of others".

In terms of interaction with face-to-face meetings (sample of 54 face-to-face meetings and 47 videoconferences), respondents felt that:
- 25% of the face-to-face meetings could have taken place by videoconferences
- 38% of the videoconferences could have taken place as face-to-face meetings
- 9% of videoconferences represented contact that would not have taken place otherwise

In addition:
- 75% felt that videoconferencing was a satisfactory alternative to travel (50 respondents), and
- 87% felt that videoconferencing had reduced the number of trips they made (31 respondents)

In general, videoconferencing was associated with shorter, more formal meetings. There was perceived to be a decline in spontaneity, which was generally regarded as detrimental. However task orientation and, to a lesser extent, cooperation among participants were seen to have increased, which was perceived to be beneficial and to have led to enhanced meeting effectiveness and time savings. The opportunity to call meetings in shorter notice and faster dissemination of information were also reported as benefits.

As a counter example of travel impacts, Mokhtarian (1988) describes the impact of a teleconference held in 1986 for the regular monthly meeting of the Southern California Association of Governments (SCAG) Transportation and Communications Committee, a planning organisation covering 38,000 square miles. This was held by setting up videoconferencing facilities in two locations. Analysis of travel changes showed that vehicle miles travelled actually increased, compared to an average meeting held at the usual single location of the SCAG offices. This was primarily because attendance increased, from its typical level of 14 people to a total of 23 people. Analysis suggested that the average distance per person to the nearest teleconference site was 24% lower than the distance to the SCAG offices (48 miles compared with 61 miles). However, because of the attendance increase, the total vehicle miles travelled was 29% higher than for a typical meeting. Mokhtarian notes the one of the main reasons for introducing the videoconference was precisely to increase attendance, and some of the survey evidence specifically showed that the higher attendance levels were due to the meeting mode. She also highlights that the travel to the teleconference sites typically took place in less congested conditions, avoiding the congested central location of the SCAG offices, and that participants were able to leave later, avoiding more of the morning peak.

11.2.2 Dodgson et al (1997) – 'Motors or Modems' study for the RAC

Moving forward another ten years, Dodgson et al (1997) report on the survey carried out by Critical Research for the 'Motors or Modems' project commissioned by the RAC. As part of this work, interviews were carried out with 303 employees (including representatives of company car drivers, people in managerial occupations, people who work from home, and people who travelled on behalf of work). Of these, 26% thought that videoconferencing could be appropriate in their job. This 26% were then asked about the proportion of business travel that could be replaced by different forms of teleconferencing, depending on the price of the equipment. Some of the results are shown in the following table:

Table 11.1: Proportion of business travel that could be replaced by different forms of teleconferencing

	Replacement by audioconferencing	Replacement by videoconferencing with perfect display and life-size image
At current prices	6.6% now 14.6% in 10 years	7.2% now 13.4% in 10 years
At low prices	11.5% now 17.8% in 10 years	15.2% now 19.7% in 10 years

Data: 79 respondents who thought videoconferencing could be appropriate in their job
Source: Dodgson et al 1997

Dodgson et al argue that these figures provided the basis for a conservative scenario about the potential impact of videoconferencing, whereby 20% of business travel for 26% of people could be replaced in about 10 years - a total of approximately 5% of business travel. They argue that a more optimistic scenario would not limit the impact to the 26% of people who believed that videoconferencing could be helpful to them, and suggest that total impact on business travel under an optimistic scenario could be 20% after 10 years. In the revised version of their report published in 2000, they reduce these estimates to suggest that teleconferencing might reduce car business travel by 3% by 2005 and 5% by 2010, although without much explanation other than the statement that "videoconferencing has not yet achieved the potential foreseen for it" and some reported technical problems to be addressed with 'transmission and switching technologies'.

11.2.3 Roy and Filiatrault (1998) – teleconferencing and air travel

Next, Roy & Filiatrault (1998) review a number of studies from the early 1990s, looking particularly at the potential for teleconferencing to substitute for business *air* travel. They quote the following results:

- teleconferencing could substitute for business air travel by between 2% in a conservative scenario and 11% in a more optimistic scenario by 2005 (Apogee Research Inc., 1994)
- teleconferencing could substitute for business air travel by 12% by 2005, 25% by 2010 and 35% in 2020 (Arvai, 1991)
- all air travel could reduce by 15% due to videoconferencing by 2030, with potential reductions as high as 40% for business trips made by air (Burger, 1995). It should be noted that as a result of this work, air traffic growth forecasts were revised downwards and plans to build a second airport in the Boston area were cancelled.
- Annual surveys from the Canadian Tourism Research Institute suggested that in 1992, 25% of respondents were making less business trips due to communications technologies and 28% were doing so in 1994, (Redekop 1994).

Roy & Filiatrault (1998) also report on their own work which involved interviews with 1139 business travellers, carried out at 7 Canadian airports, namely Halifax, Quebec City, Montreal,Val d'Or, Toronto, Calgary and Vancouver. To qualify as a respondent, the interviewee had to have completed six business trips during the last year and be a Canadian resident. Interviews took place in October 1996. Of the interviewees, 29.6% worked for organisations that use videoconferencing and 19.6% had participated in at least one videoconference during the last year. Users typically belonged to top management, and worked primarily for government, financial institutions and the communications sector.

Specific estimates of different forms of communications technologies usage, and predicted future levels of usage are given in table 11.2. Roy & Filistrault highlight the findings that 18% of respondents worked for companies with privately owned videoconferencing equipment and another 14% worked for organisations which planned to introduce these facilities in the next three years. They contrast them with a survey of Canadian firms carried out in 1990, which showed that only 2% were equipped with videoconferencing and only 5% of the non-users were planning to acquire this technology in the next three years. This is compatible with the recency of use shown in their survey (where most of the technologies had, on average, been being used for five years or less). They also state that the results showed that the proportion of respondents whose organisation had access to videoconference equipment (either through private or public facilities) could double within the next three years, compared with the current 29.6% of the sample.

Table 11.2: Current and planned usage of communications technologies

		Use now	Will use within three years	Number of years of use for existing users
Teleconferencing		49.1%	10.4%	4.5
Videoconferencing from	Private facilities	17.7%	14.2%	2.4
	Public rooms	8.1%	8.1%	2.2
	Hotel or other business facility	4.0%	8.6%	2.1
	Desktop facility	2.6%	13.9%	5

Roy & Filistrault's survey also provides some information about the impacts of teleconferencing on business travel. The findings were as follows:

- for the full sample, 24.2% claimed to be travelling less often as a result of company policy to increase utilisation of teleconferencing and 13.4% believed that their organisation would implement this policy over the next three years
- for the 19.6% of the sample (223 respondents) that had participated in at least one videoconference in the last year, on average, users stated that videoconferencing were a substitute for an air trip in 44.8% of cases. The authors argue that this represents 9.4% of all air trips by this group, and 1.8% (9.4% x 19.6%) of air trips by all respondents in the survey.
- The 29.6% of respondents whose organisation uses videoconferencing were asked about the perceived substitutability of their business air trips. On average, this was estimated to be 14.5% of these trips. Therefore the authors argue that this could represent about 4.3% of the overall business air travel market (14.5% x 29.6%).

On the basis of these figures, the authors suggest that videoconferencing could reduce air travel by 1.8% to 4.3% in the short-term and by 3.6% to 8.6% within the next three years.

In addition to these quantitative estimates, survey respondents were asked about their agreement or disagreement with a series of statements relating to videoconferencing. On average, there was agreement from the full survey for the statements that "videoconferencing saves time", "videoconferencing saves travelling costs", "telecommunications technologies will increasingly replace business trips in the future", and "videoconferencing can accelerate decision-making by rapidly linking key players". In all cases, on average, existing users of videoconferencing agreed with the statements more strongly.

11.2.4 Arnfalk (2002) – review and new analysis of Swedish companies' teleconferencing

As part of doctoral research, Arnfalk (2002) reports on the nature of business travel, based on surveys in Sweden and the USA. His work suggests that the majority of business travel is to attend meetings, and that, in large organisations with extensive geographical distributions, the majority of business trips are related to collaborations within the company. Specifically, he quotes the following:

- a national survey of business travellers in the US, where 47% reported that their last trip was to attend a meeting, trade show or convention.

- a survey of the Swedish company Skanska, where more than 80% of domestic business travel was due to collaborations within the organisation
- a survey at the Swedish company Telia Nära, where 66% of respondents travelled to meetings about company projects, 45% travelled for training or conferences, 39% travelled for network meetings and 12% travelled for customer contacts or marketing reasons.

Arnfalk also quotes a number of estimates about the proportion of business travel that might be substituted by tele-conferencing as follows:
- 30% of total Irish business travel – estimate from 1978, (Rapp & Skåmedal 1996)
- 20% of total US business travel – estimate from 1983, (Rapp & Skåmedal 1996)
- 20% of total Canadian business travel – estimate from 1983, (Rapp & Skåmedal 1996)
- 35% of German business travel – estimate from 1985, (Rapp & Skåmedal 1996)
- 35% of UK business travel – estimate from 1985, (Rapp & Skåmedal 1996)
- 25% of US business travel by air – estimate from 2010 (Cook & Haver 1994)

As part of his own research, Arnfalk carried out surveys with personnel from 4 Swedish organisations. These were the company Telia, the Scandinavian Videoconferencing User Group (SVUG), the farmers association Skånska Lantmännen and the company Tetra Pak. The results are shown in table 11.3.

Table 11.3: Respondents impressions of the effects that using videoconferencing has had on their own and others business travel.

	Telia	SVUG	Skånska Lantmännen	Tetra Pak*
Replaced my own travel	47%	45%	58%	61%
Replaced other people's travel	15%	22%	25%	19%
Some reduction but only minor effect on my travel	20%	14%	17%	39%
Participated in meetings that I would not have travelled to otherwise	16%	15%	n.a.	19%
Increased my travel	1%	4%	0%	3%
Number of respondents	158	73	12	31

* In the survey at Tetra Pak, respondents had the opportunity to tick more than one option.

Arnfalk comments that the number of respondents to this question for the latter two organisations is relatively small, yet nonetheless it was interesting that there was considerable similarity between responses for all four. He notes that "replaced other people's travel" tended to refer to the situation where managers would normally have invited staff to meetings at the head office, but instigated a teleconference instead, or where people were giving courses to employees working at different locations and chose to give these courses via teleconferencing. He concludes that the dominant effect of teleconferencing seems to be travel reduction, given that about half of the respondents said that videoconferencing had replaced their own travel and approximately another fifth said that it had reduced other people's travel.

Arnfalk also quotes traffic impact estimates made by the companies themselves.

- Tetra Pak believes that videoconferencing has reduced business travel by about 10%.
- Between 1997-2000, Telia reduced business travel by air, cutting the volume by more than a third, whilst, over the same period, their use of virtual meetings (mainly audioconferencing) increased dramatically.
- As a more specific example from Telia, three of the four quarterly meetings for top managers (60-70 people from across Sweden) were changed to become teleconferences. The company estimates that it has saved 3 million SEK in reduced costs of travel, accommodation and staff time in two years.

11.2.5 Face-2-Face – UK teleconferencing venture launched in 2003

As a final insight into teleconferencing, in 2003, a new initiative called 'face2face' was launched in the UK, (face2face, 2004). It aims to provide "*a nationwide network of low-cost, pay-as-you-go, high-quality, videoconferencing facilities.*" It was founded by Noel Edmonds, and has the backing of organisations such as the RAC Foundation, Friends of the Earth and Transport 2000. It offers a central booking system for locations nationwide, and is being run in collaboration with Cisco Systems.

By November, there were more than 60 Venue Partners in the UK offering meeting facilities, with 1800 affiliated sites globally. The organisation was aiming to offer facilities in over 200 locations in the UK by 2005 and to have more than 2000 branded sites in operation worldwide by 2006. In early publicity, the intention was stated as being to "bring videoconferencing rooms to every major town and city in the UK by Christmas [2003]".

Costs for using facilities are £50 per hour for 'local members' using their local venue for the first three hours, rising to £60 per hour after that. For local members using other venues, and 'roaming members', the costs are £65 per hour. For 'pay-as-you-go' members, costs are £100 per hour. Local and roaming members receive preferential telecoms charges, whilst pay-as-you-go members pay standard telecoms charges. The costs are described as follows "*meeting start from just £50 - the equivalent of a tank of petrol, a day in a car park at Heathrow or a round trip of approximately 50 miles on the train.*"

In June 2003, face2face carried out a survey of more than 80 regular travellers passing through London's Paddington Station in the morning. Approximately 60% were travelling purely for business purposes. The survey found that:

- the average business trip costs in excess of £2000 per person in terms of staff costs, and on average, three employees travel to a single meeting. Hence the typical costs of a meeting are claimed to be £6000 plus the costs of travel, food and entertainment.
- most business trips last more than six hours, whilst the average time spent in meetings was typically less than two hours, representing 30% of the total time spent out of the office.
- up to two hours of average meeting time is time which would usually have been spent at home.
- the business travellers surveyed typically attended meetings at least twice a week.

- almost 50% of those surveyed would consider video meetings as a preferable alternative to making their trip.

The benefits of videoconferencing are described as follows:

- *more control and better work-life balance*: the option to videoconference arguably makes planning easier and frees up time. The literature states "*satisfied users are now managing to have meetings in Edinburgh, Birmingham, Manchester and Bristol, all before lunch*". The literature also stresses that the time savings can enable a better work-life balance

- *increased effectiveness*: the loss of 'stressful or tiring' travel should arguably increase effectiveness

- *peace of mind*: the literature argues "*forget worries about being late, missing a connection, losing your way or parking your car at airports*". It also highlights freedom from "*the dangers we face travelling today - road traffic accidents, SARs, earthquakes, war or terrorism*"

- *costs savings:* the literature contrasts the estimated staff costs for attending a normal meeting (£2000, of which only about a third is spent in the meeting itself) with the cost of hiring the videoconferencing facility (starting from £50 per hour).

The face2face website is linked to the website of VMC (the Video Meeting Company, www.videomeetingcompany.com). They were founded in 1999, and describe themselves as "the UK's leading independent, fully dedicated and impartial provider of total videoconferencing solutions". They employ over 50 staff, based in four locations in the UK. They have over 300 clients, including Carphone Warehouse, Grant Thornton, Mason Williams, Origin, Richards Butler, Taylor Woodrow, and Visage Group. Each of the named clients has a short write up, which includes their perceptions of the benefits of teleconferencing. Many of their reported benefits are similar to those claimed by face2face. It is also mentioned that teleconferencing tends to make meetings more efficient, as people are already prepared when they begin a meeting (rather than starting with small talk about travel).

In particular, the website quotes information from Mason Williams, a PR agency with 45 staff and a turnover exceeding £2 million. After installing video-meeting equipment, the travel costs within the agency dropped by a third. Even using videoconferencing for London meetings with London based staff is estimated to save two hours a day (given that it can typically take an hour to travel across London to a meeting). Mason Williams estimate that the monthly cost of the video equipment is normally recouped within the first week of each month. They also believe that it enables them to offer higher levels of customer service, and increased productivity. It has also increased coordination between the London and Manchester based offices of the organisation.

11.3 Selection of teleconferencing case studies

Prior to undertaking the teleconferencing case study, we obtained a small amount of information about following;

- in 1996, as a pilot project, Nottingham County Council set up a telecentre in Walsop town hall, (SustainIT 2003). This included the latest computer systems and videoconferencing facilities. It provided a base for six staff who give clerical

287

and administrative support to departments within the County Council. It was considered a success and enabled six staff members to avoid a 46 mile round commute trip to County Hall. The telecentre became a trading organisation in 1999 as it began to generate its own income, and is now self financing. There are plans to expand and extend the telecentre in terms of staff numbers and breadth of services.

- Buckinghamshire County Council has set up 2 telecentres - one in Amersham and one in Winslow - each with ten desk spaces for County Council staff. The county would like to make the telecentres available to staff from other employers in the area. It is not clear whether the centres have teleconferencing facilities or not, (c.f. Buckinghamshire workplace travel plans case study).

- In 1997, Surrey County Council launched a new corporate development programme which included a "Surrey Workstyle ' programme (SustainIT undated, Bibby 2000). As part of this programme, they set up a telecentre in Epsom with desk space for eight people. It was set up on an initial budget of about £90,000, and was designed for use on an informal basis by all Surrey employees (and in theory, though rarely in practice, by councillors as well). Part of the thinking was to help reduce the time which staff spent driving to and from Kingston in rush-hour congestion. In practice, trading standards and social service staff have tended to be the main users, although some teachers have also made use of the centre as a convenient access point for accessing the internet. In 2000, it was replaced by an equivalent facility in Epsom town hall for staff and a separate community telecentre operated by the District Council. The inclusion (or exclusion) of teleconferencing facilities is not clear. In total, the Epsom telecentre was reported to say 30,000 vehicle miles a year.

In terms of private sector initiatives, there was information about the following:
- the Royal Bank of Scotland, which estimates that it saves more than £70,000 a month by eliminating corporate travel through the use of video and audioconferencing, (HOP Associates 2001)
- BT report that Reed Personnel have developed videoconference facilities for use between employment consultants and clients
- BT itself has extensive audio and videoconferencing facilities.

Finally, British Telecom was chosen as the case study for this initiative because there was a substantially greater volume of information available about both the nature and scale of its teleconferencing activities, and the impacts that are resulting, in comparison to any other possible candidates.

11.4 Details of chosen teleconferencing case study

In the 1990s, BT underwent fundamental re-structuring to increase the efficiency of use of their workspace. This was due to assessments showing that their desk occupancy rate was 25%, and the realisation that technological developments enabled them to re-evaluate how their employees operate. Teleconferencing is now at the heart of communications within the organisation, and is used routinely for meetings.

There are three main types of teleconferencing:

- Audio-conferencing involves multiple-person telephone meetings. There are two kinds – centrally booked conferences, where calls are booked with a central service, and "Meet me", where calls are set up through a website and users can dial in without requiring central facilitiation.
- Video-conferencing involves real-time two-way visual and audio links, generally via a dedicated videoconferencing suite.
- Web conferencing involves interaction via computing technology, including facilities such as file sharing and 'live' whiteboards.

Currently, the majority of tele-conferencing that takes place within BT is audio-conferencing.

In addition to the use of tele-conferencing for internal purposes, teleconferencing is a strong growth area of BT's business. BT is currently the number five provider internationally and number one provider in Europe for teleconferencing services provided on a commercial basis.

11.5 Staffing and budgets for teleconferencing

The costs of teleconferencing are complex since they relate to both the costs of installing facilities and the ongoing costs of using them, and are different for different types of teleconferencing. We were not able to obtain staffing and budget information for the provision of teleconferencing at BT. Those using corporate services within BT use the same system that BT provides as a commercial service, and the costs of using facilities are charged internally to account holder budgets.

The commercial rates charged by BT are as follows:

Audioconferencing -   22p per user per minute, or
                      £35 per month and 12p per user per minute
Videoconferencing -   typically £35-45 per hour for a user in the UK,
                      £1.40 per minute for a slow connection within Europe and,
                      £12.60 for a fast connection to Australasia and the Far East
Web conferencing -   35p per user per minute plus ISP charges

Providing the videoconferencing infrastructure ranges from between £5000 and £40,000 for companies, depending on the type of facilities provided.

This highlights that audioconferencing is considerably the cheapest (about £13 per hour), followed by Web conferencing (about £21 per hour plus ISP charges) followed by videoconferencing (£35-45 per hour, plus the costs of installing facilities).

As a cost comparison, face2face are offering use of video-conferencing facilities from between £50 and £100 per hour, depending on the type of membership. Local and roaming members receive preferential telecoms charges, whilst pay-as-you-go members pay standard telecoms charges.

One issue is how to put these costs in context. Face2face argue that "meetings start from just £50 - the equivalent of a tank of petrol, a day in a car park at Heathrow or a round trip of approximately 50 miles on the train." They also highlight that the average business trip costs in excess of £2000 per person in terms of staff costs, and lasts more than six hours, whilst the average time spent in meetings is typically less than two hours. Hence, teleconferencing should result in considerable cost savings.

Specific estimates of business cost savings are given in section 11.8

11.6 Scale of teleconferencing

BT employs about 108,000 people. In the last year, about 350,000 audio-conferencing calls were made with additional video and web conferencing taking place. Unfortunately, there are no data on the number of conventional face-to-face meetings to provide a context for these data. BT also report that there has been a 20% growth per annum in the use of teleconferencing up to 2002, whilst data for 2000 and 2003 suggest that recent growth may have been in the order of 30% per annum.

Hopkinson et al (2003) report on the results of a survey undertaken in October 2002 about teleconferencing at BT. Of 5457 staff contacted, 771 responded who were considered to be fairly representative of BT as a whole, in terms of business unit and age. They were asked to outline their use of teleconferencing in the previous four weeks. Tables 11.4, 11.5 and 11.6 summarise the results.

Table 11.4: Use of teleconferencing by a sample of 771 BT staff

	% using service in previous 4 weeks	Frequency of use by users				
		Once	Twice	Three times	Four times	5 and more
Meet-me audio	86.0%	14.7%	12.6%	9.1%	13.3%	50.2%
Booked audio	49.4%	21.5%	12.3%	12.1%	6.6%	47.5%
Web	13.4%	61.2%	17.5%	5.8%	2.9%	12.6%
Video	2.2%	No data				

Source: Hopkinson et al (2003)

Table 11.5: The number of participants in the respondents' last calls

Don't know	3	4	5	6	7	8	9+
3%	9%	12%	16%	16%	9%	11%	24%

Source: Hopkinson et al (2003)

Table 11.6: The number of locations in the respondents' last calls

Don't know	3	4	5	6	7	8	10
8.9%	20.0%	17.5%	17.1%	13.9%	6.8%	4.9%	11.0%

Source: Hopkinson et al (2003)

Hopkinson et al (2003) highlight that audioconferencing is very popular, being used by 92% of all staff, and, of those who use it, about 50% use it 5 times or more per month. Web conferencing is only used by about 13% of staff, but is reported to be becoming more popular, whilst videoconferencing remains a minority activity, used by only 2% of staff.

On average, conference calls involve 6-7 people, although the average number of locations was only 5, implying that many conferences involve more than one person in the same location. The majority of conferences last for under an hour.

There are currently 40 videoconference suites for BT employees spread across the country.

This information can be compared with findings from the literature as shown in table 11.7.

Table 11.7 Scale of teleconferencing

Source	Finding
BT (c.2001) and Hopkinson et al (2003)	• 92% of BT staff use audioconferencing and 13% use web conferencing • Meetings usually last up to an hour, and typically involve 6-7 participants
Roy & Filistrault (1998)	In a survey of 1139 business travellers: • 49% worked for organisations that use teleconferencing • 30% worked for organisations that use videoconferencing • 20% had participated in at least one videoconference in the last year • 18% worked for companies with private videoconferencing equipment
Bennison (1988)	In a pilot between 1983-86: • Videoconferencing was particularly useful to companies with a large number of intra-organisational contacts between people on different sites • Most videoconferences involved 4-6 people • Most videoconferences were less than 2 hours • Videoconferences fulfilled the majority of meeting functions

The available data on which to draw conclusions are sparse. Clearly, audioconferencing is the most popular and widespread form of teleconferencing. However, the work undertaken by Roy and Filistrault (1998) suggest that videoconferencing may be more widespread among senior business people than the BT data suggest. It seems typical that meetings undertaken by teleconferencing are relatively short, with a relatively large number of participants (4-7). It is also interesting that Bennison (1998) identified companies with a large number of intra-organisational contacts between people on different sites as the most fertile territory for teleconferencing, and, of course, BT are a perfect example of this. It is interesting that Arnfalk (2002) highlighted that intra-organisational contacts often constitute the majority of business travel for large, dispersed organisations.

For some types of teleconferencing (notably videoconferencing), the scale of activity may directly relate to the availability of facilities. However, facilities appear to be available to most BT staff, without widespread take-up. In contrast, Roy and Filistrault (1998) highlighted that more organisations were using videoconferencing than had their own facilities available. Face2face currently aim to provide facilities in most big towns and cities in the UK. Therefore, it is unclear how far availability of facilities will be a limiting factor in the use of such technology. Anecdotal evidence received by personal communication with an employee from one company suggested that there may be 'image problems' with videoconferencing. Specifically, in his company, facilities are placed next to the Managing Director's office and there is the perception that your meeting needs to be "very important' to justify use of such facilities. Consequently, the facilities remain relatively underutilised[2]. Bennison (1988) also highlighted that, of 14 companies provided with free videoconferencing facilities, suites remained underutilised in 11 of them, and the main reason given was that facilities were 'not strongly promoted'.

11.7 Effects of teleconferencing on car use

Unravelling the BT data relating teleconferencing to car use reduction is not straightforward due to (amongst other things):
- non-existent data on pre-teleconference meeting schedules
- limited detailed data on teleconference use and the risk of double counting
- teleconferencing changing the way that people meet (frequency, length of meeting, number of people in the meeting)

In March 2000, an sample (of unspecified size) of BT staff were contacted who had booked an audioconference call on March 30th or 31st, and asked about its impacts. This is reported in BT (c. 2001). The following results are reported:
- 75% of respondents stated that their call had replaced a face to face meeting.This comprised all local calls, 75% of national calls but only 38% of international calls
- If the sample was representative of BT, audioconferencing was estimated to be saving 135,000 face to face meetings a year, of which 120,000 involved a car journey
- Overall travel savings were estimated to be around 150 million miles, of which 59 million miles was car travel

In the survey by Hopkinson et al (2003), 71% respondents stated that their last conference call had definitely or probably replaced a meeting (with 52% being 'definite'), whilst 5% stated that it had generated a meeting. 443 of the 771 respondents provided details about the travel avoided by their last call, as given in table 11.8.

Table 11.8: Characteristics of travel replaced by teleconferencing

Mode	Number of replaced trips by respondent's last call	Mean distance of avoided travel (miles)	Total avoided miles
Petrol car	203	91.4	18558.5
Diesel car	45	102.5	4611.0
Van/LGV	15	92	1380.0
Train	143	95.3	13624.0
Plane	20	146.3	2925.0

---

[2] The employee wished both he, and his company, to remain anonymous.

Taxi	17	34.9	592.5
Tube/bus/tram	68	19.2	1306.5
Other	17	51.8	880
Total	443		41690

Source: Hopkinson et al (2003)

In addition to the information given above, the survey showed that 46% of the avoided trips would have taken place during peak congestion periods.

Hopkinson et al (2003) scale up these results as follows: "In a typical year, BT employees initiate around 350,000 conference calls. If 52% of these calls definitely replaced a meeting (the figure which we obtained from the survey) this gives a figure of 182,000 avoided meetings. If each of these avoided meetings resulted in five avoided journeys (bearing in mind that the mean number of locations participating in a conference call was 5.3) this gives a total of 910,000 avoided journeys" (p31)

A similar scaling up suggests that of the 910,000 avoided journeys, 541,735 would have been by car or van, relating to 50.56 million road miles per year. This compares well with the previous study which showed that audio-conferencing was saving 59 million miles of road travel per year. These savings are estimated to represent a 9.8 - 11.1% reduction in business mileage overall. However, BT comment: "if conference calls were not an option, work might have been differently organised to avoid any need for face-to-face meetings", and hence the mileage reductions should be seen as maximum estimates.

These conclusions can be compared with evidence from the literature, as shown in table 11.9.

Table 11.9 Impacts of teleconferencing on car use

Source	Finding
BT (BT c.2001 and Hopkinson et al 2003)	• 71% of respondents said their last conference call had replaced a meeting (with 52% being 'definite'), whilst 5% stated that it had generated a meeting. • 0.5 million car/van trips and 51-59 million miles of travel saved for 108,000 people (approx 5 trips and 450-550 miles per person per year) • 46% avoided trips would have taken place during peak periods • 10-11% reduction in business mileage
Epson telecentre (SustainIT undated, Bibby 2000)	Telecentre with 8 desks estimated to save 30,000 vehicle miles p.a. (3750 miles per desk).
Mason Williams (2004)	Video meeting equipment meant that travel costs have dropped by a third.
Tetrapak (Arnfalk 2002)	Business travel reduced by 10% due to videoconferencing
Telia (Arnfalk 2002)	Between 1997-2000, business travel by air reduced by over a third, partly due to more virtual meetings (particularly audioconferencing)

Surveys with 4 Swedish companies (Arnfalk 2002)	• 45-61% respondents said videoconferencing had reduced their own travel • 15-25% said it had reduced other people's travel • 17-20% said it had only had a minor effect • 1-3% said it had increased their travel
Canadian business travellers (Roy & Filistrault 1998)	• 24.2% said they were travelling less often as a result of company policy to increase utilisation of teleconferencing • Of those participating in at least one videoconference in the previous year, users stated that videoconferencing had been a substitute for an air trip in 45% of cases. • 1.8% of all business travel may currently be substituted by teleconferencing
Canadian employees (Redekop 1994)	25% respondents made less business trips due to communications technologies in 1992, and 28% in 1994
SCAG meeting (Mokhtarian 1988)	• Total vehicle miles increased by 29% by replacing a regional meeting for a teleconference, as shorter distances to teleconference facilities were outweighed by increased attendance. • Travel in peak-hour, congested conditions was replaced by travel in off peak, less-congested conditions
BT trial 1983-86 (Bennison 1988)	87% of respondents felt that teleconferencing reduced the amount of travel they were making

The results suggest the following:

- When teleconferencing takes place, somewhere between 45% and 90% of those involved feel that it reduces their travel. A small minority (less than 5%) feel that it has generated extra travel.
- In terms of impacts on overall company travel, reductions of between 10% and 30% are typically reported for organisations that promote teleconferencing. It is plausible that some of the differences in reported impacts may relate to the composition of the workforce (and its suitability for teleconferencing), although there is not really enough available data to assess this.
- Often, travel at peak times, in congested conditions can be avoided.

Meanwhile, the study by Mokhtarian highlights that the availability of teleconferencing facilities may alter participation in business interactions, such that measuring the effects of teleconferencing is complex.

11.8 Other effects of teleconferencing

Many of the quoted benefits for teleconferencing are similar to those quoted for telework. The main benefits are as follows:

- **Enabling people with disabilities or family commitments or from distant locations, to contribute more easily to meetings.**
In the BT study by Hopkinson et al (2003), 44% of respondents said that teleconferencing had enabled them to work when they were prevented from reaching

another work location. Of those giving reasons as to why they were prevented, 59% identified domestic issues and 43% said health or disability had been a cause. Mokhtarian (1988) reported that replacing a real meeting with a virtual meeting increased attendance at a regional event by over 60%. Reed personnel have developed videoconference facilities for use between employment consultants and clients, which will presumably facilitate job applications from people who are not resident in particular areas.

- **Reduced hassle, time savings and better work-life balance**

The option to teleconference arguably makes planning easier and frees up time for the individual, including reducing the stress and hassle of travel. The face2face literature states "satisfied users are now managing to have meetings in Edinburgh, Birmingham, Manchester and Bristol, all before lunch" and that teleconferencing enables you to "forget worries about being late, missing a connection, losing your way or parking your car at airports". It also highlights freedom from "the dangers we face travelling today - road traffic accidents, SARs, earthquakes, war or terrorism". Work on teleconferencing also stresses that the time savings can enable a better work-life balance - for example time spent travelling at unsociable hours may instead be spent with the family. In the BT study, 76% of respondents stated that teleconferencing had had either mild or strongly positive impacts on their quality of life. In Roy and Filistrault's work (1998), there was general agreement that videoconferencing saves time.

- **Cost savings**

In the study by Hopkinson et al, 54% of respondents stated that the journey they avoided would have cost over £50. BT (c.2001) estimate that audioconferencing saves £6 million a year in terms of reduced petrol claims. Mason Williams, a PR agency, estimates that the monthly cost of their video conferencing equipment is normally recouped within the first week of each month. Telia estimate that by replacing three of its four quarterly meetings for top managers by teleconferences, it has saved 3 million SEK in two years in terms of reduced costs of travel, accommodation and staff time. The Royal Bank of Scotland estimates that it saves more than £70,000 a month by eliminating corporate travel through the use of video and audioconferencing.

- **Improved organisational efficiency, cohesion and resilience**

BT argue that the introduction of teleconferencing has resulted in improved staff recruitment and retention and reduced absenteeism. Benefits quoted by staff include ease of the staying in touch with remote colleagues, ease of accessing expertise, easier decision making reduced time between an issue emerging and a solution being found, and more efficient use of worktime generally. Hopkinson et al (2003) found that 82% felt that conferencing had increased their work performance (including 44% who felt the increase was 'considerable'). At a business strategy conference, a BT representative also noted that "we can be very creative about what we used by way of computer-based training [and] we can do more and more training". However, in the study by Hopkinson et al (2003), a few respondents - less than 10% - commented that there was a tendency for teleconferencing to be overused, resulting in unnecessary meetings, and a very small minority missed face to face contact. Early work by Bennison (1988) highlighted the benefits of videoconferencing as being the opportunity to call meetings at short notice, faster dissemination of information, a greatest degree of task orientation in meetings, and greater co-operation among participants. However, there was also perceived to be a decline in spontaneity in meetings, which was generally regarded as a minor, offsetting detrimental effect. In Roy and Filistrault's work (1998), there was general agreement from their survey of business travellers that "videoconferencing can accelerate decision-making by rapidly linking key players".

11.9 Synergies between teleconferencing and other policies and issues

At British Telecom, teleconferencing had partly been promoted as part of a strategy to ensure that 'all business travel is operationally necessary and carried out in the most cost-effective manner'. This type of strategy could typically form part of a comprehensive workplace travel plan and/or fleet management initiative. The interviewee also highlighted that by providing teleconferencing, individuals are encouraged to reassess their own travel choices, which may have wider impacts than simply affecting the particular journey they are planning at the time. Conversely, policies aimed at reducing car use more generally should also help to encourage the use of teleconferencing.

In addition to its teleconferencing programme, BT encourages teleworking amongst its staff, as discussed in Chapter 10. As discussed there, it seems plausible that the two are synergetic. Ready availability of teleconferencing technology within the company makes it easier for staff to work from remote locations, and thus helps make teleworking viable. At the same time, staff who are relatively 'technology literate' from teleworking may be more willing and able to get involved in teleconferencing initiatives. Specifically, in the survey by Hopkinson et al (2003), 44% of respondents said that teleconferencing had made them more likely to think about working from home.

Where teleconferencing reduces the need for employees to start travelling early, it could be synergistic with school travel plans, since it may make it easier for such workers to not drive their children to school. Where teleconferencing reduces the need to own a car, this could contribute to more general changes to a less car dependent lifestyle.

Given that teleconferencing is associated with other business benefits, such as 'improved work life balance', it is also synergistic with a range of other initiatives that may take place within organisations for non transport reasons.

11.10 Relationship between teleconferencing spending and impact

As highlighted in section 11.5, information about overall costs of installing and using teleconferencing facilities are limited. However, the trade-offs identified by face2face suggest that teleconferencing should result in considerable financial savings to an organisation. As highlighted in section 11.8, numerous companies are quoting substantial savings from reduced travel costs and improved efficiency of staff time use. However, this does not mean that companies will automatically invest in teleconferencing facilities, or encourage staff to use them. Public sector marketing or pump priming may be necessary to encourage greater teleconferencing practice, as discussed further in section 11.12.

11.11 Future impact of teleconferencing

Within BT, teleconferencing was reported to be growing at a rate of 20% p.a., with some data suggesting recent growth rates of 30% p.a.. The interviewee felt that it was not possible to suggest how much the number of calls would increase in the future, as this would partly be a function of changes in attitudes of society to work and communications, the emergence of other ways of communicating, and, potentially, future changes in the overall working practices of the company. He felt that there was no reason to suggest that the current growth rates would not continue for the foreseeable future, but that at some point, saturation would take place.

Meanwhile, there were also some insights from BT's commercial provision of teleconferencing facilities. In 2000/01, the value of its conferencing products and services was estimated at £68 million. This grew to £83 million in 2001/02 (i.e 22% in one year). It is expected to reach £260 million in 2004/05, representing a growth rate of 260% over five years. BT also quoted a Key Note market report from 2000. This estimated that the videoconferencing market had grown by 28% between 1999 and 2000, and that it would grow from £122m to £332 million between 2000 and 2005, an increase of similar proportions (272%). Both projections assume accelerating growth. A more recent Key Note report on the subject (2003) highlights that between 2001 and 2002, market growth was actually only 14% - partly because teleconferencing products have become cheaper.

A mid range interpretation of these estimates would be that growth rates of 20% a year may be expected in terms of actual use of services.

Meanwhile, as highlighted earlier, there are numerous estimates in the literature about the potential magnitude and impacts of teleconferencing on business travel. These are summarised in table 11.10.

Table 11.10 Future scale and impacts of teleconferencing

Source	Finding
Pye 1976, Goddard & Morris 1976 and Goddard & Pye 1977	44% of meetings could be teleconferenced, including 34% by audioconferencing, and 10% by videoconferencing
Bennison 1988	25% of face to face meetings could have been replaced by videoconferencing
Dodgson et al 1997 and 2000	1997 report argues that, in about 10 years, teleconferencing could replace somewhere between <ul><li>20% of business travel for 26% of people, and</li><li>20% of all business travel.</li></ul> Their 2000 report only quotes the more conservative estimate.

Apogee Research Inc 1994	Teleconferencing could substitute for 2-11% of business air travel.
Arvai 1991	Teleconferencing could substitute for 12% business air travel by 2005, 25% by 2010 and 35% by 2020
Burger 1995	Videoconferencing could reduce business air travel by up to 40%
Roy and Filistrault 1998	• Proportion of organisations with access to videoconference equipment could be about 60% by approx 2001 • Videoconferencing could replace 15% of business air trips • Videoconferencing was reducing air travel by 2-4% in the short term and could reduce it by 4-9% in about three years
Rapp & Skåmedal 1996	Estimates of the proportion of business travel that teleconferencing could replace are: • 30% of Irish business travel (1978 estimate) • 20% of US business travel (1983 estimate) • 20% of Canadian busines travel (1983 estimate) • 35% of German business travel (1985 estimate) • 35% of UK business travel (1985 estimate)
Cook and Haver 1994	Teleconferencing could replace 25% of US business travel by air by 2010.
Face2face	50% of business travellers think that videomeetings could be a preferable alternative

There is clearly quite a wide range amongst these estimates – from assertions that teleconferencing could replace up to 50% of all business travel, to much more modest assumptions that only 15% of trips could be replaced, and that the actual impacts will be lower since many companies will not have available teleconferencing facilities.

It is notable that most estimates do not distinguish between the proportion of companies that increase their volume of teleconferencing, and the impacts on travel per company. Another problem with many of the estimates described above is that they are undated and probably relate to perceived transferability of meetings to technology, rather than the probability of this actually happening.

The only two estimates of the proportion of companies expected to have teleconferencing facilities in the future are the study by Dodgson (where teleconferencing is seen as viable for 26% of people) and Roy and Filistrault (where 60% of companies were expected to have access to videoconference equipment by 2001). This can be compared with the (relatively sparse) data from section 11.6 about the current scale of teleconferencing, which ranged from BT's experience (where 92% of staff audioconference, but only 2% videoconference), to Roy & Filistrault's survey of 1139 business travellers, where 20% had taken part in a videoconference in the past year and 30% worked for organisations that used videoconferencing.

The figures given above can also be compared with those discussed in sections 11.7 about the effects of teleconferencing. These appeared to show that teleconferencing typically reduces business travel by 10 to 30% in companies which adopt it as a mainstream business practice. This appears to be in line with many of the estimates about the overall potential of teleconferencing, and therefore 30% should perhaps be taken as an upper bound of potential impacts. However, this is unlikely to be realised given that take up of teleconferencing is unlikely to be universal.

For teleconferencing to have an impact on all business travel of this order of magnitude would clearly require a major scaling up of business activity in this area. However, this does not seem entirely implausible given the high growth rates (perhaps 20% p.a.) implied in reports by BT and Key Note. Key issues for scaling up are discussed below.

11.12 Key issues for scaling up teleconferencing

In terms of public sector involvement, the key ways to promote teleconferencing are:
- to market the benefits of teleconferencing to try and encourage organisations to undertake more teleconferencing.
- to provide both technical and managerial advice to businesses about how to undertake teleconferencing
- to offer to run training courses for staff about teleconferencing
- to provide grants for organisations to introduce teleconferencing
- to provide facilities for use by the general public and
- to encourage teleconferencing amongst their own employees.

We are currently unable to comment on the extent to which this happens, however there is clearly scope for increasing these activities. Our intuition is that, even in organisations with facilities, in many cases, there is considerable ignorance about teleconferencing, and that many staff would not know how to book an audio conference call, or how it would be charged, let alone how to get involved in videoconferencing. In some cases, as discussed in section 11.6, there may also be misperceptions about eligibility to use facilities, which result in expensive facilities being relatively underutilised, and concerns about the internal cultural acceptability of not travelling to meetings. If this is the case, there could be considerable scope for the public sector to get involved in promoting greater use of teleconferencing. Initiatives on workplace travel plans and fleet management initiatives offer a good starting point for engaging with organisations about this. There may well need to be a national lead in this area, since many local authorities may lack the internal expertise to promote and advice on teleconferencing in an expert capacity.

Meanwhile, more general policies that discourage car use for work travel will all help to encourage organisations to assess whether the business travel they undertake is a good use of resources. More explicit policy implications are given in the next section.

11.13 Policy implications relating to teleconferencing

- Information and advice about teleconferencing could be included as part of any initiative aiming to influence business travel, for example, 'fleet management programs'.
- Legislation which increases the employer's (health and safety) responsibilities for employees when they are undertaking travel in the course of work is likely to encourage a greater rationalisation of business travel.

- Demand management policies for car use, such as road pricing, fuel duties, road space reallocation etc., are all likely to encourage greater rationalisation of business travel.

- Both national and local guidance and advice about teleconferencing could be helpful, covering the range of different teleconferencing options available (audioconferencing, webcams, videoconferencing etc.), the technical issues involved in running such options, the costs of such options and the associated managerial and cultural changes needed to make such options work.

- The social benefits of teleconferencing (greater participation of those with disabilities; better work life balance) could be more widely disseminated.

- There may be a role for facilities provided by local authorities where companies can go to use some of more expensive teleconferencing facilities, such as videoconferencing. Such facilities might be particularly appropriate for small and medium enterprises, and for rural areas where business interactions are perhaps more likely to be over longer distances.

- Local authorities could be encouraged to lead by example in considering whether their own business travel is always appropriate, and whether they could make more use of electronic communication methods.

- Of all the soft factors, this is the one where there is the least literature and information, and greater empirical research could be of clear benefit.

11.14 Acknowledgements

We are very grateful for the help with the main case study from

Individual	Organisation
Ian Wood	BT Social Policy Unit
Peter James	University of Bradford

In addition to the main case study interviewees, we would like to thank:

Individual	Organisation
Andy Lake	HOP Associates

11.15 References

Arnfalk P (2002) *Virtual mobility and pollution prevention: the emerging role of ICT based communication in organisations and its impact on travel.* Doctoral dissertation, International Institute for Industrial Environmental Economics, Lund University.

Arvai ES (1991) Telecommunications and business travel: the revolution has begun. *Transportation Research Circular* 425, pp28-31, as quoted in Roy & Filiatrault 1998

Appogee Research Inc (1994) *Making connections: how telecommunications technologies will affect business and leisure air travel.* Report prepared for the Federal Aviation Administration, Office of Aviation Policy, Plans and Management Analysis, as quoted in Roy & Filiatrault 1998.

Bennison DJ (1988) Transport/telecommunication interactions: Empirical evidence from a videoconferencing field trial in the United Kingdom. *Transportation Research A* 22 (4) pp291-300

Bibby A (2000) *Surrey County Council pioneers new ways of working.* Article published in 'Flexible Working 2000'.

BT (undated – c.2001) *E-business and the environment* from Better World – Our commitment to society. BT, London.

Burger TO (1995) *Videoconferencing impacts on air travel demand.* Presentation to the ACI high-level symposium - Airport 2020, Montreal, as quoted in Roy & Filiatrault 1998

Communications Canada (1990) *Technologies in services.* Communications Canada, as quoted in Roy & Filiatrault 1998.

Cook A & Haver P (1994) "Meeting face-to-face: videoconferencing" *Airline Business* 10 (11), as quoted in Arnfalk 2002

DTLR (2002) *The impact of information and communications technologies on travel and freight distribution patterns: review and assessment of literature.* Report by HOP Associates and Transport Research Group, University of Southampton.

Dodgson J et al (1997) *Motors or modems.* Report by NERA for the RAC.

Dodgson J et al (2000) *Motors and modems revisited: the role of technology in reducing travel demands and traffic congestion.* Report by nearer for the RAC Foundation and the Motorists Forum.

Face2face (2004) All information downloaded from www.face2facemeetings.co.uk on 26/3/04. Includes press releases from their London office:
3/6/04 *'face2face teams up with Cisco systems to provide world class IP videoconferencing services.*
3/6/04 '*Most business trips last more than 6 hours and cost UK businesses £2000'*
24/10/03 *'RAC Foundation backs Noel Edmonds' face2face'*

Goddard JB and Morris D (1976) The communications factor in office location. *Progress in Planning* 6 (1) as quoted in Salomon 1985.

Goddard JB & Pye R (1977) Telecommunications and office location. *Regional Studies* 11, pp 19-30 as quoted in Salomon 1985.

HOP Associates (2001) *Travel plans: new business opportunities for suppliers of information and communication technology.* Report produced by the Energy Efficiency Best Practice Programme. General report 80.

Hopkinson P, James P & Maruyama T (2003) *Conferencing at BT - results of a survey on its economic, environmental and social impacts.* Report by SustainIT, UK CEED, Peterborough

Key Note Publications Ltd (2000) *Videoconferencing*. Key Note Publications Ltd.

Key Note Publications Ltd (2003) *Videoconferencing*. Key Note Publications Ltd.

McInroy R (1999) *Linnet Locals in Lincolnshire – electronic provision in a rural setting.* Article by the Operations Manager for Library Support Services, Lincolnshire County Council, produced by South Bank University

Mokhtarian PL (1988) 'An empirical evaluation of the travel impacts of teleconferencing'. *Transportation Research A* 22 (4) pp 283-289

Pye R (1976) 'Effects of telecommunications on the location of office employment', *Omega* 4 (3) pp 289-300, as quoted in Salomon 1985.

Redekop D (1994) *Business travel trends*. Proceedings of the 6th Aviation Forecast Conference, Ottawa, as quoted in Roy & Filiatrault 1998.

Rapp B & Skåmedal (1996) *Telekommunikationers implikationers på resandet*. Linköping University, KFB rapport 1996 (2) as quoted in Arnfalk 2002.

Roy J & Filiatrault P (1998) 'The impact of new business practices and information technologies on business air travel demand.' *Journal of Air Transport Management* 4 pp 77-86

Salomon I (1985) Telecommunications and travel: substitution or modified mobility? *Journal of Transport Economics and Policy* pp219-235

SustainIT (2003) *The UK eWell-Being Awards 2003*. Report by SustainIT. Nottingham case study p15.

SustainIT (undated) '*Surrey Workstyle: Surrey County Council*'. Case study report downloaded from www.sustainit.org

12. Home Shopping

12.1 Introduction

Home shopping, where customers have goods delivered to them, is a growing phenomenon. The nature of home shopping is discussed further in the next sections. However, one key characteristic is that it has clearly, so far, been a private sector initiative with relatively little public sector involvement.

In this chapter, we initially examine the available evidence about
- The nature of home shopping
- The current and future scale of home shopping
- The different characteristics of what people buy, and
- The transport impacts of the different sectors

However, we were primarily concerned to examine the way in which the public sector can condition the way in which the services develop, and the transport impacts which will result.

Many of the issues for optimising home delivery operations overlap with issues for optimising freight travel in general, and include, for example:
- grants to encourage investment in IT for efficient scheduling
- vehicle maintenance and driving training schemes to help companies to minimise fuel use
- national policies on fuel and travel pricing
- regulations on vehicle use within cities
- transhipment schemes
- dedicated freight vehicle lanes
- encouragement of cycling and walking couriers
- schemes to promote vehicles with more efficient engines, and that run on alternative fuels or hybrid power systems
- policies on times for permitted deliveries in residential areas
- schemes to promote local sourcing of goods
etc..

These issues have been explored in various contexts, including ECMT 1997, FTA 1997, DETR 1999, the UK TransportEnergy Best Practice[1] programme, and the EU SURFF[2] and JUPITER (1 & 2)[3] projects.

There is also a growing body of research and commentary about the overall transport and environmental impacts of home deliveries (including Handy & Yantis 1997, Romm et al 1999, Transport en Logistiek 2000, Dodgson et al 1997 and 2000, Browne *et al* 2001, Retail Logistics Task Force (2001), Hopkinson & James 2001, Kärnä 2001, OECD/ECMT 2001, Mokhtarian & Salomon 2002, Mokhtarian 2004 and

---

[1] www.transportenergy.org.uk/bestpractice/index.cfm
[2] www.euroweb.net/surff
[3] europa.eu.int/comm/energy/en/thermie/jupiter2.htm

European projects ROSETTA[4], STELLA[5] and Digital Europe[6]), together with studies relating specific sectors, as reported later in this chapter.

For this project, we were particularly keen to find evidence about local authority involvement in schemes which have focused on home shopping. Although we did not undertake a case study interview, we were able to draw on a detailed report about a pilot project taking place between the Royal Mail and Nottingham City Council. This has involved the development of a number of different delivery locations that people can have shopping delivered to, and has been written up as a case study for the Department for Transport's Transport Energy Best Practice programme, (TransportEnergy BestPractice 2004).

From the analysis work, a number of indications also emerge about other ways in which both central and local government might wish to get involved in home shopping, and the policy implications are summarised in section 12.12.

It should be noted that we were largely unable to gain any information about the public sector costs of different forms of involvement in home shopping, although some tentative statements are made in section 12.11.

12.2 The nature of home shopping

Home shopping is often taken to be synonymous with electronic commerce, or Internet shopping. In reality there are a number of different ways in which people can purchase goods from home, most of which are forecast to increase in the future. This is important since the social profile of those who use different channels is different, and therefore concentrating on Internet options alone results in a distorted picture of the potential impact of home shopping in the future. In particular, these options are:

- catalogue shopping, where the growth area is seen as specialist catalogues aiming at more upmarket clientele (compared to the traditional market which was 'middle-aged housewives' and those in need of cheap credit).
- direct retailing such as Tupperware or Avon, media advertisement with phone ordering and specialist subscription services such as book clubs.
- Internet shopping (where the main advantages are seen as being the opportunities to buy goods internationally, to get cheaper products, to readily find products requiring complex searches and to obtain new types of services and products).
- TV shopping (which has the advantage of operating on the basis of familiar technology, being watched in a comfortable environment conducive to browsing and providing a more regulated environment than the Internet).
- 'intelligent' household items such as dustbins and refrigerators (For example, Electrolux have developed a product called Screenfridge, which can be used to automatically reorder items as they run out).

In short, there are a whole range of ways that customers can and will be able to order products for delivery. It is also widely expected that technologies will increasingly merge in the future. For example, interactive TV, smart mobile phones and even

---

[4] www.trg.soton.ac.uk/rosetta
[5] www.stellaproject.org
[6] www.digital-eu.org

games consoles from Sega, Sony and Nintendo are starting to provide access to e-mail and the Internet. According to a Reuters Business Briefing quoted by Morris (2000):

> "*The likely truth is that the future is going to be dominated by neither Internet shopping nor a borne-again resurgence of high streets and shopping malls. It will, rather, be a sensible, genuinely progressive amalgam of on-line and high street businesses - what's already being called clicks and mortar*".

There is also increasing interest in the delivery of shopping to locations other than the home. This is discussed further in section 12.7.3.

12.3 The current and future scale of home shopping

12.3.1 Estimates of all forms of home shopping

Data collected by the Office for National Statistics (2003) suggests that home shopping sales (defined as 'mail order' and 'other non store retail') have constituted about 4% of total retail sales for the last 10 years, and are only just starting to become more significant. There have been some concerns about how accurately the ONS data reflect reality, particularly the newer forms of retailing such as Internet and TV shopping. Given that most home shopping is still dominated by catalogue sales, these figures provide some indication of current trends. Specifically, for example, Mintel (2003) estimates that mail order still constitutes 70% of home shopping sales, direct selling makes up 10%, whilst e-commerce (including Internet and TV sales) and other forms of home shopping make up the remaining 20%. However, there has been very rapid growth in Internet and TV retailing, compared to other home shopping sectors. For example, Mintel (2003) also quote data from a nationally representative sample of 1476 adults aged 15+, where the proportion claiming to have bought goods from the Internet has increased from less than 10% in 2000 to about 25% in 2003.

More specific estimates of the home shopping market have recently been commissioned from the Department for Transport, to evaluate the current and future scale of home shopping.

The work was conducted by Foley et al (2003b). It involved interviews with 24 key professionals and policy makers, and in-depth analysis of 5 reports from three expert organisations, namely Key Note, Retail Intelligence and Verdict. Final results from the work represent an 'average' of the results given in the reports, adjusted to take account of expert opinion. These findings are given in table 12.1

These data suggest that the scale of the home shopping market may perhaps be double that shown by ONS statistics, with rapid growth expected, particularly for Internet shopping and grocery home shopping.

Table 12.1 Estimates of the size of the home shopping market

	2000	2005	2010
Size of home shopping market	£16.3 billion	£30.5 billion*	£57.0 billion*
% of all retail sales	8%	13.8%	n/a
On line sales	£4.9 billion	£11 billion	£22.5 billion
On line sales as % of all retail sales	n/a	4.3%	7.7%
Grocery home shopping market	£530million	£4.25 billion	£13 billion
% total food retail sales	0.6%	4.0%	11%

* Inferred from predicted rates of growth between 2000 and 2005, and 2005 and 2010.

Foley et al (2003) also reviewed statistics about the prevalence of home shopping. Their review quoted studies suggesting that 52% of consumers have received at least one home delivery in the last 12 months. It argued that women were much higher users of home shopping than men, and that home shopping was most common in the middle of the socio-demographic scale (with the highest level of home shopping occurring in social group C2).

However, these results probably reflect the current dominance of mail order selling in the home shopping market at present. If the greatest growth occurs in Internet and TV retailing, the profile may change, to reflect the distribution of technology.

Access to new technology is increasing fast. According to the ONS (2004), between 1998/99 and 2002/03, the proportion of households with a home computer increased from 33% to 55%, and the proportion with Internet access rose from 10% to 45%. At the same time, 94% had a telephone and 98% had a television. Analysis of the Expenditure and Food survey (ONS, annual) suggests that income is the biggest determinant of access to all types of technology. In terms of household types, it is notable that retired households are far less likely to own the newer types of technology. The presence of children in the household increases the numbers that own a home computer, or have access to the Internet or satellite TV. This effect is more marked for two person households (probably because they have more disposable income). (Notably, this reverses the effect observed for general retailing, where the presence of children in the household means that the household behaves more like a 'poorer' household, making fewer discretionary purchases than might be expected. This implies that new technologies are not viewed as luxury goods but more as educational tools).

Take-up of new technologies is expected to continue, partly because a growth in technical literacy will probably mean that more people are able to use the new options available, and partly because the new technologies are becoming a cheaper and more ubiquitous part of everyday life. However, there are concerns that certain sectors of the population (in particular, the elderly and the poor) may remain relatively disconnected from the new technologies, with implications for social inclusion, as discussed briefly in section 12.9 and 12.12.

12.3.2 Estimates of internet shopping

As well as general estimates of the home shopping market, a comprehensive review of internet shopping was conducted by Cairns et al in 2000, including assessment of surveys from Lex Transfleet, Ernst & Young, Which ?, Continental Research, Fletcher Research (later Forrester Research), National Opinion Polls, Verdict, The Henley Centre, Bossard Consulting Group, and others. The findings are summarised below.

In general, a number of key characteristics seemed to be emerging, both about Internet users, and Internet shoppers, (who do not necessarily have the same profiles). Profiles may be expected to change, as use of the Internet progresses, and in terms of the product bought. For example, anecdotal evidence about grocery retailing suggests that 'time pressed families' from poorer households may constitute a significant segment of the home shopping market for groceries. Moreover, all surveys suggested that initial bias in Internet profiles is diminishing over time as it becomes a more 'everyday' technology - for example, the gender balance is becoming more representative of the general population. However, currently, major characteristics of Internet users and shoppers are as follows:

- More men than women use the Internet
- Internet users have a higher level of education, come from richer households and higher social classes
- Internet users are younger than average
- Internet users are more likely to live in larger cities, and particularly London.
- Internet shoppers are more likely to be experienced Internet users, and more technologically aware generally.
- Time spent on the Internet use largely replaces time spent using other communications and entertainment technologies, although people mention a wide range of activities that they substitute.
- Many people access the Internet from work, so that home penetration of computers and Internet access is not the limiting factor on the number of people who may e-shop.

In terms of numerical estimates, Cairns et al (2000) highlighted that in 1999, estimates of annual Internet sales were £0.6-3 billion (0.25-1% of total sales). Future predictions were that, by about 2005, Internet sales would account for £7-20 billion (3-7% of total sales); and by about 2010, could account for £40-113 billion (12-25% of total sales[7]). However, the reliability of future estimates was considered dubious, given the amount of variability both in current estimates, and between future estimates. Particularly dramatic increases in internet sales were tending to occur at Christmas.

In general, the findings reported by Cairns et al are in line with the recent estimates by Foley et al, except for the predictions for internet sales in 2010. Here, the figures from Foley et al are considerably more conservative, presumably reflecting the fact that experts are now more cautious given longer term experience of Internet shopping.

---

[7] £40 billion is considerably less than 12.5% of total sales, but the data source gave no estimate of what percentage of sales it did imply.

12.4 The different characteristics of what people buy

In the work by Cairns et al (2000) five main sectors of goods were defined, according to their logisitical requirement. The study excluded sales of 'special' types of products (like houses, cars, public transport tickets, theatre tickets and holidays), and services (including banking, insurance and other personal financial transactions etc).

Data from the Family Expenditure Survey was classified to provide some insights into the size of each sector. The results are given in Figure 12.1

Figure 12.1: Proportion of household spending on different sectors

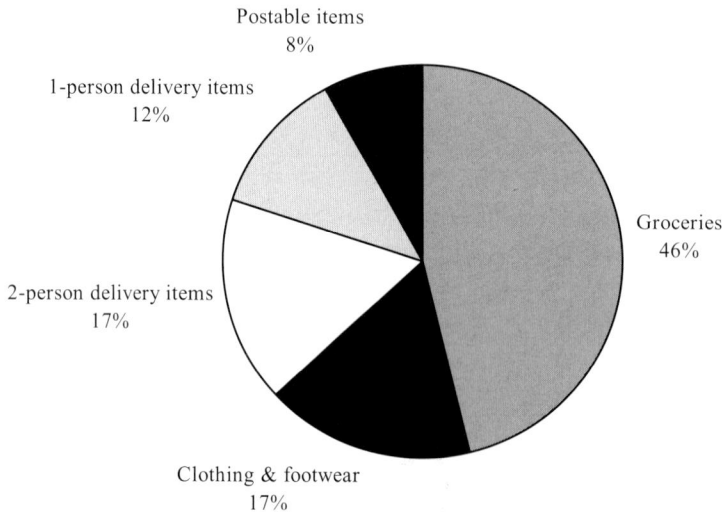

To create these sectors, data were added together as follows:
Groceries = Food, non-alcoholic drink, detergents and other cleaning materials, toilet paper, pets and pet food, toiletries, soap, cosmetics and hair products.
Clothing & footwear = Clothing and footwear
2-man delivery items = Furniture, floor covering, gas and electrical appliances, kitchen/garden equipment, household hardware and sports/camping equipment
1-man delivery items = Soft furnishings and bedding, kitchen and electrical consumables, TVs, videos, computers, audio equipment, toys, hobbies, horticultural goods, plants and flowers,
Postable items = jewellery, watches, books, maps, diaries, newspapers, magazines, photos and CDs.

It is notable that groceries account for nearly half of this expenditure. Clothing and footwear, and two-person delivery items (mainly household goods) are the second two biggest sectors, in terms of spending.

The sectors are relevant, because they have different logisticial requirements, and will have different transport impacts. These issues are considered in more detail in the following subsections.

12.4.1 Groceries

This category includes sales of food and other household items. Home shopping offerings for groceries have to deal with several distinctive features - the goods have to be delivered at three temperature regimes (frozen, chilled and ambient), and customers expect very short lead times. Purchasing is likely to occur regularly, allowing retailers to build up a relationship with their customers.

Home shopping options for groceries have been available in the UK for over 20 years, as reviewed by Cairns 1996. However, the last few years has seen a major expansion in offerings, as most of the mainstream retailers have started to offer services via the web. Most are using a logistics model whereby internet grocery orders are picked, packed and delivered using conventional stores (or facilities immediately adjacent to stores). This is the model used by Tesco, which is seen as the market leader for grocery home shopping, and now offers home delivery from stores to 95% of the UK (Tesco 2002). The only mainstream retailer using a different model is Ocado, an independent venture which delivers Waitrose goods. Although there has been the development of some independent ventures, these remain a small part of the market, and many were relatively short-lived, either closing down or being absorbed by the multiples.

Demand for the home shopping options seems to be variable. A recent Government survey of the major grocery retailers reports the following:

> *"General consensus exists among the grocery retailers that e-commerce will not exceed 10% of total UK grocery sales value by 2005, or 15% by 2010, with many of those interviewed thinking that these are very optimistic predictions. In the opinion of the retailers interviewed, a realistic estimate of the e-commerce share of the UK grocery market in 2005 appears to lie between 2.5 and 10%." (Retail Logistics Task Force, 2000)*

These figures are in line with the more specific estimates (4% by 2005 and 11% by 2010) produced by Foley et al (2003).

In terms of the transport impacts, although the total proportion of groceries which are purchased by home delivery is still very small, this sector has generated some of the greatest academic interest because of the absolute volumes involved and the regular nature of the delivery.

12.4.2 Clothing and footwear

This category is fairly clearly defined, and differs from the others in that it tends to have significantly higher return rates (typically up to 30-40%). Catalogue shopping is dominant for clothing and footwear, although the nature of the catalogue market is changing. Traditionally, the catalogue market was dominated by the 'big-book' catalogues, that were partly so attractive because they offered a source of cheap credit. However, in 1987 Next launched a more specialist home shopping catalogue, attempting to develop a more up-market image for catalogue shopping, and a number of other high street stores have followed suit. There has also been some growth in internet offerings, including sites developed by the main retailers.

As home shopping for clothing and footwear is evolving, companies are starting to offer shorter lead times, and returns policies which are more conducive to 'buying before trying'. Already, items purchased online from major clothing retailers often arrive with a pre-paid return label, and, in some cases, it is possible to take items back to a high street store, regardless of the purchasing method. Access to out of stock items and a wider range of sizes are seen as key benefits, compared with conventional shopping services.

In terms of the transport impacts, given that much of the home shopping market for clothing and footwear is catalogue sales which has already existed for some time, the growth of new delivery movements is less. It is also notable that this sector is proving to be the least successful on the Internet. However, the high return rates of this sector generate concerns about delivery movements.

12.4.3 Two-person delivery items

This category includes products such as large items of furniture (eg. sofas, wardrobes) and other large household items (eg. electrical items like washing machines, cookers and fridges; and some DIY products). The sector is distinctive in that the ordering of items, and later delivery, is already a major feature. Customers have been conditioned into waiting for goods, with deliveries sometimes taking a month or more (since many items are made to order).

However, there is evidence that customers are increasingly demanding shorter lead times, and are only really prepared to wait when they are purchasing high quality individual items. Because these types of large items are bought infrequently, the sector also relies more on advertising than on building long-term relationships with customers, and on providing high quality services and advice at the time of purchase. In general, most of the major players have developed their own websites (for example, www.comet.co.uk, www.mfi.co.uk), which offer the opportunity to purchase products. A number of dedicated e-retailers have also set up, such as www.furniture123.co.uk and www.pineonline.co.uk..

In terms of the transport impacts, the nature of these items means that home delivery has always been a major feature. Any increase in deliveries by stores is likely to represent efficiency savings, since one vehicle delivering several items is almost always likely to be more efficient than customers using their own private vehicle transporting only one item at a time.

12.4.4 One-person delivery items

This category includes many hi-tech objects like computers, stereos and TVs, together with other household/leisure items (eg. smaller electrical items like irons and some sports equipment).

Of items in this sector, computers are particularly dominant in terms of home shopping sales, and initially at least, they accounted for the highest sales value of all items sold over the Internet. A significant proportion of all computers are sold over the internet, and a high proportion of transactions are conducted directly with the manufacturers. For example, Dell only sell via the internet.

Most of the major high street players (including Dixons, Currys and Comet) have their own websites, and there are also a number of specialist e-retailers such as Dabs.com. There has also been the set up of a number of auction sites, such as e-Bay, where customers can specify how much they wish to pay for a product; and sites encouraging consumers to club together to negotiate prices, such as LetsBuyIt.com[8].

In terms of the transport impacts, this is the sector where there appears to be the biggest growth in deliveries direct from the manufacturer to the customer which is leading to the development of entirely new supply chains.

12.4.5 Postable items

This category includes all items small enough to travel via conventional postal services, like books, CDs and other leisure/gift items. This seems to be the only category containing products that could 'dematerialise'into electronic forms. It also seems to largely consist of luxury items, which are discretionary purchases, such that the increased range of options offered by home shopping is more likely to stimulate demand in this sector than in others. Third, by definition of the sector, this group of products is the easiest to transport. Hence, it is perhaps not surprising that this sector contains the some of the most popular products to buy via non-store options, and where there is most likely to be increasing international trading.

Amazon.com was one of the first Internet companies to set up, and has become synonymous with the dot.com revolution, with its sales of books, and subsequently, sales of other leisure products like CDs and videos. Meanwhile, jewellery is reported to be one of the largest selling items on TV channels such as QVC.

In terms of transport impacts, postable items, that can travel through conventional postal services are likely to have relatively little impact aside from leading to an expansion of the conventional postal market. Concerns in this sector are related to the growth of international purchasing, and aggressive just-in-time market fulfilment strategies, one example being the notorious tale of the fleet of airplanes chartered by Amazon.com to deliver the fourth Harry Potter book.

12.4.6 Overview and policy implications of sector characteristics

Different sectors generate different requirements. For groceries, temperature regimes, storage options and short delivery times are paramount. For clothing, good returns policies are vital, whilst for two-person delivery items, reliable delivery arrangements and good after-sales service are more important. Postable items are more likely to be sold internationally, and price and novelty value will be key determinants of success. Computers seem to be the only item where a considerable amount of sales are increasingly being conducted directly between the customer and the manufacturer.

Each of the different sectors generates different transport requirements. As highlighted above, postable items are largely travelling via conventional postal services, two-person items have always required delivery and home sales of clothing and footwear are dominated by the catalogue distribution networks, which have been in place for some time. Consequently, the newest and fastest growing national home delivery sectors are home shopping sales of groceries and 'one person delivery items'. The next sections look at some evidence in relation to the transport impacts of these

---

[8] These sites sell other products too, but are particularly important for one-person delivery items.

sectors. In particular, section 12.6 examines local authority involvement in a trial scheme which aimed to reduce the transport impacts of 'one person delivery items', clothing and footwear and some postable item deliveries.

12.5 Transport impacts of grocery home shopping

A review carried out by Cairns (2004) has examined the currently available evidence about the transport impacts of grocery home shopping. This material is summarised in the following sections.

12.5.1 Modelling assessments of the transport impacts of grocery home shopping

There has been modelling work about home shopping by number of commentators. The key results from these studies are shown in the following table:

Table 12.2 Traffic impacts of grocery home shopping services

	Impact on traffic generated by those undertaking home shopping	Total impact on grocery shopping traffic, depending on the proportion of the population taking up home shopping.
Cairns 1997	-70-80%	1% take-up: -0.8% 15% take up: -13.1%
Palmer 2001	Deliveries from existing stores: -75% to -91% Deliveries from mix of stores and fulfillment centres: -69% to -78%	0.5% take-up (2001): -3.7% 2% take-up (2003): -8.2 or -8.6% 5% take-up (2005): -12.6% or -11.5% 10% take-up (2010): -22.7% or -20.7% depending on fulfillment model
Punakivi et al 2001-03	-53.7% to -92.8% depending on the time restraints placed on delivery options	
Farahmand & Young 1998	-87%	
Persson & Bratt 2001		10% take-up: +0.5%* to -8.5% 25% take-up: -14% to -24% 50% take-up: -40% to -49% depending on fulfillment model, delivery destination and time restraints
Murto 1996		1 trip per week replaced: – 2% decline in total traffic (i.e. not just grocery traffic)

* It should be noted that this result is not considered to be credible given the associated descriptions in the paper.

There were additional studies by Karna (2001), Orremo et al (1999), Nockold (2001) and Freire (1999), which provide further insights, but did not produce numeric estimates of the kind that could be readily incorporated into the table. It was notable that although the various research projects were based on different software, worked at different scales, and used different assumptions, they produced some broadly similar results about the traffic impacts of grocery home delivery services. These were:

- If delivery vehicles directly substitute for car trips, the kilometres saved per shopping load are likely to be substantial – **with reductions in the order of 70% or more.** Even with very stringent operating contraints or very low levels of customer demand, reductions of 50% or more are predicted.

- The degree of savings broadly depends on the extent to which customer orders can be consolidated. Deliveries from local stores (as opposed to dedicated fulfilment centres) appear more efficient, (as shopping remains consolidated in larger vehicles for longer, only being subdivided into smaller vehicles for local delivery closer to customer homes). Delivery operations with fewer time constraints are also more efficient. There are then a number of related factors that will have an impact (including delivery vehicle capacity, the location and density of customer demand, the location of the store or fulfilment centre, etc.).

- The effect on overall travel for food shopping will largely be determined by the level of take-up of home shopping.

These conclusions are made in the context that food shopping accounts for only a small *proportion* of total motorised travel, although it generates a significant amount of travel in absolute terms. These assessments provide a starting point for considering the traffic impacts of home deliveries.

12.5.2 Behavioural responses not included in modelling assessments

In reality, changes in customer behaviour are likely to be more complex than the models assume. There are three changes in customer behaviour which are commonly discussed in relation to calculations about traffic impacts, as discussed below:

- **Car-drivers may change the frequency of their shopping**
There is concern that people may order some goods, such as dry, 'standard' products, but still make a car journey to buy other items, like fresh produce. This would mean that delivery traffic would add to existing car traffic, rather than replacing it. However, whether this happens partly depends on home delivery cost structures. Where there is a delivery charge to pay, it seems unlikely that many people will place small orders. The evidence is that, on average, the opposite effect is more dominant – with home shoppers tending to buy more and shop less often (presumably to get the most from their delivery charge). For example, Brunn-Jensen (1999) reports that, on average, Tesco home shoppers buy 120% more than store customers (an average basket size being £91 compared with £41.30 for in-store customers), whilst Iceland home delivery customers buy 500% more (the average basket size being £45, compared to the average in-store shop of £7.60). The impact of less frequent shopping should be further travel reductions[9].

---

[9] This might not apply if home shopping services are stimulating additional purchases. So far, commentators like Verdict Research (2000) have reported that this phenomenon is relatively limited (less than 10% of Internet sales) and that such 'new' purchases are largely concentrated in the 'postable' items sector, including products such as books and CDs whch are typically more

- **Non-car drivers start to use services**

If people who currently do not use a car for home shopping start receiving home deliveries, then there is no decline in car travel to compensate for the growth in delivery traffic. One counterargument is that the availability of home delivery services could, in some cases, 'tip the balance' in longer term decisions about car purchase. Moreover, the proportion of households who do not use a car for major food shopping is relatively small, with some research commissioned by Sainsburys suggesting that even 30% of non-car-owning households get a lift or take a taxi (Telephone Surveys 1994).

- **Cars 'released' from grocery shopping may be used more for other things**

There is concern that if a car is not used for the journey to the supermarket, it may be used more for other things, either because the shopper gains time, or because other members of the household will use it. Some argue that the 'time-poor households' likely to be using services will probably have 'suppressed trips' that they will want to make instead. Others suggest that such households will spend any 'time gains' by lengthening existing activities, or on in-home relaxation, (which is likely to be one of their most 'time-squeezed' activities), and that they are likely to be richer households where adults who want a car have one already. (The validity of this argument would diminish if Internet shopping becomes increasingly widespread). If it is the case that cars 'released' from shopping are used for more travel elsewhere, it is still unclear whether such additional travel should be counted in any home shopping 'traffic impact assessment'. Travel for food shopping is considered to be one of the most car-dependent trip purposes, because of the transport of bulky goods. Hence, reducing car travel for that journey purpose can still be considered a success in policy terms. Meanwhile, the 'responsibility' for reducing car-use for other trip purposes presumably depends on initiatives specific to those types of trip. Partly, the last argument simply highlights the need for an integrated transport policy. Given that people will always want to undertake some travel, the challenge is to ensure that people are provided with a more attractive alternative than the car for all journey purposes.

More generally, the scale of the behaviours described in the second two bullets are critical to their importance on overall traffic impacts[10]. Most of the models were showing reductions in travel per shopping load in excess of 70%. Crudely, this implies that even if 7 out of 10 home shoppers were not previously driving, or continue to drive for other purposes, there is unlikely to be a net increase in traffic from new services.

---

discretionary, luxury purchases. 'New sales' are not currently considered to be a significant phenomenon for grocery shopping.

[10] In one study of tele-workers (Gould and Golob, 1997), it was shown that, on days when people worked from home, on average, they spent about an hour less on work and associated travel, whilst spending 46 minutes on out-of-home discretionary activities (including travel for those activities). In contrast, those working away from home spent about an hour more on work and associated travel, and 37 minutes on out-of-home discretionary activities (including travel). This implies that when working from home, only about 15% of 'saved time' was converted into out-of-home activities. This highlights that people who gain time will not automatically wish to convert all of it into extra out-of-home activity. However, the particular focus of their study makes it difficult to draw more specific conclusions about the overall traffic impacts of home shopping.

12.5.3 Studies of the traffic impacts of grocery home shopping

To understand the complexity of behavioural responses to home shopping, studies of actual changes in customer travel behaviour are required. Although the author is aware of numerous undergraduate and MSc projects which have attempted to survey home shoppers, there has been little mainstream research or literature on the topic, partly due to the problems of accessing home shoppers for research. A few small studies are reported below, together with related surveys of relevance to the issue.

*
*   **Customers of the Food Ferry[11] (Millar 1998)**

'The Food Ferry' is an independent grocery delivery company operating in London. In 1998, in a survey of 160 customers, 61% of respondents reported that they owned at least one car, with 74% of these reporting that they were using their car less because of shopping with the Food Ferry. This implies that 45% of all respondents were reporting reduced car-use as a result of using the service. In addition, Millar reported that "two or three customers indicated they have got rid of their vehicle altogether because of the Food Ferry".

*   **Customers of James Telesuper (Tacken 1990)**

'James Telesuper' is a grocery home shopping service in the Netherlands, where, at the time of Tacken's work, customers could order goods by phone or computer. Tacken surveyed 146 customers from Amstelveen, (a town with a large central shopping area and a small shopping centre in each residential district). Survey results showed that over 50% of tele-shopping customers were still buying fresh goods from a store, but were less likely to use supermarkets, and more likely to use local shops. They were also making less trips. In general, tele-shopping customers were shopping less often than average, with 49% ordering once a month or less. Of those still visiting shops, when asked how their means of travel for shopping had changed, 28% said that they travelled less by car, 23% that they walked more often, and 14% that they travelled more by bike. 70% believed that the service was saving them time, with the average quoted saving in the order of 0.5 - 2 hours. Most did not say how the time gain was being spent, but Tacken comments: "the extra time may not have been devoted to new activities, but to more time for existing activities, including sleeping in… Most people did not mention any new activity that required travel".

*   **Members of Imperial College who use e-commerce (Snead 2001)**

Snead (2001) undertook an email survey of 95 staff and students from Imperial College, London, of whom 12 undertook home shopping for groceries. On average, the grocery home shoppers reported that using the service has resulted in a reduction of 4 trips per month. Snead comments:"Although this is not a large sample, the fact that the figure for groceries was twice as high as for any other type of shopping is worthy of note. The reason for this is probably that grocery shopping is normally the primary purpose of the shopping trip". 85% of respondents also reported that they would have travelled by car to purchase groceries, had they not shopped from home – implying that there was an average saving of 3.4 car trips per month.

---

[11] www.foodferry.co.uk

- **Customers of Schnucks Express Connection (Morganosky & Cude, 2000)**

Morganosky & Cude (2000) carried out a survey of 243 customers of Schnucks Express Connection, the internet grocery shopping service offered by a St-Louis-based store chain to parts of mid-west USA. The research did not provide any direct information about travel impacts, although it did ask about some relevant aspects of behaviour change. About 53% of people shopping from home felt that it saved them time, although 47% did not. Many (81%) reported that they were still using stores to buy food, although there was no clarification as whether these were the same stores as previously, and it is also notable that a high proportion (51%) had only started using the internet to buy groceries in the preceding month. Perhaps the most interesting finding was that many of the users identified convenience factors as reasons for using the service (including a considerable number of mothers with young children and people with physical problems lifting and carrying groceries), rather than a desire to achieve time savings in order to undertake other activities.

- **Expert views about home shopping**

In their review of research evidence and expert opinion, Foley et al (2003a) concluded that, typically, on-line grocery buyers make 3.5 fewer shopping trips per month, compared to non-buyers of online groceries. The only dissenting expert felt that the effect on travel was a slightly smaller reduction of 2 trips per month. In addition, one grocery expert stated that on-line customers typically order groceries relatively infrequently – every 15 days on average.

- **Motorists support for home shopping (Lex Transfleet 2000)**

Lex Transfleet carry out an annual survey of motorists, designed to be representative of UK motorists in general. In 2000[12], they asked 1563 motorists whether they would support home shopping if it led to a rise in the number of vans/trucks delivering goods. 22% said they would still support services, whilst 38% would be opposed. Notably, the question formulation did not include potential traffic reductions from reduced car usage – suggesting that the researchers did not consider it important in people's evaluations. To some extent, this assumption is justified by other qualitative evidence, which suggests that people are likely to perceive delivery vehicles in residential areas as noisy, dirty, and a safety risk to vulnerable road users (regardless of their actual operational characteristics), and that they are more likely to notice delivery vehicles *per se*, because, compared with cars, they are bigger, and a less common feature of the local environment.

In summary then, these surveys suggest that, whilst home shopping for groceries may generate some offsetting travel for other purposes, in general, it is likely to reduce personal car-use, with motivations for using home shopping grocery services often being about reducing hassle and having more time for existing activities. The survey of James Telesuper further clarifies that, whilst some trips may still be made to stores, the number is likely to reduce, and trips are more likely to be to local shops, by more sustainable modes. Meanwhile, the survey by Lex Transfleet highlights that perceptions of traffic impacts are likely to be skewed by concerns about delivery vehicle growth, regardless of any offsetting reductions in private car traffic. Such

---

[12] In the Lex Transfleet 2001 report, the same question was asked – but only to home shopping motorists (a total of 317 people). Opposition was significantly lower (at 24%), whilst support was higher (37%). However, given who was asked, the answers are less representative of general public opinion.

perceptual issues strengthen the business case for ensuring that home delivery services for groceries operate at maximum efficiency, using attractive, well-driven, environmentally-friendly vehicles, since this could affect whether people choose to use services, and which services they choose to use. Meanwhile, the need for research about actual traffic impacts is reinforced, since it is important that policy decisions are informed by facts about transport and environmental impacts, not simply public perceptions.

12.6 Trial scheme to minimise the transport impacts of some non-food deliveries

As discussed more generally in section 12.7.4, there is considerable interest in the use of drop boxes to increase the efficiency of delivery operations. TransportEnergy BestPractice (2004) reports on a trial scheme in Nottingham which has been effective in reducing the amount of travel generated by (supposedly) postable items, which won't go through the letterbox or need a signature, together with some deliveries of clothing and footwear and 'one-person delivery items'. The trial is of particular interest given that it is an example of public sector involvement in the home shopping sector.

12.6.1 Nature of the trial

In 2002-3, the Royal Mail undertook the trial in two postcode areas of Nottingham, in collaboration with Nottingham City Council. The trial aimed to address the problem of failed deliveries, which occur when no one is at home to receive items that either require a signature (such as time guaranteed services) or are too big to be posted through the letterbox. It included items from catalogue and Internet retailers, where such retailers were registered with Royal Mail's Local Collect service[13].

In the trial, customers were allowed to choose where items would be delivered to, both initially and following failed deliveries. The options included their own address, a neighbours address, an automated local bank (which were situated in various locations around the city), their local Post Office branch and/or Royal Mail delivery office. For some options, customers could request to be notified of the delivery by text or e-mail. The trial required the Royal Mail to ensure that the delivery facilities were in place, and to develop a database of customer preferences. An extensive marketing campaign was implemented to encourage customers to register their preferences. Initially, all unregistered customers were assigned their own address as the preferred delivery address and the nearest Post Office branch as their preferred redelivery address.

Nottingham City Council helped to facilitate the scheme as follows:
- The council helped the project concept to be swiftly introduced a wide range of prospective partners, including hospitals, universities, shopping centre management and railway station management. (This was important when identifying locker bank locations).

---

[13] This is a nationwide service, where customers ordering from registered catalogue or Internet retailers can ask to have their goods delivered directly to one of almost 15,500 participating Post Office branches.

- Locating locker banks in public places required planning permission, and a city council representative facilitated the necessary pre application discussions between Royal Mail and Development Control. This meant that any issues could be addressed as early as possible.
- The city council provided local census information and and access to city and regional partnerships including a community committee.
- The city council helped to publicise the scheme locally

12.6.2 Scale of the scheme

The trial took place in postcodes NG5 and NG9 in Nottingham. These are both mixed suburban areas, with a combined total of 68,000 residential addresses. There were 33 relevant Post Office branches located within the areas, and one Royal Mail delivery office with customer pickup facility in each. In addition, 11 locker banks were introduced into the area. In total each week 1,001,000 items are delivered into the areas of which 36,000 are packets/parcels or require a signature. This implies that there are potentially 28 relevant deliveries per household per year, which could be affected because they are not delivered successfully the first time, or because the customer would choose for them to be delivered elsewhere.

During the trial, around 2000 customers registered a delivery or redelivery preference. Some 50,000 more used the service without registering, when their undelivered items were redelivered to Post Office branches. The total number of deliveries in the scheme, either to the local Post Office branch, locker bank or neighbour, has increased over time. In February 2003, it was 6000 per month, whilst by October 2003, it was 12,000 per month and the trend was still one of upward growth. This implies growth from one item per household per year to 2 items per household per year. The majority have been redeliveries to the local Post Office branches.

A wide range of products and goods were delivered during the trial. These included books, DVDs, CDs, computer hardware and software, fishing tackle, live plants, holiday tickets, DIY kit, clothing and curtains.

12.6.3 Impacts of the scheme

With funding from the Department for Transport, 200 individuals from the trial areas were surveyed by telephone in February 2003, including half who had registered to have the local Post Office branch as their preferred redelivery option and half who had been allocated this option by default. Results from this survey were as follows:
- 25% of customers reported that they had increased the frequency of home shopping as a result of the service. A further 41% thought that they would shop from home more in the future due to the availability of the service.
- About half of the respondents stated that they used a different mode of transport to get to the local Post Office branch compared to how they would normally travelled to the Royal Mail delivery office. Over 30% of all respondents said they had changed from using a car or motorcycle.
- 71% of those using the service found that collecting items from their local Post Office branch (rather than the Royal Mail delivery office) reduced the length of

their journey, by an average of 14 minutes. Collecting items from the Post Office branch increased the journey length of only 8% of customers.

- A third of customers combined their last trip to the Post Office branch to collect their item with the trip to another location. Over 50 % of these combined their trip to the Post Office branch with a trip to the supermarket, and 19% combined their trip with a trip to work.
- On average, a customer in the trial area would have been travelling about a mile less to collect an item from their local Post Office branch, compared to the Royal Mail delivery office

The reduction in distance travelled to each local Post Office compared with travelling to the Royal Mail delivery offices, is reported to correspond to a saving in car miles of between 50,000-100,000 miles per annum, 5000 to 10,000 kilograms of carbon and equivalent savings of other polluting emissions within the trial area. Scaling up the trial to the whole of the UK is estimated to equate to an annual saving of between 30 and 60 million miles per annum (and between three and six million kilograms of carbon). Combining trips to collect goods with another journey and/or making the journey without using a car will have resulted in an even greater reduction in the number of private vehicle miles, (TransportEnergy BestPractice 2004).

An alternative calculation (not given in the case study write-up) would be as follows. Given that 96% of people live within one mile of a Post Office branch, and that the average customer would have been travelling a mile less to reach the Post Office, compared with the Royal Mail delivery office, it seems fair to assume that average journey distance has at least halved for collecting redeliveries. 30% of these journeys are no longer made by car, and some would have been made anyway. Given that 30% of journeys to the local Post Office branch were combined with another trip purpose, a mid range estimate would be that 15% of all journeys would have been made anyway. Combining the assumptions that 15% of journeys would have been made anyway, 30% are no longer made by car, and the remaining 55% are half the distance, implies that the total effect of the trial may have been to reduce customer mileage to collect unsuccessfully delivered packages by 72%.

Other impacts reported from the scheme were:
- All 33 Post Office branches in the trial saw an increase in business as a result of the trial operations.
- No new mileage was introduced into the Royal Mail operation, and significant capacity was available to absorb increased home shopping within existing services.
- Royal Mail did not reduce their operational mileage since their vehicles were driven around the trial area to maintain regular services, and these movements were independent of any home shopping deliveries or redeliveries included in the load.

Royal Mail is now conducting similar trials in different geographic and demographic areas, including rural, city centre and small town locations.

12.7 Other evidence about the traffic impacts of home shopping

As highlighted in the introduction, there have been a number of overview studies of the general transport impacts of home shopping. Opinions vary. For example, Mokhtarian (2004) argues that "there may be negative impacts due to increased travel, even if those impacts are likely to be localized and/or small in magnitude for the most part". In contrast, Romm et al (1999) comment that "we suspect the Internet economy will be no worse than neutral in the transportation sector, but could well have a large positive impact". However, the amount of empirical research or numerical estimation reported in these studies is small, with assertions often based on theory, and the majority of commentators highlight the difficulties of drawing firm conclusions given the current volatility and complexity of home shopping. The following sections report on the most relevant available empirical evidence.

12.7.1 Handy and Yantis (1997)

Handy and Yantis (1997) report on a survey of 470 people conducted in 1995, drawn from the three US cities of San Jose (California), Oklahoma City (Oklahoma) and Austen (Texas). They specifically report that their sample was not representative of the cities' populations, but argue that it does provide some insights into home shopping

Of the sample, 65% reported making a purchase from a catalogue in the preceding 12 months, with clothing, books and gifts being the main items purchased. These people were asked to think of their last purchase, and consider what they would have done if it had not been in the catalogue. 32% said they would not have bought it. 40% said they would have looked for it on their next trip to the store whilst less than 20% said that they would have made a special trip to a store. In addition, 56% of respondents said that, at some time, they have made a trip to a store because of something they saw in a catalogue (although the authors report that respondents may have interpreted 'catalogue' as 'advertisement', and there is no information about the frequency with which this has occurred).

9% reported purchasing from a home shopping channel (approx.42 people). Of these, 65% indicated that they would not have brought the item, and less than 2% indicated that they would have made a special trip.

Given the problems of survey representativeness (and the small size of some of the subcategories), it is hard to draw firm conclusions from this research. However it clearly indicates that, in some circumstances, and for some products, home shopping may stimulate extra purchases, and, even where the purchase would still have been made, it does not always replace a trip to a store. In terms of traffic impacts, the significance of this finding will partly depend on the nature of products – for example, as highlighted in section 12.4.5, increased sales of books may have little impact on overall transport where they travel by conventional postal services.

12.7.2 NOP surveys

In June 2003, British Telecom commissioned an NOP telephone poll of 538 internet shoppers, as reported by Fogarty 2003. Results were as follows:

- 78% said that Internet shopping had saved them making at least one journey by car. Of all respondents, 23% said that it had saved a journey of less than five miles; 22% said that it had saved a journey of 5-10 miles; 10% said that it had saved a journey of 11-20 miles and 23% said that it had saved a journey of over 20 miles.

- Of the 427 internet shoppers who said that they had saved a car journey, 82% said that they had not made a new replacement car journey. Of the remainder, 7% said that they had made a new journey of under five miles, 6% said that they had made a new journey of 5-10 miles, 2% said that they had made a new journey of 10 to 20 miles and 3% said that they had made a new journey of over 20 miles.

Taking these results together implies that, for those who said that Internet shopping had saved them a car journey, allowing for increased travel by some (and assuming, conservatively, that the average length of a journey over 20 miles is 25 miles) still works out as an average reduction of 8.9 miles of personal travel.

NOP subsequently conducted a more substantial poll in December 2003, as reported by Geraghty 2004. It involved interviews with 1,600 Internet users. The sample was weighted to match Financial Research Survey[14] generated profiles of Internet users, and selected from 17,931 GB adults (who were screened for Internet usage in the previous 12 months using the FRS and NOP's two Omnibus Vehicles). Of the sample, 45% reported that they had shopped on-line in the last 4 weeks, and 42% reported that they made a personal purchase.

As in the previous survey, 78% reported that Internet shopping had saved them making at least one journey by car. The distribution of trips lengths saved was also relatively similar – 26% said <5 miles; 19% said 5-10 miles; 13% said 11-15%; 5% said 16-20 miles and 15% said over 21 miles.

Geraghty (2004) reports that the average number of miles saved was 9.1. 18% of those saving a trip reported that they had used the saved time to make another journey, of an average length of 2 miles. This implies that, for those making additional trips, the average mileage saved was 7.1, and for all those who saved a trip, the average mileage saved was 8.7 miles.

12.7.3 Motors and Modems study

Dodgson et al (1997) report on a telephone survey of 303 respondents, conducted by Critical Research Ltd. This was commissioned for the RAC Motors and Modems study. They report the findings as follows:

- about 60% of people can be expected to become home shoppers to some degree over the next 20 years, whereas 40% appear to express a fundamental lack of interest in home shopping. (This conclusion was based on the premise that some

---

[14] This is one of the most respected surveys of consumer behaviour in relation to the personal financial services sector, designed to give a representative picture of the UK.

of the reasons that people gave for not using TV or Internet shopping should be overcome, such as concerns about security of credit card details, lack of information, unavailable technology and an inability to see products).

- Somewhere between 6% and 19% of regular shopping trips could be replaced by a home shopping purchase (based on the fact that 6% of respondents said that they were already purchasing food by home shopping, and 19% said they were already purchasing clothes in that way).

Dodgson et al therefore concluded that home shopping could replace 1-3% of all shopping trips after five years, 2-6% of shopping trips after 10 years, and 4-11% of shopping trips after 20 years.

In 2000, these estimates were reassessed as part of a general updating of the study. In this report, the researchers revised their estimates upwards on the basis of the rapid growth in Internet shopping. Their 2000 estimates were that tele-shopping will reduce car shopping travel by 5% by 2005 and by 10% by 2010. They comment: "We have allowed for some increase in delivery trips, primarily by light vans, but we would expect some of the delivery to be by mail, which would not necessarily increase traffic levels."

12.7.4 Information about drop boxes

Section 12.6 described a particular trial to try and increase the efficiency of delivering to customer homes, by providing customers with a set of delivery options (including locker banks and local Post Office branches). There have been a number of other experiments (as reported, for example, by Dodson 2001 and Frost 2002), and numerous commentators have highlighted generally that providing delivery to a storage unit, where the customer does not have to personally receive the goods, would allow those delivering home shopping to use wider time windows and run more efficient delivery operations. It could also enable operators to schedule more deliveries at off-peak times, helping to reduce peak-period congestion. An overview of options, and the associated security issues, is given in McKinnon and Tallam (2002).

Various products have been developed for receiving unattended deliveries at individual homes. However, a number of the private companies that have tried to provide reception boxes for customers have experienced problems with financial viability, (MacLeod 2002). Some commentators argue that the priority is to incorporate such units when new housing is built, since the marginal costs of adding such features will be less. There has also been considerable interest in delivering to intermediate points, including where people work, local shops, garages, community centres, railway stations, Park & Ride sites, etc. (as explored in detail by DTZ Research, 2000). Such intermediate points should also reduce the transport impacts of home deliveries, if they do not reinforce the need to drive for another trip purpose.

The general efficiency savings from being able to make unattended deliveries have been examined by Nockold 2001, and Punakivi et al (2001-02).

Nockold (2001) compared the effects of offering all customers a 3-hour time slot, with assuming that varying proportions of customers would accept delivery at any time during the day. In all scenarios, he argued that a reduction in delivery time constraints would result in transport cost reductions[15]. One specific result was that replacing all 3 hour time slots with delivery at any time during the day would reduce total transport costs by 27-36%

Modelling work on the issue has also been undertaken by a team in Finland, including papers by Punakivi & Saranen 2001, Punakivi, Yrjölä & Holmstrom 2001 and Punakivi & Tanskaren 2002. Their research showed that, in terms of total transport costs, compared to offering same day delivery in three 2-hour time slots:

- next day delivery, in nine 1-hour time slots would generate transport costs that were 53% more.
- next day delivery, in one 10-hour time slot (equivalent to the situation where the company delivers to a reception box) would be 27% cheaper.
- next day delivery, in one 10-hour time slot, where customers are told which day deliveries can take place (and deliveries are sorted on the basis of postcodes and divided evenly between delivery days, to present the most efficient situation from the e-grocer's viewpoint.) would be 43% cheaper.
- shared reception boxes (where deliveries for a number of customers can be made to one, unattended location) would be 55-66% cheaper.

It should be noted that their calculations of costs appear to be related (but not necessarily directly correlated) with vehicle delivery mileage, and relate only to the costs of providing the delivery, not the reception box. The work has also examined the various payback periods for the e-grocer, if they choose to invest in individual delivery boxes or shared reception boxes. It shows that, in some circumstances, the payback periods may be relatively long, which may bias a private company against investment

In brief, then, these studies suggest that encouraging greater use of drop boxes or shared reception facilities could reduce the amount of home shopping delivery travel quite substantially, compared to asking customers to opt for delivery to their home during a specific time window, with transport cost savings ranging from about a third to over 50%. However, the costs of providing such facilities may be quite substantial and it is unclear whether the private sector is likely to invest in them without public sector intervention.

These results complement the findings of the Royal Mail trial. In the Royal Mail trial, operator travel remained largely unchanged (since Royal Mail deliveries are mostly 'postable items' and so visits to individual homes are made anyway). However, there was a major impact on customer travel to retrieve unsuccessfully delivered goods. The simulations described above highlight that, for operators who are largely delivering non-postable items (of the size that could fit into some kind of locker or reception box), the main impact would be a reduction in operator travel, since they could operate considerably more efficiently. The public policy implication is that investment in facilities where goods can be retrieved by customers could help to reduce traffic by both customers and operators, depending on the situation.

---

[15] It should be noted that it is unclear how 'total transport cost' relates to vehicle mileage, and the relationship may be indirect.

12.8 Summary of information about the effects of home shopping on car use

The traffic impacts of grocery home shopping services have been examined. These could be particularly important as a considerable proportion of conventional food shopping is done by car. The results are given in Table 12.3. In summary, a number of modelling exercises and other surveys suggest that the substitution of private cars by delivery vehicles could reduce traffic by 70% or more. The (small) base of empirical evidence suggests that concerns about offsetting behaviour changes (such as increased frequency of shopping or more car use for other purposes) are unfounded - i.e. the scale of these behaviours will not be sufficient to outweigh the main impact, and there may well be reinforcing changes in the opposite direction.

Table 12.3 Evidence about the traffic impacts of grocery home shopping

Study	Finding
Modelling simulations by Cairns 1997, Palner 2001, Punakivi et al 2001-023, Farahmand & Young 1998, Persson & Bratt 2001, Murto 1996, Karna 2001, Orremo et al 1999, Nockold 2001 and Freire (1999)	• Where delivery vehicles directly substitute for car trips, the kilometres travelled per shopping load are likely to reduce by 70% or more • The effect on overall travel for food shopping will depend on the level of take up
Millar 1998	45% of Food Ferry customers are using their cars less as a result of the service, and some have given up a car
Tacken 1990	Customers of James Telesuper were less likely to go to food stores, less likely to go food shopping by car and more likely to visit local shops
Snead 2001	On average, grocery home shoppers report an average reduction of 3.4 car trips per month
Morgansky & Cude 2000	Home shoppers are mainly using services for convenience, rather than to generate time for other activities
Foley et al 2003	Experts believe on-line shoppers make 3.5 fewer shopping trips per month, and order shopping only once a fortnight
Lex Transfleet 2000	Public perceptions of the traffic impacts of home shopping are only likely to focus on the growth in delivery vehicles.

For non food shopping, there is relatively little research about traffic impacts. The information we were able to uncover is given in Table 12.4. There are a couple of studies (in particular, the NOP polls reported by Fogarty 2003 and Geraghty 2004) suggesting that home shopping may generally be reducing car use, although considerably more evidence is needed to be conclusive, and the work by Handy and Yantis highlights the importance of 'new purchasing' in some home shopping sectors. Meanwhile, it is clear that local authorities and other agencies have the opportunity to shape the impacts of home shopping by the form of support services offered. The trial undertaken between Nottingham City Council and the Royal Mail, where customers were offered a range of (re)delivery options for goods, suggested that there have been substantial reductions in customer travel as a result. Meanwhile, modelling work by several commentators suggests that public investment in facilities that enable retailers to deliver goods to dedicated facilities, rather than having to make a specific arrangement with a customer, could result in significant reductions in the amount of delivery traffic (with efficiency gains, and the opportunity to undertake more delivery trips at off-peak times).

Table 12.4 Evidence about the traffic impacts of all types of home shopping

Study	Finding
TransportEnergy BestPractice 2004	In a Royal Mail trial, offering customers alternative delivery options resulted in reductions in customer mileage to collect unsuccessfully delivered goods. Estimates suggest reductions were in the order of: • at least 50-100,000 miles p.a. for 68,000 households, or • up to 72% of car mileage for this type of journey (with current effects on 2 trips per household per year, up to a maximum of 28 trips per household per year, and a typical affected trip length of 2 miles or less)
Handy and Yantis 1995	In some circumstances, and for some products, home shopping stimulates extra purchases, and, even where the purchase would still have been made, home delivery does not always replace a trip to a store.
Fogarty 2003 and Geraghy 2004	78% of Internet shoppers say that an Internet purchase has has saved them a car journey. About a fifth of these people say that they have used the saved time to make another car journey. Taking account of this 'rebound' effect, for those saving a car journey, the average reduction in personal travel is in the order of 8-9 miles.
Dodgson 2000	Tele-shopping could reduce car shopping travel by 5% by 2005 and 10% by 2010
Nockold 2001, and Punakivi et al 2001-02	Compared to offering customers daily delivery in three 2-hour time slots, delivering to a secure box at the customers house, or a local lockerbank could reduce the delivery costs for operators by between a third to a half.

12.9 Other effects from home shopping

The literature contains many hypotheses about the 'potential' effects from home shopping, but there is relatively little evidence about observed benefits. Therefore, only a few key reported impacts from home shopping are quoted here. These are:

- **Increased viability of local shops**
The Dutch experience reported by Tacken (1990) suggests that delivery of bulk food shopping can help to increase the vitality and viability of local grocers, bakers, butchers and other small shops. The Royal Mail initiative in Nottingham generated a new function for post offices, helping to increase their viability.

- **Reduced viability for conventional high street shopping**

Initially, the growth of internet shopping was hailed as 'doom' for the high street. As highlighted earlier, this does not seem to have occurred, although there have undoubtedly been impacts on sales volume in particular sectors – notably books, music and electrical items. For example, this may have have been a factor in Dixons recent decision to close down 106 smaller stores (Dixons Group plc, 2004). For books and music, there is some evidence that the internet is generating additional demand, such that it is unclear how far it has led to problems for high street chains.

- **Improved options for customers**

For all types of customers, home shopping options potentially enable the purchase of a wider range of goods and services, including, in some cases, access to more appropriate products (e.g. clothes in unusual sizes; food for unusual dietary requirements; specialist equipment for unusual sports and other hobbies etc.). In some sectors, such as electronic goods, there is also some evidence that the advent of Internet shopping has led to significant price deflation, and that customers have benefitted from the opportunities to compare prices and to browse for product information.

- **Impacts on social exclusion**

Home shopping potentially increases the access of those in geographically remote areas to products and services. In practice, many companies offering home shopping have started by offering their services in compact urban areas – since the costs of delivering to a relatively densely clustered customer base are less. However, as offerings have expanded, more and more are offering services to the majority of the UK.

In addition, there may be benefits for those 'trapped' in the home by the lack of a car and/or responsibilities such as childcare and/or physical disabilities that make shopping difficult. For example, anecdotal evidence about grocery retailing suggests that 'time pressed families' from poorer households may constitute a significant segment of the home shopping market for groceries. Tesco has been offering a form of social service home shopping service for elderly people in Gateshead since 1980 – and Gateshead Council feel that, for one particular subset of their social service clientele, it has been more cost effective and appropriate than some of the more traditional ways of helping such people through social services.

However, these benefits are only maximised if everyone has access to the new forms of home shopping. Currently, there are some concerns that those getting 'left behind' on the internet revolution (such as the elderly) may actually experience a reduction in shopping options where there are impacts on high street stores.

Further impacts from home shopping relate to synergies with other transport policies as discussed in the next section.

12.10 Synergies between home shopping and other policies and issues

It seems likely that there would be a strong synergy effect between different types of home delivery, in that people who become more accustomed to using it for some of their shopping would become more likely to extend this to other shopping.

So far, to our knowledge, there has been no public promotion of home delivery services for food shopping. However, this could clearly form one element of wider initiatives aiming to address traffic at busy locations such as access junctions for supermarkets.

For all types of home shopping, there is clear potential synergy with freight quality partnerships and other initiatives aimed at addressing delivery traffic, which should take account of home shopping issues.

In general, levels of home shopping may increase as a result of traffic restraint policies, which increase the costs of driving to, and/or parking at, shops, or of owning and using a car more generally. In these circumstances, the cost of delivery charges is likely to be seen as more favourable that it is at present.

Home shopping clearly dovetails with other soft factors, namely tele-work and tele-conferencing, which have the potential to encourage more localised patterns of living. It could also facilitate a shift from personal car ownership to greater use of alternative modes and/or membership of a car club, since it offers the potential to reduce the need to transport bulky goods which people may see as an important reason for having their own vehicle. The need to transport food shopping as a feature of car dependence was discussed in Goodwin et al (1995).

12.11 Future impact of home shopping

For food shopping, there is a broad consensus that by 2005 perhaps 2.5 to 10% of groceries might be purchased from home, increasing to a maximum of 15% by 2010. According to analysis of 1998-2000 National Travel Survey data by Cairns 2004, shopping for groceries accounts for 40% of all car/van driver kilometres travelled per person per year for shopping. Modelling assessments suggest that, amongst those utilising home delivery services, vehicle mileage saved per shopping load is of the order of 70% or more. Assuming therefore, that perhaps 5-15% of all groceries sales swap to the internet in ten years time, this suggests grocery home shopping could reduce vehicle mileage for all shopping by about 1 – 4% over that period.

For non-food shopping, Foley et al's estimates suggest that perhaps 14% of all retail sales will be home shopping by 2005, including 4% by Internet, and that sales value might approximately double by 2010 (implying that 28% of all sales may be by home shopping, including 8% by the Internet).

Currently, there are few estimates of the overall impacts of home shopping. However it is clear, as shown by the Royal Mail trial, that the impacts from such growth will depend on the way that home shopping services develop, and the extent to which the public sector intervenes to shape their nature. The Royal Mail estimate that their trial could be scaled up nationally to almost 17,000 collection points, and that this would result in a saving of at least 30 and 60 million miles a year. Other estimates relating to the efficiency savings for operators from investment in drop boxes at individual homes or communal reception points suggest that delivery transport costs could reduce by 30-50%. Unfortunately, there is little data to suggest how much traffic this could affect. Foley et al (2003b) emphasize the lack of such data, although they highlight one estimate suggesting that that 60% of packages carried by parcel carriers are for individual homes. Further ways in which the public sector could affect the traffic impacts of home shopping are given in the next section.

We have largely been unable to obtain any information about the costs of public sector involvement in home shopping, partly because such involvement has been limited. In the Nottingham trial, the local authority primarily acted as a facilitation agent (presumably incurring minimal costs). However, it is possible that local authorities could dedicate significantly more resources to this area, by giving greater attention to instituting access regulations, offering grants for more efficient operations, paying for installation of locker banks or drop boxes etc..

Given our lack of financial information, it has been impossible to undertake cost-impact assessments to evaluate the importance of investing in such initiatives. However, it is possible to carry out a 'reverse' calculation. According to Cairns 2004, the average car/van driver travel generated per person per year for food shopping is 290 kilometres, and the reduction in travel, from undertaking home shopping, is likely to be in the order of 70% (implying 203 kilometres of car/van travel would be saved). Therefore, to reduce traffic at a cost of a 1.5 pence per kilometre, it would be appropriate to spend £3 for every new grocery home shopper. Given a city of 200,000 people where promotion work and/or the provision of better drop-off facilities might change the take-up of grocery home shopping from being 10% of the population to 15% of the population by 2010, this implies that the local authority could afford to spend £30,000 per year, or £300,000 over 10 years.

The overall traffic impacts of other types of home shopping are far less clear. However, the available evidence does suggest that investment in better drop off facilities should reduce travel for customers in some circumstances (where their alternative is travelling to a more remote collection point such as the Royal Mail delivery office), and should also improve the efficiency of freight transport (where the freight vehicles are primarily travelling to deliver home shopping, as opposed to circulating on a 'fixed round' anyway). Consequently, this strengthens the case for public sector investment and promotion of such facilities, and potentially justifies higher spending levels than those given in the preceding paragraph.

12.12 Policy implications relating to home shopping

- Consideration of home shopping could be included in freight quality partnership discussions.
- National programmes to encourage greater use of alternative fuels (for example the Powershift programme) could consider extending their remit to include grants and other promotion measures to encourage walking and cycling couriers.

- Local authorities could be encouraged to give greater consideration to the types of delivery vehicles that they allow into different types of areas - for example, allowing greater access for energy-efficient or 'clean fuel' vehicles in residential areas, or giving them greater parking rights – for example, the right to park in controlled parking zones.

- National government could consider convening discussions with the major supermarkets about the future of grocery home shopping, and the best ways to operate the delivery part of the schemes efficiently.

- Local authorities could consider tailoring some forms of home shopping services, such as grocery services, to be part of the range of options that they can offer to social service clients with problems accessing shops.

- Both national government and local authorities could be encouraged to consider funding and otherwise facilitating the introduction of local drop-off facilities for shopping. Measures could include extension of the Royal Mail trial undertaken in Nottingham; introducing lockerbanks, drop boxes at individual homes and/or requiring new housing developments to include facilities where shopping can be delivered; and, also, encouraging local shops and services to operate in conjunction with home shopping services as a way of increasing their viability. Further consideration of the most appropriate way of introducing such facilities , and possibly a range of pilot experiments, could be valuable.

- Ensuring that the whole population has access to the goods and services emerging from the internet revolution could be an important part of ensuring future social inclusion.

- Greater empirical research about the behaviour of home shoppers, and how home shopping impacts on their car travel, could be helpful.

12.13 Acknowledgements

We would particularly like to thank

Individual	Organisation
Lowri Davies	Department for Transport
Barry Fogarty	British Telecom
Eric Barker	The Royal Mail Group plc
David Bayliss	Halcrow
Mike Browne	University of Westminster
Julian Allen	University of Westminster
Tara Garnett	Wise Moves

12.14 References

TransportEnergy BestPractice (2004) *Home delivery: Meeting the needs of customers and the environment.* Case study, CS2117, Department for Transport, London. (Main author: Ric Barker, The Royal Mail Group plc).

Browne M, Allen J, Anderson S & Jackson M (2001*) Overview of home deliveries in the UK (A study for DTI)*, University of Westminster, London.

Brunn-Jensen J (1999) *Make a profit out of home delivery* Paper presented at 'The Home Delivery 99 Conference', convened by Triangle Management Services Ltd, London, 9-10/3/99.

Cairns S (in press) Delivering supermarket shopping: more or less traffic ? *Transport Reviews,* Taylor & Francis, London, ISSN 0144-1647, 38pp.

Cairns S et al (2000) *Future Trends in Shopping Behaviour in the UK.* Report to members of the European Council for Automotive Research and Development, 81pp.TSU ref. 2000/16

Cairns S (1997) *Potential traffic reductions from home delivery services: some initial calculations.* TSU Working Paper 97/45, UCL, London.

Cairns, S (1996) Delivering Alternatives: Successes and Failures in Providing Home Delivery Services for Food Shopping. *Transport Policy*, Vol 3, no 4, pp 155-176

Department of Environment, Transport and the Regions (1999) *Sustainable Distribution: A Strategy.* London: DETR

Dixons Group plc (28/4/04) *Dixons Group plc pre-close update and Dixons store closure announcement.* Press release.

Dodgson J et al (1997) *Motors or modems.* Report by NERA for the RAC.

Dodgson J et al (2000) *Motors and modems revisited: the role of technology in reducing travel demands and traffic congestion.* Report by NERA for the RAC Foundation and the Motorists Forum

Dodson S (2001) Boxing Clever *The Guardian* 11/1/01

DTZ Research (2000*) A research study into potential collection points for English Partnerships.* English Partnerships, London.

ECMT (1997) *Freight transport and the city*. Report of the 109th Round Table, OECD Publications, Paris, or www.oecd.org/cem/pub/pubrt.htm

Farahmand R & Young M (1998) *Home shopping and its future*. Paper presented at the 10th annual TRICS conference, 22-23/9/98.

Fogarty B (2003) *Telecommunications and travel substitution.* BT Strategic Business Development paper presented 7/11/03.

Foley P et al (2003a) *Experts views on statistics for the home delivery sector.* Report to the Department for Transport, De Monfort University, FTA and Associates.

Foley P et al (2003b) *The home delivery sector in the UK 1995 to 2010.* Report to the Department for Transport, De Monfort University, FTA and Associates.

Freight Transport Association & local government (1997*) Delivering the goods: Best practice in urban distribution.* FTA, Kent.

Freire I (1999) *Environmental benefits from traditional supermarket shopping versus internet/home delivery shopping.* Internship report, Amsterdam University. As quoted in Kärnä 2002.

Frost M (2002) *Success in store for hi-tech delivery box.* Daily Express 4/2/02

Geraghty C (2004) How the Internet can help ease traffic congestion. Presentation at 'Alternative Approaches to Congestion' conference convened by BT, 26/1/02.

Goodwin (ed) et al (1995) *Car Dependence.* Report to the RAC Foundation for Motoring and the Environment, London.

Gould J & Golob TF (1997) 'Shopping without travel or travel without shopping ? An investigation of electronic home shopping' *Transport Reviews 17(4)*, pp355-376.

Handy SL & Yantis T (1997) *The impacts of telecommunications technologies on non-work travel behaviour.* Centre for Transportation Research, Texas University, Austin, Texas.

Hopkinson P & James P (2001) 'Virtual traffic – will e-business mean less transport and more sustainable logistics', in Wilsdon J ed. (2001*) Digital Futures: living in a dot.com world* Earthscan, London.

Kärnä A (2001) Dematerialization potential of electronic grocery shopping. In Heiskanen E, Halme M, Jalas M, Kärnä A & Lovio (forthcoming) *Dematerialization: the potential of ICT and services.* Finnish Environment, Ministry of the Environment, Finland. www.hkkk.fi/organisaatiot/research/programs/dema/dema.htm

Lex Transfleet /Freight Transport Association (2000*) The Lex Transfleet Report on Freight Transport 2000.* Lex Transfleet, Coventry.

MacLeod M (2002) 'While you were away'. *eLogistics magazine*, October, www.elogmag.com/magazine/23/away.shtml

McKinnon A & Tallam D (2002) *New crime threats from e-tailing: Theft in the home delivery channel.* Report for the Products and Crime Task Force of the UK Government Foresight Programme. www.foresight.gov.uk

Millar J (1998) – Director of The Food Ferry - personal correspondence

Mintel (2003) *Home Shopping UK* – Retail Intelligence report, Mintel International Group Ltd, London.

Mokhtarian PL (2004) A conceptual analysis of the transportation impacts of B2C e-commerce. *Transportation* 31 pp257-284

Mokhtarian PL & Salomon I (2002) 'Emerging travel patterns: Do telecommunications make a difference ?' In Mahmassani HS (2002) *In Perpetual Motion* Pergamon.

Morgansky MA & Cude BJ (2000) Consumer response to online grocery shopping. *International journal of retail and distribution management 28 (1)* pp17-26

Morris G (5/5/00) *Supermarket's e-commerce e-cstacy.* Reuters Business Briefing, The Guardian p3.

Murto R (1996) *Päivittäistavarakaupan sijoittumisen liikenteelliset vaikutukset Tampereen seudulla.* Tampere University of Technology Transportation Engineering Research Report 15. As quoted in Kärnä 2002.

Nockold C (2001) Identifying the real costs of home delivery. *Logistics and Transport Focus 3 (10)*, pp70-71

OECD/ECMT (2001) *The impact of e-commerce.* Seminar held in Paris, 5/6 June.

Office for National Statistics (annual) *Annual abstract of statistics.* The Stationery Office, London.

Office for National Statistics (annual) *Family Spending: A report on the 'Expenditure and Food Survey',* The Stationery Office, London.

Orremo F, Wallin C, Jönson G & Ringsberg K (1999) *IT, mat och miljö – en miljökonsekvensanalys av elektronisk handel med dagligvaror.* Swedish Environmental Protection Agency report 5038. As quoted in Kärnä 2002.

Palmer A, revised by McKinnon A (2001*) The effects of grocery home shopping on road traffic.* Report to the Retail Logistics Task Force.

Persson A & Bratt M (2001*) Future CO$_2$ savings from on-line shopping jeopardised by bad planning.* In proceedings of the 2001 ECEEE summer study 'Further than ever from Kyoto ? Rethinking energy efficiency can get us there.'

Punakivi M & Holmström J (2001) *Environmental performance improvement potentials by food home delivery.* NOFOMA 2001 conference proceedings

Punakivi M & Saranen J (2001) Identifying the success factors in e-grocery home delivery. *International journal of retail and distribution management 29 (4)* pp156-163

Punakivi M & Tanskanen K (2002) *International journal of retail and distribution management 30 (10)* pp498-507

Punakivi M, Yrjölä & Holmström J (2001) Solving the last mile issue: reception box or delivery box ? *International journal of physical distribution and logistics 31(6)* pp427-439.

Retail Logistics Task Force (2000) @ *Your Service. Future models of retail logistics.* Department of Trade and Industry, London.

Retail Logistics Task Force (2001) @ *Your Home: New markets for customer service and delivery.* Department of Trade and Industry, London or www.foresight.gov.uk

Romm J (lead author), Rosenfeld A & Herrmann S (1999*) The internet economy and global warming: A scenario of the impact of e-commerce on energy and the environment.* Centre for Energy and Climate Solutions, Annandale, Virginia, www.cool-companies.org/energy

Snead C (2001) *Home shopping and its implications for travel demand.* MSc thesis, UCL, London.

Tacken M (1990) 'Effects of teleshopping on the use of time and space' *Transportation Research Record 1285* pp89-91

Telephone Surveys Ltd (1994) *Food shopping and the car.* Report produced for Sainsbury plc, London.

Transport en Logistiek Netherland (2000) *New wine in old bottles.* Transport en Logistiek Netherland, Zoetemeer.

Verdict Research (2000) Verdict on electronic shopping. Verdict Research Ltd.

13. Projections of the potential traffic impacts of soft factors and associated costs

13.1 Introduction

The preceding chapters have drawn on available evidence and detailed comment from experts in the field on each of the individual soft factors. Now, we seek to apply that evidence and information to answer two important questions:

- By how much could soft factors affect future levels or growth rates of traffic, if they were applied more intensively and on a larger scale than at present?
- How much do soft factors cost, and what value for money do they represent ?

In considering these questions, we have developed two scenarios.. The first scenario, which we call 'low intensity', is a projection of the present rate of expenditure and level of commitment, taking account of the important initiatives which already exist, and will no doubt continue, by the most committed local authorities, and of commercial initiatives being undertaken by companies. The second, which we call 'high intensity', is based on an expansion of activity, commitment and resources to a substantially higher level, which would still be consistent with practical and realistic experience, the current judgements of those working at local level in practical implementation, and feasible levels of expenditure, given the known constraints of staffing and funding generally. This scenario presupposes commitment at both local level and national level, but does allow for a degree of variation according to local circumstances.

Both scenarios are based on what we judge could be achieved by a realistic level of commitment to a programme building up over a ten year period. However, this should not be interpreted as a 'forecast for 2014', because no allowance is made for other things that will have changed by then (demography, income, economic growth, road user charging, revision and rolling forward of the Ten Year Plan, etc) and also because the effects of soft factor initiatives will certainly be influenced by other policies.

At this stage, we recognise the potential importance of induced traffic, but temporarily take this out of analysis. We do not adjust the behavioural responses in either direction, neither allowing for erosion due to induced traffic, nor enhancement of soft factor effects due to the measures to prevent induced traffic such as pricing or reallocation of road capacity. As outlined in Chapter 1, this position may be interpreted as an assumption that 'locking-in' measures are introduced at just sufficient intensity to maintain the changes brought about by soft measures, but not more.

We do not define this level in precise policy terms, but discuss it further in the next chapter. However, we note that there is now considerable empirical evidence on the scale and properties of induced traffic and suppressed traffic, arising from experience from changes in road capacity and its allocation, pricing, etc.. Consequently, this evidence base should enable the identification of quantitative estimates of the scale of implementing such measures that would be required to meet our assumption. This estimate cannot be made using the DfT's National Transport Model in its current stage of development. However, in the following chapter, we discuss some issues of analysis and method, arising from this project, which might help to move forward in solving this problem. It remains to be demonstrated how easily current modelling frameworks can be adapted to allow for soft factors, but, in any case, decisions can still be supported by a combination of formal modelling, other statistical and qualitative analysis, and judgement based on practical experience.

We do not, at this stage, make a quantitative adjustment for the effect of synergy between soft factors, or between soft and hard factors, but we do make adjustments in order to avoid double counting, especially in the case where car trips removed as a result of one soft initiative, are then not available to be removed by another initiative. This adjustment is discussed in section 13.3, and these issues are also discussed qualitatively in chapter 14.

The approach we take in the rest of this chapter is, first, to develop a range of estimates of future impact for each individual soft factor, and then to apply these, in combination, to base traffic data. We take actual traffic data for 2000 as the base, rather than forecast data for some future year, and therefore the results do not distinguish between 'traffic reductions' and 'reducing the rate of traffic growth to a level than it would otherwise have been without the initiative'[1]. This corresponds with the approach taken by other studies, as reviewed in chapter 2. Thus, the results may perhaps be interpreted as estimating what difference would exist now, if we had proceeded vigorously on this path for the previous decade or so. A judgement can then be made about future trajectories, bearing in mind that traffic growth in the more congested areas has already slowed or in some cases halted, and in these circumstances, the issue of induced traffic becomes crucial.

Finally, we bring together the data from earlier chapters on the cost-impact relationship for the different soft factors, and use this to make some inferences about value for money.

The process of estimating future impacts requires reasoned justification of many assumptions, and detailed arithmetic calculations. In all cases, these have been based on the direct and cautious judgement of the authors, rather than using behavioural or other assumptions deriving from a formal theory, or constraints imposed by the structure of an existing model. Sufficient detail is reported to enable the professionally interested reader to follow and, if desired, check the calculations and consider the impacts of alternative assumptions or methods as may seem better supported as experience develops. Those wishing to omit this rather dense narrative will find a summary of the important points arising from the calculations, and their conclusions, in the final section of the chapter.

---

[1] This distinction can only be made with a forecasting process in which soft measures are themselves endogenous within a forecasting model provided with behavioural mechanisms fully allowing for their impact, which does not currently exist.

13.2 Projections of impact for individual soft factors

This section considers what might be the impact of each individual soft factor, following about ten years of implementation. There are two dimensions to this, which we term 'coverage' and 'effectiveness'. 'Coverage' is the proportion of the population which might be affected in some way by the soft factor concerned, while 'effectiveness' is the amount by which car travel could be reduced within the affected population. The product of 'coverage' x 'effectiveness' we term 'impact'. Usually, impact is expressed as a reduction in car trips. Wherever possible, we use information enabling us to express impact in terms of car mileage, but this is not always the case, and this introduces a potential bias (often, but not always, an underestimate) of the impact, recognised in chapters 1 and 2, and discussed further in chapter 14.

We quote a lower and an upper value for coverage, and the same for effectiveness. Both of these dimensions are affected by the conditions of implementation: coverage partly reflects, for example, how many different local authorities are likely to implement such initiatives, while effectiveness is partly a function of the resources and design quality of the initiatives. Thus taken together, these two figures broadly define our low intensity and high intensity scenarios respectively. It is important to note that the difference between the two scenarios is a measure of two different sets of policies, and should not be interpreted as a 'range of uncertainty' deriving from statistical error bands, as is done for those forecasting models based on formal econometric estimation. Such uncertainty, of course, exists, but would apply to both scenarios[2].

In most cases, estimates of impact are expressed as a percentage reduction in trips or mileage for a specific journey purpose (for example, reduction in car trips to work). However, some soft factors affect more than one type of journey, and for these, the estimate of impact is a percentage reduction across all, or all relevant, journey purposes. Thus, the figures quoted for different soft factors are not immediately comparable at this stage, until brought together and applied to data reflecting the size of the different traffic segments.

The estimates of coverage and effectiveness are based as much as possible on evidence from the case studies, supplemented by data from the literature review. In particular, the case study interviews included questions on the possible future scale of implementation of each soft initiative. Where the case studies gave little indication of possible future coverage and effectiveness, we have still suggested a potential for future impact, based on judgement of plausibility or credibility, informed, where possible, by collateral evidence. We make it clear where we have had to resort to this approach.

For some soft factors, there is case study or other evidence suggesting greater coverage or effectiveness in urban areas than in non-urban areas. Where soft measures

---

[2] Uncertainty ranges are not estimated, for reasons rather similar to those which have prevented those responsible for the National Transport Model and its predecessors from making such estimates, namely that the statistical properties of a model, or a calculation procedure, which has been derived from a deliberative synthesis of many different sources and judgements, cannot be treated as a textbook case of a complete model estimated from a single coherent data set.

have a differential impact by journey purpose, there are likely also to be consequential differences by time of day. These are taken into account as appropriate.

In some cases, we have drawn on the National Travel Survey to provide a basis for current travel habits. As mentioned in Chapter 1, throughout the report, we have aimed to draw on the 1999/2001 results, to provide standardisation, although it has occasionally been necessary to use results from 1998/2000, or 2002, as these were not readily available from the 1999/2001 report.

The following sections look at each individual soft factor in turn.

13.2.1 Workplace travel plans

In estimating the impact of workplace travel plans on future car travel demand, we assume:

- The impact is concentrated in the peak period, and mainly on the journey to and from work. (There could also be impacts on business, patient, shopper, student, tourist and other visitor travel, but these have been excluded as there is not enough data to comment).
- **Coverage.** There is an upper level to the proportion of the workforce that can be readily engaged in travel plans. This is *currently* determined principally by the proportion of employees who work for public sector organisations and large companies, although the level might be increased by policies which create incentives for smaller organisations to adopt travel plans. Conservatively, we assume that the proportion of the workforce that can be readily engaged is lower in non-urban areas than in urban areas (since employment may be more dispersed and there may be fewer large employers). This is consistent with findings from our case studies. Table 13.1 sets out our projections of what proportion of the workforce might be covered by travel plans in different types of area, over the next ten years. Estimates are based on what is being achieved in the case study areas now, and what case study interviewees felt could be achieved in future, as reported in section 3.14.1. These estimates are also conservative because most interviewees' estimates of future coverage were coloured by an assumption of little change in resources, and because experience of working with clusters of SMEs is only just starting to develop.
- **Effectiveness.** In section 3.10.1 we saw that most travel plans achieve cuts in car use of 0-35%, with a few best practice plans achieving cuts of over 40% and some delivering no reduction at all. Data from the case study areas suggests that, broadly:

  > 10% of travel plans achieve no change
  > 20% reduce car use by >0-10%
  > 35% reduce car use by >10-25%
  > 25% reduce car use by >25-35%
  > 10% reduce car use by over 35%.

  The average reduction (including poor-performing, middle-range and good-performing plans) was 18%. This is consistent with results from the literature, which highlight that even minimalist plans can be expected to have some impact (as described in section 3.2).

The scenarios are based on these data (table 13.1). For both the low intensity and high intensity scenarios, in urban and non-urban areas, we assume an average effectiveness of 18%. As with our reported data, this does not mean every travel plan achieving an 18% reduction in car use. Some plans will achieve more, and some less. Equally, it does not mean that all areas will achieve the same results. Some flagship towns – for example, compact cities with well-developed traffic restraint policies – may do very well, and others may do less well. Moreover, it assumes that, even under our high intensity scenario, a large number of employers may not be prepared to engage in travel planning at all (representing 50% of employees in urban areas and 80% in non urban areas).

Combining the assumptions in table 13.1, the reduction in car commuter trips would be 5% or 9% in urban areas, and 2% or 4% in non-urban areas.

Table 13.1: Coverage and effectiveness of workplace travel plans

	Coverage Percentage of workforce covered by travel plans after ten years	*Effectiveness* Proportion of travel plans with:					*Impact* Implied reduction in car commuting trips	
		no effect~	low effect ~	medium effect~	high effect ~	very high effect ~	Expressed as % of car trips to work in companies with travel plans	Expressed as % of all car journeys to work in area
Urban areas	30 – 50%	0.1	0.2	0.35	0.25	0.1	18%	*5 or 9%*
Non-urban areas	10 – 20%	0.1	0.2	0.35	0.25	0.1	18%	*2 or 4%*

~ 'low' means a >0-10% cut in car commuting trips; 'medium' = >10-25% cut; 'high' = >25-35% cut; 'very high' = over 35% cut.

13.2.2 School travel plans

In estimating the impact of school travel plans on future car travel demand, we assume:

- The impact in the morning is entirely in the peak period. The impact in the afternoon is during the off-peak period. The entire impact is assumed to be on the journey to and from school (ignoring any potential synergy benefits with initiatives aiming to affect commuting journeys).
- **Coverage.** Evidence from the case studies suggests that in the next ten years a significant proportion of schools in all areas will have developed effective travel plans – say somewhere between 30% (a little higher than Merseyside's estimate for 2006) and 95% (close to the estimates made by Buckinghamshire and York for 2011). Coverage is likely to be similar in urban and non-urban areas (table 13.2). (It should be noted that these estimates are relatively conservative given the DfES/DfT jointly declared objective that all schools should have an active travel plan by the end of the decade).
- **Effectiveness.** The effectiveness of travel plans will vary between schools. As discussed in section 4.9.4, evidence from the case studies suggests, at current levels of engagement, typically 10-40% of engaged schools will not experience positive modal shift, 45-50% might be expected to achieve car use reductions of

Cairns S, Sloman L, Newson C, Anable J, Kirkbride A & Goodwin P (2004)
'Smarter Choices – Changing the Way We Travel'   .

*Projections
and costs*

between 0-20%, whilst 15-40% can be expected to achieve reductions of over 20%, with some schools achieving reductions of 50% or more. The proportion of high impact travel plans should increase with time, as the number of schools with fully developed travel work increases, and local authorities are able to provide more schools with measures such as safer infrastructure. Effectiveness in urban and non-urban areas is assumed to be similar (table 13.2).

Combining the assumptions in table 13.2, the reduction in car escort trips to and from school would be 4% or 20% over ten years. The effect is similar in urban and non-urban areas.

Table 13.2: Coverage and effectiveness of school travel plans

	Coverage Percentage of pupils covered by travel plans after ten years	*Effectiveness*			*Impact* Implied reduction in car escort trips to / from school	
		Proportion of travel plans with no impact~	Proportion of travel plans with an average effect~	Proportion of high performing travel plans~	Expressed as % of car escort trips to / from schools with travel plans	Expressed as % of all car escort trips to/ from schools in area
Non-urban areas	30 – 95%	0.05 – 0.2*	0.2 – 0.5*	0.75 – 0.3*	13 or 21%	*4 or 20%*
Urban areas	30 – 95%	0.05 – 0.2	0.2 – 0.5	0.75 – 0.3	13 or 21%	*4 or 20%*

~ 'no impact' means a 0% cut in car escort trips to / from school; 'average effect' = 10% cut; 'high performing' = 25% cut.
* We adopt two scenarios for school travel plan effectiveness. The first is based on the 'average' current level of engagement, and assumes that 20% of plans have no impact on traffic, 50% have an average impact and 30% are high performers. The second scenario assumes that, as local authority work in this area increases, they will be able to engage with a much greater proportion of schools on an intensive basis. In this scenario, we assume that 5% of plans have no impact, 20% have an average impact and 75% have high impact. (It should be noted that this second scenario is equivalent to a scenario where the proportion of high performers is smaller, but there are some which achieve traffic reductions considerably in excess of 25%).

13.2.3 Personalised travel planning

In estimating the future impact of personalised travel planning, we assume:
- An equal effect on all journey purposes and at all times of day.
- **Coverage.** The Nottingham and Gloucester case studies suggest that it is feasible to develop large-scale personalised travel planning programmes, covering between 10,000 and 30,000 people per year (representing approximately 10 – 20% of the population in Gloucester each year, and 3 – 5% of the population in Greater Nottingham each year). In London, a programme covering more than ten times this number of people annually is being considered, which would reach about 2% of the population per year.
- In our high intensity scenario, we assume that personalised travel planning programmes could be developed to cover around one third of the urban population over a ten year period (i.e. about 3% per year) with each programme doing whatever reinforcement is necessary for sustained impact. Not all cities would

achieve the same level of coverage – some might do more, and some much less.
We assume much lower coverage in non-urban areas (where the potential for
purely information-based measures to stimulate modal shift is less), such that
about 3% of the non-urban population is targeted over the same period (or 0.3%
per year – only a tenth of that assumed for urban areas).

- In the low intensity scenario, we assume about half this level of implementation –
  that is, around 15% of the urban population and 1% of the non-urban population
  are targeted by personalised travel planning programmes over ten years.

- **Effectiveness.** In the high intensity scenario, personalised travel planning
  programmes cut car driver trips by an average of 15% in urban areas and 6% in
  non-urban areas. These figures are at the upper end of the range of reported
  results. In the low intensity scenario, we assume personalised travel planning
  programmes cut car driver trips by an average of 7% in urban areas and 2% in
  non-urban areas. These figures are at the lower end of the range of results reported
  in sections 5.2.2 and 5.7.1.

*Using these assumptions, the reduction in car driver trips is 1% or 5% in urban areas
and less than 1% in non-urban areas.*

**Table 13.3: Coverage and effectiveness of personalised travel planning, across all
journey purposes**

	Coverage Proportion of population targeted	**Effectiveness** Reduction in car driver trips per person	**Impact** Implied reduction in car driver trips
Urban areas	15 – 30%	7 – 15%	*1 or 5%*
Non-urban areas	1 – 3%	2 – 6%	*0.02 or 0.2%*

13.2.4 Public transport information and marketing

In estimating the future impact of public transport information and marketing, we
assume:

- An equal effect on all journey purposes, and at all times of day.
- **Coverage.** We assume all areas increase public transport patronage by 0.7 – 2.5%
  per year as a result of information and marketing activity. However, their starting
  points are different, resulting in different final potential impacts. An annual
  increase of 0.7 - 2.5% is roughly half the patronage increase currently being
  achieved in Nottingham and Brighton, which case study information suggested
  was a reasonable proportion to attribute to information and marketing initiatives
  (as reported in sections 6.10.1). Our projection assumes that, on average, public
  transport quality is sufficient to enable such marketing to take place. This a
  reasonable assumption, given that our projected increases are applied to existing
  levels of public transport use (thus allowing for the fact that service provision
  varies dramatically in different parts of the country). An annual increase of 0.7 -
  2.5% is equivalent to an increase in public transport patronage of 7 – 28% over ten
  years. It should be noted that these figures are approximately consistent (to a first
  order of magnitude) with the aspirations in the Ten Year Plan for growth in public
  transport demand, taking rail and bus together. However, it is not clear whether

the projections in the 10 Year Plan already implicitly made allowance for the growth that might be expected from marketing the public transport improvements it hoped to secure, or whether those projections were mainly based on anticipated service improvements (with or without conventional levels of marketing activity), such that intensive marketing might be expected to result in additional patronage increases.

- **Effectiveness.** Based on findings from the literature and the case studies (discussed in section 6.10.2), it is assumed that 30% of patronage increases may be attributed to former car users, made up of 19% former car drivers and 11% former car passengers (in line with average car occupancy levels).

Using these assumptions, information and marketing measures could reduce car driver mileage in London and other urban areas by 0.3% or 1.1% overall after ten years (with a higher figure in London and a lower figure in urban areas outside London). In non-urban areas, car driver mileage could be reduced by 0.1% or 0.3% after the same period.

Table 13.4: Effect of information and marketing measures on public transport use in urban and rural areas

	London	Urban areas, excluding London	Non-urban areas
Current local bus trips per person per year*	115	71	32
Coverage: Annual increase in local bus trips attributable to public transport information and marketing+	8.1 – 32.2	5.0 – 19.9	2.2 – 9.0
Effectiveness: proportion of public transport trips transferred from car as driver	0.19	0.19	0.19
Annual reduction in car driver trips per person~	1.5 – 6.1	0.9 – 3.8	0.4 – 1.7
Annual reduction in car driver km per person #	21.2 – 85.0	13.1 – 52.5	5.9 – 23.7
Current annual car driver km per person**	3312	5723	8040
Percentage reduction in car driver km++	0.6 or 2.6%	0.2 or 0.9%	*0.1 or 0.3%*
Overall percentage reduction in car driver km in London + urban areas##	*0.3 or 1.1%*		

* Current local bus trips per person are derived from National Travel Survey data for 1998-2000 (as more recent NTS breakdowns were not available). The figure for urban areas excluding London is estimated, based on a mid-figure between number of local bus stages per person in metropolitan built-up areas (98) and in urban areas with a population of 10,000 or more (44). The figure for rural areas is also estimated, based on mid-figure between number of local bus stages per person in settlements of 3000-10,000 people (34) and in rural areas with less than 3000 people (29).

\+ Annual increase in local bus trips = (current local bus trips per person per year) x (percentage increase in bus trips over ten years). Lower figure assumes 0.7% growth per annum; upper figure assumes 2.5% growth per annum.

~ Annual reduction in car driver trips per person = (annual increase in local bus trips per person) x 0.19

\# Annual reduction in car driver km per person = (annual reduction in car driver trips per person) x (average mileage of a car trip). Average mileage of a car trip is derived from National Travel Survey data and was 13.9 km in both 1999/01 and 2002.

** Current annual car driver km is derived from National Travel Survey data for 2002. It is 3312 km for London residents; estimated at 5723 km for urban areas (based on a mid-figure between the figure for metropolitan built up areas and the figure for settlements with a population of 10,000 or more); and estimated at 8040 km for non-urban areas (based on a mid-figure between the figure for settlements of 3000-10,000 and for rural areas with less than 3000 people).

++ Percentage reduction in car driver km = (annual reduction in car driver km per person) / (current annual car driver km per person)

\#\# Overall percentage reduction in car driver km in London + urban areas: assumes London population = 7.6 million and population of urban areas excluding London = 34.4 million.

13.2.5 Travel awareness campaigns

The effects of general travel awareness programmes are inherently difficult to quantify, and although our one travel awareness campaign case study had some monitoring data, it does not, on its own, provide a good basis for us to feel confident of our forecast of the impact of travel awareness programmes in general. There are also different types of travel awareness campaigns, ranging from those aimed at city level (or even wider areas)[3], and those which involve intensive intervention with a much smaller group of people, such as the BikeBus'ters experiment in Denmark. Our calculations below apply to the more general type of campaign, largely due to difficulties of estimating the impacts of the specialised kinds.

The evidence we have leads us cautiously to the following:
- **Coverage.** As reported in section 7.12, in York, somewhere between 3% and 12% of drivers have probably reduced their car travel as a result of the campaign. For reasons of caution in the absence of more data, we assume that travel awareness programmes of this type might in general impact on about half this proportion (that is, a lower figure of 1.5% or an upper figure of 6%), either because such programmes are not implemented everywhere, or because they are implemented at lower intensity.
- **Effectiveness.** We assume that the reduction in car use for those people who respond to travel awareness campaigns might be 5% (as a minimum that would be noticeable), through to 20% (as a maximum, perhaps equivalent to say, foregoing car use approximately one day a week.

Taken together, these assumptions suggest 'general' travel awareness campaigns could reduce car use by 0.1 or 1% overall. We do not attempt to distinguish between effects in urban and non-urban areas, and we do not include the potential impacts of more intensive types of campaigns.

Table 13.5: Impact of travel awareness campaigns

	Coverage Proportion of car users reacting to campaign	*Effectiveness* Reduction in car use amongst those car users who change their behaviour	*Impact* Implied reduction in car trips
All areas	1.5 – 6%	5 – 20%	0.1 or 1.2%

13.2.6 Car clubs

In estimating the future impact of car clubs, we assume:
- The impact is most likely to be to reduce car use for regular trips and those where alternatives are most readily available (that is, commuting, business, school escort). This is because car club membership enables people to drive for journeys which are heavily car-reliant, such as transporting a heavy load or escorting an elderly relative. This reduces the need to own a car and leads to other journeys to

---

[3] Such campaigns often define much smaller target groups than simply a 'whole city' or 'whole region' – for example, car drivers, aged 18-25. However, they are significantly different to those that, say, aim to work intensively with a group of a few hundred volunteers.

be made by non-car modes. Pricing regimes also discourage the use of car clubs vehicles for regular journeys such as commuting. Initially at least, the impact of car clubs is likely to be concentrated in urban areas, where alternatives are more readily available, although emerging information from rural pilots suggests that car clubs may rapidly become viable and impact in these areas too.

- **Coverage**. If organisational hurdles can be overcome, already-established car clubs could become self-financing and could grow at a more rapid rate than at present. Growth will also come from more clubs being established, in cities where they are not currently operating. More clubs, and membership growth within these clubs, would result in non-linear (though not necessarily exponential) growth in car club membership.

- For our lower scenario we took the case in which 5 urban car clubs were set up per year for the next decade, each growing at 75 members per year for the first five years, and 150 members per year thereafter (in line with current growth rates in Bristol, Edinburgh and Europe). Our upper scenario takes the case in which 10 clubs are set up each year, growing at a similar rate. These assumptions seem relatively conservative since, as discussed in section 8.8, the Carplus website reports that 7 clubs launched in 2003 and 12 have launched in 2004.

- In the long run (probably requiring more than ten years), we took the case where car clubs engage 10% of the adult population in both urban and non-urban areas. This is based on evidence from the literature about the potential size of the target market for car clubs.

- **Effectiveness**. Based on international studies (as reported in sections 8.4 and 8.9), we assume that the net effect of car club membership is to reduce average car mileage of all members by about a third. This allows for the fact that some car club members will make much larger cuts in their car use, while others (especially former non-car owners) may make little change or even increase their car use.

With these assumptions, car clubs could cut urban car mileage by 0.03% or 0.06% over a decade. These low figures are because of the comparatively small number of people affected. However, in the longer term, European evidence suggests that the target market could be about 10% of the population, and if this were the case, car mileage could be cut by 3%.

Table 13.6: Effect of car clubs on car mileage

		Coverage Car club members as proportion of population	Impact Reduction in car mileage
Within next ten years	Urban areas over 100,000 people	0.1 – 0.2%*	0.03 or 0.06%
	Smaller urban and non-urban areas	0~	0
Longer-term	Urban areas	10%	3%
	Smaller urban and non-urban areas	10%~	3%

* Lower figure based on 26,000 car club members within 10 years. This could be achieved by 5 urban car clubs being set up per year for the next decade, each growing at 75 members per year for the first five years, and 150 members per year thereafter. Upper figure based on 10 car clubs being set up per year, at similar growth rates.

~ assuming that large scale car club development is concentrated mainly in larger urban areas in next ten years, but that over a longer timescale car clubs are developed in all areas

Cairns S, Sloman L, Newson C, Anable J, Kirkbride A & Goodwin P (2004)
'Smarter Choices – Changing the Way We Travel' .

*Projections
and costs*

13.2.7 Car sharing

It is difficult to judge the overall effect of car sharing, because our case studies and most of the other data we have obtained relate only to commuter car sharing schemes. Car sharing might also be important for business trips and certain types of leisure trip, but we have not been able to include this in our assessment due to absence of data. This makes our estimate of the effect of car sharing conservative.

There are successful commuter car sharing schemes in both urban and rural areas. There may be particular potential for car sharing to reduce single-occupancy commuting in rural areas and small towns, where there may be less potential for other soft interventions (workplace travel plans and public transport information and marketing) to influence car commuting.

In estimating the future impact of car sharing, we therefore used the following assumptions:

- **Coverage.** We assume that an additional 1 – 10% of urban and rural car commuters might begin active car sharing within ten years. (By this, we mean being registered with, and a regular user of, a car sharing scheme, or car sharing informally on a regular basis as a result of car sharing promotion work.) The lower figure is based on linear growth projections for the Buckinghamshire scheme indicating the proportion of potential car driving commuters that might be affected in about 10 years; the upper figure is based on projections for the Milton Keynes area indicating the proportion of potential car driving commuters that might be affected in about 10 years. (These projections are described in section 9.12.1). Compared to present car commuting patterns, this amount of increase in car sharing would be fairly modest. If an extra 10% of car commuters began car sharing, this would mean that, for every 100 people commuting by car, an extra 5-6 commuters would start travelling as a car passenger (depending on levels of car occupancy amongst sharers). This would increase the number of commuters travelling as a car passenger from 18 per 100 (the current number according to 1999/01 National Travel Survey data) to 23 or 24 per 100.
- No account is taken of the potential contribution of car sharing for journey purposes other than commuting.
- **Effectiveness.** We assume an average car occupancy of 2 – 2.5 in each car-sharing vehicle. The lower figure, equivalent to driver plus one passenger, is the minimum possible, whereas some car-sharing schemes specifically encourage three or more people per car. For comparison, 1999/01 National Travel Survey data suggests an average car occupancy of 2.4 amongst commuters who already car share.
- We assume the journey to work distance for car sharers is 1 – 1.5 times the average journey distance for people driving alone. This is based on indications from the case studies that car sharing appeals more to people who have further to travel.
- Commuter car sharing in urban areas may be developed as part of workplace travel programmes, or as a substitute for them, and, therefore, there may be some potential for double counting in urban areas with extensive workplace travel plan programmes. We deal with this issue in section 13.3.

With these assumptions, car sharing could cut car commuting vehicle trips by 0.6% or 7%, and car commuting vehicle mileage by 0.6% or 11%, over a decade.

Table 13.7: Effect of car sharing on car trips and car mileage

	Coverage	Effectiveness		Impact	
	Proportion of car commuters who begin car sharing#	Average car occupancy in car-sharing vehicles	Average journey distance to work for car sharers, relative to average for all car trips to work	Expressed as percentage reduction in vehicle trips driven to work	Expressed as percentage reduction in vehicle mileage driven to work
Urban	1 – 10%	2 – 2.5	1 – 1.5	0.6 or 7%*	**0.6 or 11%**
Non-urban	1 – 10%	2 – 2.5	1 – 1.5	0.6 or 7%	**0.6 or 11%**

Expressed as proportion of all commuters travelling by car
* At present, 1999/2001 National Travel Survey data indicates that 82 cars are used for every 100 people travelling to work by car. Of these 100 people, 69 drive alone, 13 are drivers with at least one passenger, and 18 are passengers. If 10% of car commuters (who formerly drove alone) were to begin car sharing, with an average car occupancy of 2.5, the number of cars would fall from 82 to 76, a 7% drop.

13.2.8 Teleworking

In estimating the future impact of teleworking, we assume:

- The entire impact is concentrated on the peak period, and on the journey to work. The effect is the same in urban and rural areas.
- **Coverage.** As reported in section 10.3, about 64% of the workforce is employed in occupations which currently have significant levels of teleworking (with particularly high levels in managerial, professional and technical occupations), although there is some degree of telework in all occupational groups. At present, at least 7% of the workforce teleworks some of the time, and if growth continues at current rates, around 30% of the workforce might be teleworking in a decade. While not all of those in suitable occupations are likely to be engaged in teleworking in ten years time, there are a number of trends which would support continued growth at current rates. These include the growth in the proportion of the workforce employed in 'naturally' high teleworking occupations; the growth in incidence of teleworking within those jobs most suitable for it; the development of new techniques which apply telecommunications even to those tasks previously thought unsuitable; the development of cheaper and more appropriate telecommunications technologies; and changes in attitudes to working at home as it becomes more widespread. Therefore, for the high intensity scenario, we take the case in which 30% of the workforce are engaged in teleworking to some extent (consistent with linear growth at current rates). For the low intensity scenario, we take the case in which teleworking grows more slowly than the current rate, such that 20% are engaged in teleworking to some extent within ten years.
- **Effectiveness.** For the high intensity scenario, we take the case in which 30% of the workforce are engaged in teleworking to some extent (consistent with linear growth at current rates), and working at home an average of 3 days per week.

Three days per week is is in line with the higher estimate of location-independent tasks identified in one study of a local authority workforce, current teleworking behaviour at BT, and current levels of teleworking as reported by NOP (see section 10.4). This average would certainly include some relatively intensive teleworkers, and some that are less intensive. Although we are not able to make a definite forecast for this distribution, a check on credibility is given by a possible example, such as:

> 70% of the workforce not teleworking at all
> 10% teleworking for a minority of their work, say 1-2 days per week
> 10% teleworking for a substantial part of their work, say 3 days per week
> 10% mostly working at home but with regular workplace days, or entirely home-based but with occasional meetings (say 4-5 home-based days per week).

In the low intensity scenario, we assume that teleworkers are, on average, based at home 1.5 days per week, being the lower estimate of current practice, derived from 2001 Labour Force Survey results about teleworking.

- Teleworkers' journey-to-work distance and car mode share are assumed to be similar to the national average. (This is a conservative estimate, since the literature suggests that current teleworkers typically undertake longer than average commute journeys and are more likely to be car drivers. However, as telework spreads, these tendencies may diminish, and so we have not included them here).

- We make no allowance for new car trips generated by other household members using the car left at home on telework days, or for new car trips undertaken by the teleworker. These effects are often mentioned as a particular concern for teleworking, but in fact they are merely one example of the general issue of induced traffic which we deal with in chapter 14. Evidence from the literature, as discussed in section 10.2, suggests such effects are small (and may themselves be offset by other behaviour changes such as household members adopting contracted action spaces).

- Some of the benefit of teleworking might be achieved through measures introduced as part of workplace travel plans, but a reasonable proportion might be expected to happen independently of travel plans. Nevertheless, there is some risk of double counting. We deal with this issue in section 13.3.

With these assumptions, teleworking could reduce car commuter trips by 3% or 12% in ten years.

Table 13.8: Effect of teleworking on car commuter trips

Coverage: Proportion of workforce teleworking	20 – 30%
Increase in proportion of workforce teleworking since 2003	10 – 20%
Effectiveness: Overall proportion of teleworkers' time working at home	30 – 60%
Impact: Percentage reduction in car commuter trips	**3 – 12%**

13.2.9 Teleconferencing

In estimating the future impact of teleconferencing, we assume:
- The entire impact is concentrated on business trips.
- *Coverage.* Between 25% and 60% of companies may have readily available teleconferencing facilities in the next 10 years, and start using it as part of mainstream company practice.

Cairns S, Sloman L, Newson C, Anable J, Kirkbride A & Goodwin P (2004)
'Smarter Choices – Changing the Way We Travel'   .

Projections
and costs

- ***Effectiveness***. Companies which use teleconferencing facilities reduce their business travel by between 10 and 30%.

These figures are derived from the literature and our case study, as discussed in section 11.11.

With these assumptions, we tentatively suggest that teleconferencing might reduce car business trips by 2.5% or 18% in ten years.

13.2.10 Home shopping

In estimating the future impact of home shopping, we make the following assumptions:

- **Coverage**. The home shopping literature review suggests that home delivery has the greatest potential impact on car use in the grocery sector. This accounts for 40% of personal shopping mileage by car, according to the 1998-2000 National Travel Survey.
- Estimates of the likely take-up of grocery home delivery suggest it could account for around 5 – 15% of UK grocery sales by value within about ten years, as discussed in section 12.4.1.
- **Effectiveness.** Amongst those utilising home delivery services, vehicle mileage saved per shopping load is of the order of 70% or more, as discussed in section 12.5.

This suggests home shopping could reduce vehicle mileage for shopping by 1% or 4% in ten years.

Our case study also suggests that expansion of the Royal Mail / Post Office collection points trial, (as described in section 12.6), could reduce car mileage for personal business trips. In estimating the future impact of rolling this out nationally, we assume:

- **Coverage.** In the Nottingham trial, local collection points for missed deliveries were being used twice by each household over a year, with the potential for as many as 28 uses per year, as involvement increases. Assuming an average household size of 2.3, this would be equivalent to between 0.9 and 12.2 occasions per person per year. The average person makes 105 trips for personal business in a year (including 44 as a car driver) according to the 1999/2001 National Travel Survey. We therefore assume that if rolled out nationally, the local collection points trial could affect 2% of personal business trips, or potentially up to 28% if the scheme was exploited to the full, and that the impact would fall equally on trips made by car and by non-car means.
- **Effectiveness.** In the Nottingham trial, for trips to collect goods which were unsuccessfully delivered to the home, data-supported assumptions are that perhaps 15% trips would have been made anyway (for other reasons), 30% were no longer made by car, and the average distance of remaining car trips halved. This implies that, on average overall, there was a 72% reduction in the car distance travelled to collected undelivered goods.

This suggests national roll-out of local collection points for missed deliveries from Royal Mail could cut car mileage on personal business by about 1.5% (although there is the potential for the impact to be considerably higher, up to about 20%).

Finally, there is some information suggesting that public sector investment in delivery facilities (i.e. secure drop-off points) could also reduce light goods vehicle delivery traffic by home shopping operators. As discussed in section 12.7, work by several commentators has suggested that the use of dedicated delivery facilities could reduce home shopping delivery vehicle traffic by 30-50% or more, compared to some current arrangements where retailers promise to deliver to customers within specified time slots. We have not included this in our calculation, given problems with identifying the volume of relevant delivery traffic that could be affected. However, we note that the effects could be significant.

13.3 Summary of impacts

Table 13.9 summarises the impact estimates derived above, according to area type and journey purpose.

Table 13.9: Summary of impacts of different types of soft factor~

Journey purpose	Soft factor	Impact*	
		Non-urban	**Urban**
Journey to work	Workplace travel plans	2 or 4%	5 or 9%
	Car sharing	0.6 or 11%	0.6 or 11%
	Teleworking	3 or 12%	3 or 12%
Combined impact of workplace travel plans, car sharing and teleworking, allowing for double counting		*5 or 24%*	*8 or 26%*
Journey to school	School travel plans	4 or 20%	4 or 20%
Business journeys	Tele-conferencing	2.5 or 18%	2.5 or 18%
Shopping trips	Home shopping for groceries	1 or 4%	1 or 4%
Personal business trips	Local collection points	1.5%	1.5%
Multiple journey purposes	Personalised travel planning	<1%	1 or 3%
	Public transport information and marketing	0.1 or 0.3%	0.3 or 1.1%
	Travel awareness campaigns	0.1 or 1%	0.1 or 1%
	Car clubs		0.03% - 0.06% (up to 3% long term)

* Impact is expressed as a percentage reduction in car mileage for the relevant journey purposes for car clubs, car sharing, home shopping for groceries and local collection points. For all other measures, the impact is expressed as a percentage reduction in car *trips* for the relevant journey purposes, and we suggest that these figures are also applied to car mileage, as there is no information from either the literature or the case studies that would enable the reliable calculation of different figures for mileage.
~ Note that for soft factors which affect multiple journey purposes, the impact is expressed relative to all car travel. For soft factors which affect only one journey purpose, it is expressed relative to car travel for that purpose.

For most soft factors, we have insufficient information to give different estimates according to area type. The exceptions are workplace travel plans, personalised travel planning, public transport information and marketing, and car clubs: for these the non-urban estimates are mostly lower because of the generally poorer quality of public transport there.

In most cases, the impact is expressed as a percentage reduction in car *trips*. However, there are a few exceptions, where we had information that enabled an estimate of the impact on car *mileage*. On the whole, car mileage data is more useful. Where it is lacking, we assume that mileage is reduced by the same proportion as trips. As mentioned above, this may introduce a bias, usually but not always an underestimate, especially important where the combined effects of soft measures (and other policies) are such as to encourage a greater proportion of local travel, as well as a shift in mode.

Some soft factors are assumed to only affect one type of trip: for example school travel plans are assumed to only affect car use for the journey to school. (This is a simplification, since mode change for one journey purpose may well have second-order effects, particularly for linked trips.) Other soft factors affect trips for a variety of purposes. Equally, some trip purposes can be affected by more than one soft factor.

In section 13.4, we combine the impact of several soft factors to derive journey change factors for different trip purposes. Before doing this, we were keen to make adjustments to avoid the possibility of double counting. By double counting, we mean the incorrect assumption that several soft factors acting together will each reduce car travel by an independent percentage, when in fact the target market of people willing or receptive to respond to each of them overlaps. For most trip purposes, this is not likely to be an issue. For example, home shopping affects a fairly small proportion of car mileage for shopping trips, and so it is plausible that any impact from personalised travel planning, public transport information and marketing, travel awareness campaigns or car clubs would simply be additive.

However, the journey to work can be influenced by six or possibly seven soft factors, of which three (workplace travel plans, car sharing and teleworking) could each have a substantial impact. Here, there does seem to be some risk of double counting. We therefore make the following adjustments:

- We assume that car sharing will largely be developed as part of workplace travel programmes, or as a substitute for them. Arbitrarily, we assume around two-thirds of the impact of workplace travel plans will come from measures other than car sharing in the high intensity scenario. This would make the combined impact of workplace travel plans and car sharing schemes 3 or 14% in non-urban areas and 6 or 17% in urban areas.
- We assume that the growth in teleworking will be uniformly spread across public and private sector bodies, and across small and large organisations, but that in organisations which have a travel plan, half of the impact of teleworking will 'overlap' with the travel plan. Thus in non-urban areas, where we estimate 10 – 20% of the workforce may be covered by a travel plan, the net effect of teleworking will be to cut car commuting trips by 3 or 11%. In urban areas, where we estimate 30 – 50% of the workforce may be covered by a travel plan, the net effect of teleworking will be slightly less, cutting car commuting trips by 3 or 9%.

13.4 Applying the projections to national traffic data

The calculations above have produced a set of low figures corresponding with a low intensity scenario, and a set of higher figures for a high intensity scenario. The reviews and discussion indicate that useful calculation of the effects of soft measures must to some extent distinguish different contexts, not deal at very general national totals.

The Department for Transport forecasting model, the National Transport Model (NTM), operates at the level of individual trip-making for journeys by each mode of transport for each journey purpose, and freight traffic, travelling on a road network which distinguishes areas of the country, times of day, different types of road (motorway, trunk, etc) and different types of area (big cities, small towns, etc), but not specific roads in specific locations.

Ideally, the impact of soft measures would use the same classification system, but the research results only partly overlap with the model categories, and do so differently for the separate instruments. The main issues this presents for projection include the following:

- It is possible to distinguish impacts by journey purpose for some initiatives, namely workplace and school travel plans, teleconferencing and home shopping. In some cases, this also allows differentiation by time of day. In contrast, personalised travel planning, public transport information and marketing, travel awareness campaigns and car clubs are assumed to affect more than one journey purpose.
- It is possible to provide different estimates of impacts in different areas for workplace travel plans, personalised travel planning, public transport information and marketing and car clubs.
- Nearly all the measurements relate to changes in the volume of car use for a specific subset of traffic. We have no direct evidence from the case studies of the total traffic volumes represented by each subset, but this information is available in the NTM model, broken down in some detail by the areas and times it occurs.
- Policy impacts on behaviour within the NTM model are calculated at the level of the trip, driven mainly by generalised cost changes, distinguishing mode but not time of day, which is introduced at a later stage of the calculation. Soft measures are not fully defined by generalised cost, and in some cases hardly at all.

Therefore we proceeded as follows:
1. We defined a table of traffic data that was consistent with the dimensions of discrimination we are able to make from the research results, *and* the data used in NTM for the year 2000. (To some extent, this data also embodies some grossing up and adjustments performed by the Department's modelling process. This complication is ignored: we treated the tables as though they were real data).
2. We calculated the percentage changes to appropriate subsets of traffic that would be caused by different soft factors, at a level of intensity corresponding to the high intensity and low intensity scenarios built up over a notional ten year period.
3. We applied these percentage changes to the traffic table created in stage one.

As discussed above, we used an implicit assumption that just sufficient locking in is

Cairns S, Sloman L, Newson C, Anable J, Kirkbride A & Goodwin P (2004)
'Smarter Choices – Changing the Way We Travel' .

*Projections
and costs*

implemented to prevent induced traffic from eroding the impacts, but not more, and that there is no synergetic addition or subtraction to the figures other than those reported in sections 13.2 and 13.3.

13.4.1 The source National Transport Model data

The source data used for the first stage of our calculation is drawn from the National Transport Model and is for a base year of 2000. The tabulations available to us differentiated vehicle mileage by time of day, urban / non-urban roads and vehicle type (car, goods vehicles and public transport vehicles). Car mileage was further divided into six categories according to journey purpose: home-based work; home-based employers' business; non-home based work/employers' business; home-based essential other; home-based discretionary other; and non-home based discretionary other. While some of these categories clearly correspond to more familiar descriptions of journey purpose such as commuting and business travel, this categorisation was not very helpful for soft factors which affect journeys to school, shop and for personal business. We explain below how we have dealt with this.

The time of day data was simplified into two bands: 'peak weekday' traffic (traffic between 8-9am and 5-6pm Monday – Friday); and 'rest of week' traffic (all traffic outside peak weekday hours).

'Urban' traffic was defined as all traffic in urban areas with a population of over 10,000. 'Non-urban' traffic was defined as all traffic in areas with a population of 10,000 or less.

HGV and bus traffic was converted into passenger car units (pcus) using the standard factors applied by Department for Transport.

Table 13.10 summarises the source data.

Table 13.10: Year 2000 traffic data derived from National Transport Model

	Urban			Non-urban		
	All traffic	Peak weekday	Rest of week	All traffic	Peak weekday	Rest of week
Cars work	57.53	16.76	40.76	52.97	15.20	37.77
Cars business	20.16	3.01	17.15	32.98	5.67	27.31
Cars other	107.43	6.69	100.74	105.25	6.39	98.86
Cars total	185.11	26.46	158.65	191.20	27.26	163.93
Other traffic	53.79	6.03	47.76	79.77	8.96	70.81
Total	238.90	32.49	206.42	270.97	36.22	234.75

Units are billion pcu kilometres
'Peak weekday' = 8-9am and 5-6 pm Monday – Friday; 'rest of week' = all traffic outside peak weekday hours
'Cars work' = home-based work
'Cars business' = home-based employers' business + non-home based work / employers' business
'Cars other' = home-based essential other + home-based discretionary other + non-home based discretionary other
'Other traffic' = LGVs + rigid HGVs + articulated HGVs + PSVs, converted to pcus.

13.4.2 Journey change factors

For each of the journey purpose categories, 'work', 'business' and 'other', we derived two journey change factors, based on summation of the impacts of the relevant soft factors[4]. The lower journey change factor represents the case in which the coverage and effectiveness of each soft factor are the lower figures corresponding with the 'low intensity' scenario. The higher journey change factor represents the case in which coverage and effectiveness of each soft factor are of higher value, the 'high intensity' scenario.

We had difficulty in estimating the contribution of two soft factors, namely school travel plans and shopping home delivery / local collection points. This is because we did not know what proportion of 'cars other' mileage was for escort education, shopping or personal business. To enable calculations for these soft factors, we used an approximate breakdown based on 1999/2001 National Travel Survey data[5].

The journey change factors are derived from tables 13.11 and 13.12.

The final journey change factors used are as follows:

- **High intensity scenario**
'Cars work' journey change factor = 0.67 in urban areas; 0.75 in non-urban areas
'Cars business' journey change factor = 0.75 in urban areas; 0.81 in non-urban areas
'Cars other' journey change factor = 0.92 in urban areas; 0.97 in non-urban areas.

- **Low intensity scenario**
'Cars work' journey change factor = 0.91 in urban areas; 0.95 in non-urban areas
'Cars business' journey change factor = 0.96 in urban areas; 0.97 in non-urban areas
'Cars other' journey change factor = 0.98 in urban areas; 0.99 in non-urban areas.

---

[4] Our journey change factors are expressed as the proportion of traffic that remains after our projected reductions are applied. For example, a journey change factor of 0.66 implies that 66% of the car traffic would remain, if our projected traffic reductions from soft factor initiatives were realised.

[5] This approximation assumes that 'cars others' is broken down into: 2.2% escort education; 18.7% shopping; 10.0% personal business; 69.1% other. This approximation is based on National Travel Survey data about the breakdown of annual miles travelled by all modes (excluding travel for commuting and business). Ideally, we would have preferred to use a breakdown based on annual mileage travelled *by car* for different trip purposes, but this was not readily available. Given the size of the final volumes of potentially affected traffic, and the magnitude of potential traffic reductions that we were applying to these, it is our impression that using that alternative breakdown would not have had a significant effect on our final estimations.

Cairns S, Sloman L, Newson C, Anable J, Kirkbride A & Goodwin P (2004)
'Smarter Choices – Changing the Way We Travel'   .

*Projections
and costs*

Table 13.11: Journey change factors in a 'high intensity' scenario

		Non-urban areas	Urban areas
Cars work		Workplace travel plans, car sharing and teleworking together cut car travel to work by 24%; personalised travel planning cuts it by 0.2%; public transport information and marketing by 0.3%; travel awareness campaigns by 1%; car clubs by 0%. Total reduction of 25.5%	Workplace travel plans, car sharing and teleworking together cut car travel to work by 26%; personalised travel planning cuts it by 5%; public transport information and marketing by 1.1%; travel awareness campaigns by 1%; car clubs by 0.06%. Total reduction of 33.16%
Journey change factor		**0.75**	**0.67**
Cars business		Teleconferencing cuts business travel by 18%; personalised travel planning cuts it by 0.2%; public transport information and marketing by 0.3%; travel awareness campaigns by 1%; car clubs by 0%. Total reduction of 19.5%	Teleconferencing cuts business travel by 18%; personalised travel planning cuts it by 5%; public transport information and marketing by 1.1%; travel awareness campaigns by 1%; car clubs by 0.06%. Total reduction of 25.16%
Journey change factor		**0.81**	**0.75**
Cars other	'escort education = 2.2% of 'cars other' 'shopping' = 18.7% of 'cars other' 'personal business' = 10.0% of 'cars other'	Personalised travel planning cuts 'cars other' travel by 0.2%; public transport information and marketing cuts it by 0.3%; travel awareness campaigns by 1%; car clubs cut it by 0%; school travel plans cut the escort education portion of 'cars other' by 20%; home delivery cuts the shopping portion of 'cars other' by 4%; local collection points cut the personal business portion of 'cars other' by 1.5%. Total reduction of 2.84%	Personalised travel planning cuts 'cars other' travel by 5%; public transport information and marketing cuts it by 1.1%; travel awareness campaigns by 1%; car clubs by 0.06%; school travel plans cut the escort education portion of 'cars other' by 20%; home delivery cuts the shopping portion of 'cars other' by 4%; local collection points cut the personal business portion of 'cars other' by 1.5%. Total reduction of 8.50%
Journey change factor		**0.97**	**0.92**

Table 13.12: Journey change factors in a 'low intensity' scenario

		Non-urban areas	Urban areas
Cars work		Workplace travel plans, car sharing and teleworking together cut car travel to work by 5%; personalised travel planning cuts it by 0.02%; public transport information and marketing by 0.1%; travel awareness campaigns by 0.1%; car clubs by 0%. Total reduction of 5.22%	Workplace travel plans, car sharing and teleworking together cut car travel to work by 8%; personalised travel planning cuts it by 1%; public transport information and marketing by 0.3%; travel awareness campaigns by 0.1%; car clubs by 0.03%. Total reduction of 9.43%
Journey change factor		**0.95**	**0.91**
Cars business		Teleconferencing cuts business travel by 2.5%; personalised travel planning cuts it by 0.02%; public transport information and marketing by 0.1%; travel awareness campaigns by 0.1%; car clubs by 0%. Total reduction of 2.72%	Teleconferencing cuts business travel by 2.5%; personalised travel planning cuts it by 1%; public transport information and marketing by 0.3%; travel awareness campaigns by 0.1%; car clubs by 0.03%. Total reduction of 3.93%
Journey change factor		**0.97**	**0.96**
Cars other	'escort education = 2.2% of 'cars other' 'shopping' = 18.7% of 'cars other' 'personal business' = 10.0% of 'cars other'	Personalised travel planning cuts 'cars other' travel by 0.02%; public transport information and marketing cuts it by 0.1%; travel awareness campaigns by 0.1%; car clubs by 0%; school travel plans cut the escort education portion of 'cars other' by 4%; home delivery cuts the shopping portion of 'cars other' by 1%; local collection points cut the personal business portion of 'cars other' by 1.5%. Total reduction of 0.65%	Personalised travel planning cuts 'cars other' travel by 1%; public transport information and marketing cuts it by 0.3%; travel awareness campaigns by 0.1%; car clubs by 0.03%; school travel plans cut the escort education portion of 'cars other' by 4%; home delivery cuts the shopping portion of 'cars other' by 1%; local collection points cut the personal business portion of 'cars other' by 1.5%. Total reduction of 1.86%
Journey change factor		**0.99**	**0.98**

Cairns S, Sloman L, Newson C, Anable J, Kirkbride A & Goodwin P (2004)
'Smarter Choices – Changing the Way We Travel' .

*Projections
and costs*

13.4.3 Combined impact of the soft factors on future traffic levels

The result of applying the journey change factors to the NTM data is as follows:

Under the 'high intensity' scenario, traffic in urban areas could be cut by 14% overall, and 21% at peak times. Traffic in non-urban areas could be cut by 8% overall, and 14% at peak times. Nationally (that is, across both urban and non-urban areas), traffic could be cut by 11% overall, and 17% at peak times.

Under the 'low intensity' scenario, traffic in urban areas could be cut by 3% overall, and 5% at peak times. Traffic in non-urban areas could be cut by 2% overall, and 3% at peak times. Nationally, traffic could be cut by 2-3% overall, and 4% at peak times.

These conclusions are summarised in table 13.13:

Table 13.13: Impacts of soft factors on future traffic levels

Impact on...	Low intensity scenario	High intensity scenario
National traffic	2%	11%
Peak-time national traffic	4%	17%
Off-peak national traffic	2%	10%
Urban traffic	3%	14%
Peak-time urban traffic	5%	21%
Off-peak urban traffic	3%	13%
Non-urban traffic	2%	8%
Peak-time non-urban traffic	3%	14%
Off-peak non-urban traffic	1%	7%

We emphasise again that these are projections of what *could* happen. Achieving these reductions in traffic (especially those in the 'high intensity' scenario) will depend on the priority and support accorded to soft factors, and the extent to which their benefits are locked in by other measures to control induced traffic.

Table 13.14 summarises the relative contribution made by the different soft factors to the overall traffic reduction figures. The biggest contributions come from measures targeted at the journey to work (workplace travel plans, teleworking and car sharing), personalised travel planning, and teleconferencing. This does not mean that the other measures are unimportant. In particular, school travel plans could have great significance by influencing attitudes to car use amongst children, which may be translated into greater awareness and behavioural change when they are adults. Car clubs are very unlikely to have a major impact on car use within the next ten years because they are relatively new, but, as noted earlier, in the longer term they could cut car use by as much as 3% and have the potential to become self financing.

Table 13.14: Contribution made by each soft factor to overall traffic reduction figures, national average

(with adjustment to avoid double-counting; columns are additive not multiplicative; no adjustments to allow for synergy of impact; assumption that there are 'just enough' supporting measures to lock in effects without enhancing them)

	High intensity scenario	Low intensity scenario
Measures targeting the journey to work, of which:	5.4%	1.4%
Workplace travel plans	*1.2%*	*0.7%*
Car sharing	*2.0%*	*0.1%*
Teleworking	*2.2%*	*0.6%*
Personalised travel planning	1.9%	0.4%
Teleconferencing	1.9%	0.3%
Travel awareness	0.7%	0.1%
Public transport information and marketing	0.5%	0.1%
Home shopping	0.3%	0.08%
School travel plans	0.2%	0.04%
Local collection points	0.06%	0.06%
Car clubs	0.02%	0.01%
Total*	**11%**	**2.5%**

* Figures in this row may not match column totals, due to rounding

13.5 Relationship between impact, cost and value for money

Chapters 3 to 12 used case study data on current levels of spending and impact for each soft factor to derive a cost-impact ratio: that is, an estimate of the current cost per car kilometre taken off the road to the public sector. Table 13.15 presents a summary of that data. We emphasise that the figures it contains should be treated as indicative of orders of magnitude only. Making assessments about the relative effectiveness of the different soft measures, or of soft measures in different case study areas, will be sensitive to the various simplifications and assumptions made as listed in the calculations in chapters 3 – 12, and the figures are likely to vary in different local contexts. This means that we are *not* able to say that, for example, there is a general rule that workplace travel plans are 'cheaper' or 'more effective' than, say, car clubs. We can however say that the costs of workplace travel plans and car clubs are of a similar order of magnitude.

The figures given reflect experience to date. There are some logical reasons for expecting the relationship between costs and level of implementation to be non-linear. There may be economies of scale which reduce the unit costs of large initiatives; there may be learning and the development of better methods which increase the effectiveness of soft measures; and there may be diminishing returns especially as the achievable limits to behavioural change are approached. The first and second of these would lead to unit costs becoming lower as a programme of soft measures is built up, and the third would lead to the unit costs becoming higher. A sensible hypothesis might be that in the early stages of extensive soft factor implementation, unit costs will fall, and at later stages as saturation of effect is approached, they will increase. There are insufficient data and experience fully to check this hypothesis at present, but we comment on evidence and indications about this issue below.

We also note that the cost-impact ratios we have used are based on the reduction in car vehicle kilometres, as an indicator of congestion and environmental benefits. The costs quoted do not include any changes in personal expenditure by the individuals modifying their behaviour, or spending by the private sector (unless a direct grant or contract by the public sector). The figures also take no account of the social value of resulting changes in congestion, pollution, social inclusion, health improvement etc. The measures we have used are those without any discounting to allow for erosion of benefit due to induced traffic, in line with the general appraoch used in the study, and therefore their achievement does depend on whether supportive measures are implemented.

Table 13.15: Indicative public sector costs, in terms of pence/vehicle kilometre reduced, for soft factors

Factor	Source	Indicative Cost* pence/vehicle km reduced
Workplace travel plans--	Birmingham case study	0.1 – 0.3
	Bristol case study	0.6 – 1.6
	Buckinghamshire case study	0.7 – 1.5
	Cambridgeshire case study	0.4 – 0.9
	Merseyside case study	0.4 – 0.7
	Nottingham case study	0.6 – 2.0
	York case study	0.4 – 0.6
School travel plans	Buckinghamshire case study	1.4 – 2.6
	Merseyside case study	2.0 – 3.8
	York case study	5.3 – 9.9¬
Personalised travel planning	Gloucester case study (pilot)	3.3
	Bristol case study (Vivaldi phase 1)	3.4
	London proposed large-scale	1.2
	Nottingham proposed large-scale	0.7
Public transport information and marketing +	Brighton case study	4.4
	Nottingham case study	4.1
Travel awareness	York case study	0.2 – 2.7
Car clubs#	Edinburgh case study	4.8
	Bristol case study	5.1
Car-sharing	Buckinghamshire case study	3.3
	Milton Keynes case study	0.7
Teleworking Tele-conferencing Home shopping	In all three cases, private sector investment is needed, but cost savings should outweigh investment costs. However, public sector intervention may be needed to stimulate developments and changes in business practice^.	

* Use of decimal places (eg in 0.2p) should not be read as greater precision than 1p, 5p etc.. Capital costs have been annualised at 3.5%. No allowance has been made for induced traffic.
¬ York's school travel figures are high because they include a substantial amount of safer routes work, as well as the 'softer' elements of school travel plans. Such engineering work is often essential to school travel plans, but, in many authorities, it is partly borne by the road safety budget, not simply by the school travel plans budget.
-- Excludes spending by the private sector. We assume that private employers will only invest in travel plans if they see offsetting benefits, such as reduced parking requirements, improved staff recruitment and retention, obtaining commercially valuable planning permissions, etc. In some cases, employers have managed entirely to fund travel plans from car parking charges.

[+] Costs include public investment only. Investment by commercial operators is assumed to be motivated, and therefore at least offset, by revenue generated by additional passengers. (However, net costs would be even less where revenue from additional passengers exceeds investment by the public transport operator).

It is likely that car clubs will become cheaper, and eventually 'free', at the point when they become self-financing.

^ For telework, we estimated that the BT initiative had reduced travel at a cost of 1.2 pence per km, in terms of the costs to BT of facilitating teleworking. However, this calculation did not include offsetting savings. For example, BT estimate that telework has contributed to their office space savings worth £180 million per year.

For teleconferencing, one company reported that videoconferencing equipment paid for itself within the first week of each month in terms of reduced travel costs and staff time savings, and numerous other companies also reported financial savings from adopting teleconferencing. However, public sector promotion, advice and grants may be needed to encourage greater adoption of teleconferencing as mainstream practice, which are currently impossible to cost.

For home shopping, provision of services is largely occurring for commercial reasons anyway. However, public sector promotion of home shopping for groceries could help to increase take-up, and funding for local drop-off facilities could help to make freight operations more efficient. One 'back of the envelope' calculation suggested that, to achieve traffic reduction at a cost of 1.5 pence per kilometre, in a city of 200,000 people, it would be possible to justify spending at least £300,000 over 10 years.

On these assumptions, cost-impact ratios vary from about 0.1 pence to about 10 pence expenditure per vehicle kilometre reduced, with most figures tending to be at the lower end of this range. Those at the upper end of the range typically include some supporting hard measures implementation. The approximate average soft factors cost was 1.5 pence per vehicle kilometre saved.

Although the development of a full cost benefit analysis of the value for money represented by these figures is beyond the scope of the study, we can make use of other studies which calculate the congestion relief and other benefits which derive from a reduction in vehicle traffic in various conditions. There is a large literature on this subject, and naturally a range of different estimates are made, some of which have already been used in comparable applications of assessing the value for money of Department for Transport initiatives. For example, the evaluation of the school and workplace travel plan site specific advice programme (Potter et al 2003) used a value of 20.5 pence per mile, equivalent to 12.8 pence per kilometre, based on an update of figures from Samson et al 2001[6].

The most authoritative and complete figures available to date which are actually used for the purpose of assessing value for money in the allocation of public funds, are those agreed between the Strategic Rail Authority and the Department for Transport for use when assessing the benefit of shifting 'sensitive' lorry miles from road to rail. These figures, published by the Strategic Rail Authority (2003) include estimated values for congestion costs for a variety of different road conditions, and also values for accidents, noise, pollution, climate change, infrastructure costs, a quantitative estimate for other unquantified factors, and adjustments for taxation. The total value per lorry mile reduced was given as 51pence, and £1.74 on local roads in London and other conurbations. Over 85% of the net benefit per lorry mile reduced was accounted

---

[6] Samson et al's figures included some valuation of the effects of reducing accidents, local air pollution, noise and climate change, although the bulk of their figure (over 10p per kilometre) was based on congestion benefits.

for by the congestion element, the proposed environmental values being rather low in comparison (and based on less well established evidence).

The best established figures used, in practice, are those for congestion. These are shown in table 13.16.

Table 3.16 Values of road congestion benefits resulting from reduction of traffic.

	Congestion Benefits (pence per lorry mile)
Motorways	
High congestion	79.0
Medium congestion	37.0
Low congestion	6.3
London & Conurbations	
Trunk & principle	121.9
Other roads	135.5
Rural and Other Urban	
Trunk & principle	45.8
Other roads	10.6
Weighted Average	43.9

Source: SRA 2003

For the purpose of calculating congestion effects, standard PCU factors enable conversion from lorries to cars: these are currently assessed as 1 for light vans, 1.68 for HGV rigids, and 2.46 for HGV articulated vehicles. While the actual traffic mix will vary according to type of road and context, to a first approximation we can convert from lorry miles to car kilometres by dividing the figures in table 3.16 by 3.

This suggests that each car kilometre removed by soft measures brings an overall average benefit in reduced congestion of about 15 pence. This figure varies with location, ranging from about 45 pence in city streets, to over 3 pence in rural and other urban streets. These figures do not distinguish by time of day: since the benefits of reducing traffic are very sensitive to the level of congestion, the figures would be higher at peak periods. They would also be higher if other external benefits, such as environmental impacts, are included.

The implication of these figures, even taking account of their range of uncertainty, is that taking a proportion of traffic off the roads by soft measures appears to give robustly good value for money: the margin of estimated benefit over cost is large enough that even quite major errors in assumptions about costs and impacts (which, as discussed above, have themselves been on the conservative side) would still leave a positive net benefit.

However, we should caution that the estimated benefits are not necessarily robust to induced traffic. For the same reasons as pointed out by SACTRA (1994) in the case of road building, a small amount of induced traffic, in conditions of relatively high congestion, can have a disproportionately large effect in eroding the initial benefits.

The costs of achieving reductions of congestion by soft measures appear to be less than by other 'carrots' such as public transport infrastructure or service improvements (other than those brought about by low cost capacity reallocation such as bus priority measures). They are also typically very much less than the cost of seeking to achieve comparable reductions in congestion by increasing road capacity more than traffic growth. (Demand management by price, on the other hand, can, if desired, raise more money than it costs, so the comparison is different in nature). We caution that such comparisons would always need to take account of the extent and cost of the supportive measures necessary for success, and also that such policies are not entirely independent of each other. For example, public transport improvements and public transport marketing are often linked.

Further quantification of these considerations would go beyond the terms of reference of this study, but the orders of magnitude are such that this conclusion will be reasonably robust to more detailed analysis. Over the coming years, it should also be possible to estimate empirically the hypothesised relationships of changes in soft factor unit costs due to economies of scale, improvement of methods, and diminishing returns, for which there is qualitative and logical evidence but not yet clear quantitative evidence. At present, there is no evidence that unit costs have started to rise due to these effects, and indeed there are some indications that returns from soft factors are currently increasing due to the development of knowledge and skill in devising more effective methods of implementation, and economies of scale. We therefore speculate that we are currently still in the increasing returns part of the hypothesised curve, although further research would be needed to conclude this with certainty.

In summary, there is a prima facie case that expenditure on soft measures could represent very good value for money in terms of the absolute benefits obtained per pound spent. We have indications that the ratios of benefits:costs are in the order of 10:1 on average, and many times this in congested urban conditions. There is also a likelihood that comparisons with other methods of achieving similar objectives would also be very favourable for soft factors. Logically, at some stage, diminishing returns should set in, but there is no indication that this is imminent, or that it would erode benefits sufficently to offset the very positive margin of net benefit considered likely to occur within the time frame and policy range of this study.

13.6 Summary of findings on projections and costs

In this chapter, we have developed two scenarios for the possible future impact of soft factors, termed 'high intensity' and 'low intensity'. The high intensity scenario represents the conditions in which local and national policies support the widespread implementation of all soft factors, and lead to each individual soft factor having an effect at the high end of what experience suggests is realistically achievable in a period of approximately 10 years. In the low intensity scenario, implementation of soft factors is presumed to be less widespread over the next ten years, and their effect is presumed to be at the lower end of what is suggested by current experience.

The scenarios make no explicit adjustment for induced traffic or for particular synergy between soft and hard factors, or for positive reinforcement between individual soft factors. These issues have been mentioned in earlier chapters, and are discussed again in chapter 14.

Using evidence from the case studies and elsewhere, we derived estimates of future impact for each of the individual soft factors. Some allowance was made to avoid any possibility of double counting for the journey to work (the only journey purpose where the risk of this was considered significant), by reducing the combined impact of three soft factors which, in practice, are likely to interact closely. These were workplace travel plans, car sharing and teleworking.

We combined the impact estimates for the individual soft factors to produce journey change factors for work trips, business trips and other trips, differentiated by urban and non-urban areas. The journey change factors were applied to traffic data used for the National Transport Model, and suggested that (in the high intensity scenario), the reductions in car use brought about by soft factors could amount to something in the order of 14% of traffic in urban areas and 8% in non-urban areas. Impacts would be higher (21% and 14%, respectively) during peak periods.

The biggest contribution came from measures targeted at the journey to work (workplace travel plans, teleworking and car sharing), personalised travel planning, and teleconferencing, although there are clearly reasons why it is may also be considered important to invest in the other soft factors, in particular their effects over a longer timescale than the next ten years.

In terms of pence per vehicle km taken off the road, all soft factors had costs in the range from about 0.1 pence to about 10 pence. Most figures were at the lower end of this range, such that 1.5 pence per vehicle km taken off the road represents a reasonable average figure for soft factors. In terms of congestion relief, the ratios of benefits:costs were in the order of 10:1 on average, and many times this in congested urban conditions.

13.7 References

Potter S, Lane B, Parkhurst G, Cairns S & Enoch M (2003) *Evaluation of school and workplace travel plan site specific advice programme* Department for Transport, London.

Samson T., C. A. Nash, P. J. Mackie, J. D. Shires, S. M. Grant-Muller (2001) *Surface Transport Costs and Charges*. DETR, London.

SACTRA (1994) *Trunk roads and the generation of traffic*, Report of the Standing Advisory Committee on Trunk Road Assessment, HMSO, London

Strategic Rail Authority (2003) *Sensitive Lorry Miles: results of analysis*, SRA, London.

14. Conclusions

14.1 Overview

In recent years, there has been growing interest in a range of transport policy initiatives which are now widely described as 'soft' measures. Soft measures usually seek to give better information and opportunities which affect the free choices made by individuals, mostly by attractive, relatively uncontroversial, and relatively cheap improvements. They include:

- Workplace and school travel plans;
- Personalised travel planning, travel awareness campaigns, and public transport information and marketing;
- Car clubs and car sharing schemes;
- Teleworking, teleconferencing and home shopping.

Following this review, we can say that sufficient evidence now exists to have some confidence that soft factor interventions can have a significant effect on individual travel choices.

In this concluding chapter we bring together both the research conclusions from the literature and case studies, and also the policy issues, barriers and difficulties which the case study interviewees discussed with the study team.

The assessment focuses on two different policy scenarios for the next ten years. The **'high intensity'** scenario identifies the potential provided by a significant expansion of activity to a much more widespread implementation of present good practice, albeit to a realistic level which still recognises the constraints of money and other resources, and variation in the suitability and effectiveness of soft factors according to local circumstances. The **'low intensity'** scenario is broadly defined as a projection of the present (2003-4) levels of local and national activity on soft measures.

The main features of the high intensity scenario would be

- A reduction in peak period urban traffic of about 21% (off-peak 13%);
- A reduction of peak period non-urban traffic of about 14% (off-peak 7%);
- A nationwide reduction in all traffic of about 11%.

These figures represent a cautious estimate of the impacts of significantly scaling up work on soft factors from its current level. The scenario described is one where soft measures have benefited from a high intensity policy build-up over a period of about ten years. This would require commitment at local government level (though at a varying scale in accordance with local conditions) and by national government also.

It would necessarily involve more resources than are currently committed to this area, but at a level which we judge, based on the interviews carried out, to be within the range of what could feasibly be made available and used efficiently, should local and national government choose to do so. We have not estimated an upper limit of how much could be achieved by seeking to go beyond these short and medium term constraints.

We emphasise that, even under our scenario of intense implementation, there will be particular types of location where certain soft factor policies would be less appropriate, and that it would be unrealistic to assume that all authorities could achieve the same effects as those particularly impressive individual achievements that have only occurred in a small minority of cases.. Therefore we assume more widespread, but not universal, application of soft factors, achieving results from soft factor interventions which are in line with *typical* current achievements from authorities that have prioritised such interventions.

With these rather cautious assumptions, our calculations suggest that soft factor interventions offer very acceptable value for money. Using current DfT practice for estimating the value of the effects on travel times of a reduction in the number of vehicles, each £1 spent on soft measures could produce benefits of about £10 on average, and considerably more in congested conditions. Inclusion of values for potentially positive effects on safety, health or the environment would further increase the value for money. This gives a good margin of robustness to changes in assumptions or methods of calculation.

The figures are subject to a number of caveats. They are based on a generally conservative interpretation of the evidence, analysed by 'hands-on' methods which do not depend on the assumptions, simplifications and mechanisms of traditional transport modelling. However, there is inevitably a degree of doubt as to their robustness. We would broadly recommend that the margins of statistical error assumed (upwards as well as downwards) should be similar to those applied to policy assessments from the Department's National Transport Model generally.

In addition, the review has also revealed the critical importance of the policy context, with specific issues that are so fundamental that they should always be emphasised at the same time as the optimistic picture described above:

First, these figures do not represent a forecast, they represent a potential. If implementation is at a lower level, inadequately funded, or inconsistent, the effects, unsurprisingly, will be substantially less. Calculations we have made about 'low-intensity' implementation, in which soft factors are not given increased policy priority compared with present practice, are estimated to be considerably less than those of the high intensity scenario, including a reduction in peak period urban traffic of about 5%, and a nationwide reduction in all traffic of 2%-3%. These smaller figures also assume that sufficient other supporting policies are used to prevent induced traffic from eroding the effects, notably at peak periods and in congested conditions. Without these supportive measures, the effects could be lower, temporary, and perhaps invisible. Effects at this scale could still be worth having from a cost-benefit point of view, because of the benefits brought to the individuals affected, but might not be seen as making a significant contribution to mainstream transport strategy.

Thus, the difference between the high and low intensity scenarios is not a statistical error band driven by uncertainty about economic trends. It derives from the different assumptions about the policy priority and momentum that local and national government may, in future, choose to give to soft factor initiatives.

In either case, soft measures, which, in intent and style, are so different from road construction, do share one important feature with it: any substantial initial reduction in congestion has the potential to cause induced traffic, which erodes the benefits. To spell this out, those individuals choosing to reduce their car use may be simply replaced by other individuals who are attracted by the freer road conditions to increase their car use.

In 'Managing our Roads' (DfT 2003), the Government stressed the importance of 'locking-in' the benefits of congestion reduction policies by demand management measures to control induced traffic. This review has found that the same condition is vitally important for delivering the full potential of soft measures. Without this, soft measures can still succeed in changing *which* individuals are using cars, therefore potentially resulting in benefits for individuals, but may have much less effect on area wide traffic levels, congestion or environmental impacts. Broadly, those experienced in the implementation of soft factors locally support this logic of 'locking-in' usually expressing it in terms of soft measures being part of an integrated transport strategy, or needing to be supported by complementary measures. They frequently emphasise that achieving overall reductions in traffic depends on some or all of such supportive policies as re-allocation of road capacity and other measures to improve public transport service levels, parking control, traffic calming, pedestrianisation, cycle networks, congestion charging or other traffic restraint, other use of transport prices and fares, speed regulation, or stronger legal enforcement levels.

14.2 Summary results of research literature and case studies

14.2.1 Overall impacts

Seven separate published estimates of the overall effect of differently defined packages of such measures were examined (including the Halcrow study leading to the 5% figure given in Department for Transport guidance on the multi-modal studies). The results of these studies, about the potential traffic reduction from soft factors, range from a lowest figure of 4% of national traffic and a highest of 20% overall, and up to about 30% for some specific urban locations (although the latter figure also included the effect of additional supporting hard measures). These results can be interpreted in relation to our low and high intensity scenarios. They suggest that, at the lower intensity application, there is scope for soft measures to reduce traffic levels by about 4% or 5% at the national level, with a range around this according to local circumstances. Taking the studies as a whole, they suggest that, with higher intensity application (and emphasising the importance of supportive hard measures either by assumption or explicitly) the estimated potential effect of soft factor interventions on traffic levels would be a reduction of 10% to 15% as a national average, and 15% to 20% in favourable local conditions. (These figures represent only the central bands that emerge from the 7 studies – the full distribution was wider).

Our own high intensity estimate of 11% falls towards the lower end of the central band of the other studies, and our estimated 22% for urban peak periods is slightly above the central band, but well within the range of results as a whole. Our low intensity estimate of 2%-3% is somewhat lower than the 5% figure given in the Department for Transport guidance to the multi-modal studies (derived from Halcrow, 2002), although the difference is probably within the range of uncertainty of both studies.

Thus, both our low intensity and high intensity estimates appear to be in line with informed professional opinion.

14.2.2 Impacts of soft measures considered separately

For the present study, the overviews mentioned above were augmented by examination of detailed international published literature on specific instruments of policy, and case studies based on twelve UK local authority areas, and also the experience of British Telecom. These case studies covered 24 different single or combined soft factor initiatives.

The main findings were as follows.

- Workplace travel plans typically reduce commuter car driving by between 10% and 30%, though the best ones achieve significantly more than that. Typical cost to the local authority is £2-£4 per head. So far, city authorities prioritising workplace travel plans have typically managed to engage with organisations representing about 30% of the workforce, whilst county authorities have managed to engage with organisations representing about 10%.

- School travel plans, on average, cut school run traffic by between 8% and 15%, with high performing schools commonly achieving reductions of over 20%, and, sometimes, considerably more. Many local authorities are devoting more resources to school travel work than to workplace travel plans, and some expect to reach nearly all schools in their area in the next 10 years.

- Personalised travel planning initiatives typically report reductions in car use of 7%-15% in urban areas, and 2-6% in rural and smaller urban areas. Costs for large scale implementation are likely to be considerably cheaper than pilot projects, being in the order of less than £20 per head, (with some suggesting figures of half this magnitude).

- Public transport information and marketing has delivered clearly recorded increases in bus use, with evidence suggesting that it can cause patronage increases from service improvements to double. City-wide budgets for such work of £60,000-£300,000 per year (including public and private sector investment) have helped to deliver city-wide increases in bus use of 1.5%-5% a year, when combined with other improvements.

- Travel awareness campaigns vary in nature, from relatively general campaigns to closely targetted intensive approaches. Both types report evidence of car use reductions, although intensive approaches tend to achieve higher levels of individual change. Many are now focusing on the positive health benefits from alternative transport policies. In many cases, travel awareness campaigns are used to win support for, and perhaps intensify, other specific initiatives, and the value of national awareness campaigning was identified in relation to many of the other soft factor initiatives.

- Car clubs have been associated with a reduction of about 5 private cars per car club vehicle. They require start-up funding in the order of £50,000 to £150,000 per club which should lead to them becoming self-financing. In the absence of evidence, there has been a tendency to set unrealistic timescales for breaking even, perhaps partly to justify public funding. Initially, car club initiatives have been focused on high density urban residential locations, although emerging information from rural pilots suggests that low-cost operational models can make clubs viable in rural areas too.

- Organised car-sharing has effects on overall car use, but these depend on other factors, including parking regimes, the balance of users drawn from car driving or from other modes, and the amount of informal car sharing already taking place. Set up and running costs vary significantly and are primarily determined by the extent of associated publicity and marketing that takes place.

- Teleworking is growing rapidly, and typically currently results in a reduction of between 2 and 6 home-work journeys per teleworker per week. Evidence suggests that changes in car use for other purposes, or by other household members, or due to changes in home location, do not substantially offset these reductions, and, in some cases, there may be further cuts in car use. Costs are likely to be offset by business savings.

- Teleconferencing typically reduces business travel by between 10% and 30% in organisations that promote its use. Many commentators suggest that there is great potential for more widespread use of teleconferencing, however public sector promotion may be needed to ensure mainstream adoption. Business savings could be substantial, in terms of reduced travel costs and more efficient use of staff time.

- Home shopping currently accounts for less than 5% of the grocery market, but is estimated to reach 10%-15% over the next decade, leading to potential reductions of 7-11% of all food shopping traffic. Meanwhile, investment in better drop off facilities for all types of home shopping could reduce travel for customers in some circumstances (where their alternative is travelling to a more remote collection point) and could also substantially improve the efficiency of delivery vehicle operations.

14.2.3 Costs of implementation

For the different soft factors, the cost of facilitating choices by individuals to reduce their car use in most cases ranged from about 0.1 pence to 10 pence per vehicle kilometre saved, depending on the soft factor and method of cost attribution. Our calculations suggest that it is reasonable to take a public expenditure cost of 1.5 pence per vehicle kilometre saved as an indicative figure for a well-designed package of different soft initiatives, i.e. £15 for removing each 1000 vehicle kilometres of traffic. Current official practice calculates the benefit of reduced traffic congestion, on average, to be about 15p per car kilometre removed, and more than three times this level in congested urban conditions. Thus, as outlined in section 14.1, on average, every £1 spent on well-designed soft measures could bring about £10 of benefit in reduced congestion alone, more in the most congested conditions, and with further potential gains from environmental improvements and other effects, provided that the tendency of induced traffic to erode such benefits is controlled. There are also opportunities for private business expenditure on some soft measures, which can result in offsetting cost savings.

There are reasons for expecting the relationship between cost and impact not to be linear. There may be economies of scale which reduce the unit costs of large initiatives; there may be learning and the development of better methods which increase the effectiveness of soft measures; and there may be diminishing returns especially as the achievable limits to behavioural change are approached. The first and second of these would lead to unit costs becoming lower as a programme of soft measures is built up, and the third would lead to the unit costs becoming higher. A sensible hypothesis might be that, in the early stages of extensive soft factor implementation, unit costs will fall, and, at later stages, as saturation of effect is approached, they will increase. Although available data do not yet allow these hypotheses to be fully checked, there are some indications that, currently, in some situations, the unit costs of implementing soft factors are falling, consistent with the reality that most soft factors interventions have so far only been implemented in a relatively small scale way. Within the time scale and assumptions of the high intensity scenario, we would not expect that diminishing returns are likely to set in.

14.3 Issues of implementation and policy

All the literature reviewed, and the case study interviews, have stressed the importance of the policy context of soft factor interventions, and have also discussed various problems, constraints, barriers to successful implementation, and 'wish-lists' of improvements that would make implementation easier. At local level, officials concerned with developing soft measures often feel that their work is still not recognised as being of central importance in transport strategy, which is affecting resources, political support, career expectations and profile. There is also a perception that the relevant professional skills are not widely available or given sufficient importance.

The discussion below attempts to synthesise the main policy arguments and issues from the case study interviews and published literature, though it should be remembered that there is a range of different views on all these matters, with consensus not yet having been widely tested.

14.3.1 National strategy

Soft measures are always described as making a contribution to overall transport policy, but this is often an aspiration rather than embedded reality. There could be greater use of specific practical applications in which hard measures (a) create a greater demand for the new opportunities given by soft measures, and (b) 'lock in' their benefits so they are not eroded by induced traffic. This would arise naturally from traffic reduction targets such as those provided for in the Traffic Reduction Acts, where a long term strategy for an area would be implemented by coherent use of all available policy instruments. Most of the interviewees have suggested to us that they would welcome a clear national strategy about traffic reduction as this would help to integrate separate initiatives, an issue which we did not pursue for this study. In any case, local traffic reduction could be supported by national guidelines, information and advice on how soft measures might contribute to this goal: there is a widespread local view that national support can help to give credibility, demonstrating both that traffic reduction is an officially approved policy objective, and that soft measures can make a valuable and concrete contribution to this.

14.3.2 Funding mechanisms

Most soft measures are funded via local authority revenue budgets, and most specific initiatives are locally designed and launched. Therefore the views, priorities and constraints in local authorities are likely to be decisive in determining what happens in practice. Some local authorities have successfully made the case to their district auditors that soft measures, being part of a package of hard and soft measures, can be funded from capital budgets, and this has given them a great flexibility which they see as important. Others cannot do this, or think that they cannot. If soft measures are to be applied more intensively and extensively than at present, greater flexibility in funding them via capital programmes would be required, or alternative revenue sources would need to be found. This is particularly true to avoid short term contracts, and associated rapid turnover, of staff with the skills to implement soft factors.

14.3.3 Requests for supportive national policies

Many soft measures require stronger supporting action from other areas of local and national policy. Those national policies most frequently mentioned by our interviewees were:

- More employers could be persuaded to develop workplace travel plans if further tax incentives were offered. One mechanism mentioned by interviewees was business rate rebates; alternatives might include tax credits for travel plan revenue measures, or enhanced capital allowances for infrastructure.
- Some interviewees argued that travel plans could be made a statutory requirement for schools (as part of their health and safety responsibilities to pupils) and for other organisations (drawing parallels with legislation on disability and social housing, which, although initially seen as an unacceptable burden on the private sector, are now widely accepted).
- Planning policy guidance was felt to be inconsistently applied, and two tier authorities in particular felt that PPG13 could be strengthened to ensure planning authorities required effective travel plans as part of new developments. It was suggested that Section 106 planning gain agreements could be used more frequently to secure personalised travel planning programmes and car clubs for new residential developments – and that, as innovative use of the planning system occurred, it was important to disseminate good practice.
- Public transport information and marketing can only be as good as the product, and if bus services are poor quality, infrequent, or do not connect, marketing will not deliver significant patronage increase. The lack of directive powers for local authorities and PTEs to set the framework for public transport was felt to be an

obstacle to the provision of good public transport services. It was also argued that OFT constraints are perceived to inhibit cooperative arrangements on joint information, marketing, ticketing, and timetabling arrangements between operators. National clarification that this is encouraged would be welcomed.

- There are some groups that local authorities find hard to engage with – for example, leisure providers, property developers and trade unions for workplace travel planning; and retailers for home shopping. Greater work with these groups at national level might make achieving local buy-in from such groups easier. Technical advice for companies interested in telework or teleconference solutions might also be appropriate.

- The majority of interviewees commented that it was often hard to gain credibility for soft policies – not least because knowledge and evidence about them was sparse. Consequently, greater dissemination of existing national experience could be helpful for achieving local acceptability.

14.3.4 Need for other local policies which support soft measures

The most important local policies to support soft measures were identified as follows:

- Reallocation of road capacity, parking restraint, congestion charging and workplace parking levies were all felt to be important in order to 'lock in' the benefits of soft measures; to motivate organisations to become involved in travel planning; and to provide the space necessary for high quality public transport, walking and cycling provision.

- Traffic calming, 20mph limits, safe crossing facilities and parking restrictions outside schools were felt by some interviewees to be an important part or counterpart to school travel planning programmes.

- Traffic orders for dedicated parking spaces for car club vehicles could be fast-tracked, to reduce the long time gap between canvassing potential car club members in a new locality and providing a car. Special parking arrangements for car sharers could also help to substantially generate interest in car sharing schemes.

- For home shopping, vehicle access restrictions, specific parking rights, and investment in local drop-off facilities could all help to persuade retailers to invest in more efficient and less polluting logistics systems.

14.4 Issues of analysis, methodology, and implications for modelling and forecasting

As foreshadowed in chapter 1, the work has revealed a number of quite serious measurement problems, which affect all calculations of the impact of soft measures, in some cases substantially – though it should be said that similar issues will also need to be addressed for many other types of transport initiative. The five most important identified problems are described in the following sections.

14.4.1 Recognition of responses other than mode switching

Many of the policy objectives, reviews and individual studies have expressed their targets and outcomes in the form of shifts in the proportion of trips by each mode, then converting these into traffic impacts by re-calculating the figures as vehicle kilometres. However, they have done so in different ways, in some cases simply by assuming that all origins, destinations and average journey distances stay the same, others by allowing for differential impact on journeys of different lengths, and a few by allowing for an effect on wider dimensions of choice such as destination, number of journeys, time of day, and patterns of trip tours at the household level. Analysis which treats mode shift as the only behavioural response is unlikely to be able to make a full assessment of the impact.

Overestimates of impact may occur if a particular soft measure is only effective for short journeys, but is assumed to be equally effective for journeys of all lengths. For example, a health awareness programme specifically aimed at encouraging people to walk instead of driving for short trips might have a large effect on number of car trips but a small effect on car mileage.

Underestimates may occur because:
- no allowance is made for average distance or longer car journeys switching to closer destinations, which then make switching to walking or cycling more realistic;
- switching from car to public transport is most likely to be associated with a shift from diffuse patterns of origins and destinations to more concentrated patterns reflecting public transport routes, with, for example, a focus on city centres.

The former effects mainly apply when considering shifts in mode within a stable pattern of journey length, and the latter to shifts in the distribution of journey length itself, which is especially likely over the periods of time in which people change their home, job and shopping preference for other reasons. It is therefore a logical hypothesis that overestimating effects might be more likely in the short run, and underestimating them might be more likely in the longer run. However, we have not yet found evidence to confirm this.

14.4.2 Dynamic build-up of effects over time

Most studies of the effects on behaviour of hard measures, such as studies of changes in price (involving econometric analysis of time series data) or studies of the expansion or contraction of road capacity (involving analysis of traffic counts), have concluded that effects on behaviour can build up over a period of several years. Theory, logic and intuition, but little evidence, suggests that this build-up process could also apply to the similar behavioural responses involved in some soft measures, and, if so, those studies with a short period will underestimate the impacts of such measures, after allowing also for the effects in the longer term of other factors (eg income, car ownership etc) which may be operating in the opposite direction.

Other soft factors, however, may have the effect of shortening the behavioural response period, by making immediate information available, and alternatives worth considering, which would otherwise only filter through to some travellers much more slowly, or not at all. Further, some soft initiatives seem to need reinforcement or refreshment after a period.

Although some studies have continued empirical monitoring for a longer period, when considering future impacts, it is most common only to allow for delays due to feasible timescales of implementation, not those due to the behavioural timescales of response.

14.4.3 Synergy and interactions

A recurrent theme in earlier reviews has been the strong argument that synergies and interactions are likely between soft measures, and between soft and hard measures.

Local experience rarely if ever presents a 'pure' experimental context where only one instrument is changed at a time, or controlled combinations of instruments are implemented. Therefore the observed effects will always, to some extent, include effects of a combination of variables, but not in a way which allows definite attribution of importance to each, or the statistical measurement of interaction effects.

In local experience the initiators of soft policies have formed a strong impression of specific synergies and interactions at work, as reported in Chapters 3 to 13. The most frequently cited examples of positive synergistic interactions are those in which (a) one soft measure increases the effectiveness of another and (b) soft measures interact with hard measures. In each case, the main mechanisms are: strengthening awareness, intent, or the range of opportunities available; reaching thresholds enabling larger responses; or reducing offsetting effects which would undermine the impact of the soft factor intervention. There are also often synergies with non-transport policy objectives.

There were some concerns about circumstances where the interaction may be negative, namely:

- Car-based initiatives such as car clubs or car-sharing are intended to encourage a less car-based lifestyle, but they may have the opposite effect for some people, subtracting from public transport, walking or cycling. For car clubs the available evidence suggests the net effect so far has been small (that is, non car owners who join car clubs show little change in their travel patterns), partly because cost regimes make car use unattractive for regular trips. For car-sharing, the evidence is less clear, but common sense suggests that car-sharing might be more appropriate in areas where public transport is relatively poor (e.g. rural areas) than in areas where it is good.

- When approaching saturation levels of effect for particular markets, further reductions in car use will be increasingly difficult, and it would then risk double counting to assume that the effects of separate soft factor initiatives, aimed at the same journeys, would be additive. It is unlikely that this applies often at present, but it would become material in the event of intensive, sustained and successful implementation of soft measures over a number of years.

- If soft instruments succeed in reducing car use in conditions of congestion, sufficiently to have a noticeable effect on that congestion, induced traffic effects must become important. This has been identified as a potential problem throughout the report. As highlighted, if this occurs, soft measures may have large effects on individual behaviour but small or zero eventual net effects on traffic levels. Consequently, demand management measures aimed at avoiding induced traffic offsetting the results of soft measures are a key requirement to achieving their full potential.

- It has been suggested that enthusiasm for soft factors is enhanced by high congestion and related problems. To some extent, success in overcoming these problems could reduce their potential effectiveness, though the other benefits from soft factor measures would still apply.

Overall, the main significance of arguments about both synergies and negative interactions is that consistent application of soft and hard measures will increase the speed at which maximum realistic behavioural shifts are achieved, and inconsistent or partial application will substantially undermine the likelihood of having much effect at all at the network level, though effects at the individual level could still occur.

14.4.4 Prospective and retrospective bias

When carrying out systematic comparisons of alternatives for policy appraisal, it is usual to imagine or model a world of identical base conditions, where the same people with the same economic and social circumstances are making different travel decisions because of different transport costs, opportunities or information. There are some features of soft policy instruments which make it difficult to fit real world observations into this framework.

One case applies prospectively, when selecting in advance a specific sample of the population for information or opportunities not aimed at everybody. When a reduction in car use is then observed, it is necessary to distinguish how many of the target group would have made the observed change in their behaviour even without the intervention. It is known that, in any two time periods, a substantial proportion of the population will reduce their car use even without policy intervention, though they will be offset, or more than offset, by different people who increase their car use. This is important both for calculation of the overall change, but also for attribution of the size of the soft impact.

Another case applies retrospectively, especially when relying on research methods asking 'what did you do before?' or 'why?'. There is a well-documented tendency for people to recall and describe events and motives in such a way as to justify their current choices, to themselves or to the interviewer, which can influence both estimation of the size of a change and its attribution to different causes.

Both of these effects can be allowed for, in principle, by suitably rigorous controls. Not all studies have attempted to do so, and those that have frequently record controversy and argument about whether the controls are well defined and the inferences valid. It is worth noting that similar caveats and issues of interpretation apply to assessment of conventional or 'hard' policies, though are often not taken into account.

14.4.5 Monitoring

As a new area of policy, there is a wide range of practice on monitoring, and a sensitivity to its cost. There is some wry puzzlement about expectations or requirements that a much larger proportion of the overall expenditure should be spent on monitoring soft measures than has ever been considered for traditional hard policies. This is seen as a barrier to implementing cheap, potentially good value measures which is not imposed on expensive, potentially poor value measures. Moreover, there is also an increasing awareness of the difficulty of measuring complex changes to travel behaviour with precision, for the reasons discussed above.

Guidelines on monitoring methodologies could help ensure useful data was gathered at least cost. However, to be useful, this should not be seen as an additional burden of proof required for soft measures, but part of a general approach to monitoring the effects of all important policy initiatives and projects. (This is especially important since it is now argued that the degree of certainty about the impacts of traditional hard measures is no greater than that for the new policy packages).

There is a particular lack of empirical evidence about the traffic impacts of tele-conferencing; car sharing schemes (in particular, what participants 'did before'); travel awareness campaigns (in terms of behaviour change, not simply attitude modification); and home shopping schemes. It is also clear that nationally funded pilot projects on some of the other soft factors (notably the personalised travel planning pilots and the original Sustrans Safe Routes to School project) have played, or are playing, a key role in helping to increase the knowledge base about the role of such measures in the UK. Further pilot projects, with careful monitoring, could help to reduce the current lack of data about some of the less well understood soft factors. The 'Sustainable Travel Demonstration Towns' project should also provide an invaluable source of data about the combined impact of introducing a co-ordinated package of such measures.

14.5 Recommendation

Although 'soft factors' still remains, in part, a label of convenience rather than being coherently and rigorously defined, there is nevertheless a growing body of practical experience and theoretical understanding of the role for such measures in transport policy. Soft factor interventions provide a number of different ways of giving more reliable information, better informed traveller attitudes, and more benign or efficient ways of travelling.

Such policies, separately or together, have been undertaken for a wide range of different objectives including reducing congestion; increasing revenue for transport companies; improving health by encouraging more physical activity; improving social inclusion; reducing environmental damage and saving commercial costs for employers. The most common specific feature linking these different policies has been that they have the potential to impact on levels of car use.

We conclude that these soft measures, in a favourable wider policy context, could be sufficiently effective in reducing traffic that they merit serious consideration for an important role in transport strategy for the foreseeable future, prima facie offering very good value for money, and few disadvantages.

We stress that the substantial future traffic reduction identified here should be seen as the potential that soft factor interventions offer, not a forecast of probable impacts. Particular attention would be needed to ensure the benefits from soft factor interventions are 'locked in', via demand management measures to control induced traffic. Such measures, if well designed, could also have further beneficial effects on travel choices and traffic conditions in their own right. In this report, we have not taken any of these further effects into account.

It is important to include the impact of soft measures in national forecasting exercises, though we do not find helpful the practice that this can be done simply by subtracting a certain percentage of traffic, whatever figure that may be. The effects of soft policies will depend on the scale of implementation chosen, as an act of policy, by central and local government, associated, and interacting, with other policies being assessed, including prices, service improvements, traffic control and management, and infrastructure changes.